Transmissions

Nick Mauss

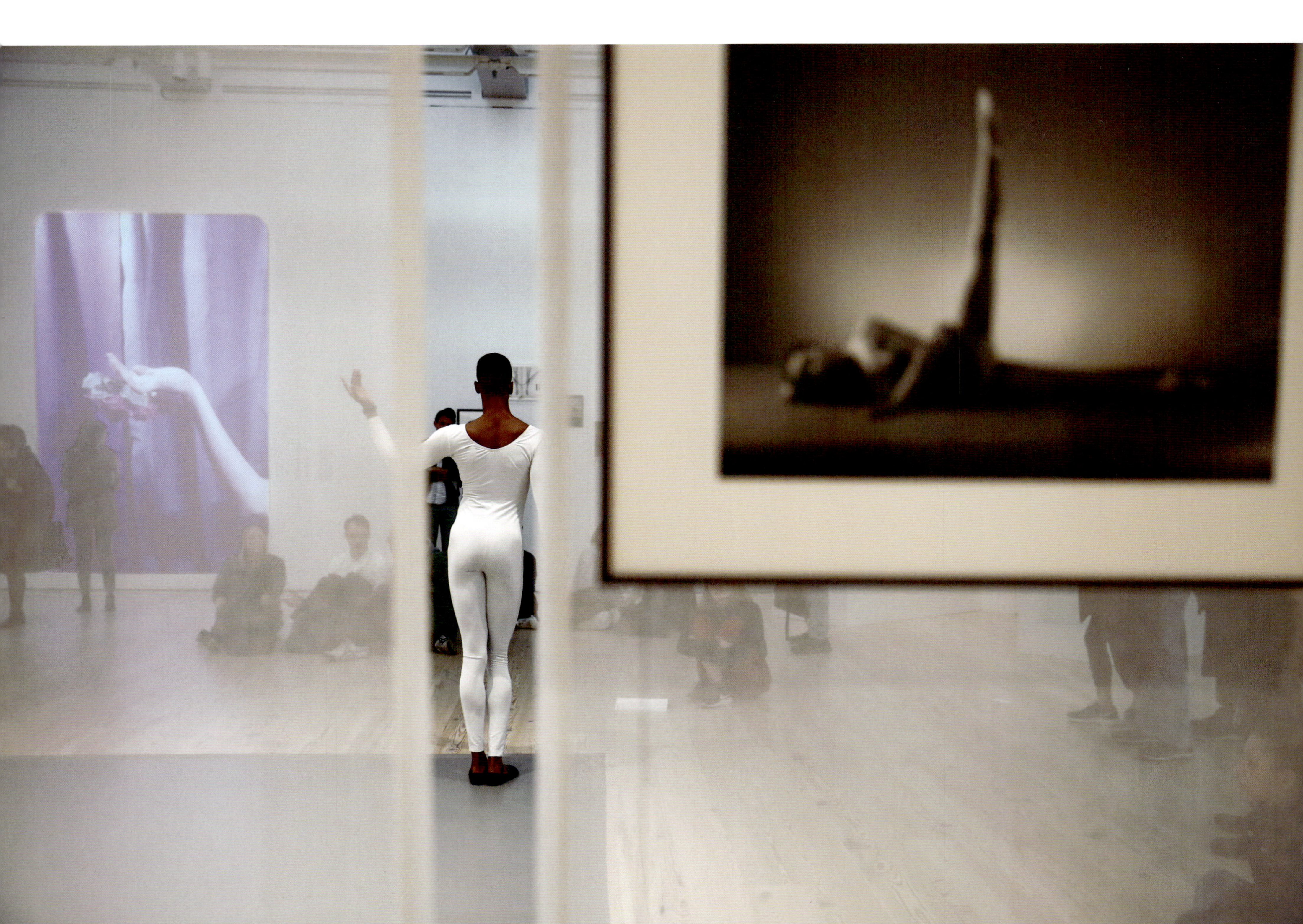

Dancing Foxes Press, Brooklyn, New York
Whitney Museum of American Art, New York

Distributed by Yale University Press, New Haven and London

Contributions by Joshua Lubin-Levy, Scott Rothkopf, Elisabeth Sussman, and Allie Tepper

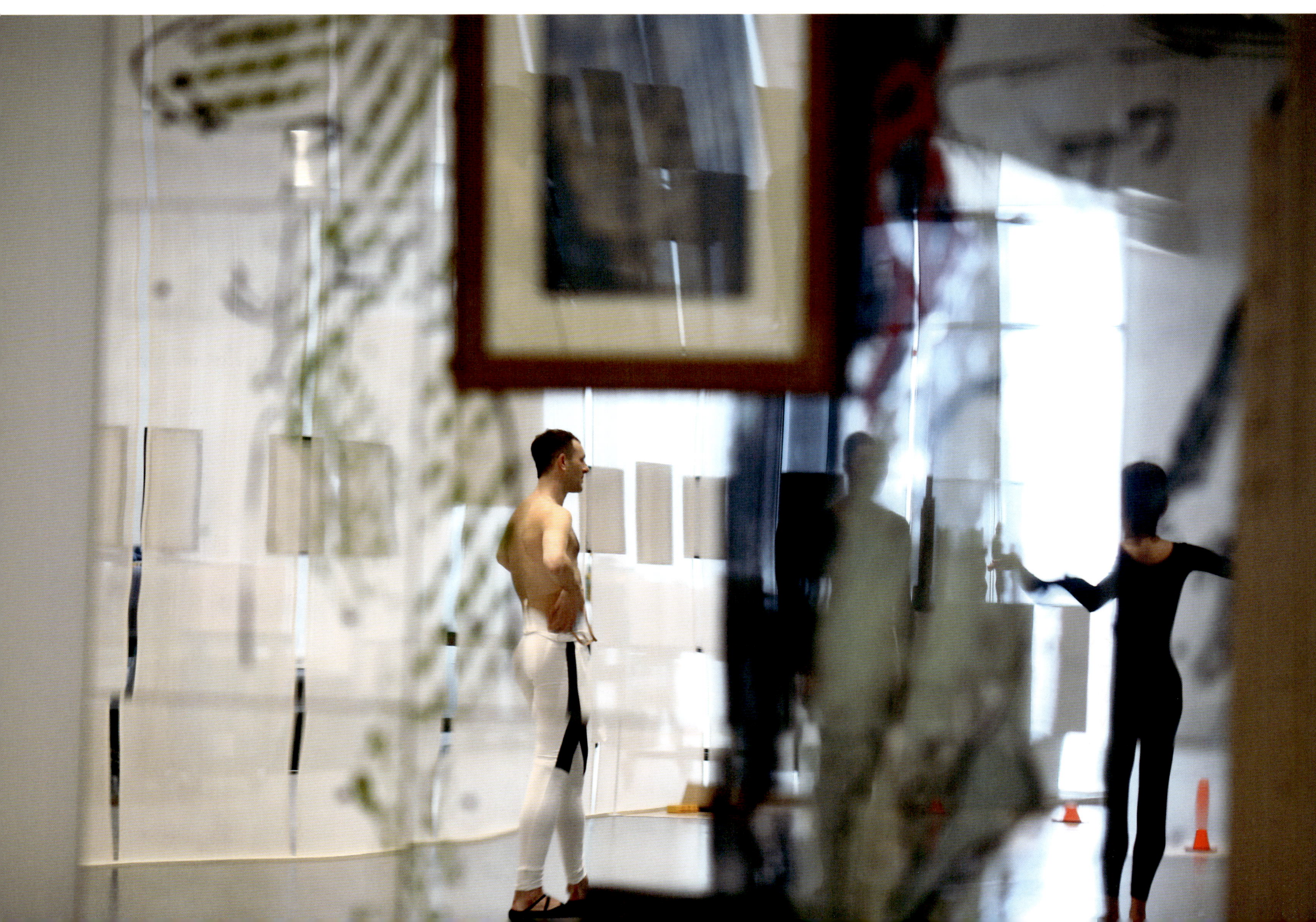

Contents

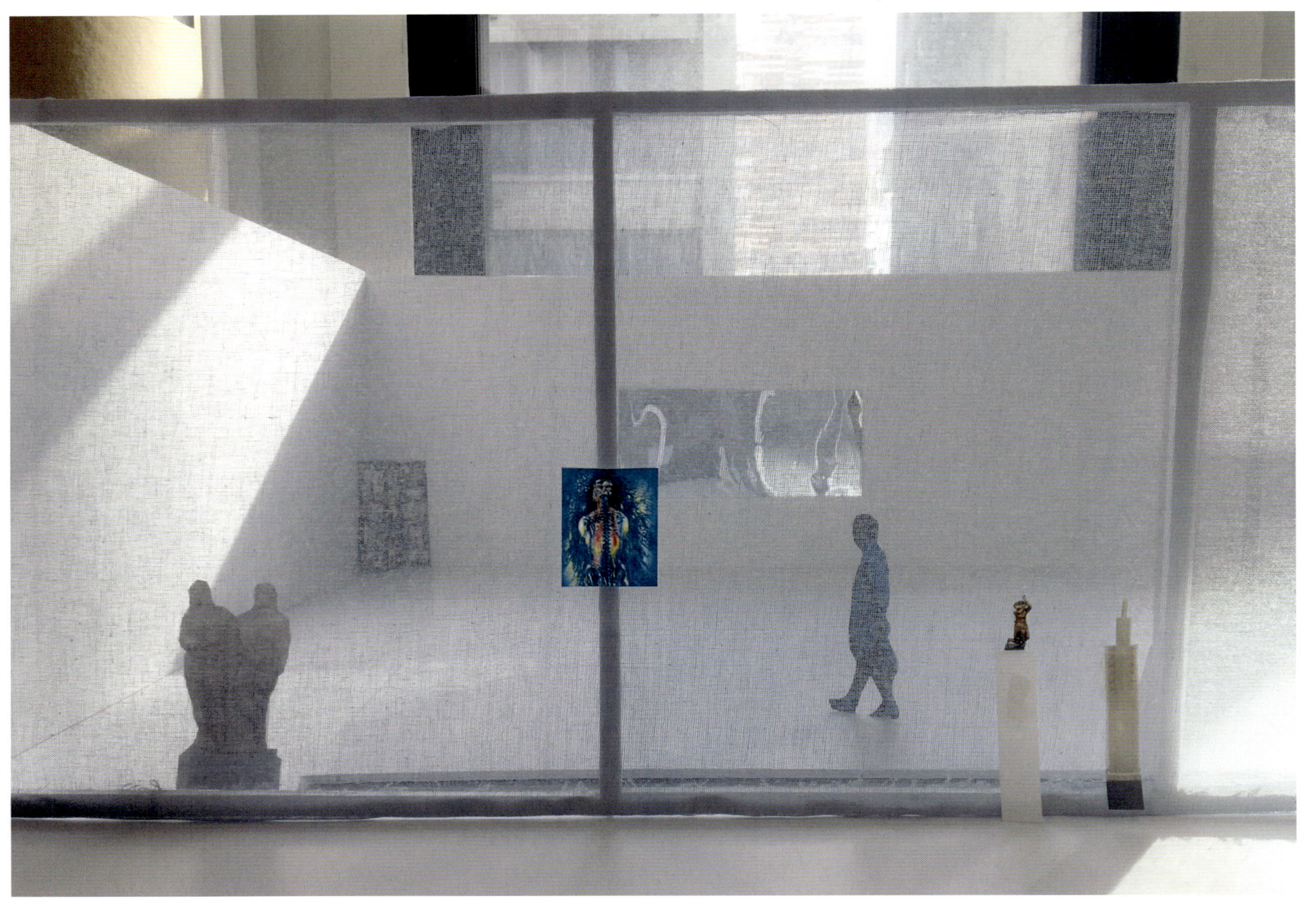

Nick Mauss's *Transmissions* is a collage, a collection of forms affiliated through content and brought together piece by piece. The link between these forms—drawings, paintings, costume studies, costume re-creation, sculpture, painting, looped videos, models of stage sets, an ensemble of live dancers, and photographs—is a particular world of ballet that flourished in New York from the 1930s through the 1950s. Mauss chose the objects and wrote the lengthy and precise texts of the labels affixed to the wall in the exhibition and the captions in this book (these weighty descriptions are significant elements of the collage and include facts about the objects, such as their provenance and use, social history, and biographies of the artists and their subjects), but Mauss neither narrates nor theorizes the history of ballet of the New York of this era. As artist, ballet-omane, historian, queer theorist, and choreographer, Mauss is diffused as a subject here among his choices, only one of which comes from his own hand, a large mirror mural fabricated to his design and on which he has painted. Nothing else is overtly made by him; the artist is not present through objects of his own making.

While photographs are prominent participants in Mauss's mix, their roles vary depending on the modes of presentation. The usual way to show photographs in an exhibition is to hang them more or less in a row on the wall. Mauss sometimes did this in *Transmissions*, mingling them with other objects. Hung in this way, the images—works by photographers with widely different styles—can be taken in individually: Lincoln Kirstein, the person responsible for bringing George Balanchine to the United States in 1933 and founding what became New York City Ballet, was photographed by Walker Evans in a pose that mimics that of a mugshot. Cecil Beaton captured Charles Henri Ford, poet and editor of the journal *View* (a vehicle for Surrealists in America), in costume as Harlequin. Author, photographer, critic, and dance aficionado Carl Van Vechten, who took more than 2,800 slides, mostly of dancers posed in costumes against fanciful

backgrounds in his apartment to compile a near-anthropological record of figures in the worlds of dance between 1940 and 1964, was represented by over eight hundred of these images, projected at life-size in an ongoing loop in the gallery. They were a monopolizing centerpiece to the rich interplay of works in Mauss's ensemble, evoking the social-creative web of New York.

It was in the selection and presentation of the works of George Platt Lynes where Mauss radically departed from the conventions of exhibiting photography. The entry to the exhibition was to be a seventy-foot plane; rather than constructing a wall, which would have blocked the view into the gallery, Mauss chose to extend a stiff gauze, like a theatrical scrim, that allowed visitors to see immediately into the galleries and imaginatively find their own bodies in relation to the bodies in the exhibition, whether those of the images and artifacts or those of the live, moving performers. Lynes's photographs hung in front of the translucent barrier, animating the point of entry. Though static, they performed in dynamic exchange with viewers, the dancers in the galleries, the images mounted on the gallery walls, and the sculptures and other objects that occupied the space.

Known first for his portraits of celebrities, shown at the Julien Levy Gallery in 1932, and then for his career as a fashion photographer in the 1930s and 1940s, Lynes was also celebrated for images of New York City Ballet in its various formations from the mid-1930s until his death in 1955. But Mauss didn't only choose photographs of dancers for *Transmissions*. He more broadly focused on images that demonstrated Lynes's profound and daring ability to portray the plasticity of the body and to stage, boldly and erotically, the male nude, singly or in intertwined poses. In fact, Balanchine wrote in a souvenir program published after Lynes died in 1955: "Lynes's secret was his sense of plasticity, his genius for lighting figures in space."[1] Lynes's studio—where the photographer himself became choreographer, dramatically lighting bodies to emphasize their lines and silhouettes—haunted the

exhibition space. The photographer's brother, Russell Lynes, has described the studio: "The space George rented was (or he made) ideal. Its center was a large high-ceilinged squarish room, a studio with space for creating substantial background and for props stacked in the corner."[2] The bodies were posed in a spare set consisting of "anything that took light handsomely."[3]

In sourcing images from Lynes's extensive oeuvre of nude male photography, Mauss turned to the holdings of the Kinsey Institute for Sex Research. While sexologist Alfred Kinsey himself had commissioned some of these images, Lynes, near the end of his life and in need of money, sold others to Kinsey's research center. In assigning such an active role to the prints in *Transmissions*, Mauss located Lynes squarely within the canon of photography, challenging his status on the margins, either as a footnote or, at best, an early influence for Robert Mapplethorpe.[4] Though sidelined in the history of modernism, Lynes's principal subjects—fashion, celebrity, nudity—register a bold and beautiful narrative of the time, aspects of which Mauss marshals in *Transmissions*.

Among the Lynes images that hung on the scrim were two striking photographs occasioned by the staging of *Four Saints in Three Acts* (1934), an opera by Gertrude Stein and Virgil Thompson that premiered at the Wadsworth Athenaeum in Hartford, Connecticut—a watershed moment in the introduction of modernism to America. Mauss selected two nude studio photographs of the three black principal dancers, Maxwell Baird, Floyd Miller, and Billie Smith. In one, the young and elegant British choreographer Frederick Ashton stands in profile, clothed in formal suit and tie, his arm draped around the shoulders of the nude dancers. In the other, the dancers lie on a horizontal surface, their bodies choreographed for the camera by Ashton. Showing the men intertwined, as if in sexual play, the photograph imparts a blithely erotic undertone to the standard account of the opera. What exactly this photograph captures is unclear: an extemporaneous performance beyond the protocols of studio photography, or

1. George Balanchine, quoted in Michael Novak, "Composition and the Artistic Icon: The Beauty, Mystery, and Legacy of George Platt Lynes' Dance Photography" (thesis, Senior Seminar in Dance, Barnard College, 2008), 7, https://www.yumpu.com/en/document/read/6713619/by-michael-novak-dance. Novak, now artistic director of the Paul Taylor Dance Company, thinks Lincoln Kirstein may have ghostwritten Balanchine's statement.

2. Russell Lynes, quoted in David Leddick, *Intimate Companions: A Triography of George Platt Lynes, Paul Cadmus, Lincoln Kirstein, and Their Circle* (New York: St. Martin's Press, 2000), 97.

3. Ibid.

4. See Philip Gefter, *Wagstaff: Before and After Mapplethorpe* (New York: Liveright, 2015), 149.

a (momentary) kinship between Lynes, Ashton and Baird, and Miller and Smith.

While Lynes's photographs took on a leading role in the exhibition, his prominence in the imbricated worlds of *Transmissions* is further emphasized in this book, which includes not only additional images from the Kinsey Institute but also more in-depth visual and textual context, such as a press release written by his lover Glenway Wescott and an invitation for a two-person exhibition that surprisingly paired Lynes with Walker Evans. Such ephemera finds apt staging on book pages. Ballet generated a wealth of such printed material (programs, magazines), which could carry photographic portraits of dancers, various photographic experiments in capturing dance, as well as painted or drawn work by famous and lesser-known artists (not to mention textual ekphrases by various authors). By contrast, the position Van Vechten's images assume in this book is quite distinct from their central spot in the exhibition; slipped into the pages on an accordion poster that can be removed from the rest of the materials, they manifest here in a way that is peripheral but no less consequential.

Two books influenced the shape and logic of this volume. The first was Alexey Brodovitch's iconic 1945 book *Ballet*, with an introduction by Edwin Denby and motion-blurred photographs by Brodovitch, laid out in pairs across the stagelike space of the book's oblong format. Brodovitch's role as art director for *Harper's Bazaar*, where he commissioned work by avant-garde artists, also tied into the many reciprocations between purportedly separate worlds (fashion and fine art, museum and magazine, dance and art) explored in *Transmissions*.

Let's Take Back Our Space: "Female" and "Male" Body Language as a Result of Patriarchal Structures, Marianne Wex's systemic 1977 study comprising photographs of "involuntary and unconscious" gestures and styles of comportment from "real life" and art history, also resonated conceptually and formally with the expansion of *Transmissions* from exhibition into book. The work of an artist in the guise of a hybrid sociological study, *Let's Take*

Back Our Space was originally exhibited as an installation of collaged panels (inspired by Aby Warburg's *Mnemosyne Atlas* [1924–29]). In 1979, Wex's project was published—like Brodovitch's—in an oblong format that allowed for the arrayed images to unravel formal relationships and rhymes and to argue for the persistence of certain coded poses through history and across cultures. The influence of Wex's project can be seen here where images of the idealized study of ballet in the 1940s bleed into caricature and abstraction, time-travel into Tanagra figurines, then leap forward into Peter Hujar photographs of Elie Nadelman sculptures and finally into a display of the Nadelman figures themselves, receding behind the faint reflection of several *Transmissions* performers in the exhibition's Nadelman vitrine.

Poet Ange Mlinko recently identified the poet's "project book" as a form that disperses the "monological personal utterance . . . known as 'voice'" by interspersing the poet's own words with associatively interrelated texts by others. She could be describing *Transmissions* when she extols its "array of forms." In such a project, she claims, "the author is less creator than curator," an artist who documents by way of "a decentered presence."[5]

5. Ange Mlinko, "Holding It Together," review of *Hey, Marfa*, by Jeffrey Yang, with paintings and drawings by Rackstraw Downes; and *Baby, I Don't Care*, by Chelsey Minnis, *New York Review of Books*, January 17, 2019, 34. Poets Claudia Rankine and Susan Howe have also adopted the form of a project book.

Installation view of *Nick Mauss: Transmissions* (Whitney Museum of American Art, New York, March 16–May 14, 2018). Left to right: Carl Van Vechten, Al Bledger of the Von Grona American Negro Ballet, 1938; Carl Van Vechten, Al Bledger of the Von Grona American Negro Ballet, 1938; Carl Van Vechten, Carl Van Vechten slideshow, 1940–64; New York City Ballet souvenir program from the company's second European tour, 1952; Charles Henri Ford, "Ballet for Tamara Toumanova," in "Americana Fantastica," *View 2*, no. 4 (January 1943), 1943; Ballet Theatre program for the 1951–52 season, 1951; Ruth Page photographed by Maurice Seymour in costume designed by Pavel Tchelitchew for Page's *Variations on Euclid*, in the publication *Ruth Page and Harald Kreutzberg*, with poem and introduction by Mark Turbyfill, c. 1936; George Platt Lynes, dancer Jacques d'Amboise in a costume designed by Paul Cadmus for *Filling Station*, choreographed by Lew Christensen for Ballet Caravan, 1937; George Platt Lynes, cabaret performer James Leslie Daniels, c. 1937; Pavel Tchelitchew, *Anatomical Painting*, 1946. Photo: Ron Amstutz

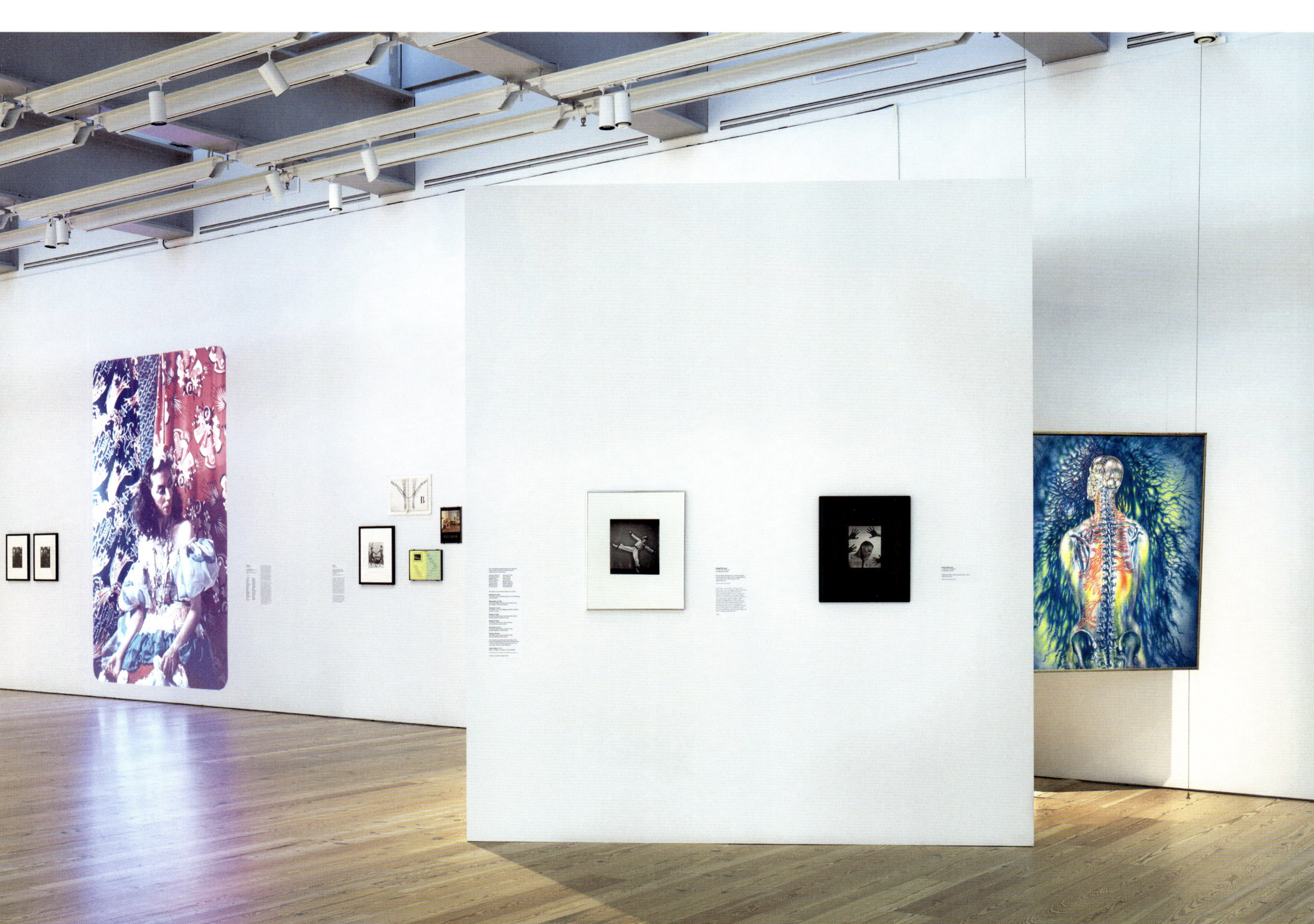

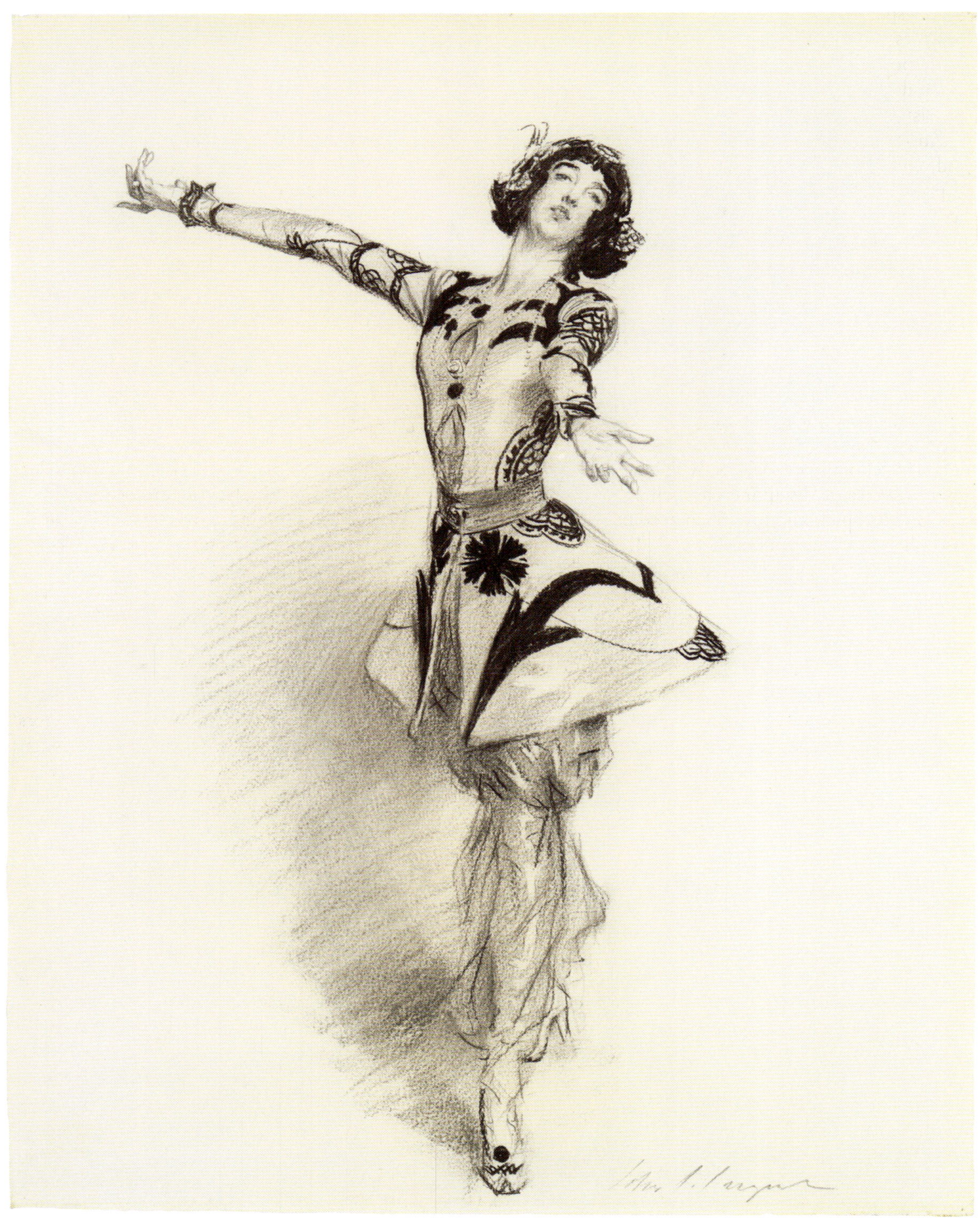

It's Mother's Day 2018, and Fran Lebowitz is onstage at the Whitney complaining about museums packed with strollers. New York used to be smaller—*her* New York anyway, in the seventies and eighties—and it was full of people who truly cared about culture before culture cared much about them. They were artists and gallerygoers, dancers and balletomanes, writers like her and readers, who all existed symbiotically with and for one another. The passion and erudition of the audience was what made the work so good. All of them lived for art. Many of them died of AIDS. That incalculable loss, she insists, tore a hole in the avant-garde's family tree, leaving mentorless the next generation of misfits, homosexuals, immigrants, aesthetes, dreamers, and acerbic connoisseurs. "Almost the entire audience died off. . . . If you had bombed Lincoln Center, it would have had the same effect," Lebowitz says, her trademark wit not quite cauterizing the wound. She is explaining all this to her interviewer, the artist Nick Mauss, whose exhibition *Transmissions* is on view upstairs. Born exactly thirty years before him, in 1950, she is old enough to be, well, his mother, and his questioning recalls how an orphan might one day inquire about parents lost at war. Behind them, tall windows look out onto the West Side Highway, with the taillights of yellow cabs and the Hudson River flowing by under a dimming sky.

Transmissions, as Mauss's title elliptically suggests, grew in part from the artist's desire to bridge a chasm. The word evokes a passage in time and space from transmitter to receiver: whether via radio waves or Wi-Fi, gossip or scholarly account, dance notation or performance. All are relevant examples here, as is the intimate observation and emulation of one generation by the next. The ostensible subject of Mauss's exhibition was the New York avant-garde of the 1930s through 1950s, viewed through the lens of American ballet. It was a time of great invention, when George Balanchine, working alongside impresario Lincoln Kirstein at what would become New York City Ballet, proved that he was not just the greatest choreographer of the

twentieth century but one of the greatest creative minds that ever lived.

Writers, composers, painters, costume designers, architects, and polymaths simultaneously occupying several of these roles were drawn into the new ballet's orbit and, in turn, irradiated their respective fields. Yet standard art histories of the period say relatively little about ballet and its catalytic force in the development of modernism across the visual and performing arts (largely because such histories privilege painting and sculpture in general and abstraction in particular). Conversely, academic accounts of ballet emphasize Balanchine's purity—the almost oxymoronic classicism of his contemporaneity—with nods to the early interdisciplinary collaborations of the Ballets Russes and to the later jazz and vaudeville references that spiced his art. But his work in America developed in closer proximity to fields including commercial fashion, photography, and illustration than is generally acknowledged in scholarly chronicles, which still tend to segregate disciplines, as well as the so-called high and low. Such accounts also often bracket, or entirely overlook, the gay erotics that fueled so much of the period's aesthetic efflorescence, albeit long before the broader understanding and openness associated with a category like "queer" today. With *Transmissions*, Mauss aimed to recenter ballet amid these impure cultural and social networks, as well as within the lifeblood of midcentury American art history—all while making a new and challenging work of art.

Transmissions was an exhibition of artifacts, film footage, and artworks that Mauss selected largely from the Whitney's collection, which he arranged in a mise-en-scène encircling a flat gray vinyl "stage," populated by live dancers. Although Mauss performed all the traditional functions of a curator—from researching, choosing, and installing objects to writing explanatory wall labels—to classify his work as "curating" or his show as yet another "artist-curated project" would be to sorely miss the point. Rather, Mauss conceived of an artwork in the guise of an exhibition, and in this sense expanded a strain of

practice pioneered by the likes of Marcel Broodthaers or Pierre Huyghe, who have used the form and conventions (in space and time) of the exhibition itself as pliant raw material. Curating then becomes just one of his chosen mediums, along with painting, sculpture, choreography, writing, and design—all brought together in an insistently interdisciplinary artwork that one could be forgiven for not recognizing as such. And if Mauss was the artist and the show was his work, then my colleague Elisabeth Sussman and I might rightly be seen as the curators, albeit operating in some unfamiliar capacity that blended the roles of executive producer, dramaturge, and shrink with a fair amount of ventriloquism.

Although *Transmissions* appeared at the Whitney in 2018, the roots of the project and Mauss's relationship with the museum trace back to the 2012 Whitney Biennial. For that exhibition, co-organized by Sussman and Jay Sanders, Mauss embarked on a newly theatrical way of working that merged his previous sculptural and pictorial interests with more overtly architectural and curatorial impulses. *Concern, crush, desire* consisted of a room-size installation with velvet-covered walls appliquéd with ribbons that approximated a 1930s ornamental interior by French scenic artist and illustrator Christian Bérard at the Guerlain Institute in Paris. One entered the chamber through a pair of low doors and suddenly found oneself, as if onstage, within a proscenium-like space opening onto a larger gallery. Around the installation, Mauss displayed works by other artists, including double-sided drawings by writer and furniture designer Eyre de Lanux, an Andy Warhol crotch-shot photocollage, and Marsden Hartley's 1940 portrait of a hunky boxer whose smoldering gaze is rendered with only slightly less loving attention than his outsize nipples. Bérard was an openly homosexual part-time Surrealist, part-time fashion illustrator, and full-time creative force who had the dramatic flair to drop dead of a heart attack at the age of forty-six on the stage of Paris's Théâtre Marigny. It's safe to imagine that these details were as much a source of Mauss's fascination as

John Singer Sargent, *Gertrude Vanderbilt Whitney* (in a Léon Bakst costume), c. 1913. Charcoal and graphite pencil on paper, 24 5/8 × 19 5/8 inches (62.5 × 49.8 cm). Whitney Museum of American Art, New York; gift of Flora Miller Biddle, Pamela T. LeBoutillier, Whitney Tower, and Leverett S. Miller

the proportions of Bérard's moldings and pediments. Mauss has an acute if meandering instinct for how biography and art intermingle, and how a real setting—whether 1930s France, the twenty-first-century Whitney, or their evocative cross-contamination—can engender a realm of fantastical projection, heightened attention, indirect desire, and the possibility of feeling differently alive.

You may have guessed by now that Mauss is gay. I don't mention this fact to draw a direct line between his personal proclivities and his artistic ones. There are—don't get me wrong—the homoerotic images that have long and intermittently populated his work and that have been made doubly alluring by the sensitive touch of his hand. But far more crucial is Mauss's devoted attention to the stories and protagonists too often excluded from mainstream histories still largely populated by straight white men. He often casts his eye just offstage, beyond the main drama of modernism as we've received it, whether to the pages of a French fashion magazine, forgotten love triangles among artists and writers, or lesser-known examples of deco interior design. A byway is only a side street, Mauss suggests, because of where one chooses to build the main road. What if the history of modernism weren't told through a progression of easel pictures and freestanding sculptures but via one of Lanux's lacquered end tables or a pastel-hued Marie Laurencin curtain for the stage? What if, Mauss asks, the history of modernism were told so that

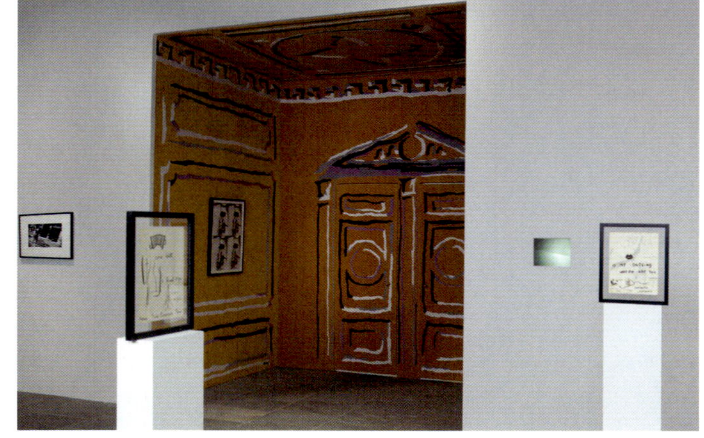

Installation view of intervention by Nick Mauss in the 2012 Whitney Biennial, with the artist's *Concern, crush, desire* (2011) and *Untitled* (2011), and works by Garry Winogrand, Eyre de Lanux, and Andy Warhol. Photo: John Berens

the things once held as extrinsic to its development were seen, by contrast, as *intrinsic* to its creative force?

Here one must be mindful not to read Mauss's work as a nostalgic recitation of effete or obscure references, as such a designation would only serve to reify the very biases he aims to upend. He is less interested in particular subjects than in aesthetic strategies, and for the latter he might look anywhere from the protean performances of Kim Gordon and Ralph Lemon to the semiotic gambits of Lorraine O'Grady and Jasper Johns. In this regard, Mauss's queer sensibility has less to do with an indexing of proper names than with his dismantling of traditional hierarchies and the disruptive operations he brings to bear on static artworks and exhibition formats. In the years following *Concern, crush, desire*, he dedicated himself even more fully to the strange imbrication of a particular class of subject matter within an increasingly unclassifiable process. He exploded his artistic practice to encompass live music and dance at the 2014 Frieze London art fair; architectural interventions in the Portuguese Casa de Serralves and in an Italian Brutalist lobby; and the designing of a show of Léon Bakst's work for the stage. All the while, he paired open formal structures with aleatory processes involving materials such as mirrors, lattices, sheer textiles, and kiln-fired ceramics, which left whatever was left of his "work" vulnerable to various physical contingencies, including our shifting visual and aural regard.

Transmissions represents the culmination—at least until now—of Mauss's work with these intertwined methods and stories. The project began in earnest in 2014 when he proposed to the Whitney a show featuring live dancers in proximity to works from the collection that related more or less directly to ballet's midcentury New York milieu. Given the complexity of Mauss's concept, Sussman and I couldn't quite say yes, but we didn't want to say no. So we dispatched Mauss for further R & D. Undaunted, he delved into the museum's archive and storage rooms, focusing on artists who played some role in his story. He studied, for

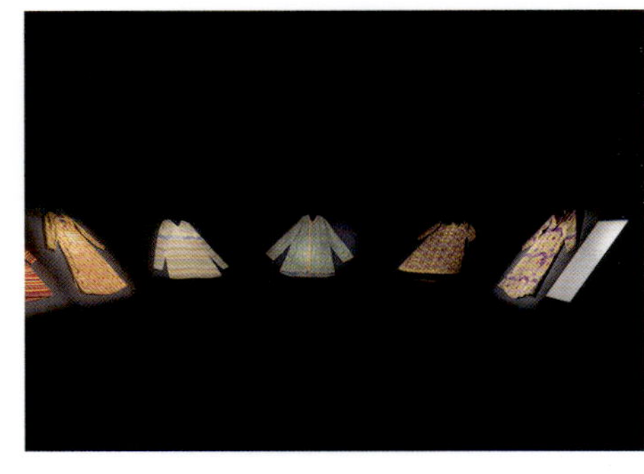

Exhibition design by Nick Mauss for the display of costumes for the Ballets Russes opera-ballet *Ivan the Terrible* (1909), in the exhibition *Designing Dreams: A Celebration of Léon Bakst*, Nouveau Musée National de Monaco, 2016

example, a cache of miniature plaster figurines, reminiscent of dancers, by Elie Nadelman, an artist championed by Kirstein, as well as Nadelman's husky *Two Circus Women* (c. 1928–29), a towering version of which architect Philip Johnson installed in the New York State Theater at Lincoln Center in the 1960s, when it became home to City Ballet. Mauss also turned up two 1930s portraits of Kirstein: a sultry Walker Evans photograph and a diminutive robotic bronze (nude!) by Gaston Lachaise. The trail of breadcrumbs led to a delirious Technicolor X-ray-like painting by the Russian émigré Pavel Tchelitchew, who created costumes and sets for Balanchine in the 1930s and later introduced him to Dorothea Tanning, who herself would later design ballets for the choreographer and whose large rhythmic abstract canvas from the Whitney's collection also fell into the mix. And so the anecdotes and artifacts accumulated in a loose daisy chain that would soon extend to the holdings of the Philadelphia Museum of Art, the Yale University Art Gallery, and various far-flung archives and private collections.

Although Mauss had originally proposed to site his selected works and their accompanying performance in the Whitney's theater, Sussman and I came to realize that his ambition exceeded this container, in terms of both his installation objectives and the modes of spectatorship he hoped to engender. He was angling not for the laser-like focus of a circumscribed theatrical event but for the more quotidian, contrapuntal attention one brings to an evenly lit gallery full of diverse stuff. Sussman and I had never staged—nor, for that matter, ever seen—a live performance in a museum in proximity to historical artworks, which come with their own display demands, from low lighting and crowd control to safeguards like plexiglass cases and costly insurance. In this sense, Mauss's conversations with us became a form of pointed, if unintentional, institutional critique, forcing the museum to reconsider the calibration of the exhibition's physical, temporal, and operational parameters, as well as our respective roles. What was the longest period our staff and the performers could sustain the desired level of activation? And what was the shortest run that could justify the transport and installation of precious artworks from our storage and collections up and down the Eastern Seaboard? Ultimately we rolled the dice and carved out eight weeks in the calendar for the museum's top-floor open-plan gallery, which we hoped would hit the sweet spot of the artist's interwoven aspirations—though they weren't yet fully known to us or even to him.

One thing we were certain of was that Mauss's inchoate concept needed to crystallize further under the pressure of greater expertise. In 2015, he was appointed a fellow at the Center for Ballet and the Arts at New York University, founded by ballet historian and critic Jennifer Homans to foster dialogue among scholars, artists, choreographers, and dancers. During his fellowship, Mauss heard firsthand from the likes of former Balanchine ballerina Heather Watts and delved into the rich holdings of the Jerome Robbins Dance Division of the New York Public Library for the Performing Arts, where he researched film footage by dancer and critic Ann Barzel, as well as drawings and models of costumes and sets for Balanchine ballets by Eugene Berman, Tanning, and Tchelitchew. These suggest far more inventive and fantastical productions than many better-known efforts: think Surrealist costume party in a Palladian ballroom as opposed to the bare stage and practice clothes or gossamer Disney on Ice confections one sees today. The same is true for the delirious original 1946 costumes of the Balanchine landmark *Four Temperaments*, which Mauss discovered documented in a trove

of 2,800 jewely slides of "photographic séances" by Carl Van Vechten, America's first dance critic in the daily press and a pioneering if problematic proponent of the Harlem Renaissance. Shot for his clandestine pleasure from 1940 to 1964, they feature a veritable who's who (and who's *that*?) of ballet dancers, collaborators, and hangers-on striking poses in exotic costumes and makeup before gaudy backdrops in Van Vechten's Central Park West apartment, where he would project the images during private salons.

The photographer George Platt Lynes emerged as a central character in Mauss's tale. Born in New Jersey, Lynes found his way to the Berkshire School in Massachusetts, where he first met Kirstein before decamping to the Paris beau monde of Jean Cocteau, Julien Levy, Gertrude Stein, and transient expats including writer Glenway Wescott and his boyfriend Monroe Wheeler, who would later wind up at the Museum of Modern Art in New York. Lynes's taste for vanguard talent was exceeded only by his appetite for beautiful men. Upon his return to New York, he became known publicly for his portraits and covers of *Vogue* and *Harper's Bazaar*, and privately for images that would have run afoul of decency laws. Having been appointed City Ballet's official photographer by Kirstein in 1935, he shot dancers in poses by Balanchine and choreographer Frederick Ashton by day, as well as in more immodest scenarios of his own invention by night. And sometimes artist and writer friends joined the scene. After his premature death in 1955, Lynes's archive was saved by Alfred Kinsey, founder of the Kinsey Institute for Sex Research at Indiana University, where Mauss also undertook extensive study. If I dwell on Lynes and his pictures, it is because they occupy the dead center of the Venn diagram of Mauss's research: pellucid indices of the overlapping worlds of fashion, ballet, modern art, and gay New York, embodied by bodies that summon various personal and professional histories at once.

As Mauss's exploration of these artifacts and accounts unfolded, he turned his attention to their living correlate in the present—the dance that would

occupy the center of *Transmissions*. His aim, emphatically, was not to create a ballet. Rather, he hoped to evoke the *idea* of ballet through its vexing inheritance in the muscles and minds of young dancers active in the downtown scene. Mauss began with a casting call, seeking dancers who had some background in ballet, and who, more importantly, were open to responding creatively to the visual sources he had assembled. Ultimately, he selected sixteen individuals of differing body types and training, from the dance companies of Merce Cunningham and Karole Armitage to regional academies. For all of them, ballet was a charged touchstone. It could represent youthful aspiration as much as alienation, especially for bodies that refused—intentionally or not—to comply with its athletic or aesthetic codes of behavior. Mauss and the dancers collaboratively authored a set of poses and movements as solos, trios, and pas de deux and quatre inspired by Van Vechten's and Lynes's photographs, as well as by sequences captured in various archival performance and rehearsal tapes. Working in a borrowed space right off the sidewalk near Astor Place, they relied on their intuition, experience, and one another as much as on Mauss's erudition and eye. Warm-up stretches arched into achingly erotic partnering. A moment on pointe abutted more intentionally pedestrian movements in a visual collage of styles and ability. Gender configurations seemed to both matter and not. And then to matter in seeming not to. These were young New Yorkers in 2018 making something new.

The dance at the heart of *Transmissions* unfolded within a multilayered mise-en-scène that held together the many facets of Mauss's daedal work of art. One was greeted upon arrival by a row of translucent cheesecloth panels stretched from floor to ceiling. In front of them hovered on wires framed Lynes photographs printed to Mauss's specifications from digital files provided by the Kinsey Institute. A famed ballerina, Paul Cadmus and his boyfriend, beautiful men in careful tangles, Ashton in a natty suit, a butt stretched open to reveal a clenched hole. Before a window overlooking the

Hudson, Nadelman's gilded *Dancing Figure* (c. 1916–18) crouched provocatively on a revolving pedestal beneath a diaphanous re-creation of Cadmus's transparent mechanic's costume for *Filling Station*, a 1937 one-act ballet *succès de scandale*. Through the milky cheesecloth scrims, one observed a palimpsest of images, actions, and histories piling up. Constellations of objects orbited the gray dance floor. Sculptures by Man Ray and John Storrs summoned the skyscrapers of New York; Nadelman figurines, mounted upright, shimmied in mute choreographies; and a group of Tanning's surreal costume drawings astonished in slightly creepy frames sheathed in pink ballet-slipper leather. Each grouping floated in the room like a beguiling archipelago, full of arcane stories and surprising seductions illuminated by labels in Mauss's digressive yet limpid prose.

In the far corner of the space opposite the entry, Mauss installed the only work by his own hand: a panoramic *verre églomisé* with painted abstractions and fragments of figures sandwiched between glass and silver gilding that mirrored the entire room. A television propped on a metal folding chair faced the mirror so that its footage of a Balanchine rehearsal could be viewed only in reflection, recalling a training trick that Watts had told Mauss dancers use to see simultaneously their models and themselves in the proper stage orientation. On the far side of the mirror, a late nineteenth-century ivory figurine with upstretched arms held aloft a gold dish bearing a calling card printed with the words SERGE DE DIAGHILEW. This artifact had stood for years in the drawing room of Kirstein's East Nineteenth Street town house before being bequeathed to a friend and ballet patron who anonymously lent it to Mauss's show. One could imagine the elegant object with its unusual transliteration of Diaghilev's Russian name passing indirectly from the founder of the Ballets Russes's hands to Kirstein's. And here it sat quietly emitting its invisible aura—a talisman, a transmission, a witnessing ghost.

Four dancers in street clothes passed daily amid unaware visitors and took

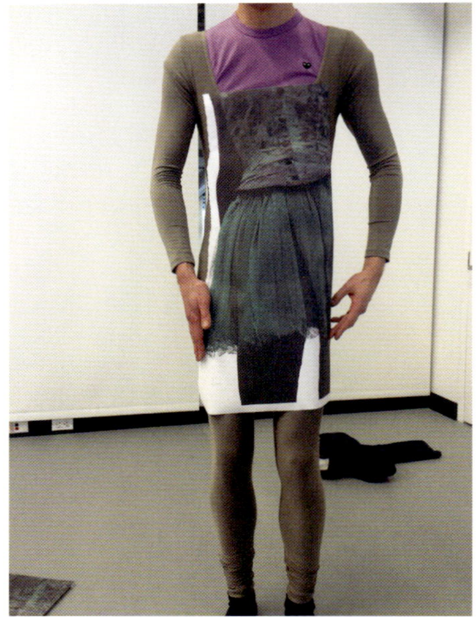

Preliminary study for dancers' unitards in *Transmissions*, printed with Louise Lawler's *Marie + 90*, (2010/2012), 2018

their positions on the vinyl flooring. Unannounced, they warmed up in plain sight on two freestanding ballet barres that guarded the empty stage. After about an hour, they moved the barres aside and stripped down to their leotards. One leotard was black. The other three were white, and Mauss had had each printed with an enlarged photograph by Louise Lawler—in magenta, green, or blue—of Marie, Edgar Degas's iconic *Little Dancer Aged Fourteen* from about 1880. Marie's tulle skirt wrapped their hips while her bronze bodice stretched across their torsos as if they were literally clothed in the sculpture, as if they had become her. Then they danced. They moved and posed to the ambient music of the rehearsal tapes, the sounds of the visitors shuffling about, and the occasional cough or baby's cry. They danced to the sounds they made with their footfalls, claps, and breaths of exertion. During solos, duets, and trios, those not dancing left the stage and crossed the space to stand like sentinels, or to lounge on a large white staircase structure inspired by a set in some of the Lynes pictures. Glances ricocheted from dancer to audience to artwork to dancer, their bodies juxtaposed with those of the slide projections, sculptures, photos, videos, and other people in the space. Visitors were unwittingly turned into audience

members. Some squatted or sat cross-legged around the action, while others stared at the artworks as though oblivious to the performance going on. The vinyl floor was but one stage within the larger stage of the exhibition, its edge a porous membrane transgressed by flows of energy and attention that activated all the bodies within the space of the gallery—whether real or depicted. Those who had been captured on camera were by now mostly dead, lost to age, AIDS, or greater or lesser degrees of obscurity. But somehow, in the moment, they felt present and close.

After repeating the fifty-minute sequence, the dancers stopped their labor and began a cooldown. They stretched, lounged, and chatted among themselves, smiling with relief and accomplishment or maybe grimacing at the recollection of a leap that had fallen flat. We witnessed them transform from performers back into people, which always felt strangely more touching and magical than the other way around. Then, without applause, they left the room and got on the subway and on with their lives, yet the exhibition remained somehow altered by the memory of their work. And the next day all this happened again, a little differently, in a shiny new museum with old wood floors, adjacent to the last meatpacking plant in Manhattan, around the corner from Merce Cunningham's former dance studio, across the street from the crumbling piers where people used to cruise, make love, and make art.

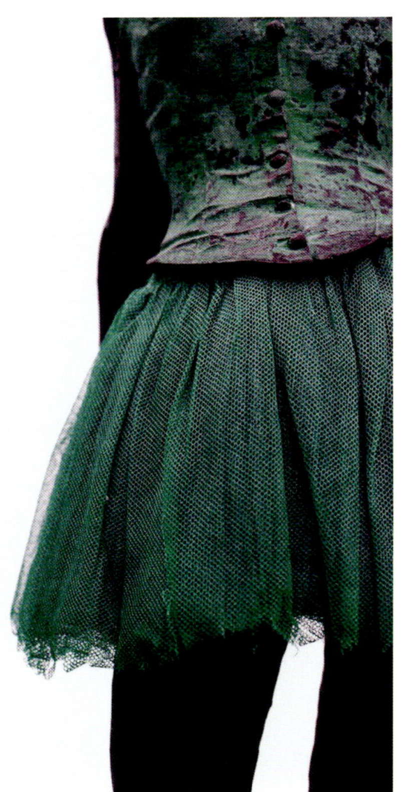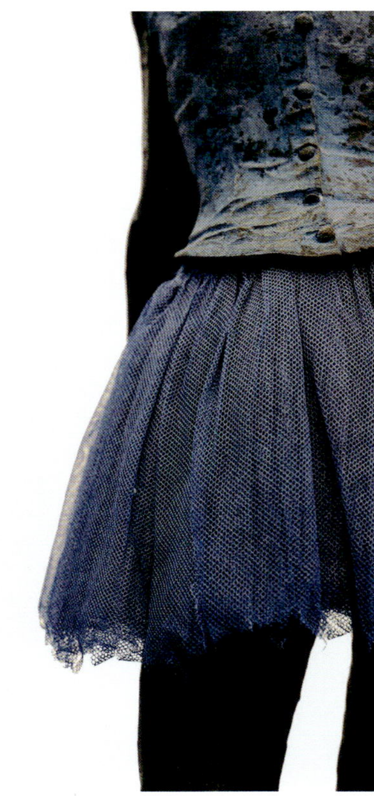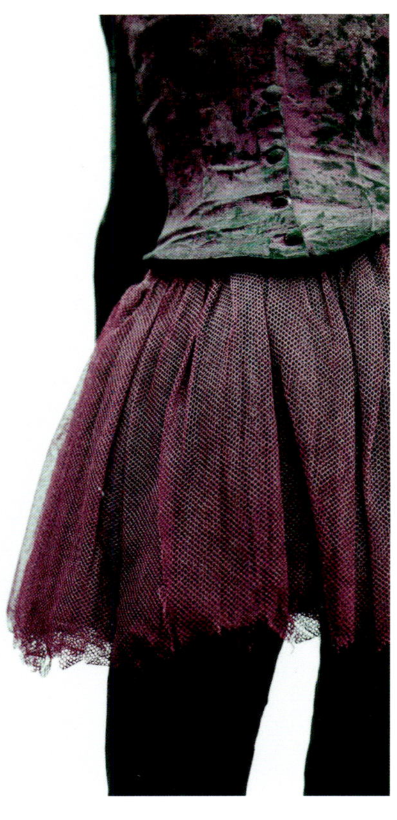

Left to right: Louise Lawler, *Marie + 90*, *Marie + 180*, and *Marie + 270*, 2010/2012. Silver dye bleach prints on aluminum, 59⅛ × 45½ × 1¹³⁄₁₆ inches (150.2 × 115.7 × 4.6 cm) each. Whitney Museum of American Art, Purchase, with funds from the Photography Committee (*Marie + 90*); Courtesy the artist and Metro Pictures, New York (*Marie + 180* and *Marie + 270*)

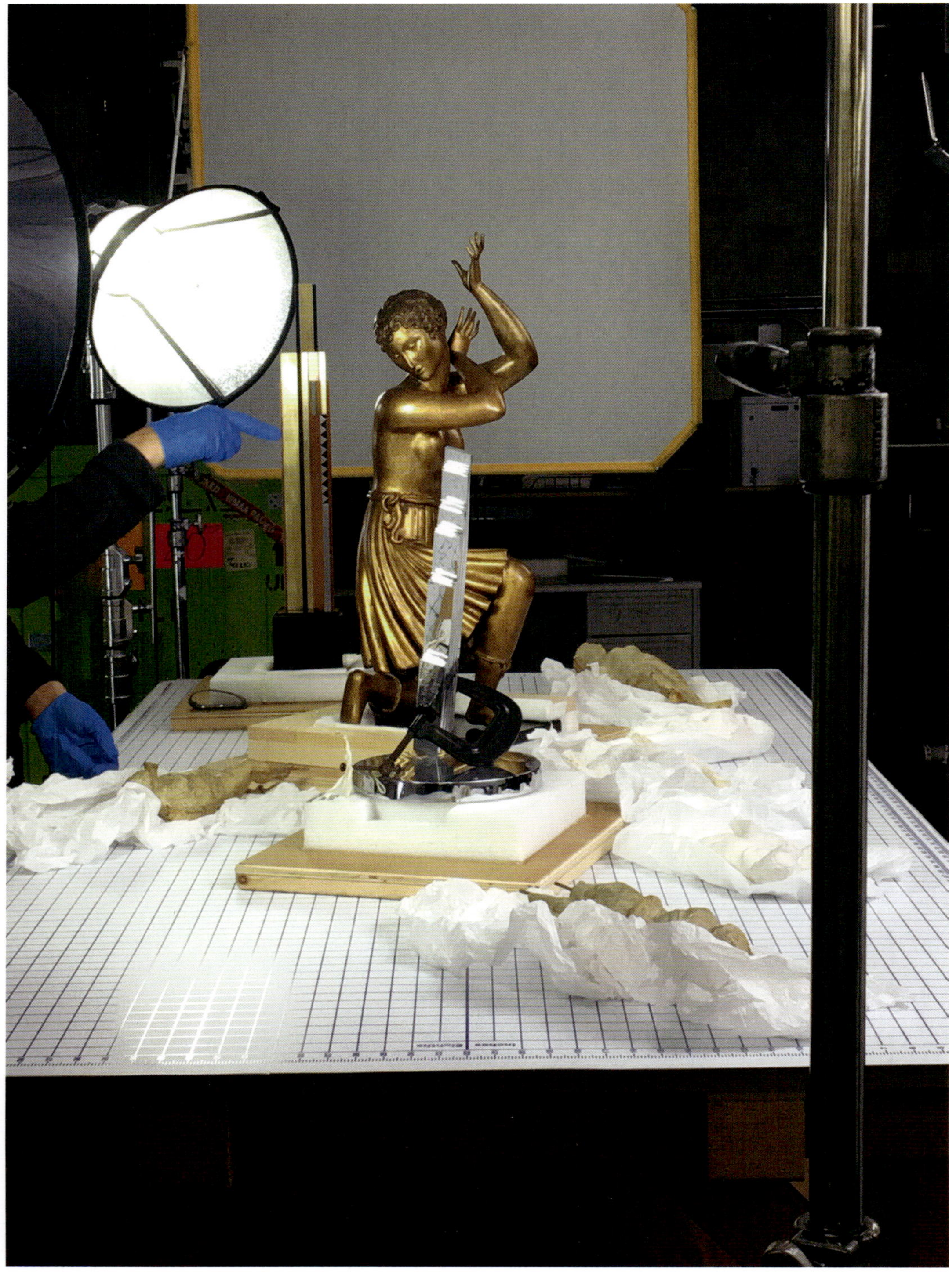

I came to ballet late and in reverse—I didn't grow up with it. My first exposure to live dance was through the 2001 White Oak restagings of Judson dances, which made me a devotee of Judson Dance Theater and post-Judson dance. Ballet seemed reactionary, far away, and of no use to me. But my interest in dance was kindled at about the same time I had begun to grow suspicious of a naturalized art-historical canon. The discrepancy between that canon and my own interests or possible artistic antecedents drove me to fashion a new frame of reference for myself. I began to pull at loose threads in the modernist narrative, and these drew my attention to theater, couture, architecture, and decoration, as well as to practitioners who were seldom or no longer spoken of but who opened up worlds outside of given categorical limits. It was in reconsidering standard histories of modernist painting that I encountered Natalia Goncharova's and Marie Laurencin's designs for the Ballets Russes, which taught me that the unassailable version of modernism I had learned could be destabilized when seen from a different point of view where the relation to performance, collaboration, and intersecting media was made primary. Through a succession of different overlays of genealogies, I eventually arrived at the flamboyant intersection of modernist ballet and art in New York in the 1930s through the 1950s. I was surprised to find that this nexus not only articulated an overtly queer erotics long before the emergence of a public language around "queerness" but also engendered experimental cross-media collaborations and dialogues that presaged many of the techniques that are commonly assumed to have emerged in the 1960s. Indeed, as Gerald Murphy, the expatriate American artist who had designed sets for the Cole Porter jazz ballet *Within the Quota* (1923), remarked, "Ballet was the focal center of the whole modern movement in the arts."[1]

If ballet really had been "the focal center," I wondered, then why was ballet only mentioned as an aside in histories of modern art? When had the centrality of ballet to the avant-garde been occluded from the historical narrative, and to whose benefit? By looking elsewhere—to the peculiar images and words sparked by ballet—I found what I had been looking for: traces of a wholly different conception of the reciprocity between visual art, dance, and life than the one I had been taught. It is a story that is not often told—one that poses as many questions about how history is constructed as about how it is disfigured and, of course, about how we occupy our own time.

I wondered how the jarring effect of reading accounts, such as the following *Theatre Arts* article from 1951, could be made visible in the form of an exhibition:

List the artists who have been responsible for the settings and costumes of modern ballet and you have a Who's Who of modern art. Picasso, Matisse, Dalí, Rouault, Chagall, Leger, Braque, Dufy, Utrillo, Juan Gris, and Marie Laurencin, all would be included. It is no accident that the rise of the one art form coincides with the rise of the other. It is in large part due to the glamor, color, and excitement with which modern art invested it, that ballet, which traditionally had been the private amusement of aristocrats, became during the past two or three decades the delight of millions. It is also true that modern art won new converts for itself when an audience which normally would have little or no personal contact with the new art to be seen then mostly in small galleries, came under the spell of its brilliant fantasy and dazzling color at public ballet performances.[2]

* * *

Like modern art, ballet was not endemic to the United States and would have to be imported, its audience invented. The early twentieth century had produced a new paradigm for ballet in Europe, most notably in the production model of Serge Diaghilev, who invited avant-garde composers and painters to collaborate on ballets whose choreography borrowed as much from Greek vases, cinema, the machine age, and tennis as from the classical vocabulary handed down from the Imperial Russian Ballet. Ballet and painting, both art forms of the royal courts, subverted their classical conventions in tandem through the frame of the proscenium. The future proselytizer of an American ballet idiom, Lincoln Kirstein, wrote in 1937 about Diaghilev's catalytic genius: "Revolutionary cubism hit the ballet with its ton of bricks and horrified the old guard ballet-ballet lovers, which was Diaghilev's earnest intention. Social satire, American jazz, the everyday continental vacation and boulevard life of the nineteen-twenties; dada, neo-classicism, the falsely naïve, the falsely archaic, and decorative folklore . . . were all exposed to the caprice of Diaghilev's ingenious combinations."[3] A panoply of alternate designations for ballet stagings of the early twentieth century attests to the rigorous disarrangements to which this traditional form was subjected, as well as to the various attempts to think dance *through* its kinship dynamics with other media: choreographic poem, burlesque scenes, danced legend in six pictures, choreographic picture, choreographic fantasy, romantic reverie, the first paranoiac performance, sculptural poses in three tableaux, entertainment, danced poem, mythological poem, pantomime in ten pictures, games and dances, rehearsal without décor, scenic work, a ballet document in one act.[4]

1. Gerald Murphy, quoted in Calvin Tomkins, "Living Well Is the Best Revenge," *New Yorker*, July 28, 1962.

Elie Nadelman, *Dancing Figure* (c. 1916–18); Man Ray, *New York* (1917/1966); and plaster figurines by Elie Nadelman (c. 1938–46) in the Whitney Museum of American Art storage space. Photo: Nick Mauss

2. Emily Genauer, "Modern Art and the Ballet: The Trend Is toward Separation," *Theatre Arts* (October 1951): 16.

3. Lincoln Kirstein, *Blast at Ballet: A Corrective for the American Audience* (New York: Marstin Press, 1938), 15.

4. The descriptors enumerated here are appended to the titles of the following ballets: *The Afternoon of a Faun*, 1912; *Petrushka*, 1911; *Nobilissima Visione*, 1938; *Le Spectre de la rose*, 1911; *Les Sylphides*, 1909; *Bacchanale*, 1931; *Mercure*, 1924; *Le Bal*, 1929; *Scheherazade*, 1910; *Jeux*, 1913; *Narcisse*, 1911; *The Triumph of Neptune*, 1927; *Midnight Sun*, 1915; *Romeo and Juliet*, 1938; *Le Train Bleu*, 1924; *Filling Station*, 1937.

Flyer (recto) signed by André Breton and Louis Aragon condemning Max Ernst and Joan Miró's collaboration with Serge Diaghilev, 1926

Prone to capitalize on public scandal, modernist ballet also inflamed controversies along ideological lines, such as the one that arose on the opening night of *Romeo and Juliet* in 1926, when André Breton and Louis Aragon, while chanting, "Long live the Soviets, long live the Russian Revolution!" scattered protest leaflets from the balcony over the ballet audience, accusing their former peers Max Ernst and Joan Miró of selling out Surrealism by collaborating with Diaghilev for the sake of entertainment.

Protest

It is inadmissible that ideas should be at the behest of money. Not a year goes by but that someone whom one thought to be unshakeable submits to forces to which he was opposed until then. Those individuals who capitulate to the point of disregarding social distinctions are of no importance, for the ideal to which they paid allegiance before their abdication survives without them. That is why the participation of the painters Max Ernst and Joan Miró in the forthcoming production of the Russian Ballet can never imply that although they have abandoned

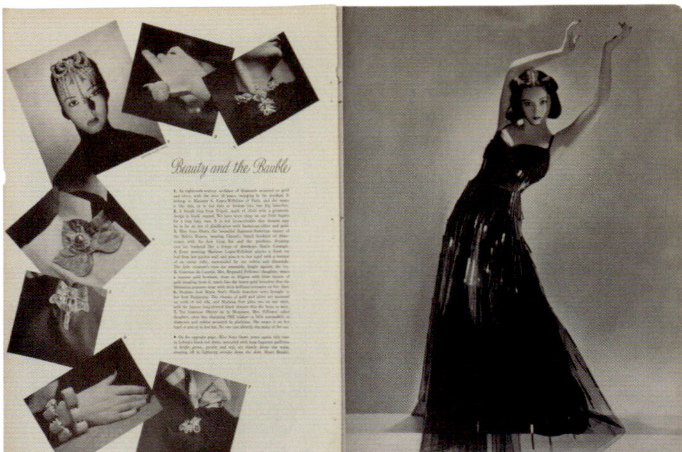
Interior spread from the May 1938 issue of *Harper's Bazaar* featuring dancer Sono Osato photographed by George Platt Lynes

their class the surrealist ideal *has done likewise. It is essentially a subversive ideal which cannot come to terms with such enterprises, whose goal has always been to tame the dreams and rebellions of physical and intellectual hunger for the profit of the international aristocracy.*

It may have seemed to Ernst and Miró that their collaboration with M. de Diaghilew, legitimised by the example of Picasso, would not have serious consequences. However, it puts us under the obligation—we who have all the worry of maintaining slave-ships of every kind of advanced thought out of reach—of denouncing, without consideration of the people involved, an attitude which arms the worst partisans with questionable ethics.

We know that we are only making out a very relative case for our artistic relationship with such and such. Give us the honor of believing that in May 1926 we are more than ever incapable of sacrificing our sense of real revolution.[5]

* * *

I looked to American magazines of the 1930s and 1940s as carriers for multiple dissonant messages, their covers often featuring works by the same artists who intervened on transatlantic ballet stages, as well as in museums and galleries. The pages of fashion magazines, in particular, provided both a conduit for the popularization of vanguard European aesthetics, as well as a stage for certain kinds of performance, in which the frozen pose

of the model had clearly been lifted from a repertoire of danced gestures, as in a spread devoted to jewelry modeled by the Ballet Theatre dancer Sono Osato photographed by George Platt Lynes. In another instance, an invocation of ballet's recent past appears in an advertisement for American Enka brand rayon (transformed by the Hollywood costume designer Adrian into a "Greek-style" dress), via a cameo appearance by the dancer Leon Danielian costumed in the title role of Vaslav Nijinsky's iconic *Afternoon of a Faun*.[6] The interplay of glamour, vanguard art, ballet, and stylized history made a potent cocktail, most poignantly blended by Lynes, for transmitting aesthetic innovation, coded desire, and commerce. During the course of his lifetime, Lynes created a vast body of studio photographs of ballet dancers in poses excerpted from their dances and of models in fashion tableaux or other allegories of war, mythology, and eros. Lynes's artistic output describes a double life of sorts, encompassing works made for public and commercial dissemination as well as private works made for friends or for a distant future. Often Lynes's models—including visual artists, lovers, and cultural icons—spanned both dimensions. Despite their high artifice, or maybe because of it, Lynes's photographs

6. I invoke the concept of the "recent past" as it is analyzed in Walter Benjamin's *Arcades Project*: "This unrelenting confrontation of the recent past with the present moment is something new, historically. Other contiguous links in the chain of generations have existed within the collective consciousness, but they were hardly distinguished from one another within the collective. The present, however, already stands to the recent past as the awakening stands to the dream." Walter Benjamin, *The Arcades Project*, trans. Howard Eiland and Kevin McLaughlin (Cambridge, MA: Harvard University Press, 1999), 898.

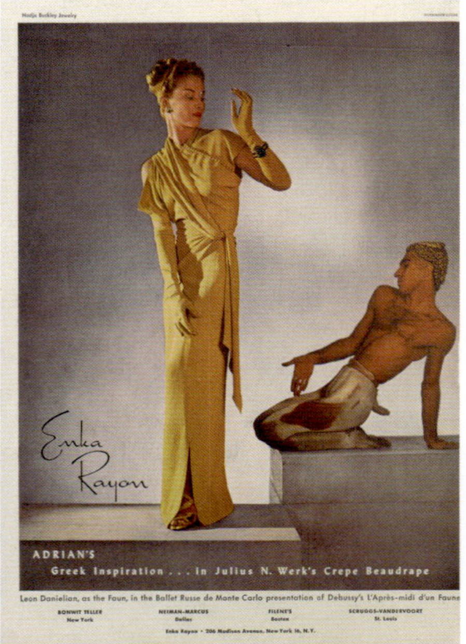

Advertisement for American Enka rayon in the November 15, 1944 issue of *Vogue*, with photograph of unknown model and Ballet Russe de Monte Carlo dancer Leon Danielian by George Hoyningen-Huene

et les révoltes de la famine physique et intellectuelle.

Il a pu sembler à Ernst et à Miró que leur collaboration avec Monsieur de Diaghilew, légitimée par l'exemple de Picasso, ne tirait pas à si grave conséquence. Elle nous met pourtant dans l'obligation, nous qui avons avant tout souci de maintenir hors de portée des négriers de toutes sortes les positions avancées de l'esprit, elle nous met dans l'obligation de dénoncer, sans considération de personnes, une attitude qui donne des armes aux pires partisans de l'équivoque morale.

On sait que nous ne faisons qu'un cas très relatif de nos affinités artistiques avec tel ou tel. Qu'on nous fasse l'honneur de croire qu'en mai 1926 nous sommes plus que jamais incapables d'y sacrifier le sens que nous avons de la réalité révolutionnaire.

Louis ARAGON — André BRETON

Flyer (verso) signed by André Breton and Louis Aragon condemning Max Ernst and Joan Miró's collaboration with Serge Diaghilev, 1926

5. André Breton and Louis Aragon, translated in Alexander Schouvaloff, *The Art of Ballet Russes: The Serge Lifar Collection of Theater Designs, Costumes, and Paintings at Wadsworth Atheneum, Hartford, Connecticut* (New Haven, CT: Yale University Press, 1997), 196.

serve as crystalline documents of the interchange between him and his subjects, archiving tensions between intimacy and distance.

The Kinsey Institute for Sex Research houses one of the largest collections of Lynes's prints and negatives, a testament to its judicious founder, Alfred Kinsey, who understood the reciprocity between aesthetics and human sexuality as much as the need to preserve for future study all manner of images that produced or documented pleasure. Thus, Lynes's work, in which erotics and aesthetics are tuned to the same pitch, was saved from destruction by censorship laws that would have deemed it pornographic, housed in a heterogenous collection that would expand to include photographs of Nijinsky; dancers from the Denishawn School of Dancing and Related Arts; charts of tattoos; Japanese woodblock prints; scientific films of onanism, fellatio, sodomy (and more); as well as avant-garde films such as Jack Smith's *Flaming Creatures* (1963) and Kenneth Anger's *Kustom Kar Kommando* (1970). In looking through thousands of Lynes's images, I began to read them like a telephone book of artists, patrons, writers, models, impresarios, and dancers, and a highly enlivened view of New York's explicitly sexual cultural scenes emerged.

The dance critic, novelist, and cultural advocate Carl Van Vechten produced his own intimate archive of ballet in New York, photographing dancers, choreographers, lighting designers, and costumers in his apartment. Unlike Lynes, whose photographs' overt sexual content is intensified by their studio gloss, Van Vechten was an amateur in Roland Barthes's sense of "one who loves and loves again";[7] the photographer often privately circulated his images as self-made postcards or presented them to visiting friends as slideshows.[8] In these highly staged "photographic séances," Van Vechten's evident delight in set dressing and costuming—in selecting fabrics of an intense opticality as backdrops and evocative props to suit a subject's innate or performed character—heightens the sense of a playful rapport between the photographer and his

Carl Van Vechten, photograph of dancer Lenwood Morris, 1940. Kodachrome slides with hand-labeled frames. Jerome Robbins Dance Division, The New York Public Library for the Performing Arts, Astor, Lenox and Tilden Foundations

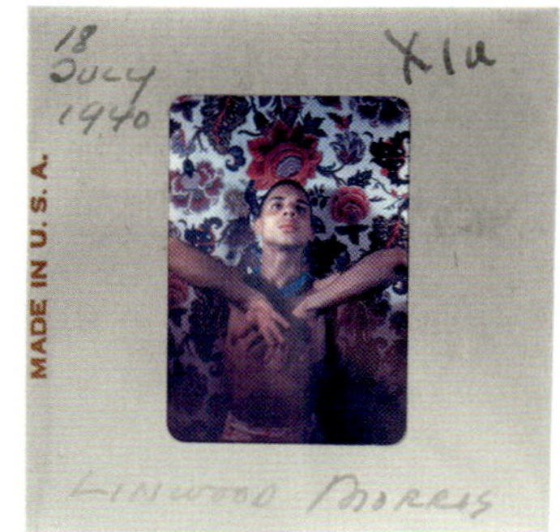

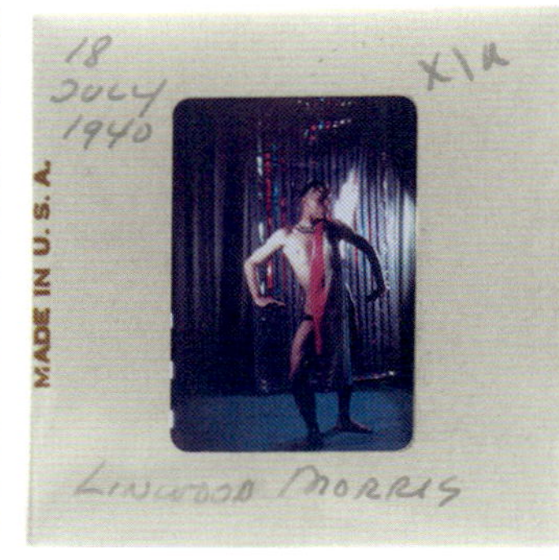

subjects that led to digressions from balletic description into mutual fantasies of identity (de)construction. His subjects include the costume designer Barbara Karinska, prima ballerina Janet Collins, Alicia Markova's legendary hands isolated in classic ballet gestures, the young Arthur Mitchell flanked by Swedish Christmas angels, Hugh Laing posing in improvised costumes, and Nora Kaye as the ax murderer Lizzie Borden in Agnes de Mille's *Fall River Legend* (1948). The artists portrayed in Van Vechten's slides range from some of the most famous in twentieth-century ballet to people who are all but forgotten. Many re-create for the camera instances from ballets that are still performed today, though with costumes that were shed from the repertoire long ago. As a repository of outmoded styles and lost languages of gesture and camp, Van Vechten's slides constitute an archive of singular importance.[9] It is fitting that Van Vechten's efforts to immortalize dancers and their dramatic roles lives on in immaterial form, as a succession of projections. The undeniable presence of these images shivers between the camera, the subject's gaze, and the contemporary viewer, who sees these larger-than-life slide-projection figures as if they are performing live. The brilliant color of the Kodachromes nearly shocks. Studying the backlit images through a loupe in the dance division of the New York Public Library, I couldn't help but dialectically conjure, like some kind of catechism, Yvonne Rainer's "No Manifesto" of 1965, to laugh at the glorious defiance of each of its provocations, which I and so many other inheritors of 1960s art and performance history had mistakenly internalized as unassailable

tenets: "NO to spectacle no to virtuosity no to transformations and magic and make-believe no to the glamour and transcendency of the star image no to the heroic no to the anti-heroic no to trash imagery no to involvement of performer or spectator no to style no to camp no to seduction of spectator by the wiles of the performer no to eccentricity no to moving or being moved."[10]

But I *was* moved by these performances for the camera.[11] I had been looking for antecedents for recent queer, experimental, collaborative, transdisciplinary practices, and I had been looking for a certain New York—one that I didn't have any evidence of and that nobody ever spoke about. It is no accident that this search fixated on a historical blind spot, somewhere between Van Vechten, Judson, and Stonewall, though it also kept shifting depending on where I placed emphasis. I wanted to know what an art history of pre-Stonewall New York would look like, and both Van Vechten's intimate images and Lynes's tableaux offered visual evidence of sensibilities, complex interrelationships, modes of exchange, and ways of being that did not conform to the streamlined narratives of art or its progress through the twentieth century as we have internalized them.

* * *

When I came upon the dedication in Charles Henri Ford's volume of selected poems from 1972, *Flag of Ecstasy*, I found remarkable its address not to *one* but to *many* distinct individuals from the author's past and present who may or may not have known each other—and may or may not have even liked each other if they did. It is not a list of people one would necessarily think of as associated, and it gives its many unknowns the same weight as its luminaries. It begs questions: who are they, and how are they all related? In Ford's configuration, even those I was already familiar with had new significance. After some time spent reading the list over and over, I couldn't help but notice that nearly all these artists and writers seemed to be linked into this transatlantic network/milieu via Gertrude Stein: the mother of us all.[12]

7. Roland Barthes, *Roland Barthes by Roland Barthes*, trans. Richard Howard (Berkeley: University of California Press, 1994), 52.
8. See Paul Padgette, introduction to *The Dance Photography of Carl Van Vechten* (New York: Schirmer Books, 1981), 14. *Transmissions* was the first instance in which Van Vechten's slides of dances were publicly presented, and I am grateful to the Jerome Robbins Dance Division of the New York Public Library for the Performing Arts, Peter Kayafas, and Edward Burns of the Van Vechten Trust, for preserving them so beautifully and making it possible to share them with a greater public.

9. The fact that some of Van Vechten's images of performing artists date from the early 1960s verifies the persistence of those languages and their overlap with not only modern but early postmodern dance aesthetics. One of Andy Warhol's assistants from the later years, Benjamin Liu (aka Ming Vase), remembers that Van Vechten was discussed in an early issue of Warhol's *Interview*, a context in which he registered no longer as a mainstream cultural commentator but as a kind of subcultural curio. Liu, conversation with the author, April 2018.

10. Yvonne Rainer, "Some Retrospective Notes on a Dance for 10 People and 12 Mattresses Called 'Parts of Some Sextets,' Performed at the Wadsworth Atheneum, Hartford, Connecticut, and Judson Memorial Church, New York, in March, 1965," *Tulane Drama Review* 10, no. 2 (Winter 1965): 178.
11. I do not intend here to enforce an opposition between Rainer's work and the images of a lost aesthetic captured by Van Vechten. In the context of the essay in which it originally appears, the "No Manifesto" carries a different valence. Rainer herself revised the manifesto in 2008 to give greater flexibility to "the rules and boundaries of my own artistic game of the moment," as she had described the litany of refusals in 1965, pointing to an anxiety about the way an excerpt from her essay had been received, taught, and distorted as dogma. If anything, my confrontation with Van Vechten's images revealed a bridge between these hitherto antithetical practices, an unexpected juncture allowing for the implications of each philosophical proposition to come into greater relief. Additionally, during the final edit of this book, I had the opportunity to rehearse with Yvonne Rainer for Emily Coates's and Rainer's reconstruction of "Parts of Some Sextets," in which I performed movements that originated with Robert Morris. How this affects my thinking I hope to address at a future point.
12. Gertrude Stein was a "mother" to a number of figures in this book, including Charles Henri Ford, George Platt Lynes, Virgil Thompson, and Carl Van Vechten, to name only a few of the figures who she introduced to one another and whose work she supported.

```
TO

A. EVERETT AUSTIN, JR.
CHRISTIAN BERARD
ANDRE BRETON
GERTRUDE CATO
JEAN COCTEAU
CARESSE CROSBY
E. E. CUMMINGS
ISAK DINESEN
MARCEL DUCHAMP
BILLIE HOLIDAY
EUGENE JOLAS
MARIE LAURE
MARIE MENKEN
ZACHARY SCOTT
EDITH SITWELL
GERTRUDE STEIN
FLORINE STETTHEIMER
PAVEL TCHELITCHEW
CARL VAN VECHTEN
PETER WATSON
WILLIAM CARLOS WILLIAMS
STARK YOUNG
```

Dedication page in Charles Henri Ford's *Flag of Ecstasy: Selected Poems by Charles Henri Ford* (Los Angeles: Black Sparrow Press, 1972)

I drew multiple webs of interrelationships, elective affinities, and echo waves of influence, focusing as much on the social, professional, sexual, and collaborative points of contact as on transhistorical resonances that were in some cases perhaps fantasy—eschewing standard mappings of modern art. To contravene the bizarre authority invested in Alfred H. Barr's diagrams of art of the modern period, I embraced anachrony and distortion over apparent objectivity. Ultimately, the most inspired social diagram arrived in the form of a drawing by Natalie Clifford Barney, inserted between the endpapers and frontispiece of her 1929 collection of essays, *Aventures de l'Esprit*. Barney's map details the many guests who came over the years to the salon she hosted in the Doric "temple of friendship" beside her house in Paris starting in 1910. It's nearly impossible to read or figure out. As such, it not only represents the open form of this kind of gathering but also indexes with humor and charm and in a kind of chaotic complexity the passage of a few people through a particular place in time (notice the teapot around the tiny table at the center). The map admits its own insufficiency. I can decipher a few names: here too are Gertrude Stein, as well as Djuna Barnes, Colette, Eileen Gray, Rainer

Maria Rilke, and even some who moved from this social scene in Paris to the overlapping New York circles of my research: Isadora Duncan, Darius Milhaud, Virgil Thompson, and Carl Van Vechten. This *Temple de l'Amitié* gave me a conceptual model for the swarming that I hoped to picture in the form of an exhibition and, later, in that of this book. I was beginning to understand that I wanted neither to conclusively portray early ballet in New York nor to glorify a lost sensibility but to transmit multiple simultaneous relations (among works of art and among people). Though punctured by voids and elisions, this construction would have to hold up against the irremediability of certain histories, figures, anecdotes, circumstances, artworks, dances, gestures, events, speech acts, and biographies.

* * *

It occurred to me that the history of dance in America, like the history of modern visual art that was ringing increasingly false, was marked by a rift: the most daring practitioners of dance in the United States in the first half of the twentieth century were women, many of whom made their careers abroad.[13] These were makers of modern dance, even if some of what they made was termed ballet (in the US, the blanket term tended to be thrown

13. Josephine Baker, Isadora Duncan, Katherine Dunham, and Loie Fuller are among the American dance makers who left an indelible mark on early twentieth-century visual culture in Europe.

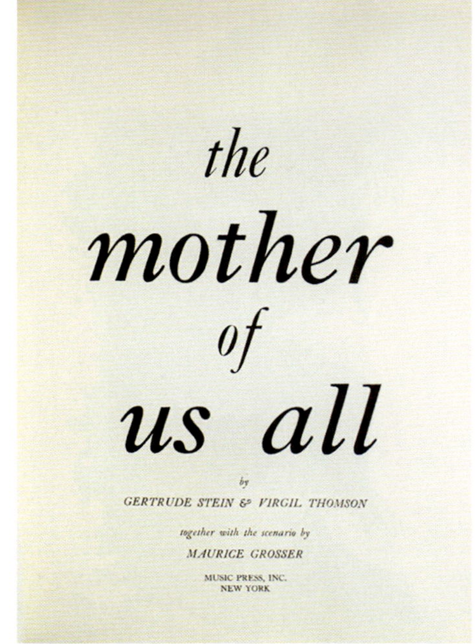

Frontispiece of *The Mother of Us All*, a piano-vocal score for Virgil Thompson's second opera, with text by Gertrude Stein (New York: Music Press, 1947)

on almost any artistic arrangement of bodies on a stage). Jill Johnston, the radical public intellectual who began her career as a dance critic and had worked in the dance division of the New York Public Library, narrates the fissure in the story of American dance as follows:

> *I had a powerful subconscious understanding of dance in America as a matriarchal tradition. Isadora Duncan was our founding matriarch. I saw her at the head of some family tree consisting of women. The story I had developed, and at length updated, went something like this: There had been something awful going on in Europe called the ballet, which was punitive toward women. But the ballet was the only form of respectable professional dance that existed for women. In the meantime, women in America were tasting greater freedom through the early feminist movement. The ballet had not taken hold here. A woman from California called Isadora, who knew all about ballet and had a free sort of California spirit, invented a dance that didn't bind the body or depend on men to look good. She was succeeded by other pioneering-type women, St. Denis, then Humphrey and Graham, who applied their intellects to dance making to invent whole techniques and formal approaches to choreography. . . . Then somewhere along in there the European ballet got a foothold in America. Modern dancers welcomed the opportunity to go to ballet classes and strengthen themselves or increase their range, but were powerless to stop an invasion that eventually obscured the through line of the American modern dance. . . . Ballet companies sprang up everywhere. The money went to ballet. Modern dance became a poor sister. And women were returned to the pedestal and made to appear silly in tutus and dependent on men to look good.[14]*

14. Jill Johnston, "How Dance Artists and Critics Define Dance as Political," in *Secret Lives in Art: Essays on Art, Literature, Performance* (Chicago: A Capella, 1994), 96.

Johnston's intentionally partisan account rhymed with my own initial aversion to ballet as a restrictive tradition, but by now I was convinced that the story of modernist ballet was much more lawless and unconventional than received ideas

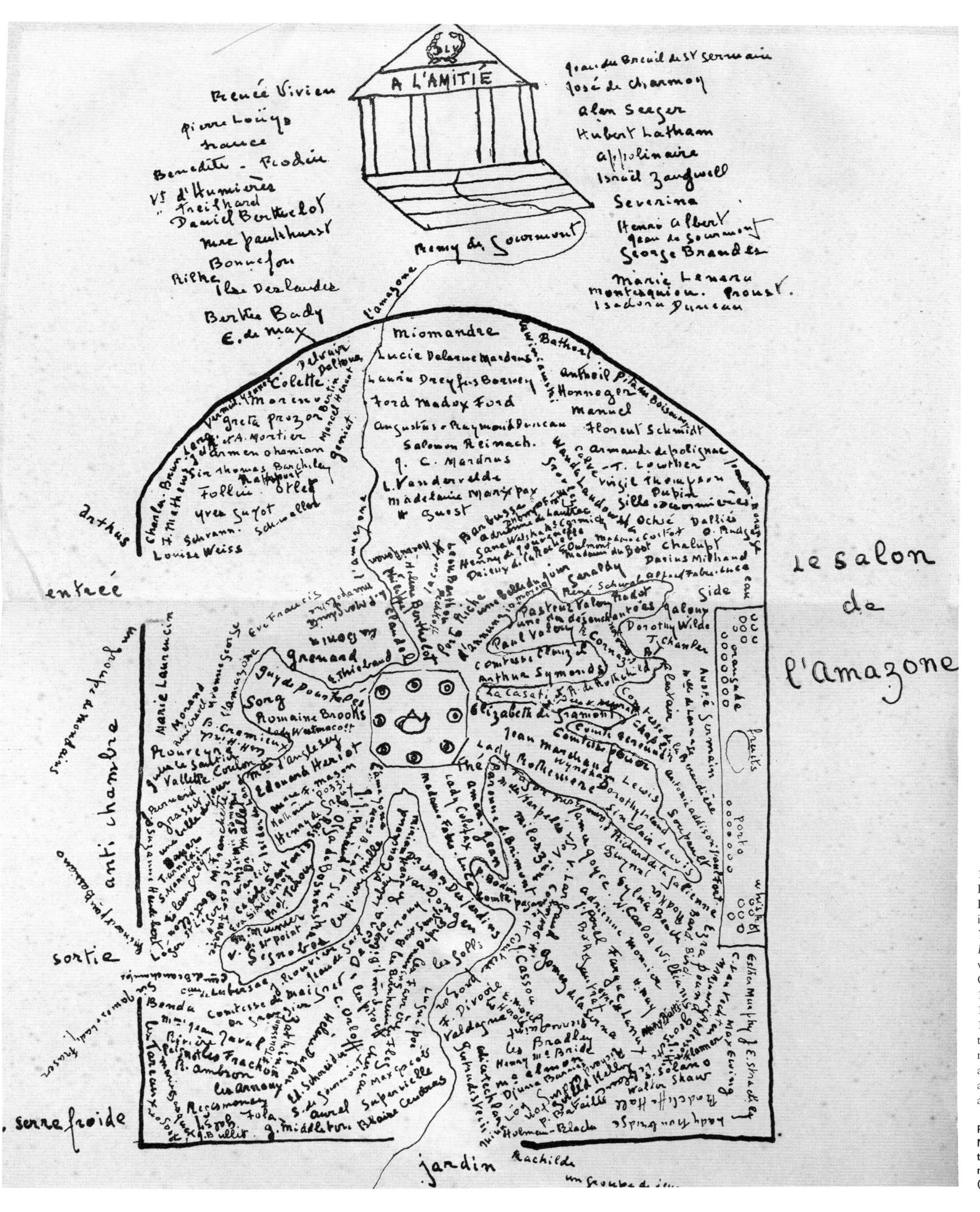

15. Sally Banes, "Sibling Rivalry: The New York City Ballet and Modern Dance," in *Dance for a City: Fifty Years of New York City Ballet*, ed. Lynn Garafola with Eric Foner (New York: Columbia University Press, 1999), 74.
16. Ibid., 78.
17. It is the problems in history that are interesting to me, not the ways in which a cleaned-up past might affirm our fantasies about a desired present.

Foldout map drawn by Natalie Clifford Barney for the frontispiece to her 1929 memoir *Aventures de L'Esprit* (Paris: Emile Paul, 1929)

would have me believe. Dance historian Sally Banes dispels the assumption that ballet and modern dance developed in opposition to one another, suggesting a relationship of reciprocal parasitism: "More like a sibling rivalry than the unadulterated hostility of enemy camps, it has been threaded through with similarities as well as sharp distinctions, love as well as envy, collaborations and incessant jostling for dominance."[15] Thanks to a novice audience, American ballet was freed from the strictures of European protocols and could try out anything and take from anyone. The resulting magpie aesthetic often made it difficult to discern the frayed borders between ballet, modern, and social dance.

In the 1920s, decades before ballet's naturalization into the culture, the form was "colonizing the sister arts in various ways: borrowing techniques, styles, moves, structures, themes, ideas, and values, as well as composers and designers from modern dance and synthesizing it with classical ballet, as well as jazz and social dancing."[16] I find Banes's use of the term "colonizing" in this context astute, in that it names the problematics.[17] Modernist ballet's ascendancy roughly coincided with the waning of the Jazz Age, and many of its productions were laced with quotations and appropriations from African American dance forms and their derivatives. Such "borrowings" may have been motivated by a certain American flair for the exotic as much as by an urgent desire on the part of choreographers to articulate, desegregate, and revise what constituted American concert dance or even American art in general. The questioning of all terms, including the term *American art*, carries into *Transmissions* in emphasizing the crucial cultural contributions made by artists who were not considered wholly American—owing either to exile or emigration from their country of origin or to the fact that they live(d) as second-class citizens in "America." And though ballet has been yoked to an ideology of "whiteness," many images of modernist ballets in America attest to a reality in which deep-seated segregation came up against earnest (and often problematic) endeavors to create modern dances that reflected the totality of a riven yet miscegenated culture, both in its dancers and in the gestures they articulated. The fact that American ballet was often produced by European or Russian émigrés working with American (*American* here meaning performers of the African diaspora, as well as of Caribbean, European, Japanese, and Native American descent), European, and Russian dancers to broadcast a jumble of national themes through various caricatures makes it difficult, from our current vantage point, to adequately parse the tangled politics of these productions.

The question of black influence and of what Erin K. Maher terms "black self-representation in concert dance"[18] under Jim Crow laws is also hard to track, especially given the number of avant-garde dance productions featuring all-black casts during the interwar period (from Gertrude Stein and Virgil Thompson's opera *Four Saints in Three Acts*, notable for its casting of performers in roles that were not race-typed, to Agnes de Mille's first ballet, an exoticist production called *Obeah*, also known as *Black Ritual*, featuring sixteen African American female dancers who were not trained in ballet). These productions coincided with the emergence of "performances of theatricalized African diaspora social dance" by Katherine Dunham, one of several independent black choreographers with all-black companies.[19] Needless to say, critical scrutiny of a modern visual culture addicted to exoticism and primitivism must extend to modernist dance in order to assess the more brutal terms of representation and embodiment in these interconnected fields.

* * *

My decision to insist on ballet as the fulcrum in *Transmissions* was also a response to the ubiquity of postmodern dance derivations within the contemporary museum environment and the reductive version of modernity that these prequalified dance idioms signify and cement. Contemporaneity is reduced to a "look" of modernity. Modernist ballets

make for engaging historical documents precisely because their own relationship to history is a kind of suspension of disbelief; they are intrinsically modernist, even if they don't "signal" modernity to contemporary eyes. But I had also noticed an undeniable difference in the images produced by ballet as compared to those produced by modern dance. While modern dance appeared enigmatic, cold, and intellectual, ballet was allowed to be highly sexualized and eclectic. Ballet images also tend to focus on and exalt the individual dancer/subject, whereas the modern dancer (unlike the auteur choreographer) was often made anonymous through universalization. The ballet dancer's headshot or full body shot—a new type of image convention borrowed from Hollywood—set in motion a peculiar ritual. Since this mechanically produced portrait was only "complete" with the depicted subject's autograph added, the image activated a circuit: seeing, admiring, dreaming about, seeing again, and finally being with the photographed subject, obliging the dancer to autograph their likeness as proof of the completed cycle.[20] In ways I didn't anticipate, *Transmissions* became a historical recoding of a particular genre not only of art dance but also of art photography. Debates around photography's status as an art form (as in

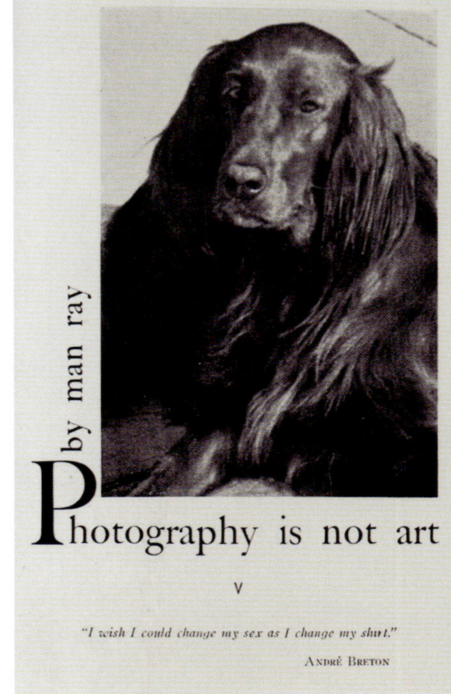

Detail of Man Ray's "Photography Is Not Art," in the April 1943 issue of *View*

Man Ray's self-ironizing multipart text "Photography Is Not Art," published serially in *View* magazine)[21] dovetailed with the contestation of this other new art form, which happened to be a central subject of modern photography: the work of the dancing body. But the nascent status of photography as art meant that the schism between commercial and high-art photography was not yet entrenched, so that photographers made use of all venues and surfaces, from catalogues and magazines to galleries and museums. That kind of porosity allowed for poses to filter back and forth between ballet, fashion, and high art in a style gradient that relied heavily on neoclassicism spiked with commercialized Surrealism and a penchant for the "unusual"—the invention of modern glamour paving the way for camp.[22]

By the end of World War II, thanks to the efforts of innumerable ballet academies and companies both imported and native, ballet had established itself as a vastly popular form of entertainment in America. An article in *Fortune* magazine, published just months after the end of World War II, "The Boom in Ballet," announces triumphantly:

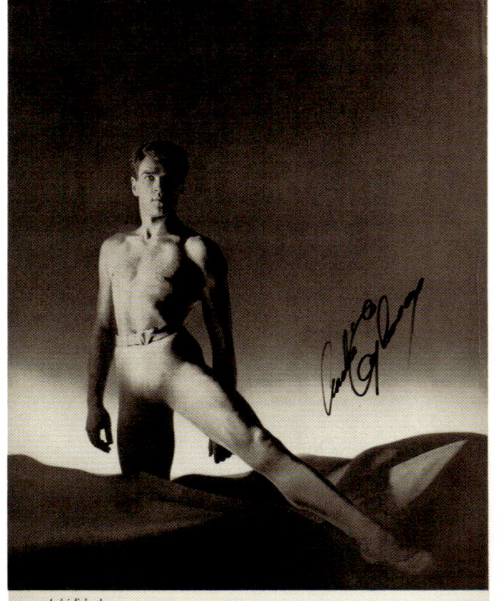

George Platt Lynes, photograph of André Eglevsky, with Eglevsky's autograph, New York City Ballet program, 1951

18. Erin K. Maher, "Ballet, Race, and Agnes de Mille's *Black Ritual*," *Musical Quarterly* 97, no. 3 (Fall 2014): 415.

19. Thomas F. DeFrantz, "Visualizing Dance of the Harlem Renaissance," in *Dance: American Art 1830–1960*, ed. Jane Dini (New Haven, CT: Yale University Press, 2016), 185.

20. Prephotographic ballet fetishes include the collecting of feathers, blossoms, and sequins that had fallen from costumes and, in one apocryphal instance, the boiling of the slippers of cult ballerina Marie Taglioni by her devotees to make a soup for their delectation. See Molly Engelhardt, "Marie Taglioni, Ballerina Extraordinaire: In the Company of Women," *Nineteenth-Century Gender Studies* 6, no. 3 (Winter 2010), https://www.ncgsjournal.com/issue63/engelhardt.htm.

21. Man Ray, "Photography Is Not Art," *View* 3, no. 1 (April 1943): 23, and no. 3 (October 1943): 77–78, 97. 22. In this way, the dates of many photographs included in *Transmissions* might cause flashes of surprise. For example, images from the 1940s might, at first glance, be misrecognized as from the 1960s or even 1980s.

There can be little doubt that the most striking artistic development of the past American decade has been the new popular success of ballet. . . . The total audience for these troupes may be estimated at over 1,500,000, and the gross take at $2 million . . . . Even Hollywood has been infected; some of the leading ballerinas have been seen along Wilshire Boulevard. . . .

Some people feel the magic at once. Others require considerable educating as to what they are supposed to see. But learning has been proceeding rapidly in the past decade. A whole new American audience has been discovering the fine art whose diaphanous graces have been rugged enough to withstand every world upheaval since 1700. Aside from the audiences on the road, it is estimated that at least half the ballet's metropolitan public are people who had never seen a pirouette ten years ago. . . .

The delirious prose describing America's newfound balletomania abruptly swerves to warn of the underlying threat posed by the practice of this art form, by which dancers might easily be "infected":

In Virgil Thompson's classic observation: "Dancers are autoerotic and have no conversation." They are professionally obliged to have a preoccupation with their own bodies, and there can be little doubt that a narcissistic degree of it has often helped to promote the extraordinary graces the great soloists achieve. But if dancers spend much of their time in that erotic direction that Sigmund Freud declares is natural to all in infancy, it is a truism that many male dancers are also homosexual. This is perhaps very largely due to the middle-class prejudice against dancing as a male profession; few boys are encouraged in a dancing bent that might lead to a ballet career. In any case, the androgynous effect provided by many male ballet dancers is not admired by ballet specialists any more than it is by steam fitters who have wandered in out of curiosity. The ideal is the pliant vigorous masculine air.[23]

23. "The Boom in Ballet," *Fortune*, December 1945, 226.

A surprisingly public reckoning with the specter of homosexuality, the fear of aberrant sexuality (and its class inscription) elaborated in this fantastical diatribe threatens to "out" dancers deemed too androgynous or even "feminine"—evidence of the tacit, though fragile, cover that ballet provided homosexual men on many fronts. To spectators, it offered a meeting place at a time when public congregation by homosexuals was forbidden; to performers, amateurs, or fans, it gave license to a complex negotiation of image, self, and desire behind the strict hetero-binary coding of ballet's narratives; to visual artists, it gave free rein to an erotic object, more naked than nude but appropriately cloaked in culture.

***

The world of the spectator, the receiver, was a primary lens through which I constructed *Transmissions*, and the flux of the exhibition's daily audience over the course of two months took on a central role within it. This book is similarly directed at the wholly different—private, rather than social—negotiations of the reader. A number of visitors commented that the eighth-floor gallery of the Whitney Museum felt more like a studio or some other space between public and private than like a museum. The visitors to *Transmissions*—their impressions, anecdotes, memories, questions, and consternation—completed what was from the outset an experiment in juxtaposing protocols of an historical exhibition with more porous artistic processes (including a collaboration with sixteen dancers).[24] And in my interactions with visitors, I understood the subject of *Transmissions* to be the memory of the body against the memory of the institution.

Transmissions became an exhibition (in its literal sense: a public display) of what the museum, as an extension of the culture, had repressed. This book is intended as a continuation of that project. I also would like to state emphatically that the histories addressed in *Transmissions* are not, as many people would like to continue to believe, minor histories. These artists and performers operated at the very center of American culture, with a high degree of visibility, popularity, influence, and support. What

24. See Allie Tepper, "Legacies of Exchange," in this volume, 170–71; and "Nick Mauss in Conversation with Dancers Alexandra Albrecht, Kristina Bermudez, Maggie Cloud, Brandon Collwes, Jasmine Hearn, Elizabeth Hepp, Forrest Hersey, Alexandra Jacob, Burr Johnson, Maki Kitahara, Evelyn Kocak, Benedict Nguyen, Matilda Sakamoto, Quenton Stuckey, and Anna Thérèse Witenberg," in this volume, 172–80.

I laid bare in *Transmissions* is the process of my own realization that American modernism is constituted by the very forms and protagonists that are claimed to fall outside its scope. In treating ballets as connective tissue, I began to see a kind of looping correlation everywhere. The myth of single authorship evaporated in countless collaborations, as did the phantom of purity that seemed to enshroud ballet and modern art. Every object I looked at opened up a new set of social, professional, sexual, and intellectual affinities and contradictions among protagonists who were often also spectators of the multiauthored, time-based artworks they contributed to, so that the cliché of an artist-as-set-designer proved too one-sided to account for the dedicated synergy and tension between these imbricated worlds. I searched through collection databases for works of art that emerged from this pluralized moment, works that are usually put in the service of a neutralized history. But it was the artifacts of dance history that uncovered what had been obscured by art history, pronouncing how false it is to speak of one without the other.

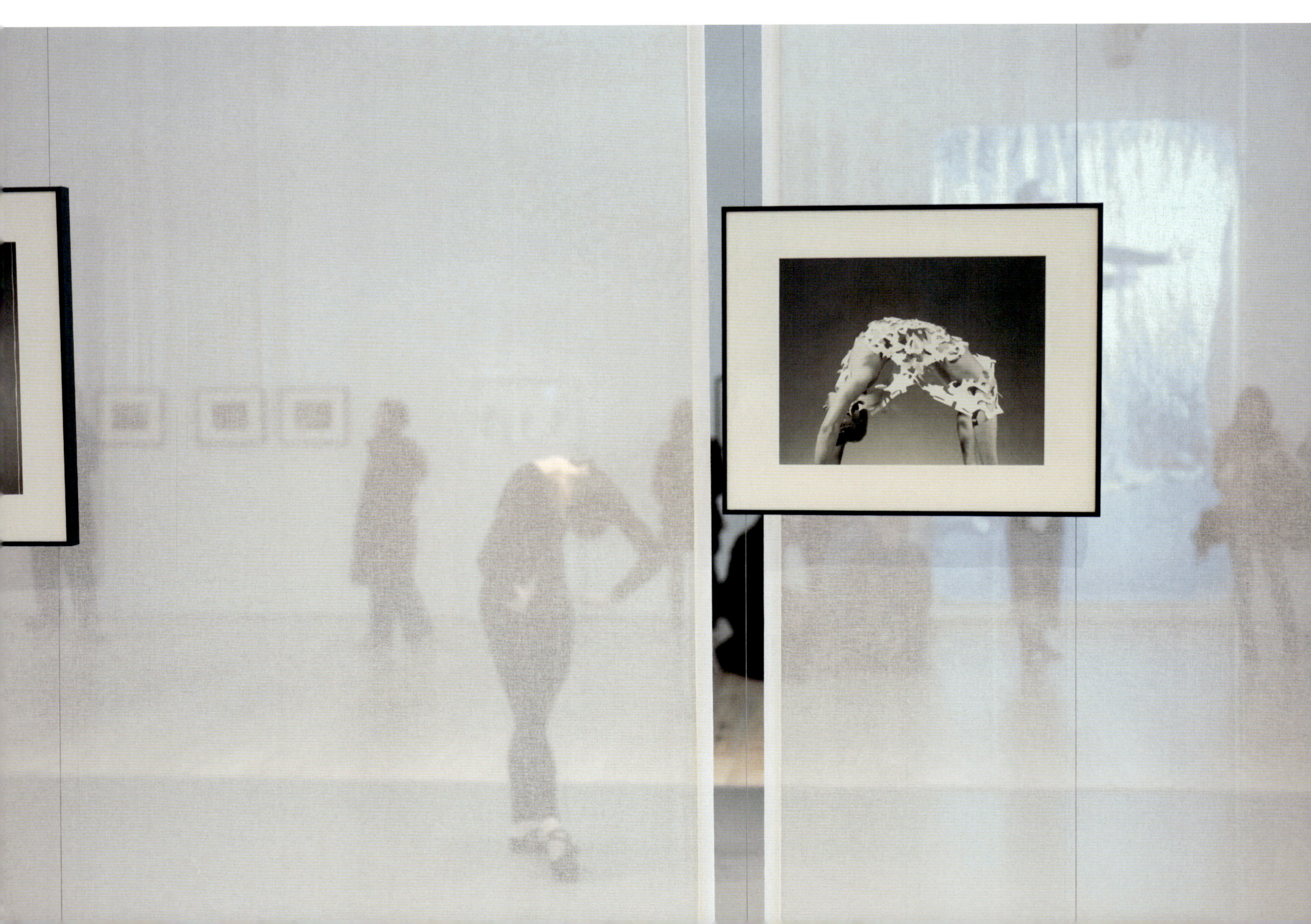

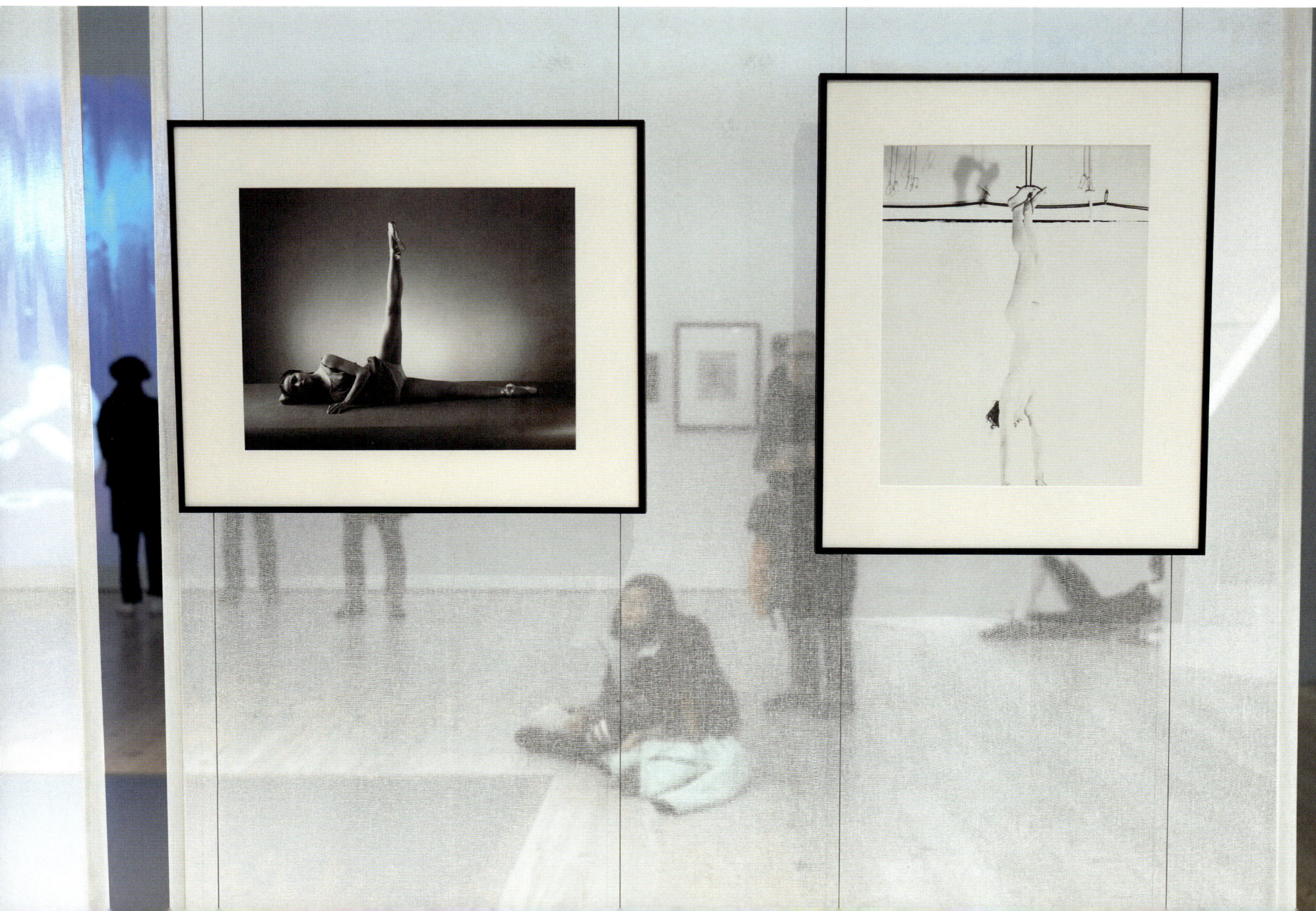

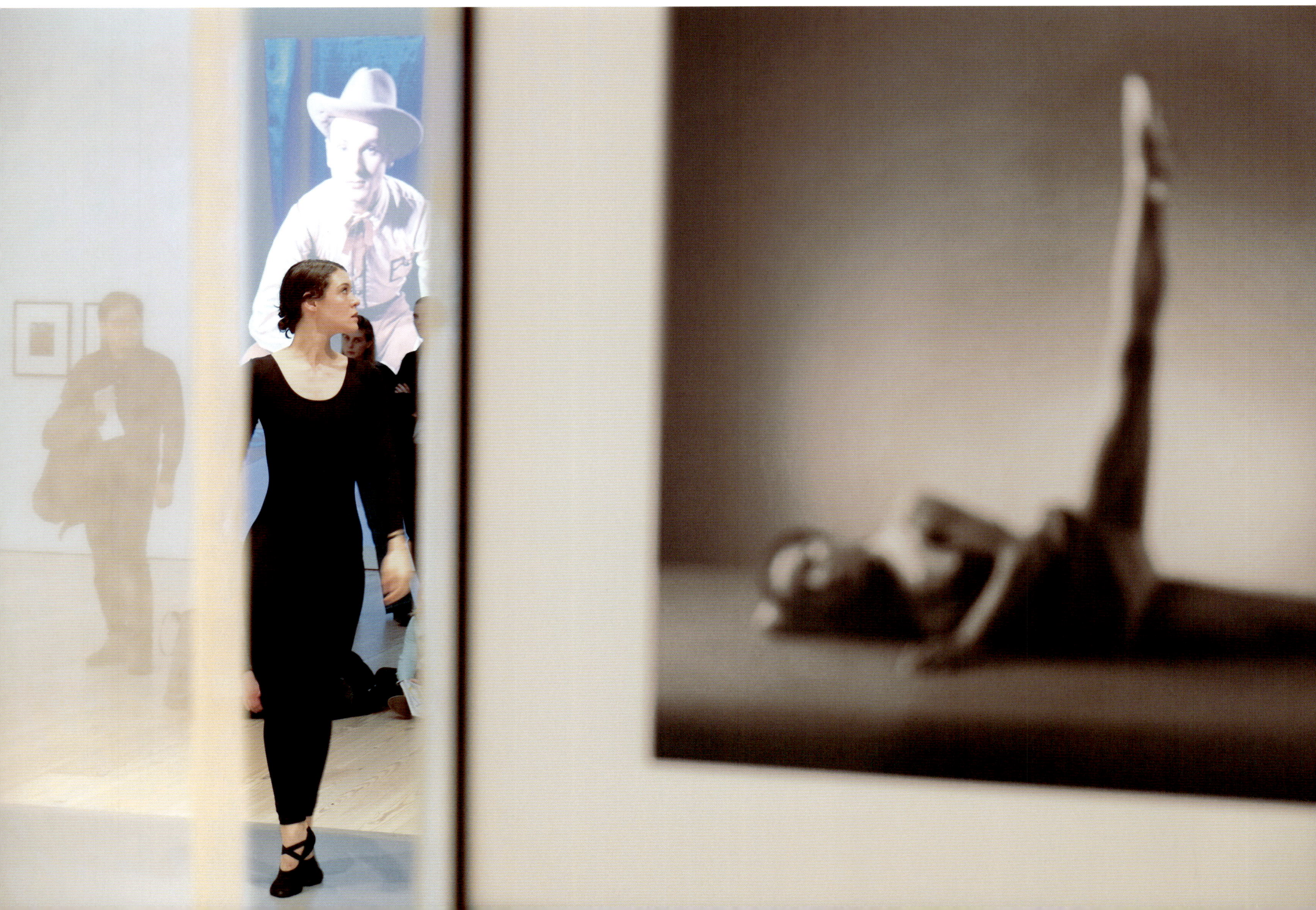

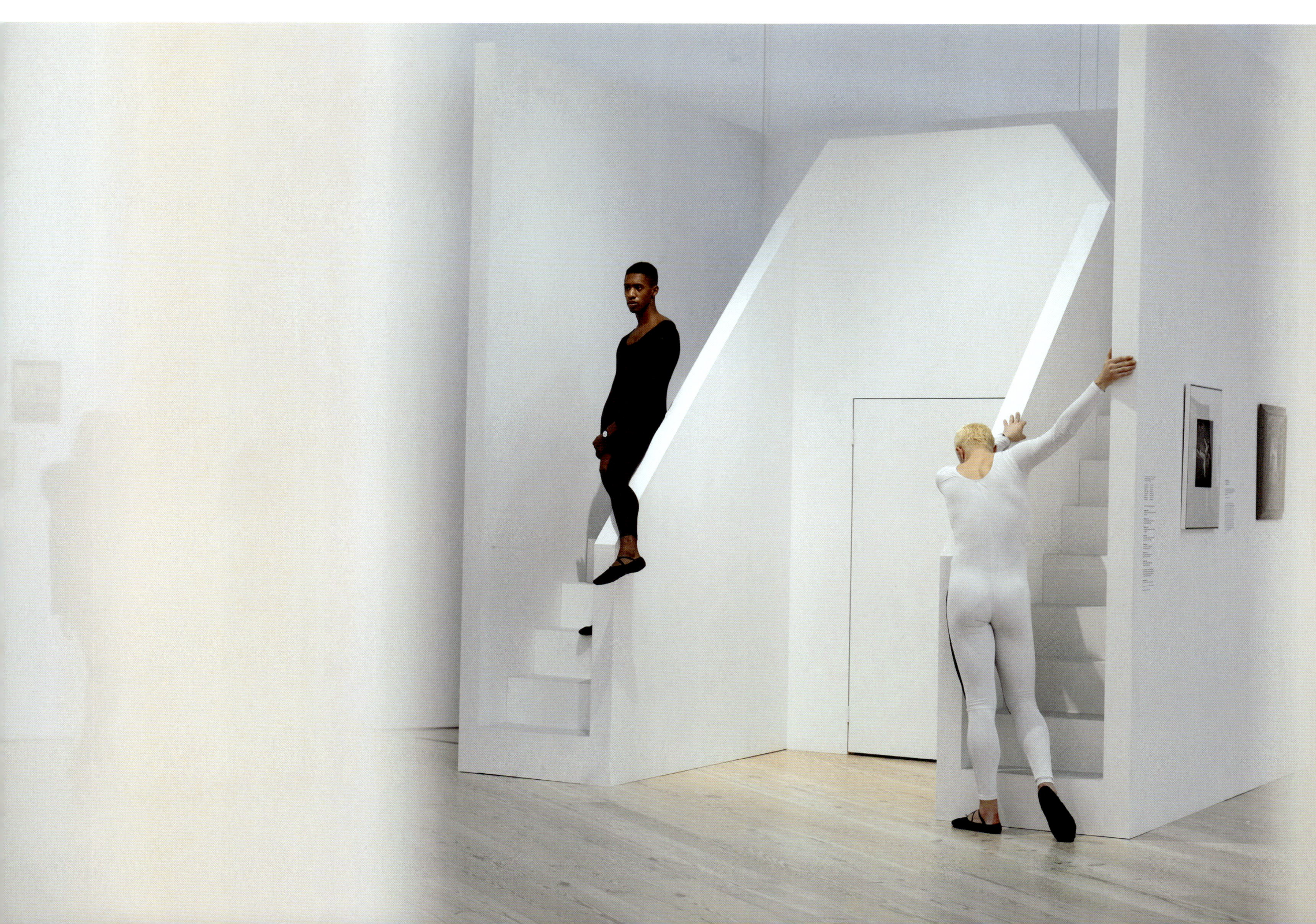

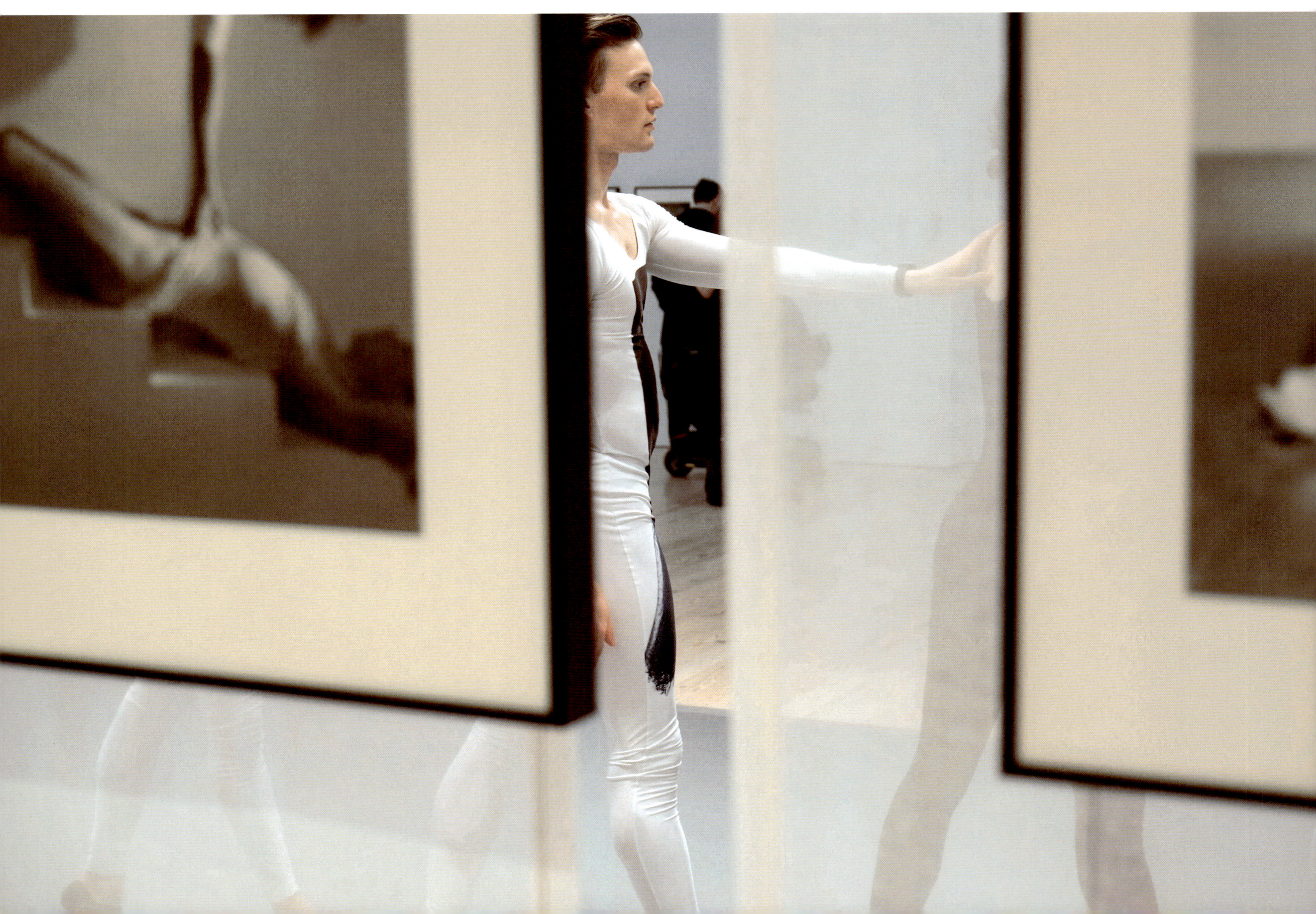

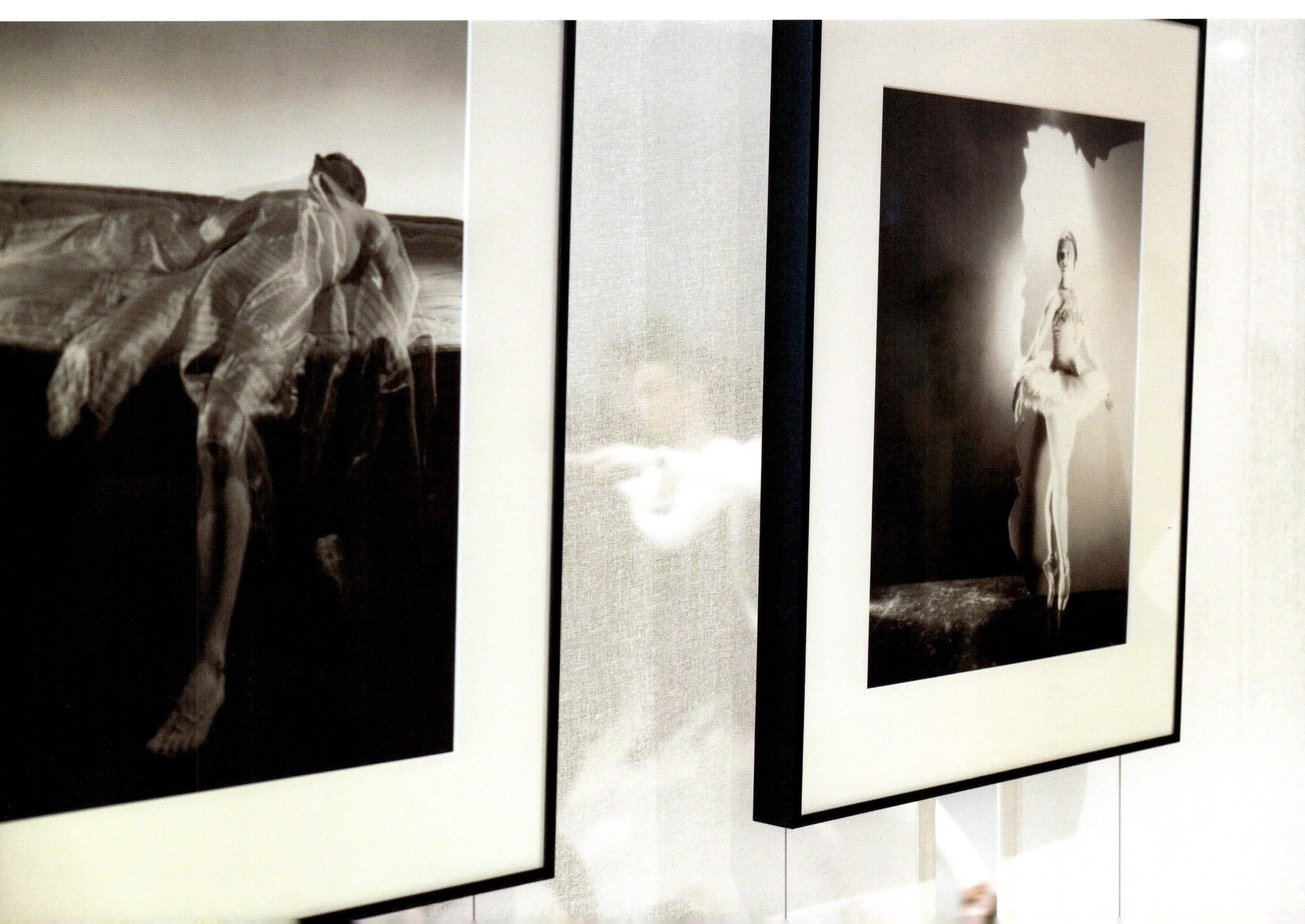

The most vivid documents of the Americanization of ballet are photographic but not necessarily documentary. Though figures such as writer, critic, curator, and cofounder of New York City Ballet Lincoln Kirstein and art dealer Julien Levy championed photography as an art form by the 1930s, its still-uncertain status allowed for experimentation and an unconventional imaging of the newly conceived language of American ballet. Ballet photography supplemented live events to create particular and erotically charged star images, aiding in ballet's dissemination across not just the United States but the world. The direct interplay between staged photography and choreography was especially visible in the studio of George Platt Lynes, where choreographers, including George Balanchine and Frederick Ashton, often posed dancers for photographs. Balanchine commented that Lynes's "pictures will contain, as far as I am concerned, all that will be remembered of my own repertory in a hundred years."

Hired by Kirstein as the official photographer of the American Ballet (precursor to New York City Ballet) in 1935, Lynes mixed the pop Surrealism he had gleaned from Man Ray and Jean Cocteau as a young student in Paris with the cold glamour of Hollywood studio photography. He piggybacked unofficial, personal work (what he called "nonprofit-making ventures") on his commercial jobs for the ballet, *Vogue*, and *Harper's Bazaar*, often using the sets he'd created for daytime shoots to photograph "ballet boys" and other models in dishabille later that night. Lynes's unofficial works were saved from destruction by Alfred Kinsey (sexologist and founder of the Institute for Sex Research at the University of Indiana), who commissioned and purchased thousands of prints and negatives spanning Lynes's oeuvre that explored themes such as mythology, allegories of war, commissioned family portraits, nudes, portraits of literary figures, ballet dancers and choreographers, and headshots of models at the moment of sexual climax.

George Platt Lynes, photograph of dancer Fred Danieli, 1937. Scan from original negative. Collections of the Kinsey Institute, Indiana University

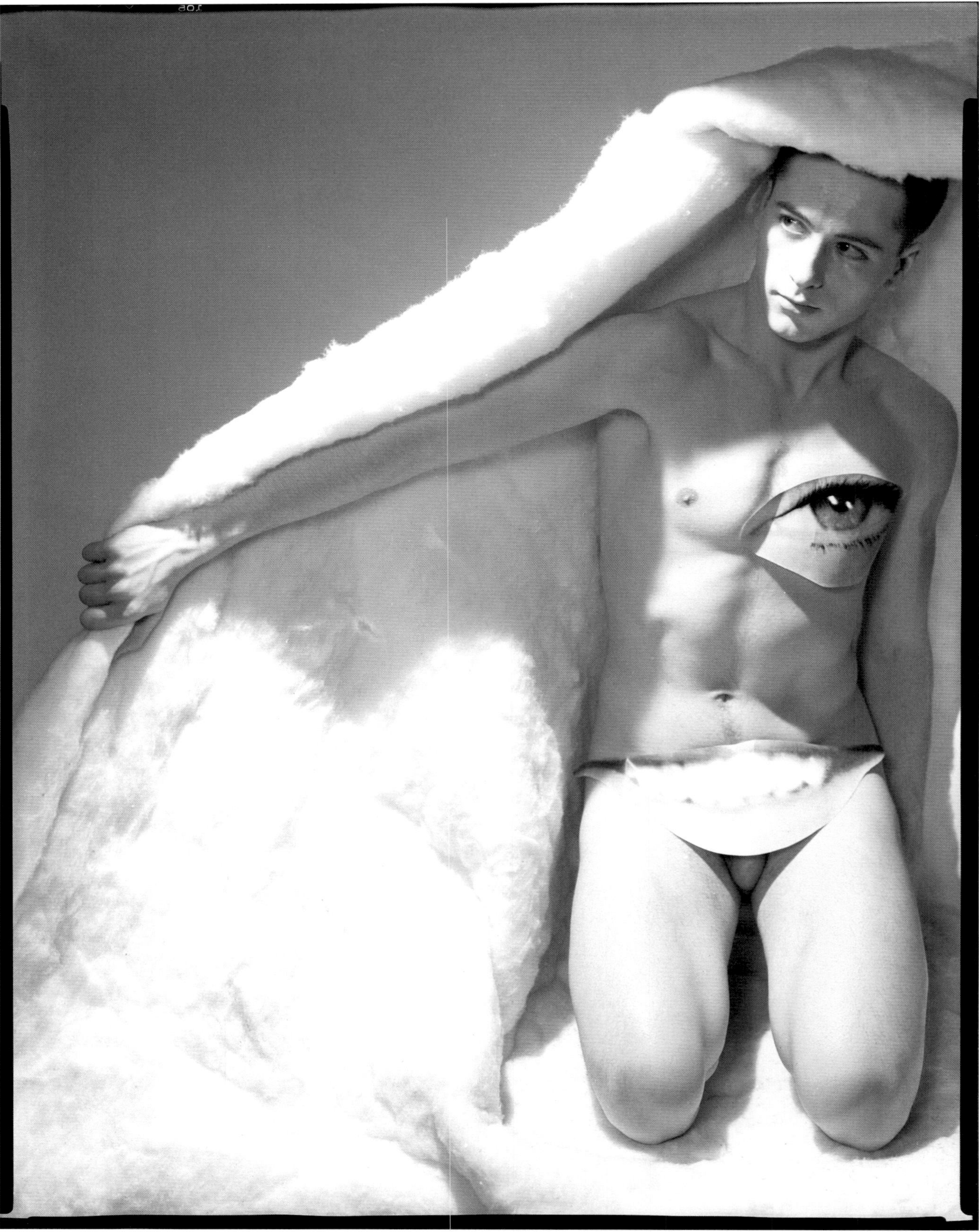

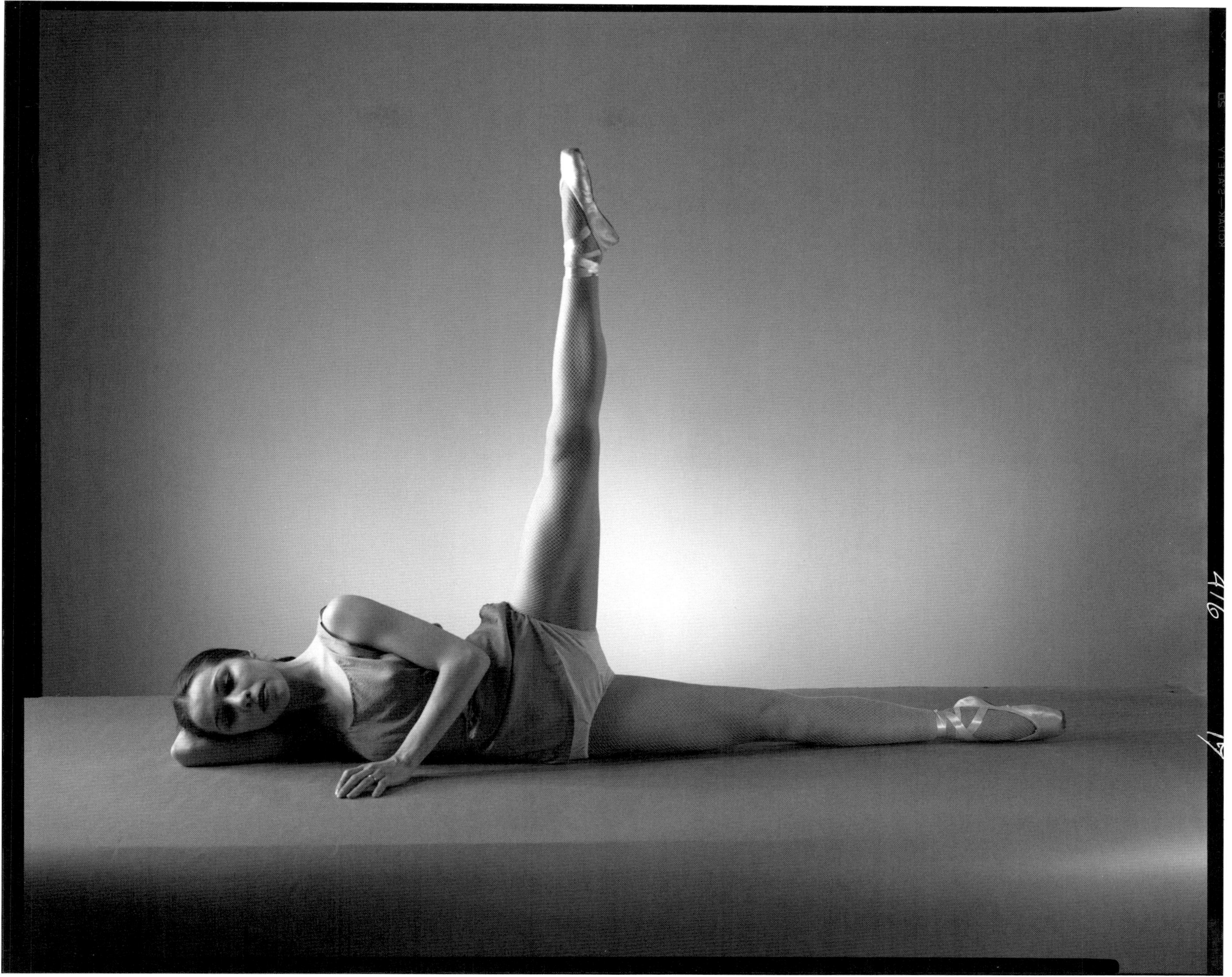

George Platt Lynes,
photograph of dancer
Maria Tallchief, 1953. Scan
from original negative.
Collections of the Kinsey
Institute, Indiana University

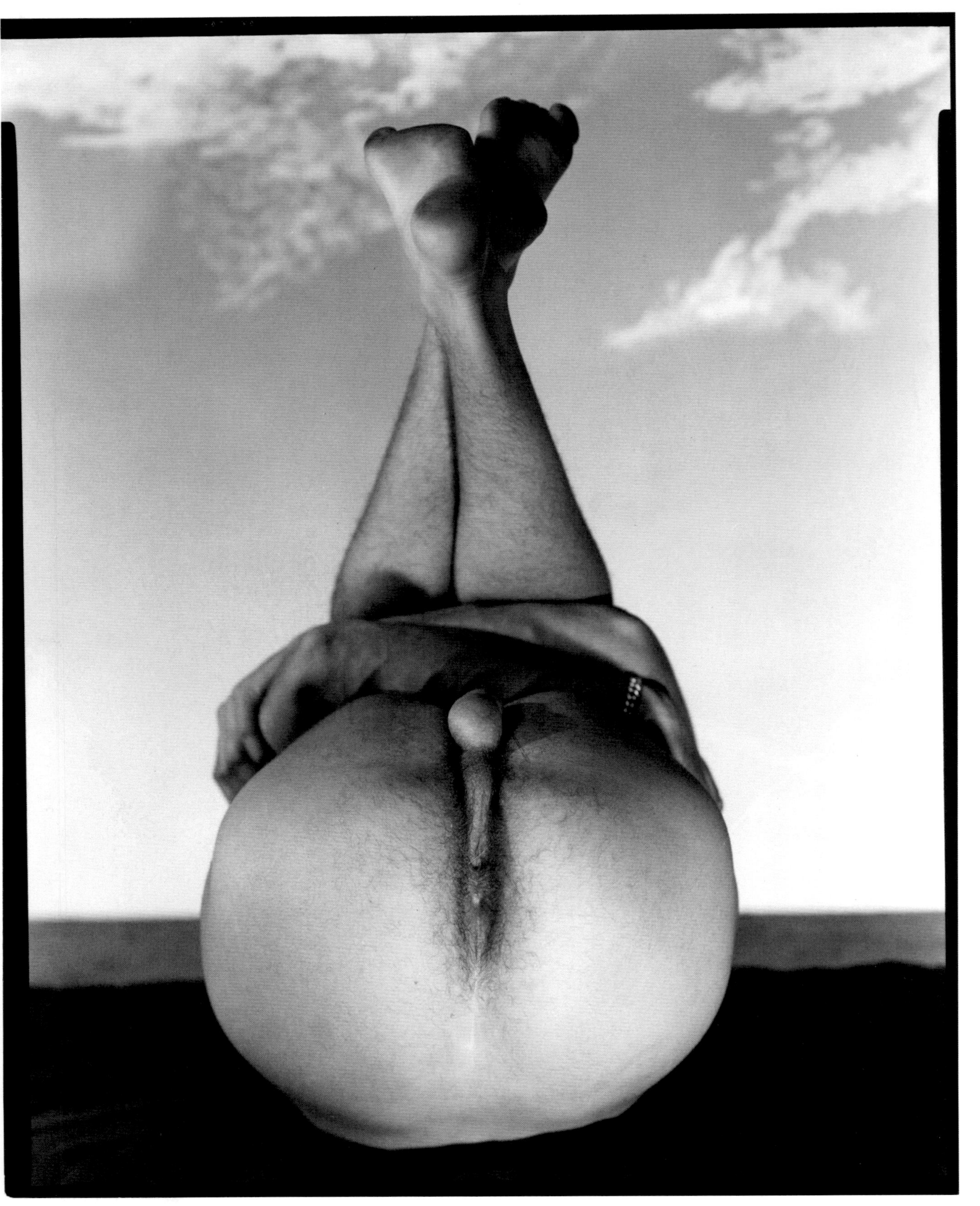

George Platt Lynes,
photograph of unknown
subject, n.d. Scan from
original negative. Collections
of the Kinsey Institute,
Indiana University

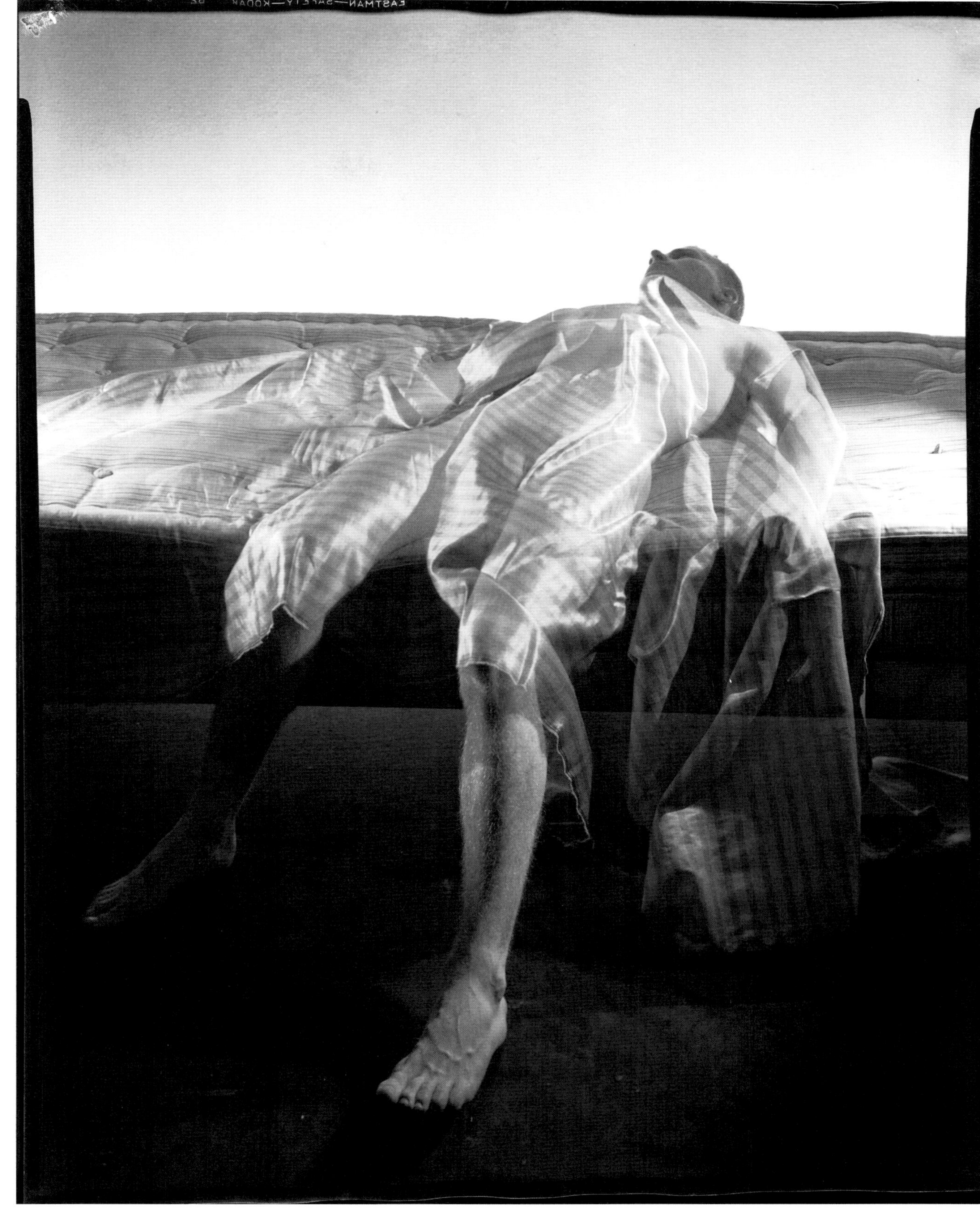

George Platt Lynes,
photograph of John Ferenz,
1936. Scan from original
negative. Collections
of the Kinsey Institute,
Indiana University

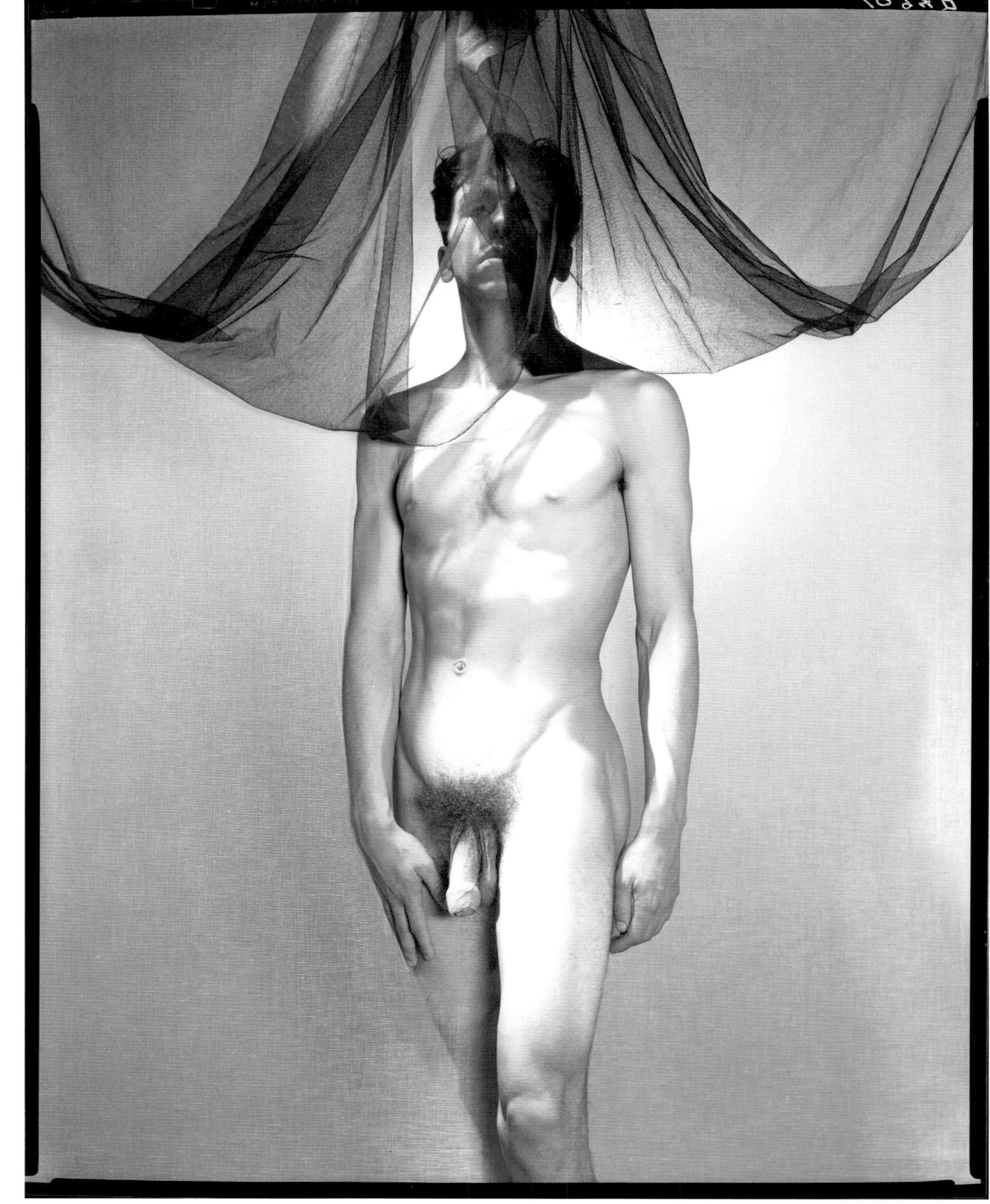

George Platt Lynes,
photograph of dancer
Nicholas Magallanes,
c. 1938. Scan from original
negative. Collections
of the Kinsey Institute,
Indiana University

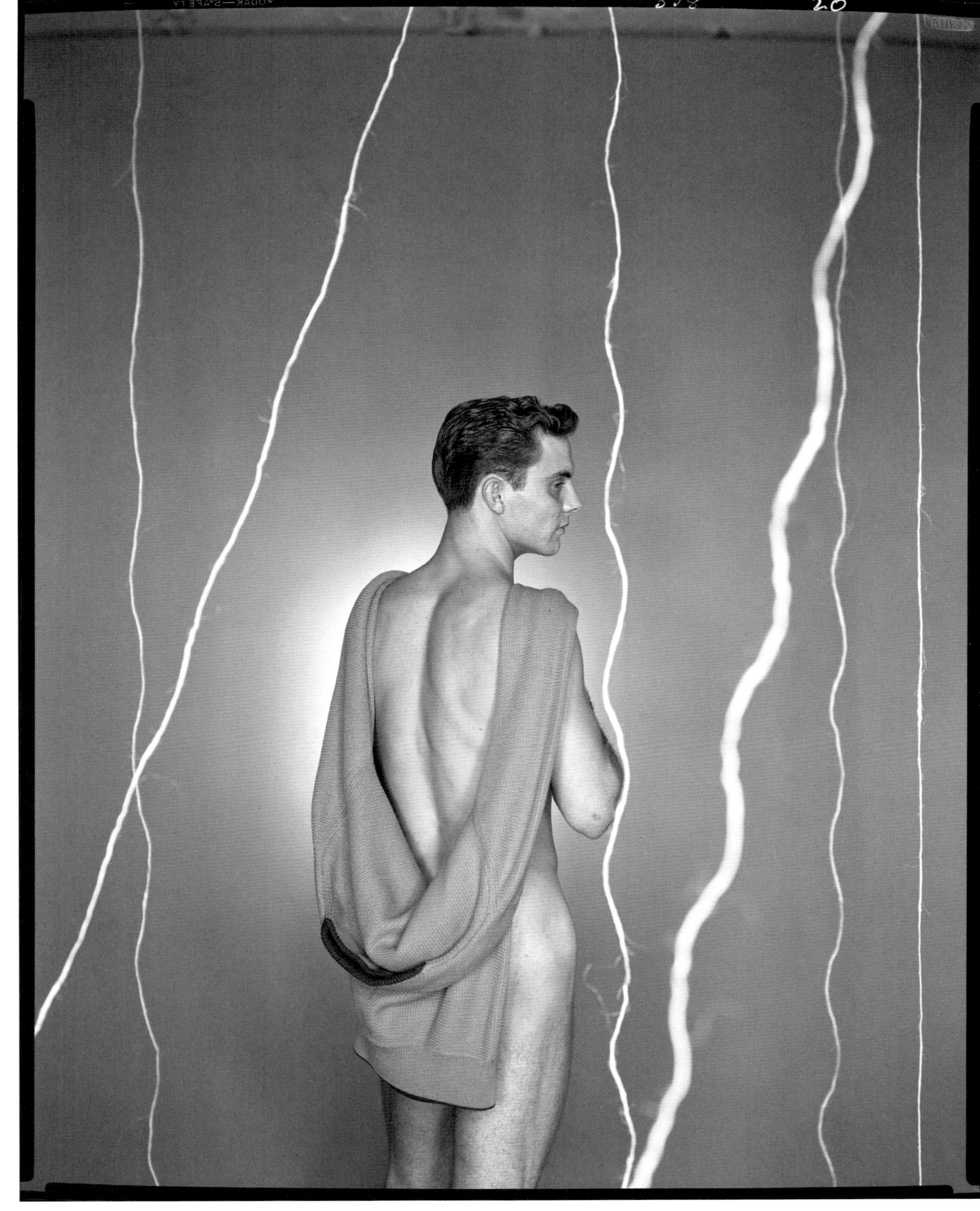

George Platt Lynes, photograph of dancer Ralph McWilliams, 1952. Scan from original negative. Collections of the Kinsey Institute, Indiana University

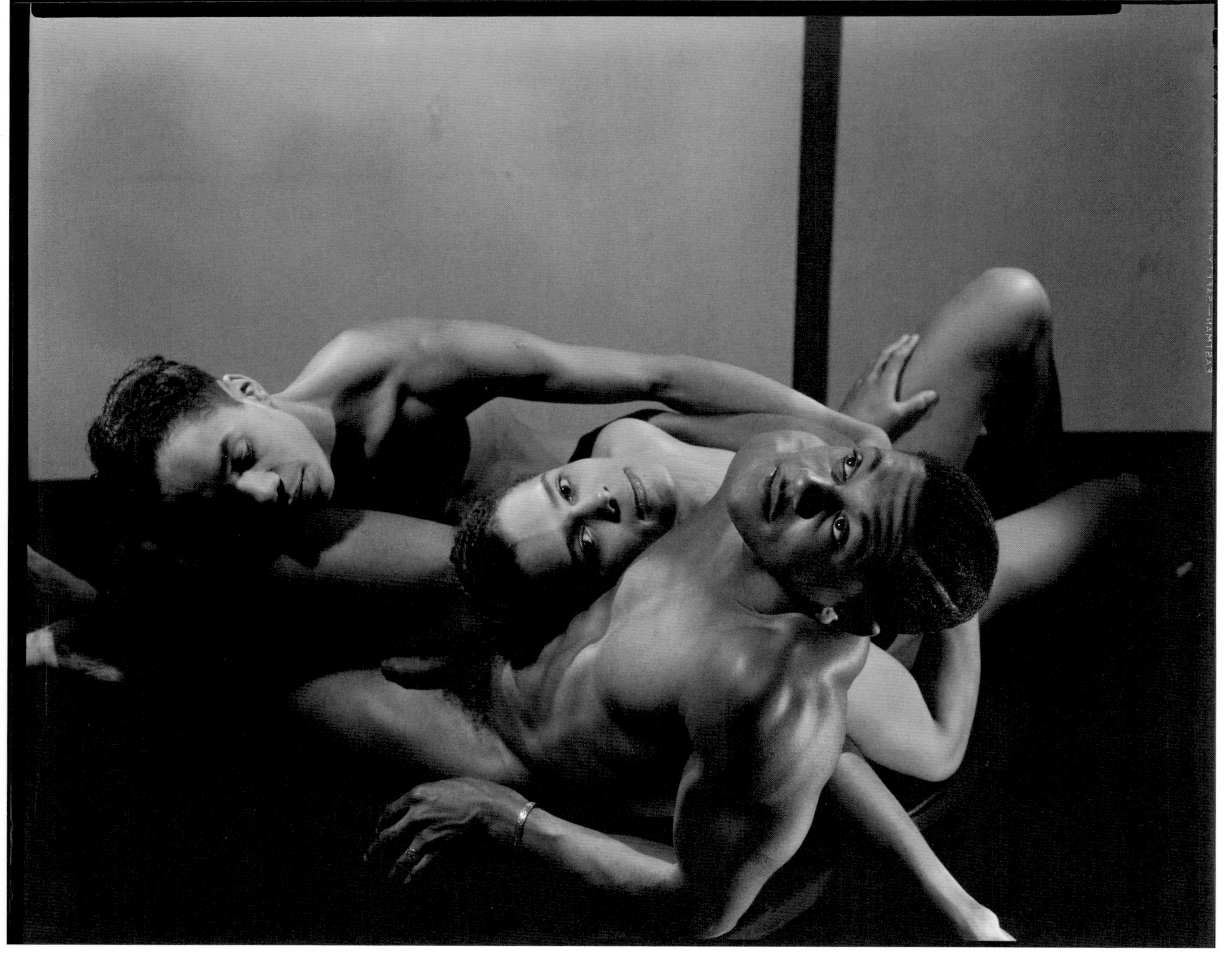

George Platt Lynes,
photograph of dancers
Floyd Miller, Billie Smith,
and Maxwell Baird,
posed by choreographer
Frederick Ashton, 1934.
Scan from original negative.
Collections of the Kinsey
Institute, Indiana University

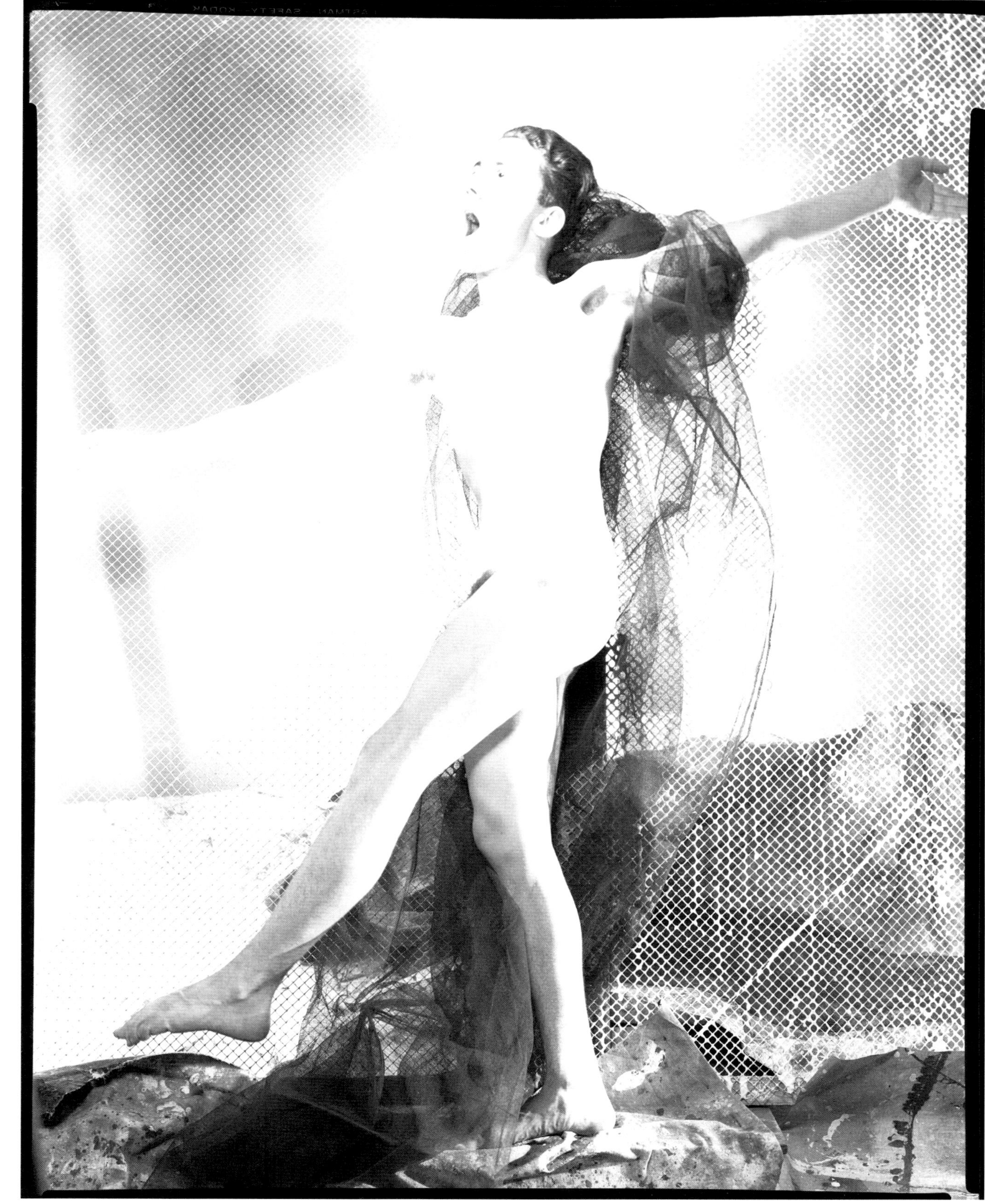

George Platt Lynes, photograph of Bradbury Ball, 1941. Scan from original negative. Collections of the Kinsey Institute, Indiana University

George Platt Lynes, photographs of John van Sikken, c. 1940. Scans from original negative. Collections of the Kinsey Institute, Indiana University

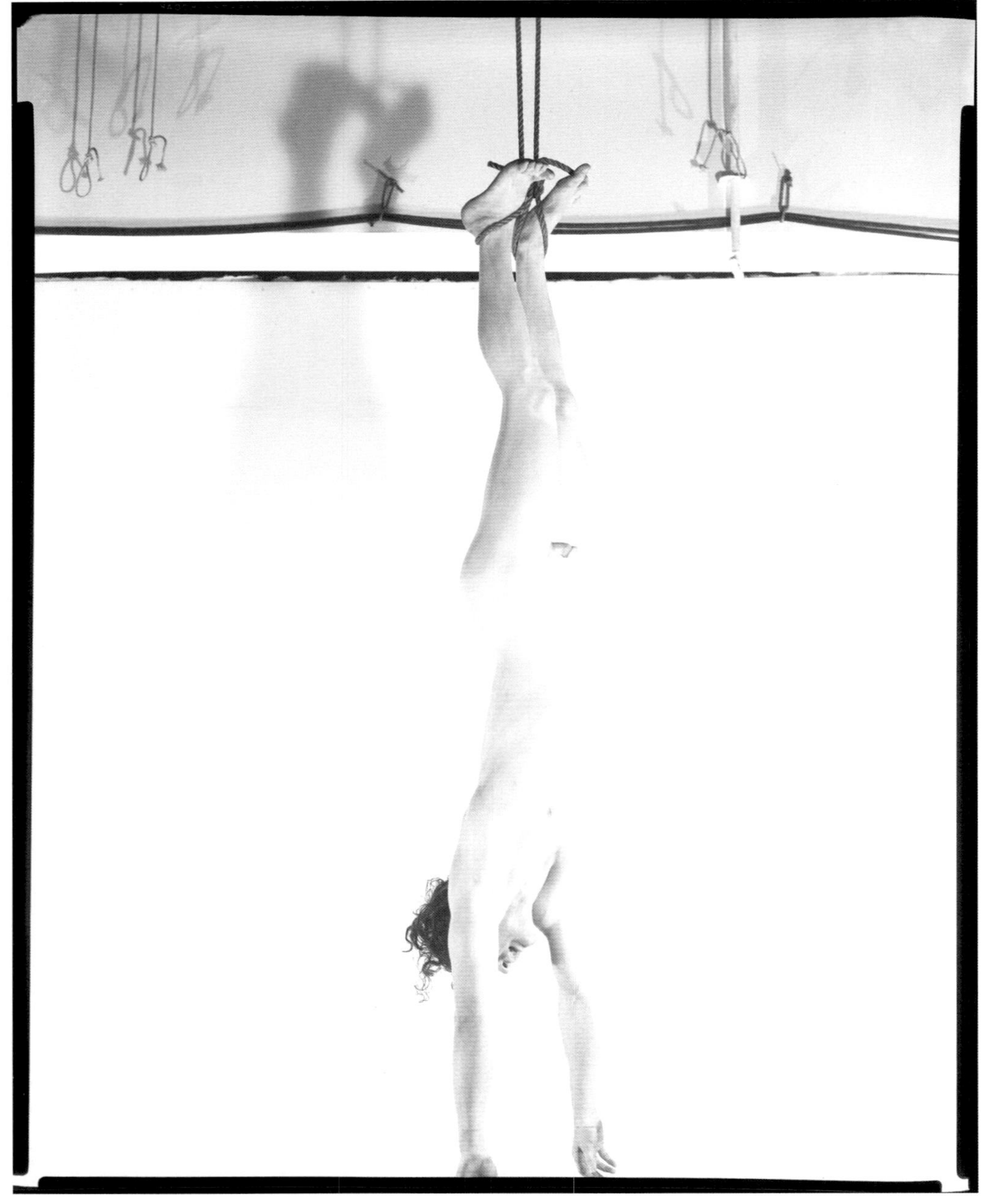
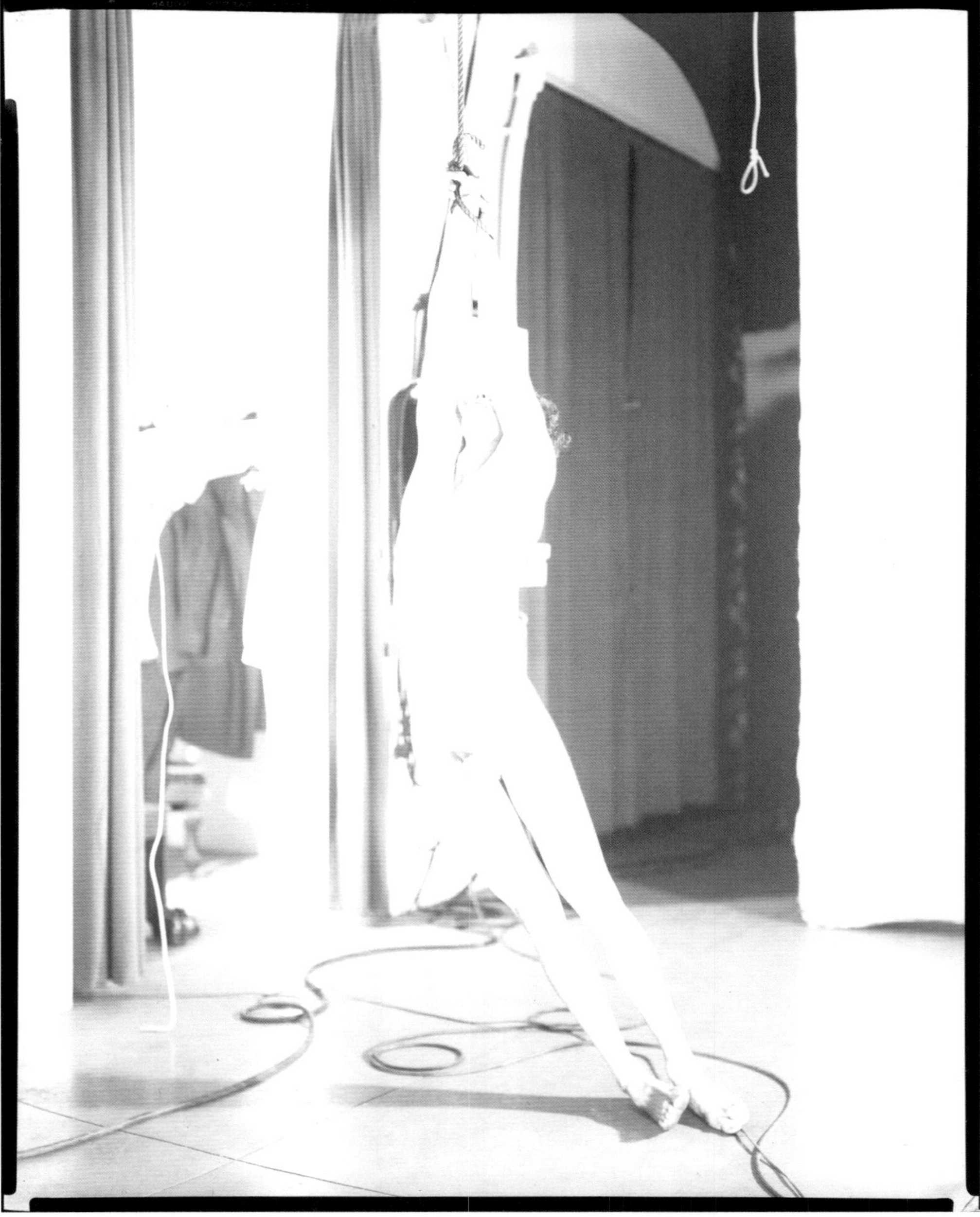

George Platt Lynes,
photograph of Charles
"Tex" Smutney, 1941. Scan
from original negative.
Collections of the Kinsey
Institute, Indiana University

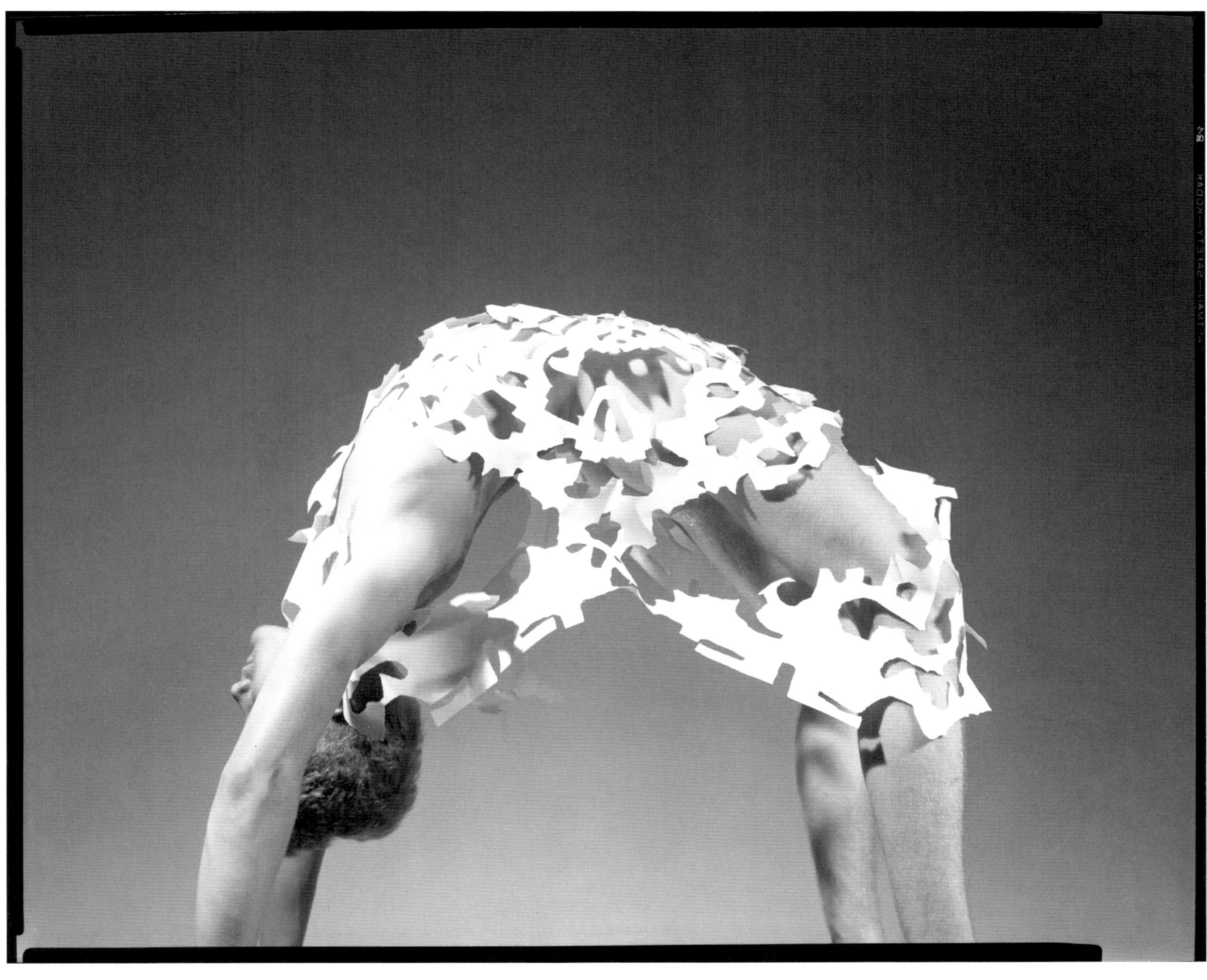

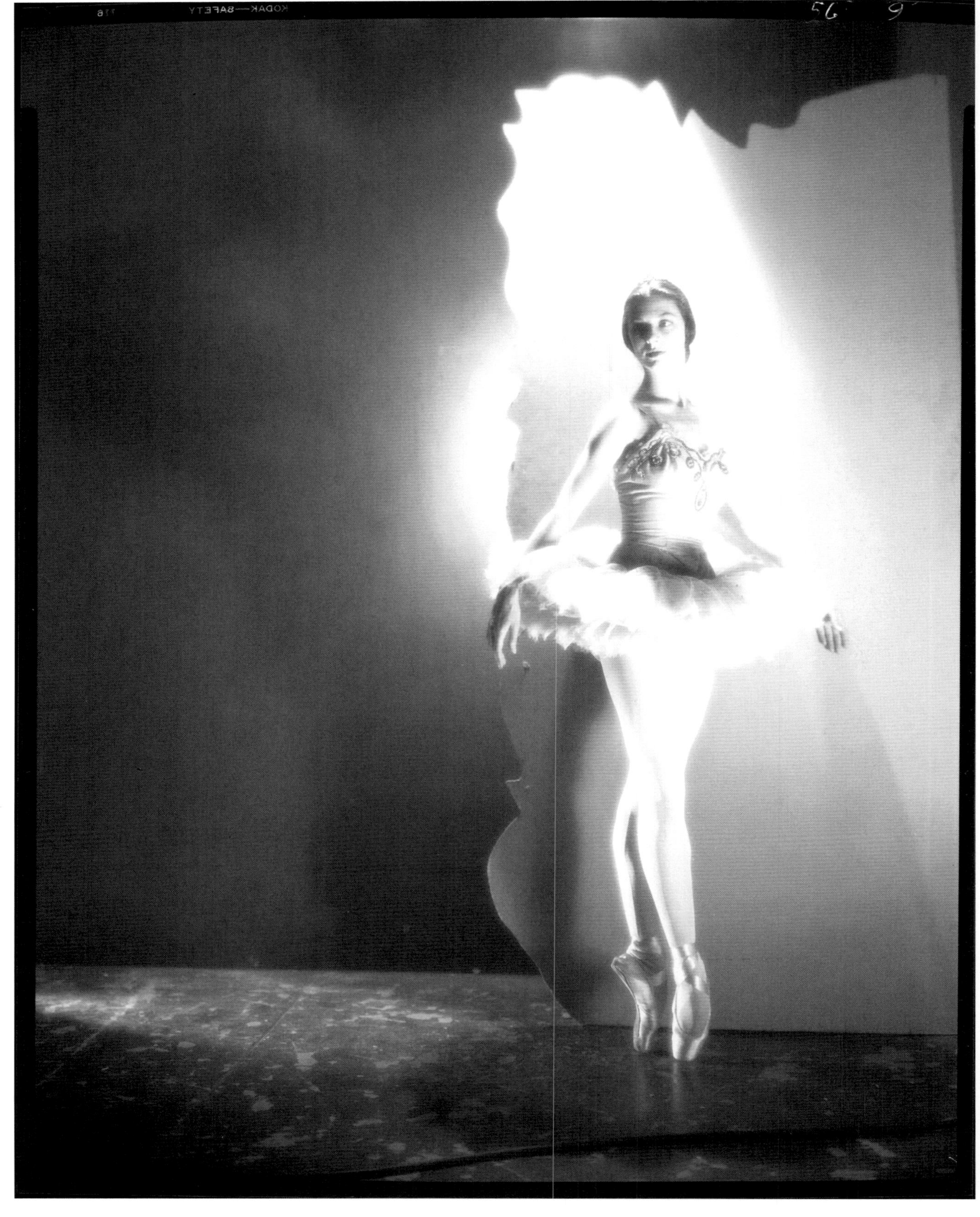

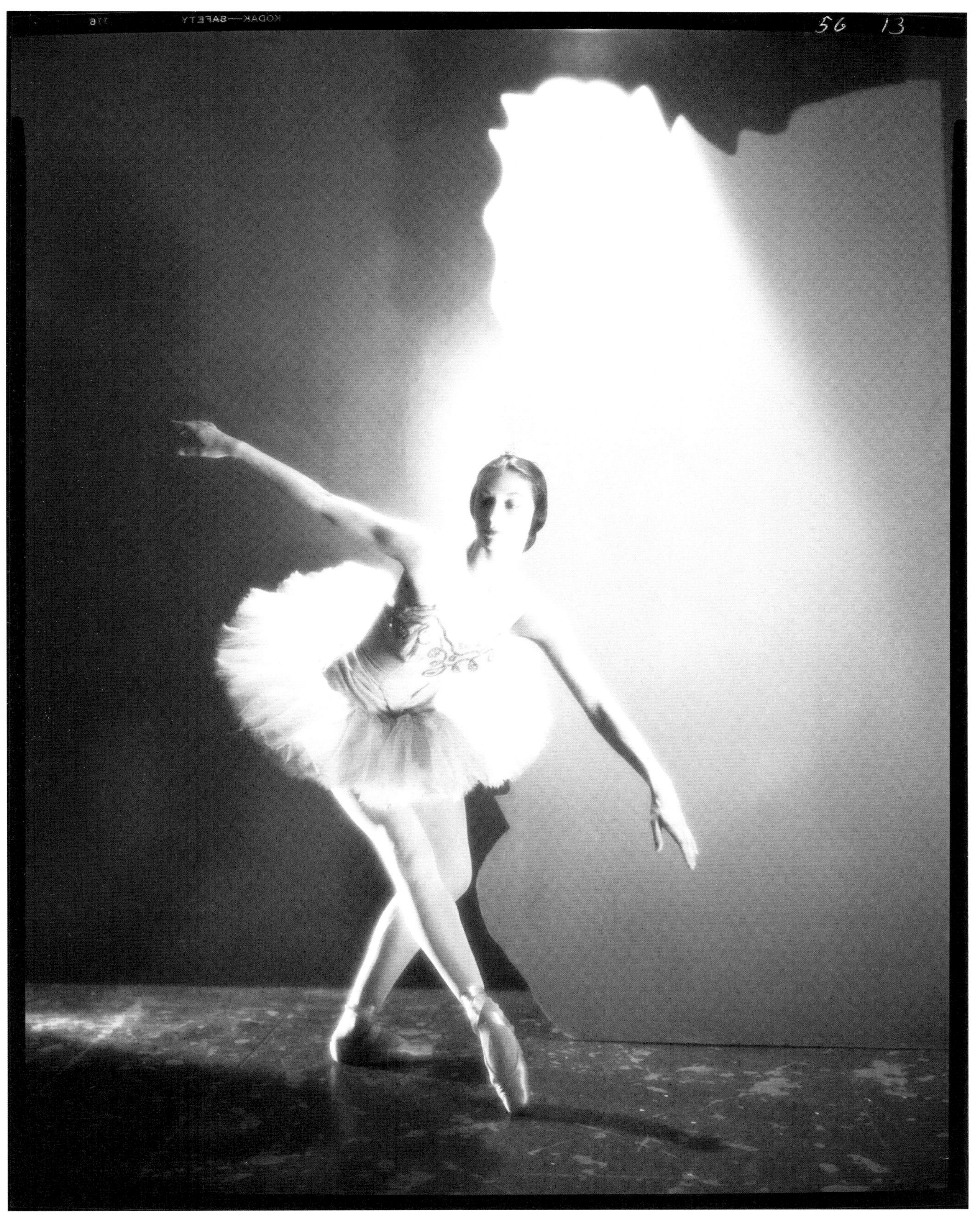

Opposite and left: George Platt Lynes, photograph of dancer Mary Ellen Moylan, 1941. Scan from original negative. Collections of the Kinsey Institute, Indiana University

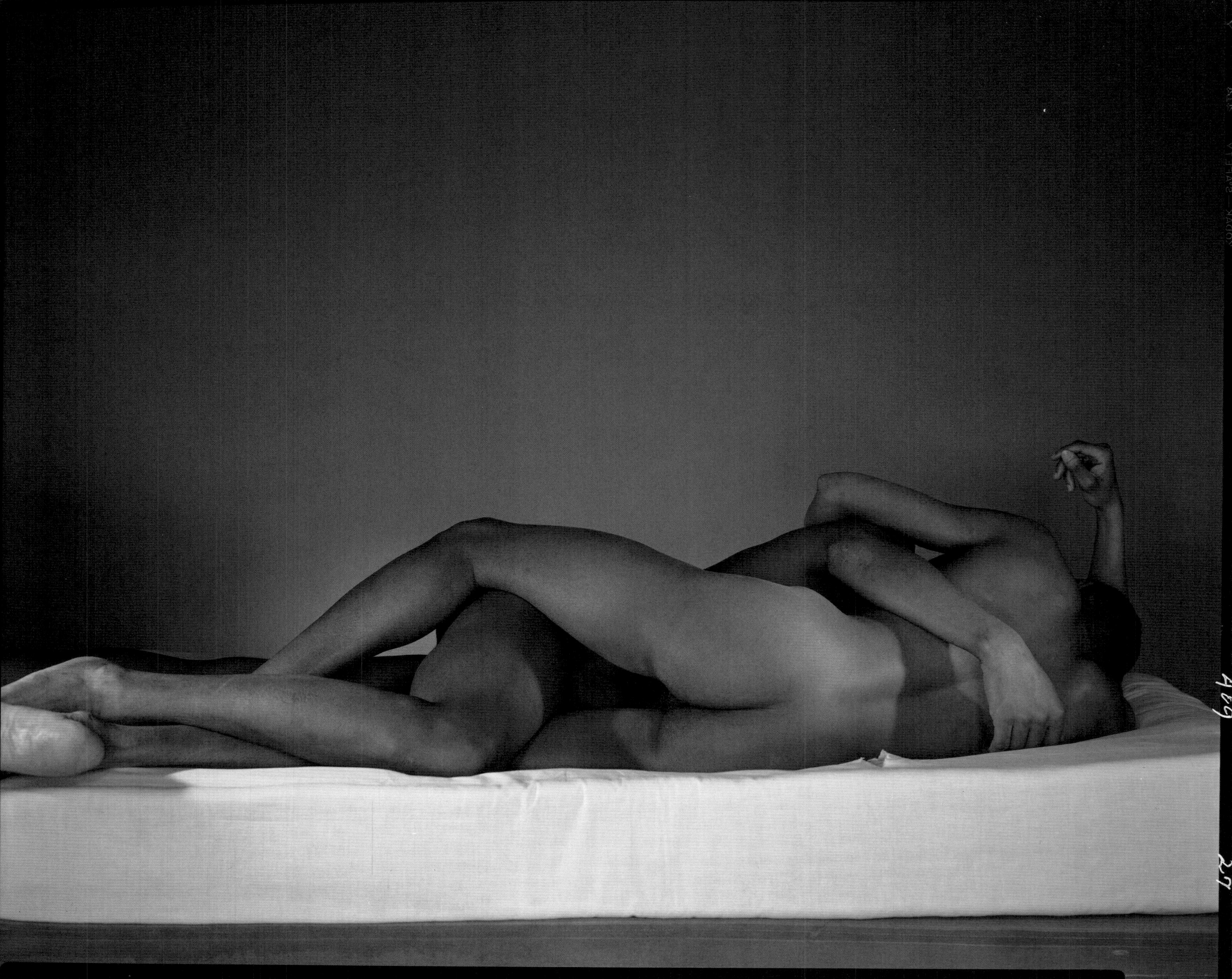

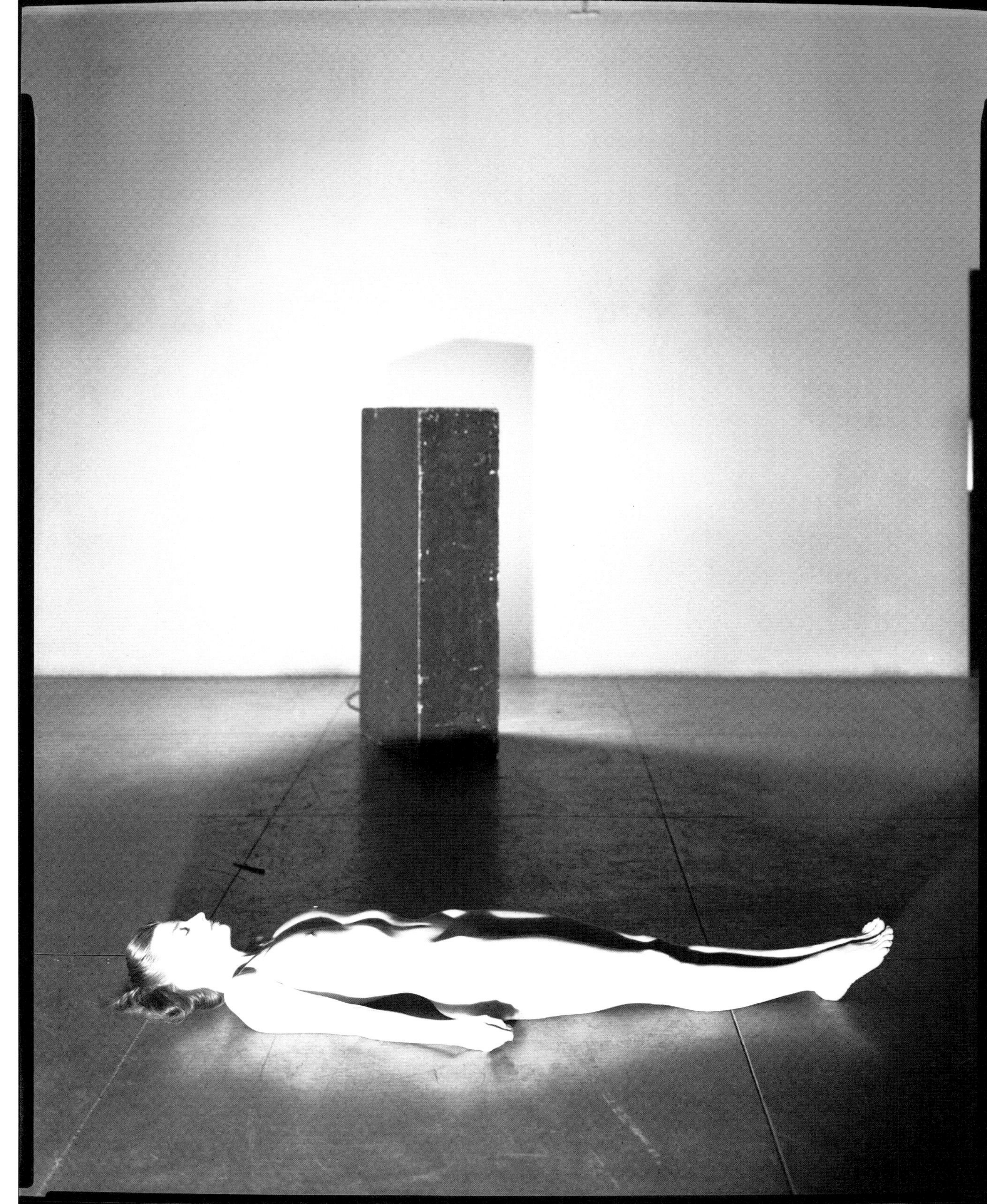

Opposite: George Platt Lynes, photograph of John Leaphart and Bill Blizzard, 1953. Scan from original negative. Collections of the Kinsey Institute, Indiana University

George Platt Lynes, photograph of model Laurie Douglas Harbach, 1944. Scan from original negative. Collections of the Kinsey Institute, Indiana University

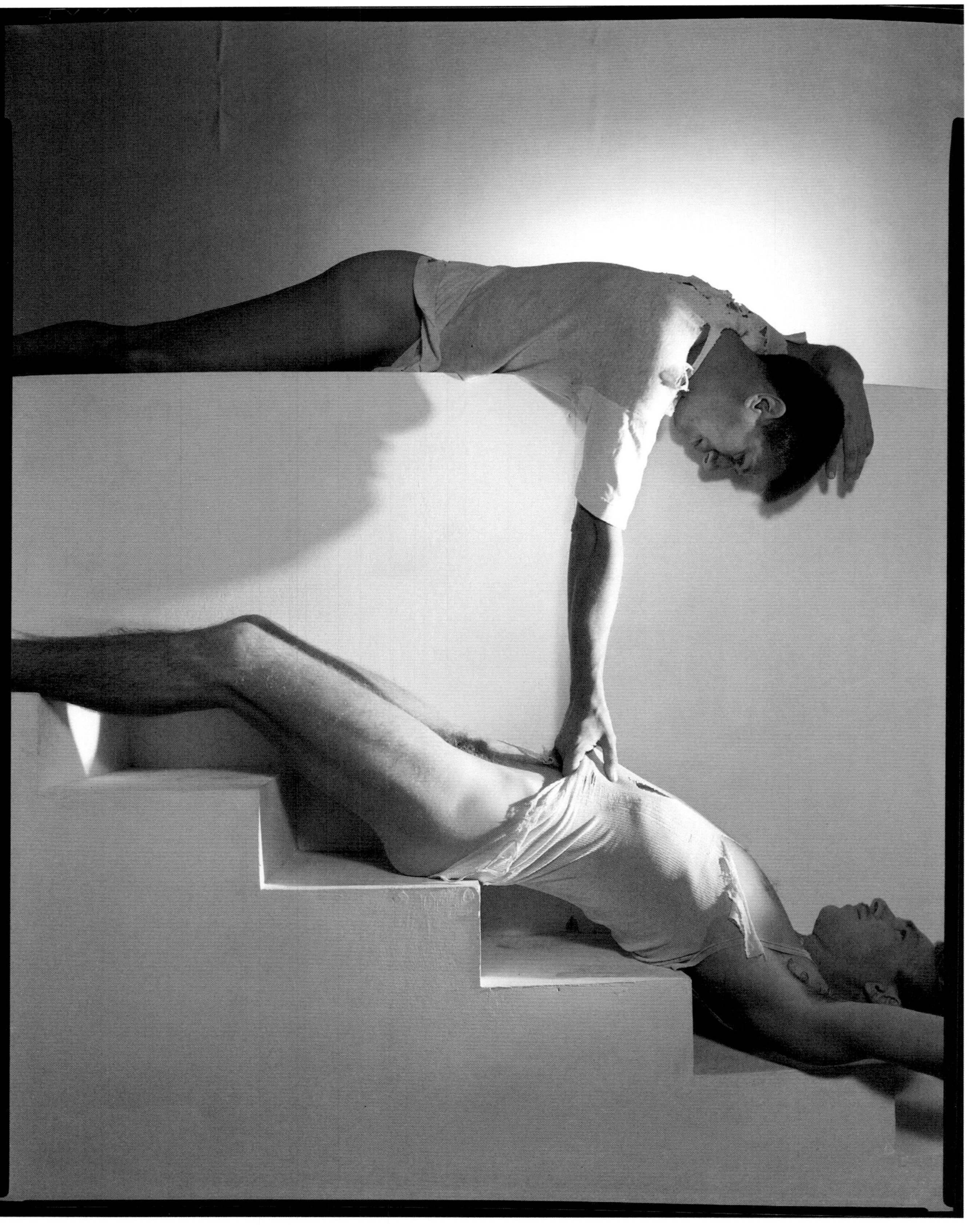

George Platt Lynes,
photograph of artists Paul
Cadmus and Jared French,
1937. Scan from original
negative. Collections
of the Kinsey Institute,
Indiana University

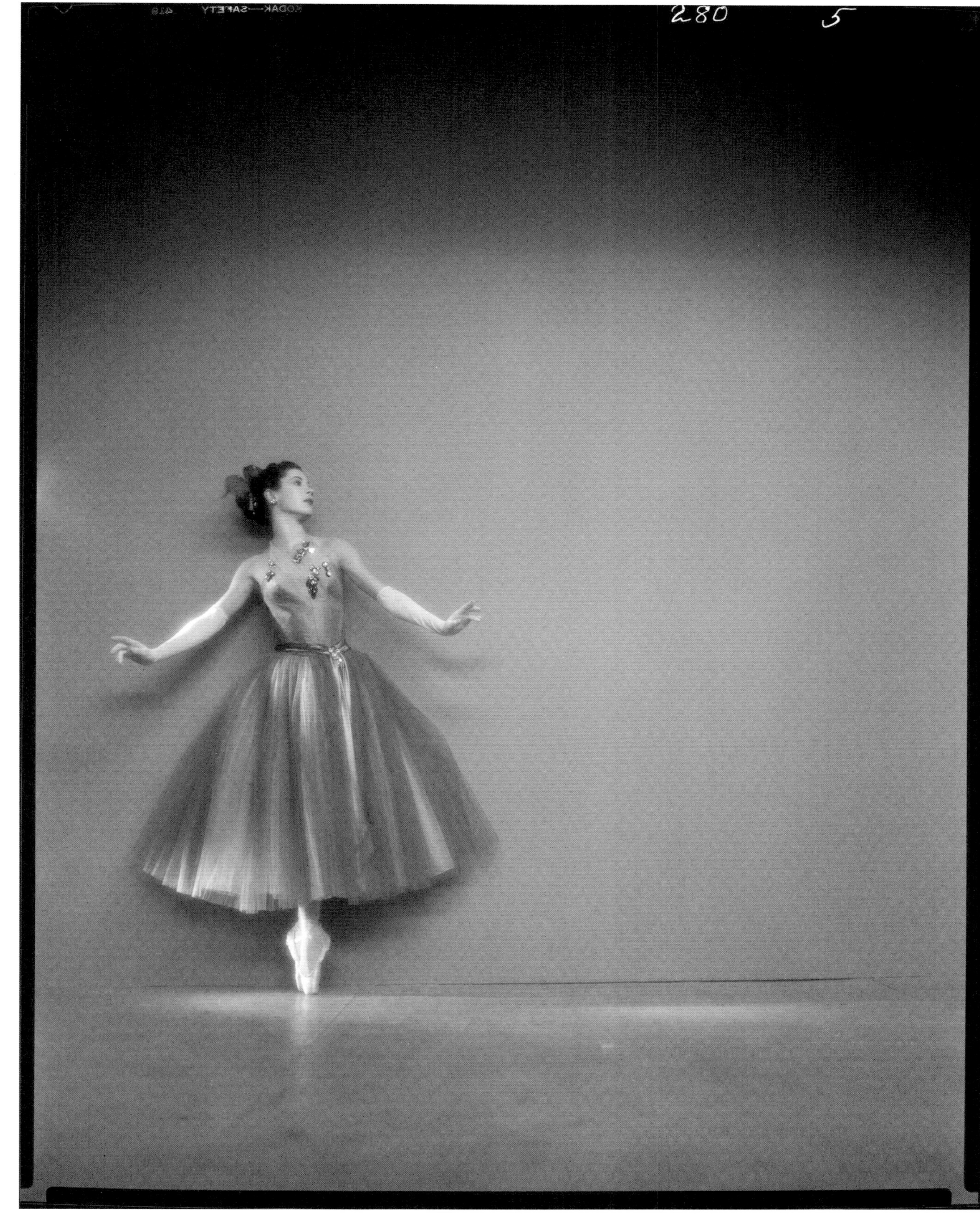

George Platt Lynes,
photograph of dancer
Diana Adams, 1951. Scan
from original negative.
Collections of the Kinsey
Institute, Indiana University

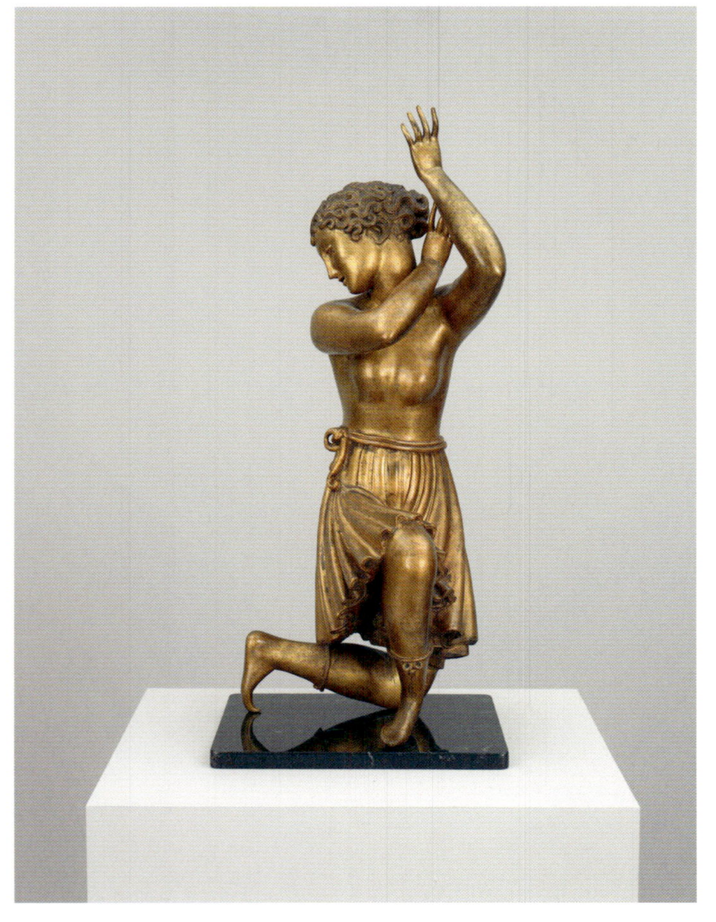

Left: Elie Nadelman, *Dancing Figure*, c. 1916–18. Gilded bronze, 29⅝ × 13⅛ × 11½ inches (75.2 × 33.3 × 29.2 cm). Whitney Museum of American Art, New York; gift of an anonymous donor

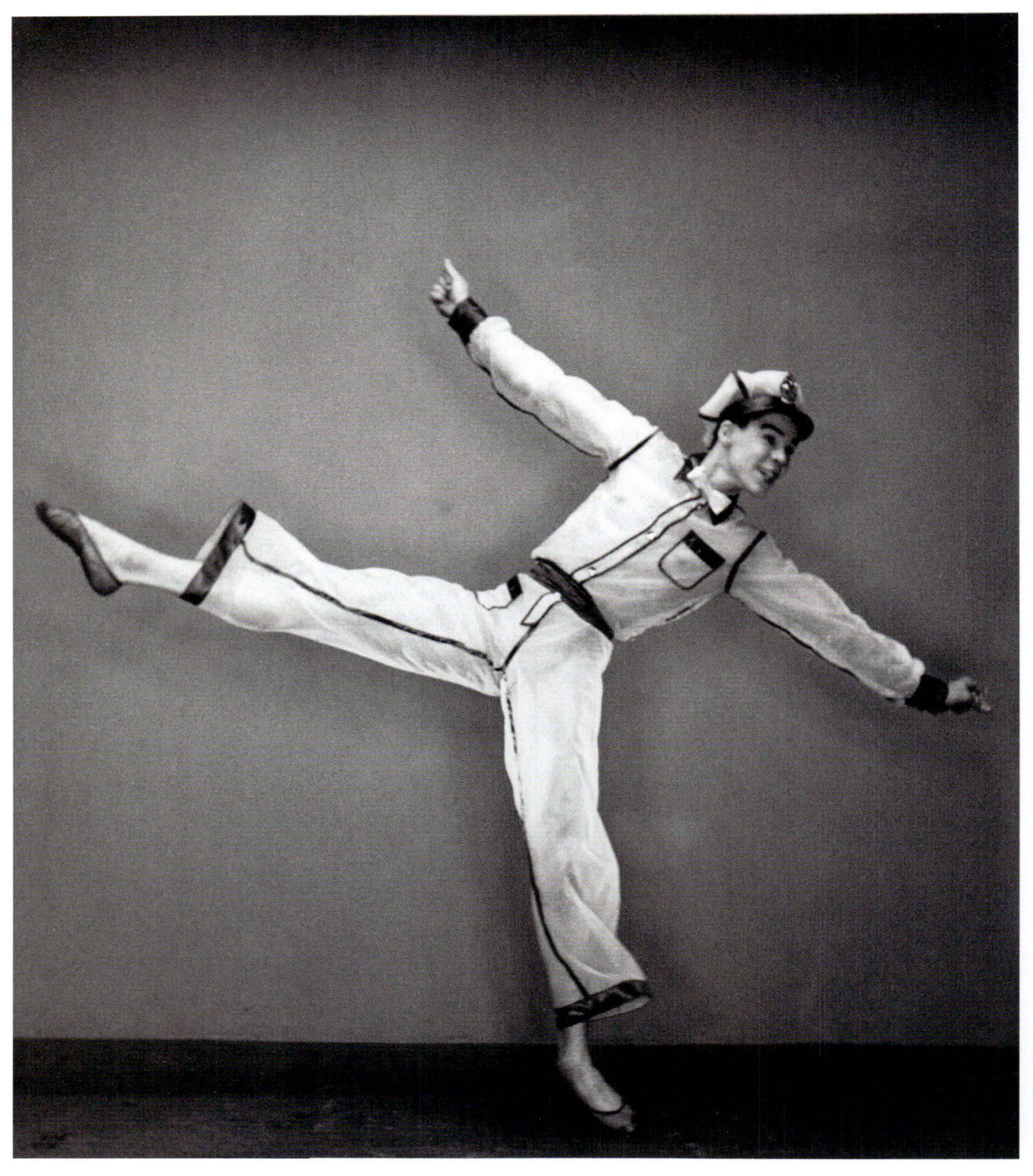

Above: George Platt Lynes, photograph of dancer Jacques d'Amboise in a costume designed by Paul Cadmus for *Filling Station* (1937), choreographed by Lew Christensen for Ballet Caravan, 1950. Gelatin silver print, sheet: 12 × 10¼ inches (30.5 × 26 cm). Collection of Beth Rudin DeWoody

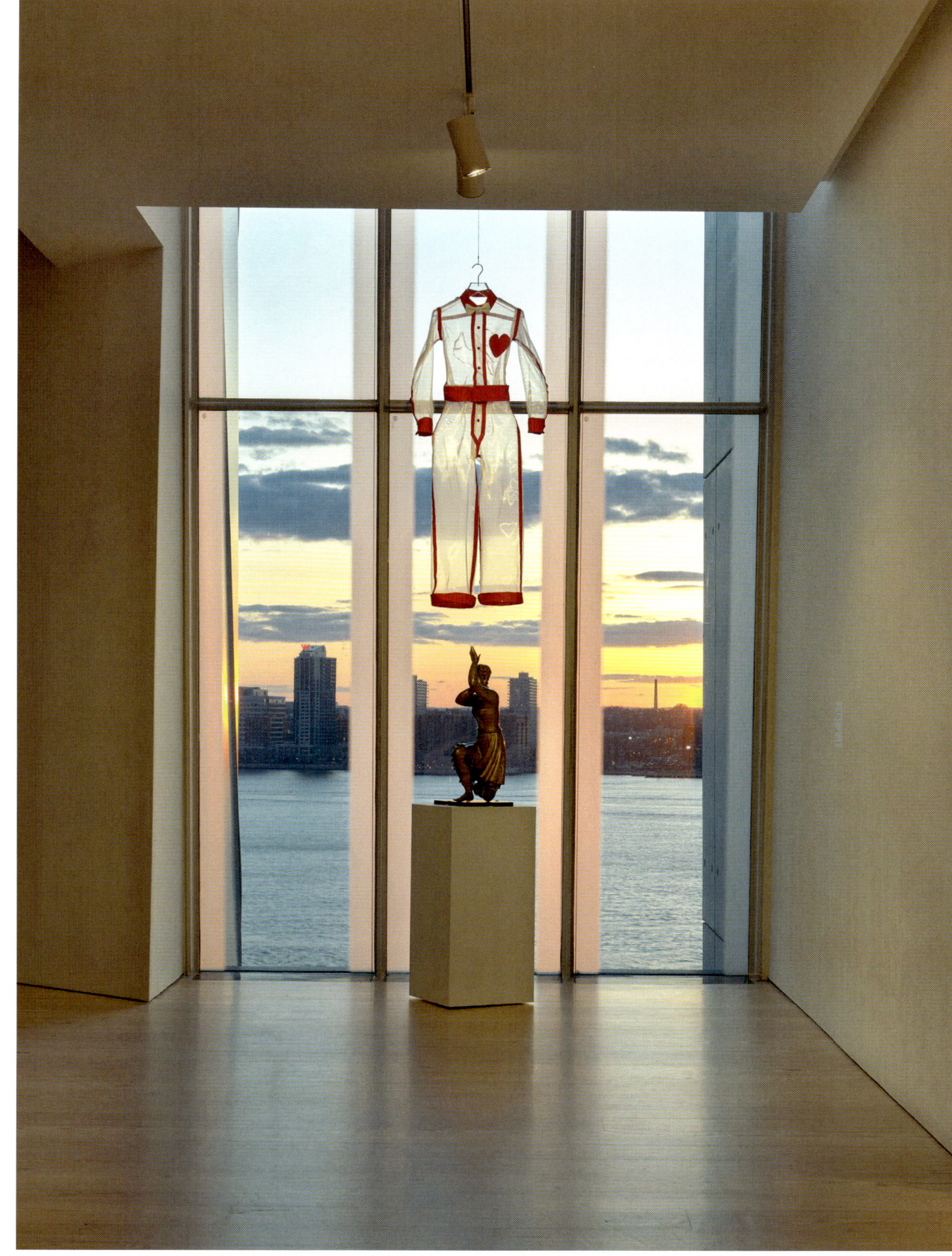

Paul Cadmus's painting *Fleet's In* (1934) aroused public controversy over its flagrant depiction of sailors on shore leave. Lincoln Kirstein, who was married to Cadmus's sister, Fidelma, seized on the artist's notoriety by commissioning him to design the sets and costumes for his American folklore ballet production of *Filling Station* (1937), with music by Virgil Thompson. The dance featured a wholesome gas station attendant jetéing in a costume made of sheer material. Like many artists of the period who exploited transparent fabrics, cellophane, plastics, or glass, Cadmus equates transparency with modernity by way of this see-through costume.

Installation view of *Transmissions*, with Nick Mauss's re-creation of costume designed by Paul Cadmus for *Filling Station* (1937), fabricated by Andrea Solstad, 2018; and Elie Nadelman, *Dancing Figure*, c. 1916–18. Photo: Ron Amstutz

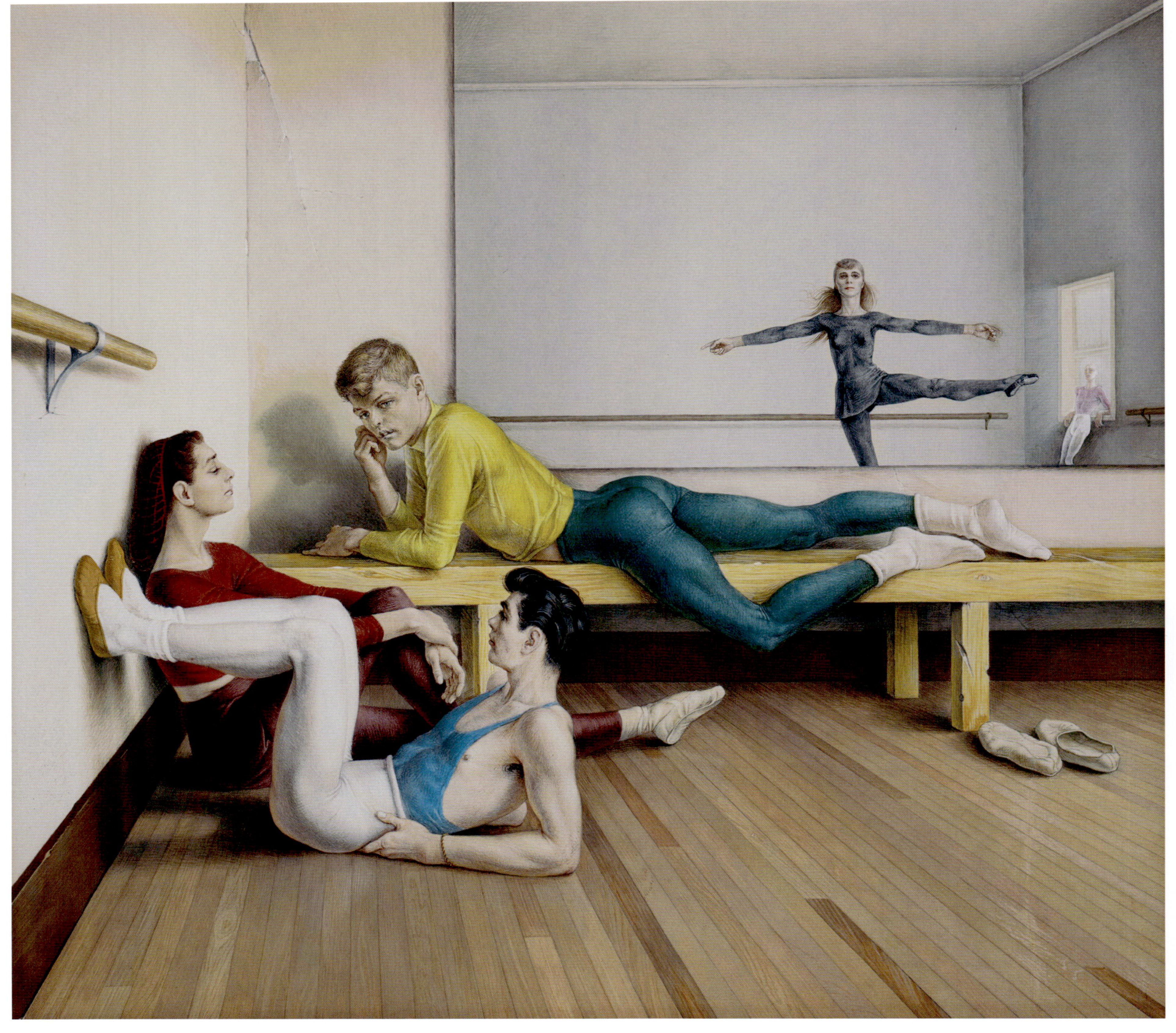

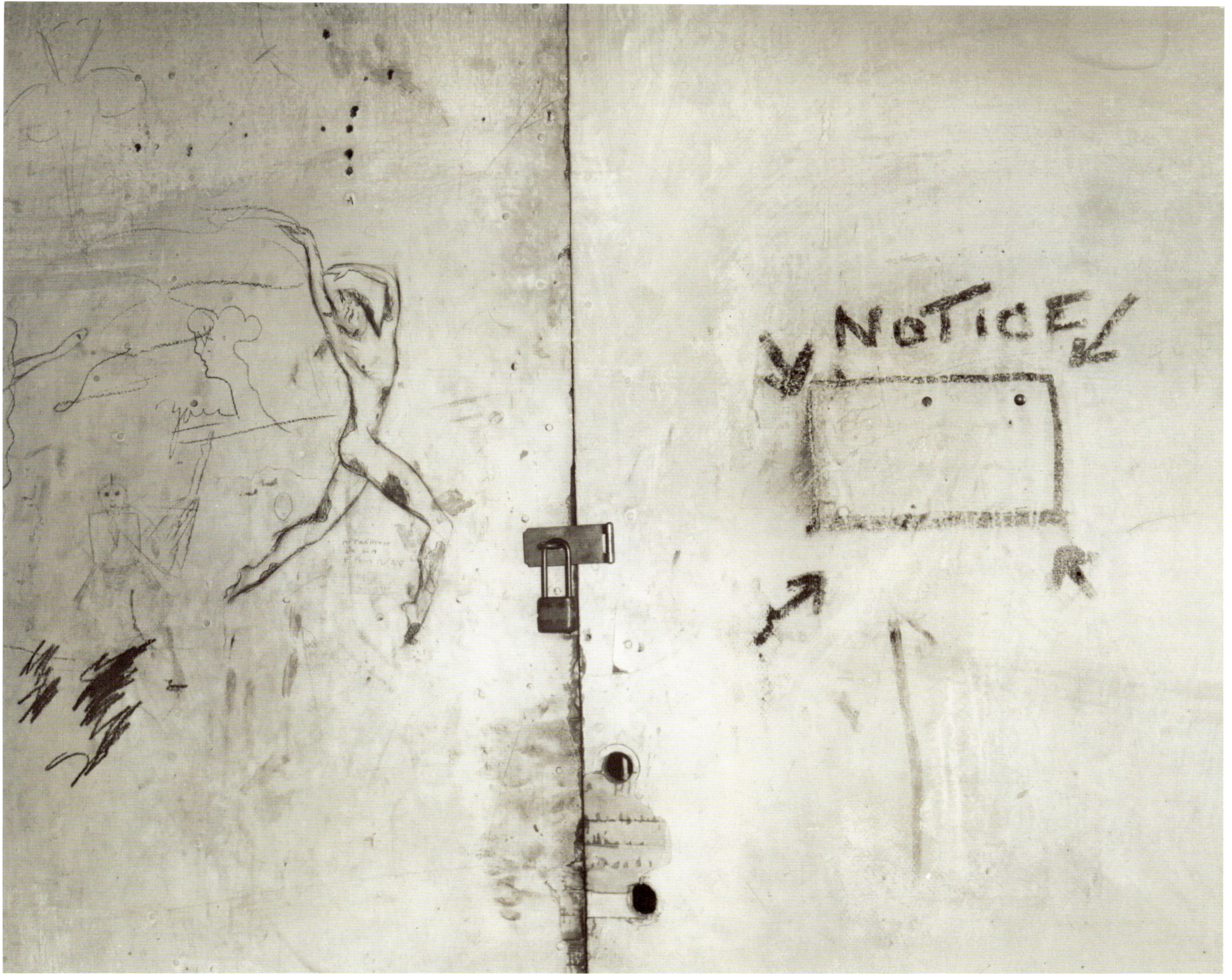

NOTICE

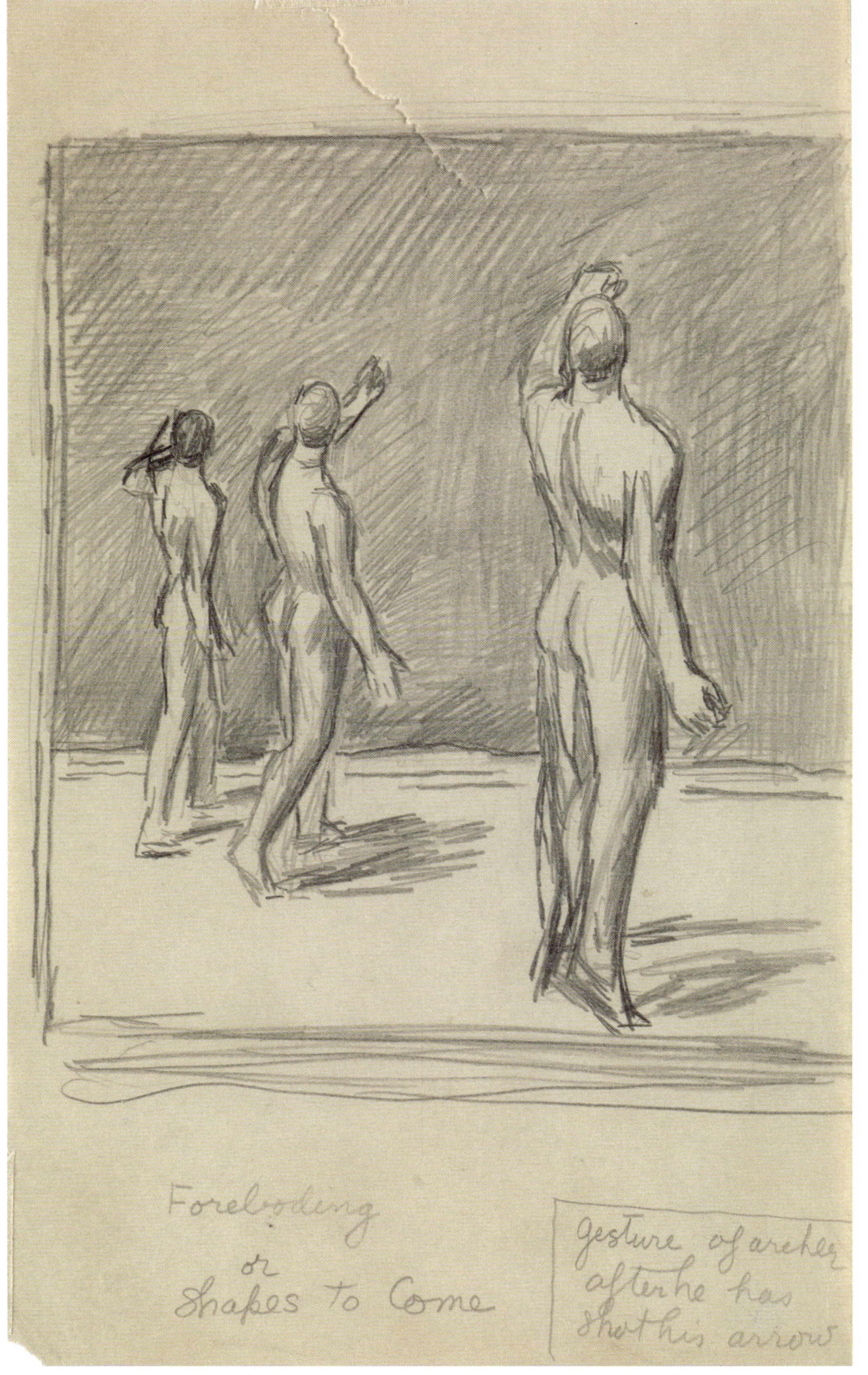

Page 48: Paul Cadmus, *Reflection*, 1944. Egg tempera on composition board, 16¾ × 19 inches (42.6 × 48.3 cm). Yale University Art Gallery, New Haven; bequest of Donald Windham in memory of Sandy M. Campbell

Page 49: Walker Evans, graffiti on backstage door of the School of American Ballet, 1945. Gelatin silver print, 9⁷⁄₁₆ × 12 inches (23.9 × 30.5 cm). The Metropolitan Museum of Art, New York. Gift of Paul F. Walter, in memory of Christopher Hemphill, 1987

Jared French, *untitled*, n.d. Pencil on paper, 8 × 5 inches (20.4 × 12.6 cm). Private collection

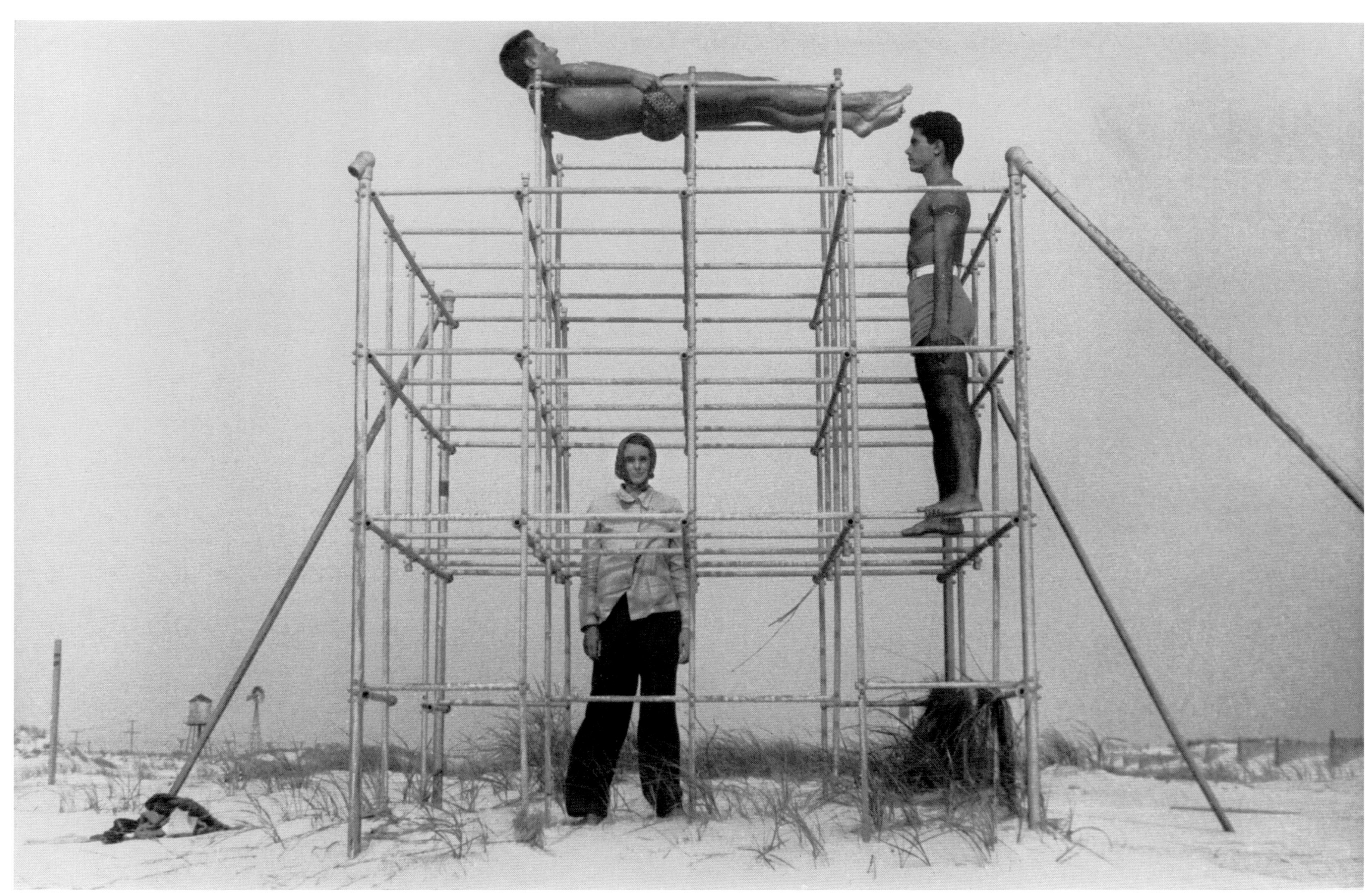

PaJaMa, *Margaret French, Paul Cadmus and José Martinez, Fire Island*, 1939 Gelatin silver print, 11 × 14 inches (27.9 × 35.6 cm). Whitney Museum of American Art, New York; promised gift of Jack Shear

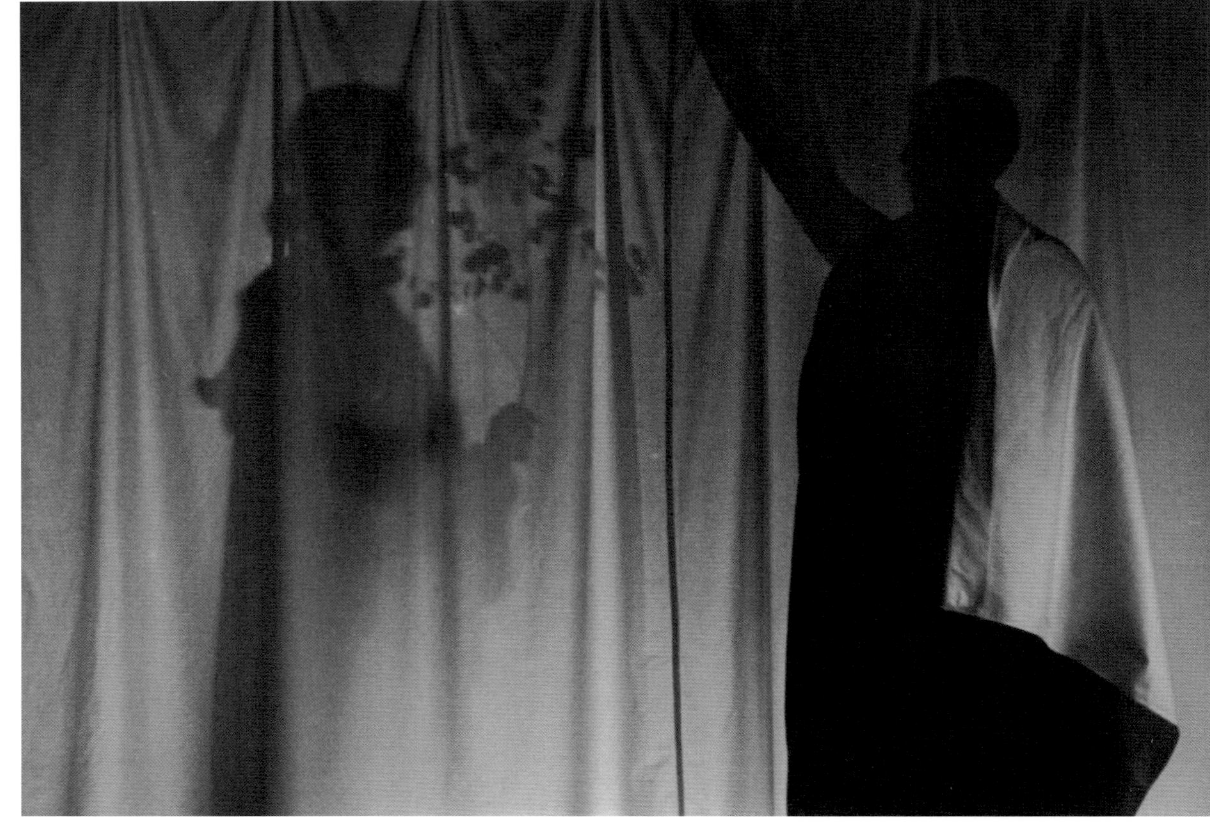

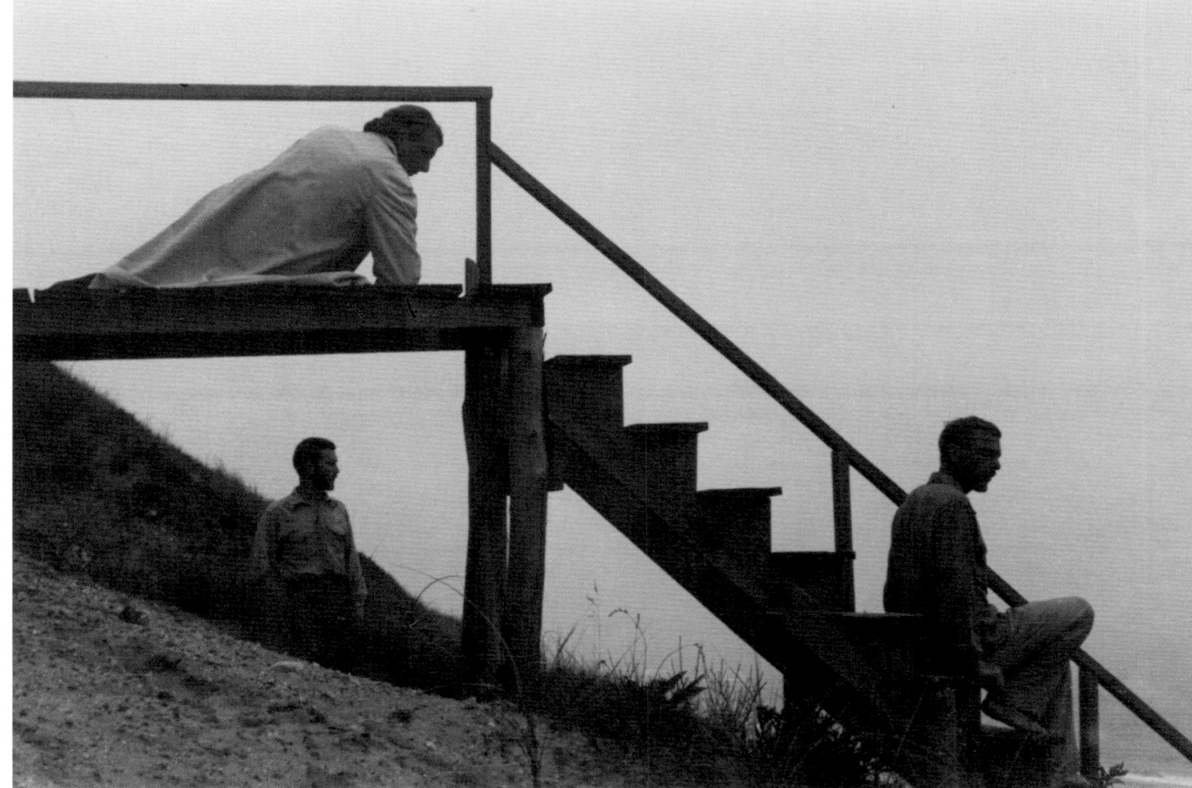

Top: PaJaMa, *Margaret French and Paul Cadmus, Provincetown*, c. 1947. Gelatin silver print, 11 × 14 inches (27.9 × 35.6 cm). Whitney Museum of American Art, New York; promised gift of Jack Shear

Bottom: PaJaMa, *Margaret French, George Tooker and Jared French, Nantucket*, c. 1946. Gelatin silver print, 4 ½ × 6 ¾ inches (11.4 × 17.1 cm). Whitney Museum of American Art, New York; promised gift of Jack Shear

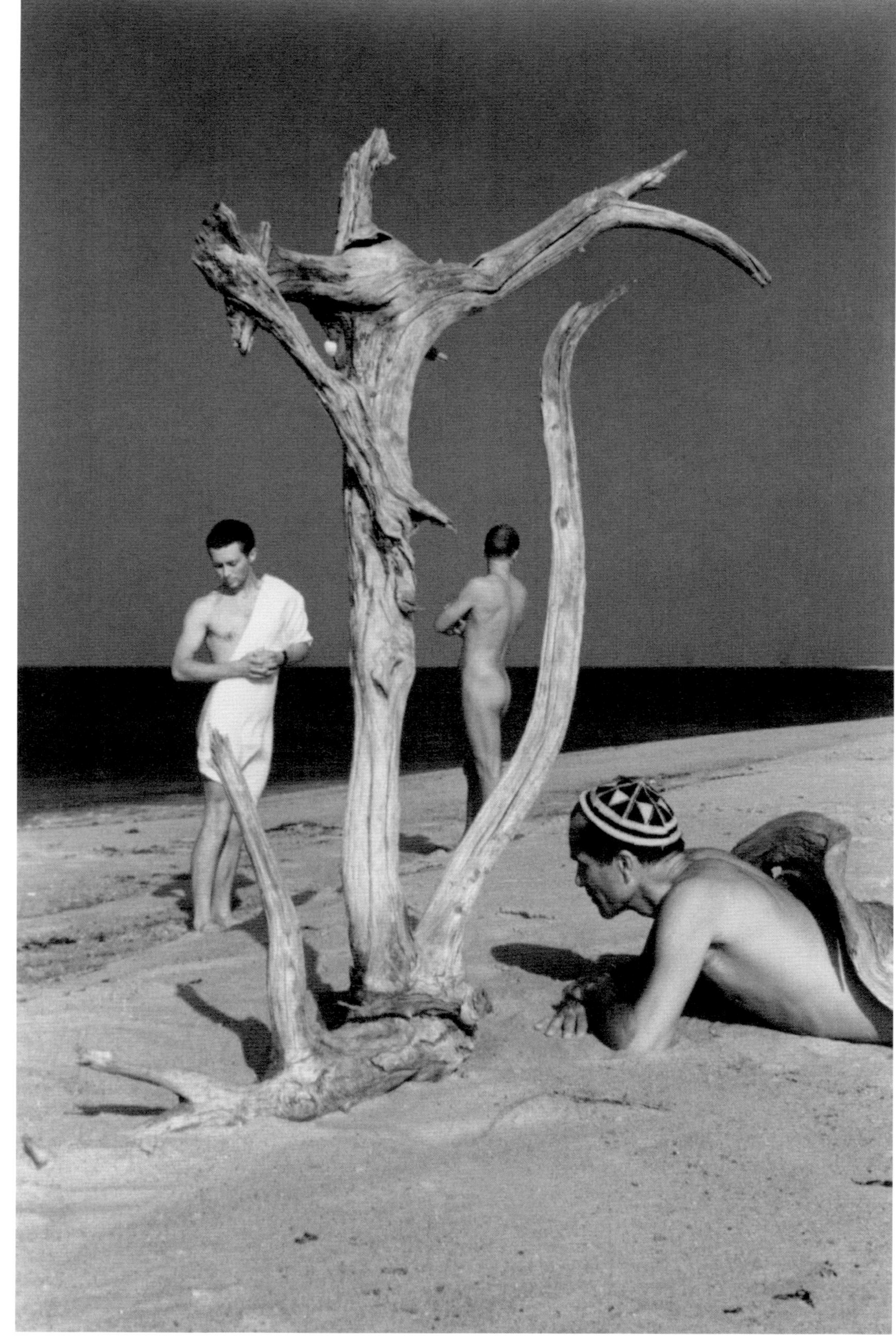

Lovers Paul Cadmus and Jared French, along with French's wife, Margaret Hoening French, formed a photographic collaborative known as PaJaMa (an acronym composed of the first two letters of each of their first names). Together they staged mythical daydream tableaux against beachscapes in Fire Island, New York; and Provincetown, Massachusetts. Intended only for circulation among an inner circle of friends, PaJaMa's photographs dramatize vectors of desire, isolation, betrayal, déjà vu, and apprehension, evoking the more ambiguous psychosexual dynamics of their triad and the nonconformist liaisons of their peers.

PaJaMa, *George Tooker, Jared French and Monroe Wheeler, Provincetown*, c. 1947. Gelatin silver print, 6⅜ × 4¼ inches (16.2 × 10.8 cm). Collection of Eric Ceputis and David W. Williams

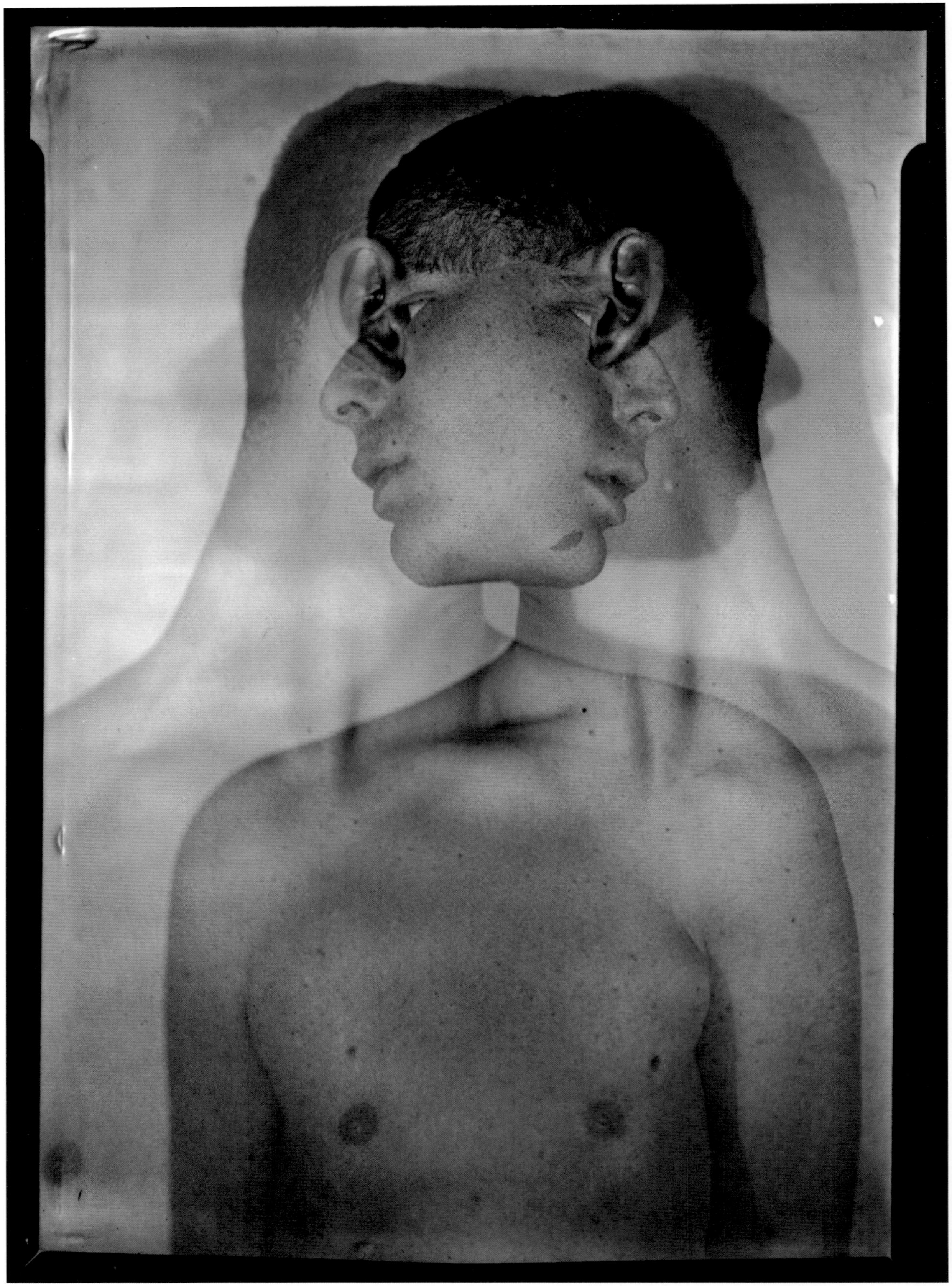

Walker Evans, *Double Exposure of Lincoln Kirstein, Left and Right Profiles*, 1930–31. Scan from original negative, 7 × 5 inches (17.8 × 12.7 cm). Walker Evans Archive, The Metropolitan Museum of Art, New York

Walker Evans's ingenious portrait of a young, bare-chested Lincoln Kirstein contrasts with the more detached work that Evans is known for and that he would himself call, at the end of his life, documentary-style photography. Evans's doubled portrait captures the spirit of experimentation between the young photographer and the even younger impresario as much as it conjures the notion of a split self. Artists in Kirstein's circle reimagined the conventions of the portrait as a form of communication and gift exchange, producing for one another portraits of imagined subjects, caricatures of friends, devotional studies, and oblique dedications. Examples include a head with transparent skin by Pavel Tchelitchew and a stylized profile by Elie Nadelman (both artists championed by Kirstein), as well as a portrait of Kirstein's lover and favorite dancer José "Pete" Martinez, drawn by Paul Cadmus, brother of Kirstein's wife, the artist Fidelma Cadmus Kirstein (portrayed as a ballet dancer at rest in Cadmus's *Reflection* [1944; page 48]). An inscription on Tchelitchew's 1941 costume study for George Balanchine's *Balustrade* reads: "To Fidelma and Lincoln, a souvenir of pink in a gray time."

Clockwise from top left:

Elie Nadelman, *Head of a Woman*, c. 1925. Graphite pencil on paper, 10 × 7⅞ inches (25.4 × 20 cm). Whitney Museum of American Art, New York; purchase with funds from Joanne Leonhardt Cassullo and the Dorothea L. Leonhardt Fund at the Communities Foundation of Texas in honor of Gilbert C. Maurer

Pavel Tchelitchew, *Head of Man (Interior Landscape)*, 1944. Pen and brush and ink and ink wash on paper, 10 ¹⁵⁄₁₆ × 8⅜ inches (27.8 × 21.3 cm). Whitney Museum of American Art, New York; gift of Dr. Richard and Carole Rifkind

Pavel Tchelitchew, design for *Balustrade* (1941), choreographed by George Balanchine for the original Ballets Russes (inscribed "To Fidelma and Lincoln, a souvenir of pink in a gray time"), 1941. Gouache and pencil on paper, 13¾ × 11 inches (34.9 × 27.9 cm). Jerome Robbins Dance Division, The New York Public Library for the Performing Arts, Astor, Lenox and Tilden Foundations

Paul Cadmus, *José Martinez*, 1937. Pen and ink and graphite pencil on paper, 12⁷⁄₁₆ × 10¾ inches (31.6 × 27.3 cm). Whitney Museum of American Art, New York; purchase with funds from the Drawing Committee

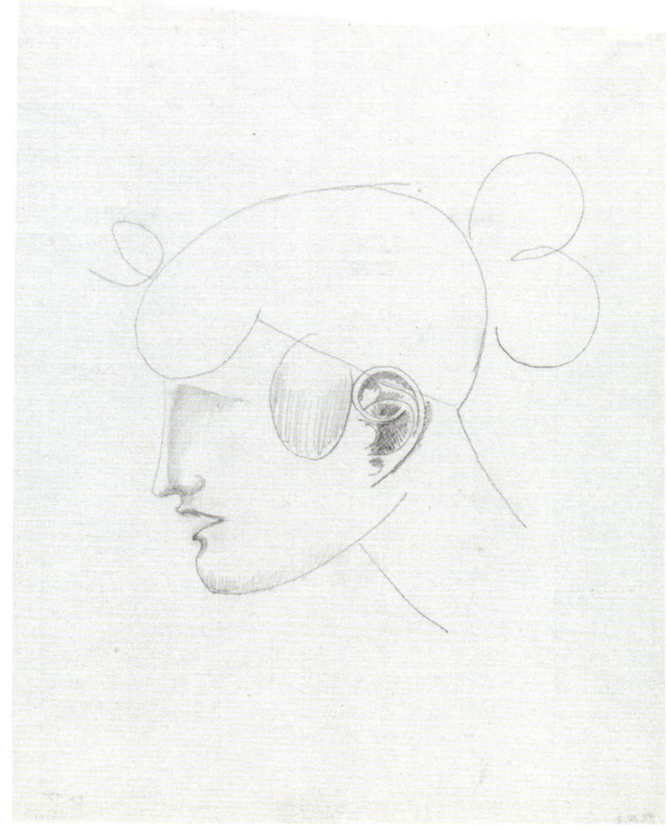

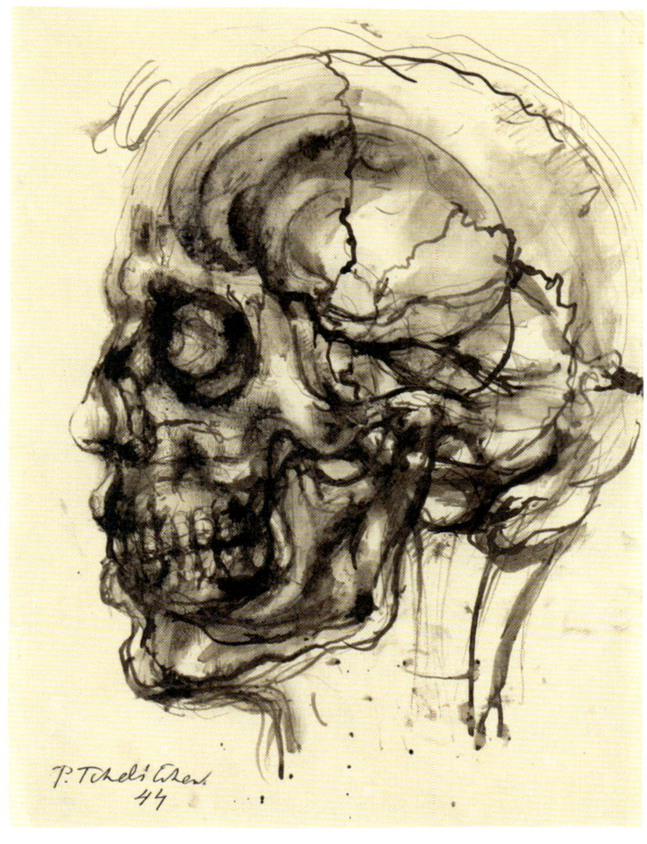

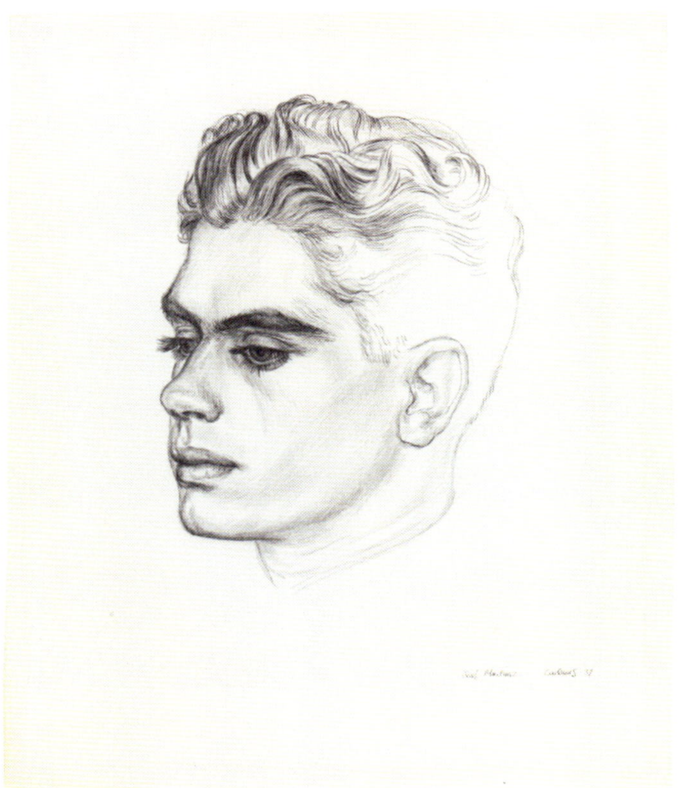

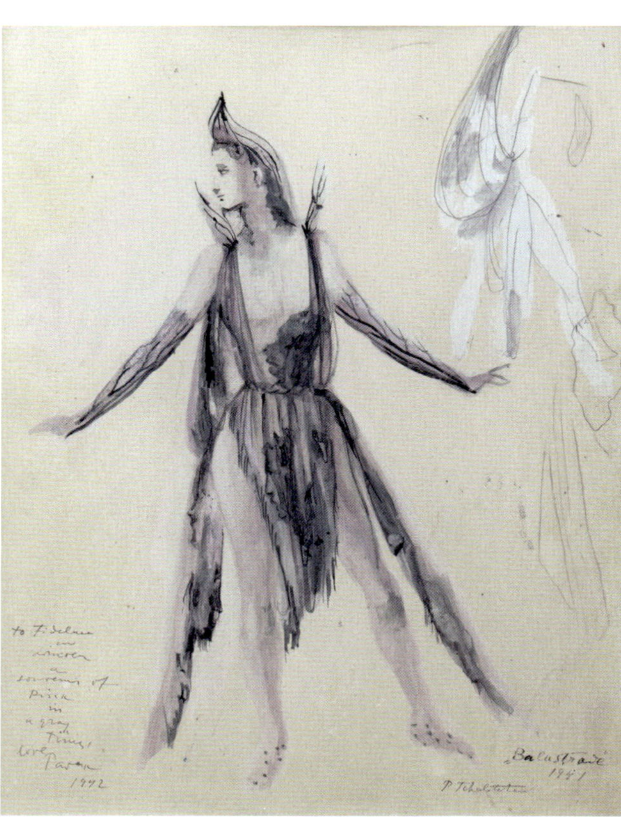

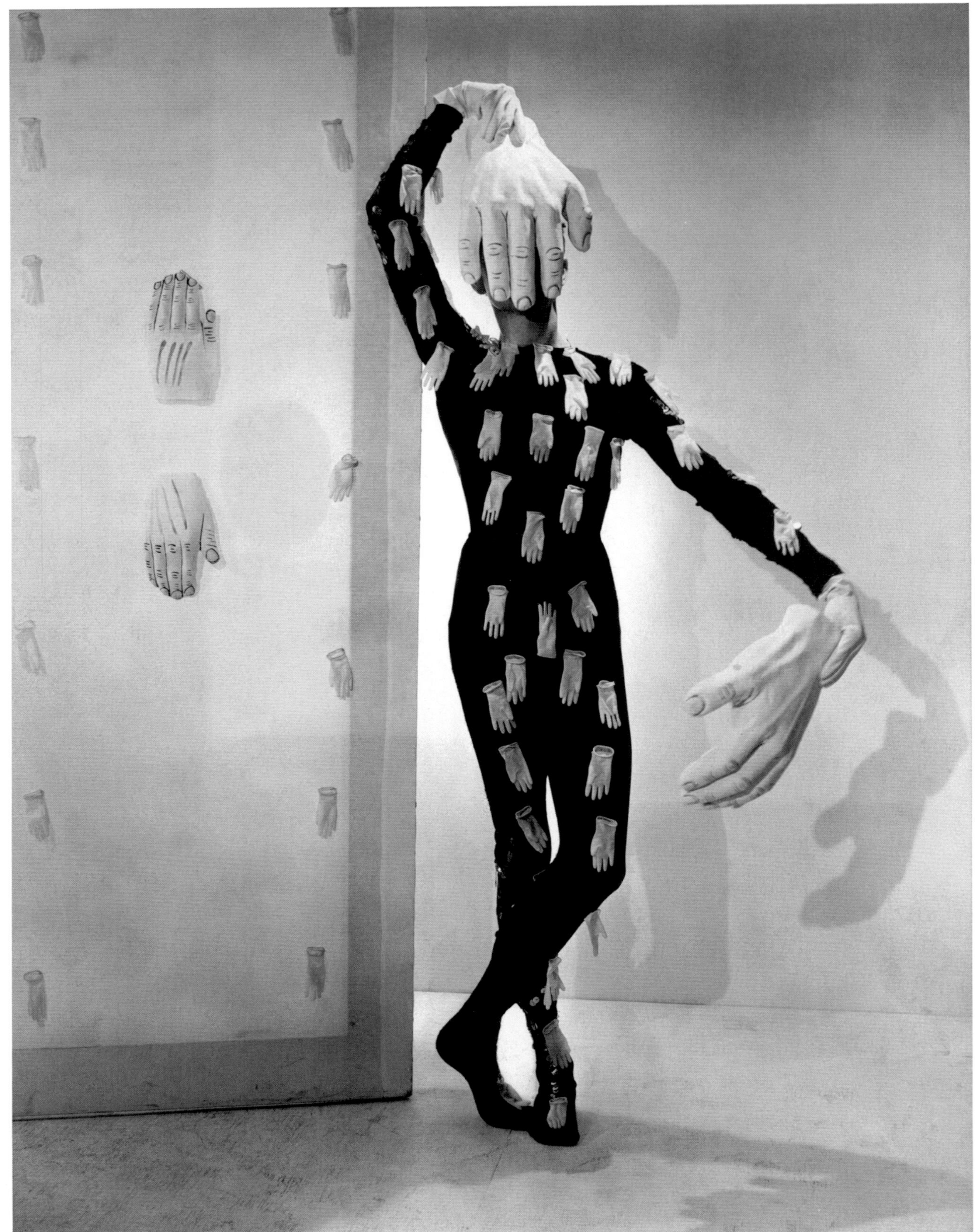

Cecil Beaton, photograph of poet Charles Henri Ford in a Salvador Dalí–designed costume, 1937. Gelatin silver print, 18⅔ × 14⅔ inches (47.2 × 37.1 cm) framed. Collection of Beth Rudin DeWoody

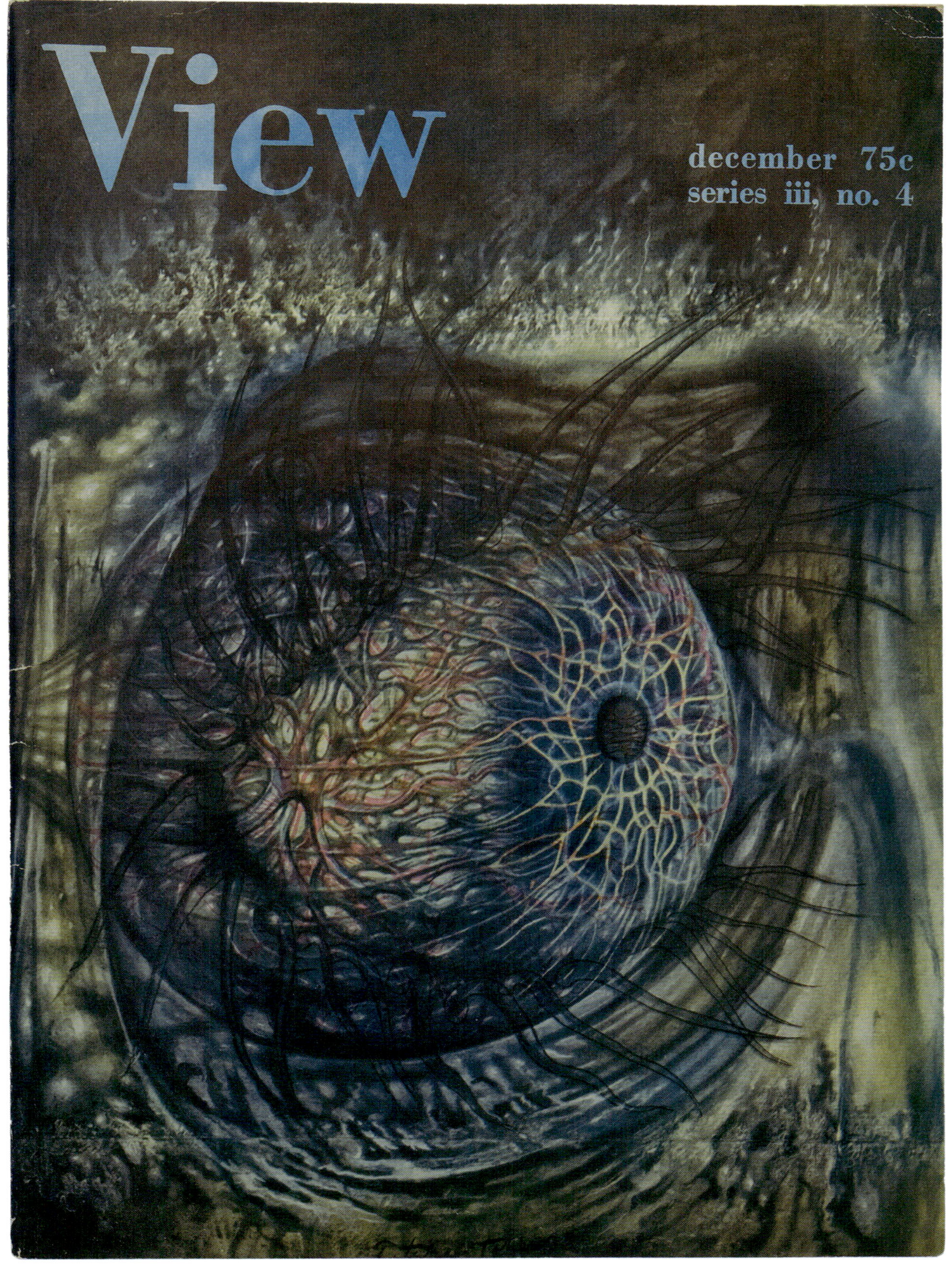

Charles Henri Ford was a precocious poet, publisher, and artist and a coauthor (with Parker Tyler) of *The Young and Evil* (1933), which has been credited as the first novel to treat the daily lives of homosexuals without shame. Championed by Gertrude Stein, it was later described by Tyler as "the novel that beat the Beat Generation by a generation." (Tyler would go on to become the most original film critic of the twentieth century, and the loquacious biographer of Elie Nadelman, Florine Stettheimer, and Pavel Tchelitchew.) Ford's greatest gifts to modern American culture were the two pathbreaking magazines he edited: *Blues* (1929–30) and, later, *View*, an iconoclastic vehicle for Surrealist art and literature as well as vernacular American art forms, which he coedited with Tyler from 1940 to 1947. In an article on Jean-Paul Sartre published in the *New Yorker* in 1946, Ford "said that he would describe *View* as avant-garde if that didn't sound so old-fashioned. 'We are for all advanced points of view,' he said. 'Advanced Catholic, advanced Anarchist, advanced Leftist. And we are Surrealist, of course, but *advanced* Surrealist.'" Paintings and photographs by Ford's peers filled the pages and graced the covers of *View*, including several works by his partner, Russian émigré painter Tchelitchew. The magazine's advisory board included composers Aaron Copland and Ramón Sender, Surrealist ethnographer Pierre Mabille, critic Henry McBride, poet Edith Sitwell, curator James Johnson Sweeney, and writer Stark Young. *View*'s editorial secretary, Betty Cage, would later become the general manager of New York City Ballet.

Cover of December 1943 issue of *View* by Pavel Tchelitchew

View

one east fifty-third street
new york 22, n. y.
telephone: plaza 3-7522
cable address: viewmag

Charles Henri Ford, Editor
Parker Tyler, Associate Editor
John Myers, Managing Editor
Betty Cage, Editorial Secretary

ADVISORY BOARD: Aaron Copland, Marcel Duchamp,
Henry McBride, Pierre Mabille, Ramon J. Sender,
Edith Sitwell, James Johnson Sweeney,
Stark Young

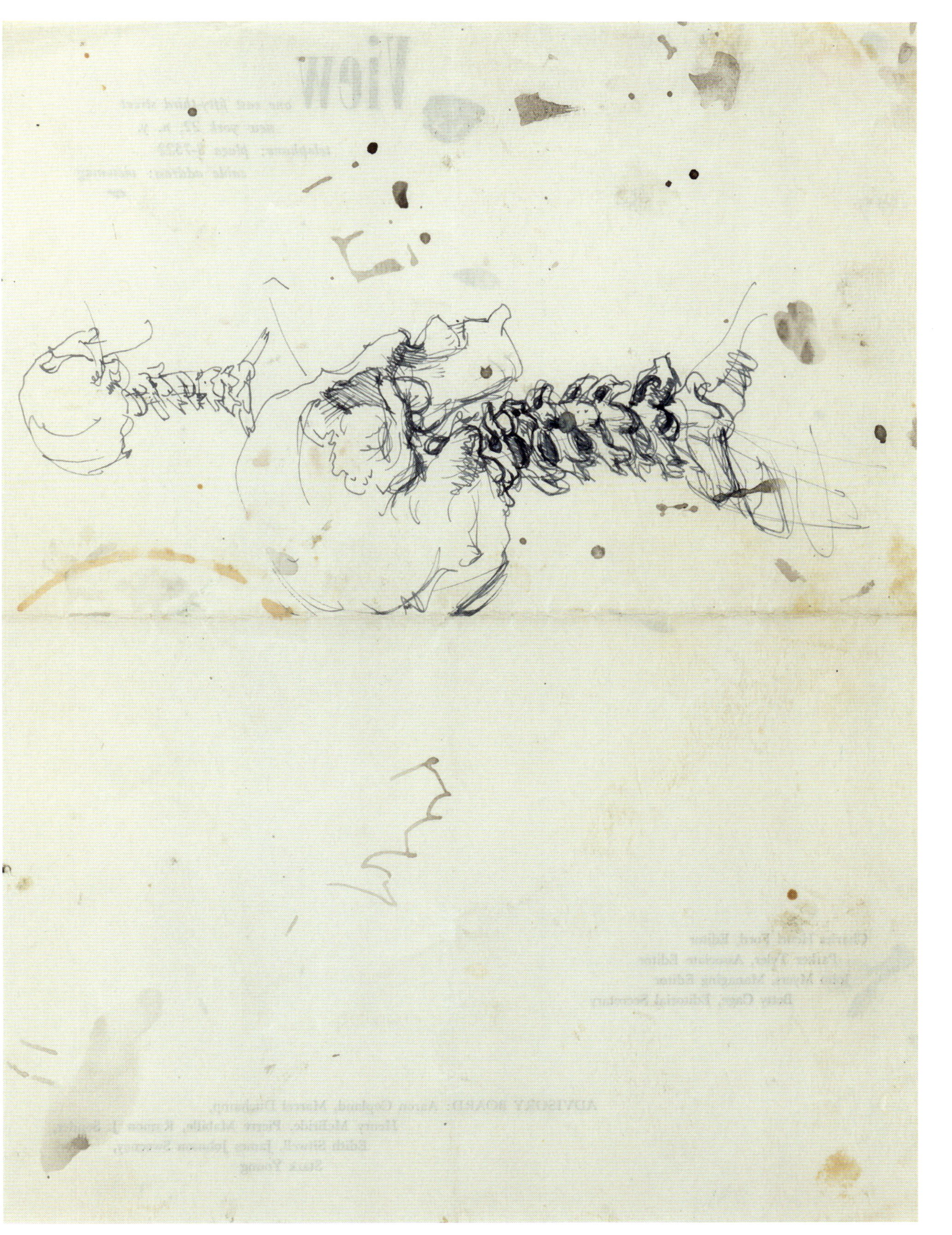

Opposite and left: Letterhead of *View* with sketch by Pavel Tchelitchew on the reverse, n.d. Private collection

FIFTY PHOTOGRAPHS BY GEORGE PLATT LYNES

Julien Levy Gallery, 602 Madison Ave., New York

Monday, October 1, to Saturday, October 13, 1934

A foreword: I think that photography is an art. Intelligent friends say it is not. Yet it can take in more than the mere human eye at any one glance can, and as it were in black and white memory convey this visual experience briefly, or intermittently, to no matter whom, at once or when the time comes. What do the other admittedly fine arts propose? Each to outdo one or more of our five senses, our parlous faculties, in some such fashion. Disinterested emotion is what we judge by; the effect of disinterested emotion on our subsequent thinking is what we want. Indeed that aroused by a photograph is not primarily disinterested as a rule, but inherent in the subject: face of greatness, breasts of beauty, scene of crime, etc. Or it depends on the person to whom it is shown, his or her mood of the moment, the drama of that particular image's appearing where it does not naturally belong: beloved physique far far away, for example, or beggar's hands in soft drawing-room, or wrecked ship in rural paradise. And though the photograph be mediocre, it may have an effect nevertheless, but as any old fetish or keepsake does, on one person or two, for a while. So a poor love-letter all out of grammatical and logical focus yet will turn its trick; of course, we say, that is not art. Whereas the same communication well-rendered makes, for unacquainted populations throughout fitful centuries, a sort of mental music; and we call it art then. In photography, as in grander work and play of civilized man, the noblest effort is like the lowliest to start with. The difference between whatever the postman happens to deliver and literature, between fine photography and hack-work, lies in the answers to obvious questions: How many people does it interest, and for how long? How lasting is its language, the material of its embodiment? Of how much consequence in their civilization are the people whom it interests, and how important in each individual scheme of things is the emotion aroused?

Now beauty makes things interesting. Photographic beauty is rare. In any case this is a very restricted art, dangerously like and unlike several others. A lot of blundering goes on in imitation of painting, classic painting or Parisian painting as the case may be. Intelligent friends say, for example, that Titian painted out of focus, and of course idle or incompetent photographers like to hear it said. But a painting literally cannot be out of focus: a very real wash or daub of pigment has to be placed on the canvas, which the eye then looks at, definite as mosaic or enamel, whether or not what it represents amounts to anything. In spite of the paraphernalia—orb of pressed glass, and hysterical film, and doped paper, and poisonous pharmacopoeia, and dark vessels in dark-room—the photographer has really very little medium or raw material to work with: a thin sort of emanation of the model or subject precariously relayed from lens to plate, from plate to paper. He cannot do just what he likes. One of the things he cannot do is to fill up waste space in his composition with sumptuous nothing; he is poor. What he fails to bring clearly to the attention of the lens might better not be in the picture at all; it is just so much soiled paper. Unfortunately the horrors of contemporary photography are not all of mechanical origin. The sawed-off chunks of nude or other commodity, and the drunken abstractions, and the cigarette-butts and cellophane in still life, and the sweet ectoplasmic studies, and the dressmakers' dreams in a flatulence of tulle, and the poor female faces all flattened out by electric light but with hairy eyes and greasy mouths, amid extremities of this and that, composed like an egg around its yolk, against blear background—vulgarity on the one hand to please the purchaser, who is bored anyway, minor mania on the other hand for art's sake: it is an infinitude of rote and sham, lethargy and advertisement. A technician by nature, an honest and fussy man, Mr. Lynes will not ask us to put up with anything of that sort, fortunately.

What is most interesting in the present exhibition is the evidence of his effort to enlarge upon photographic beauty, to solidify and clean up and limber up its petty aesthetics, in practise. There is a variety of hard jobs involved. He never will settle down to two dimensions, or even two and a half, photography seeming to him more akin to sculpture in low relief than to any other representational art. Natural space, he thinks, must be established before and behind and beside the subject. Though in camera-work true perspective must appear mechanically, all too often you cannot see any; in a gelatinous dimness, or cramped area merely cut out, it is left to your imagination. A look of abundant light is also very hard to get. Blaze of bulbs directed at the subject tend to produce just some tiresome mist; whereas the Rembrandt formula, the soul shining away in a dark corner, has been overworked ever since the invention of the camera. There is the problem of embellishment, of the flattering likeness. In theory the sitter has a right to have his or her ideal self represented, the photographer to express the enthusiasm about the sitter which characterizes him, if this can be done without causing other ugliness. In general practise retouching clogs the negative, deadens or dirties the print. Mr. Lynes has thought of some new ways of making people look fine, though it may be said that pre-war or post-Hollywood prettiness is not his ideal. His severest undertaking is the reduction of waste space; so that, if you like, when you get around to it, you may take an interest in everything that there is in his picture, every square inch. No doubt a picture ought, like a sentence, to be reasonably and smoothly tied up, with subject and predicate, with every incidental bit in intelligible relative place, all according to a sort of grammar of location. That is the great pictorial mystery called composition. Having specialized in portraiture has simplified that problem for Mr. Lynes somewhat, complicating the rest. It is a good specialty: the male or female face, the most variable and the most mobile thing in nature, focal point in a way of everything else there is to photograph, and almost impossible to describe, often looks intimidated or tired in painted pictures.

Glenway Wescott

1. Capt. Harold Balfour
2. Miss Ruth Bolton of Boltonville, Wisconsin
3. Mr. Nelson Brinckerhoff
4. Miss Rosemary Carver
5. Mr. Jimmie Daniels
6. Miss Lucy Martin Donnelly
7. Mrs. Winsor Brown French, II.
8. Mr. Denham Fouts
9. M. André Gide
10. Mr. C. G. Hope Gill
11. Miss Billie Haywood
12. Miss Billie Haywood
13. Miss Muriel King
14. M. Serge Lifar
15. M. Serge Lifar: L'Aprés-Midi d'un Faune
16. Mrs. Li Ming
17. Miss Marya Mannes
18. Miss Lois Moran
19. M. Louis Moyses
20. Mr. Lewis Mumford
21. Princess Nathalie Paley
22. Mlle. Lily Pons
23. Miss Mildred Pope
24. Miss Katherine Anne Porter
25. Mrs. Langdon W. Post
26. Mr. & Mrs. Sergei Soudeikine
27. Miss Gertrude Stein
28. Miss Mamie Sze
29. Mr. Carl Van Vechten
30. Mr. Pavel Tchelitchew
31. Mr. Bruce Peters Wescott
32. Mr. Monroe Wheeler
33. Miss Virginia Winmill
34. Parisian
35. Under the Pont-Neuf
36. Notre-Dame-la-Grande, Poitiers
37. Sleeping Beggar, Valladolid
38. Annunciation, San Vicente, Avila
39. Vultures
40. Baskets and Broom
41. The Green River Mill
42. Old Vehicles
43. Tree, Massachusetts
44. Taxi-Driver
45. The American Navy
46. Miss Minnegerode in Travesty
47. Mr. Isamu Noguchi
48. Male Nude
49. Female Nude
50. Self-Portrait

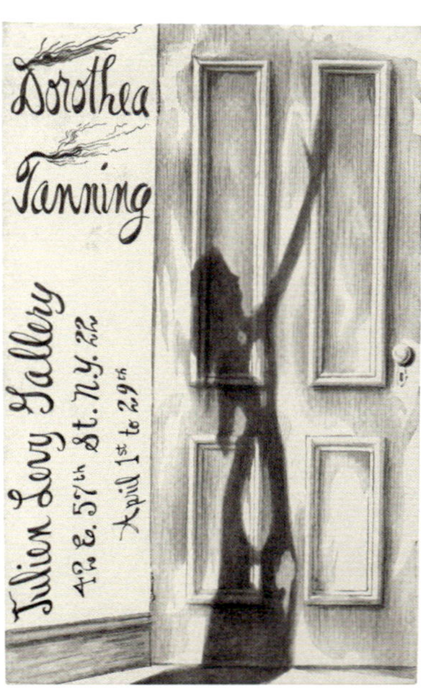

MURALS BY

JARED FRENCH

JULIEN LEVY GALLERY, 15 EAST 57 STREET, NEW YORK

JANUARY 24 TO FEBRUARY 7, 1939

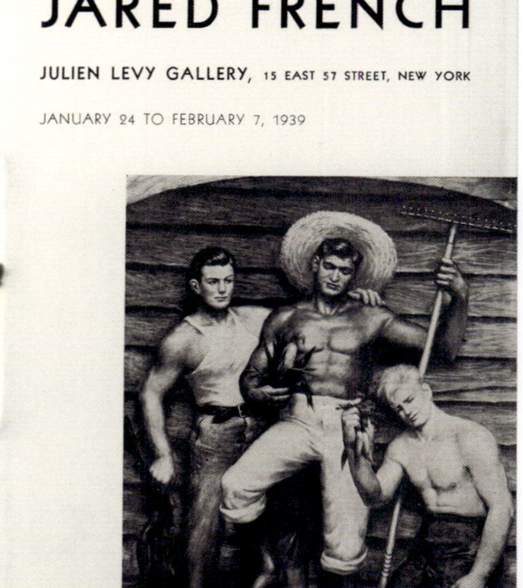

WALKER EVANS
GEORGE LYNES

Opposite, left: Exhibition checklist for *Fifty Photographs by George Platt Lynes*, with essay by Glenway Wescott, Julien Levy Gallery, New York, 1934

Opposite, top right: Exhibition invitation to *Walker Evans/George Lynes*, Julien Levy Gallery, New York, 1932

Opposite, bottom left: Exhibition invitation to *Dorothea Tanning*, Julien Levy Gallery, New York, 1944

Opposite, bottom right: Cover of exhibition brochure for *Murals by Jared French*, Julien Levy Gallery, New York, 1939

Below: Back and front of exhibition brochure for *Man Ray: Objects of My Affection*, Julien Levy Gallery, 1945, featuring a reproduction after Marcel Duchamp, after Alexander Hackenschmied

As curator Ingrid Schaffner has noted, gallerist Julien Levy was an early advocate of photography (the "supreme expression of our epoch"), Surrealism ("the photography of the mind"), and Neo-Romanticism ("the camera of the soul"), exhibiting works of these genres alongside theatrical posters, American folk art, experimental films, and ballet costume and stage designs. Levy's gallery was notable for its singularly anachronistic ethos and its focus on Surrealist automatism, which might be seen to have prognisticated Abstract Expressionism. Active from 1931 to 1949, the gallery was a vibrant nexus for European and American artists, and Levy himself played a central role as artistic and romantic matchmaker. One of Levy's exhibition invitations includes a checklist of subjects depicted by photographer George Platt Lynes beneath an essay penned by novelist Glenway Wescott, with whom Lynes and curator Monroe Wheeler shared a seventeen-year romantic triad. Wescott's text begins with a contradiction: "I think photography is an art. Intelligent friends say it is not." An invitation to Man Ray's exhibition features an artwork by Ray's friend and collaborator Marcel Duchamp. The image, however, is "after" filmmaker Alexander Hackenschmied, who was married to another of Duchamp's collaborators, filmmaker Maya Deren.

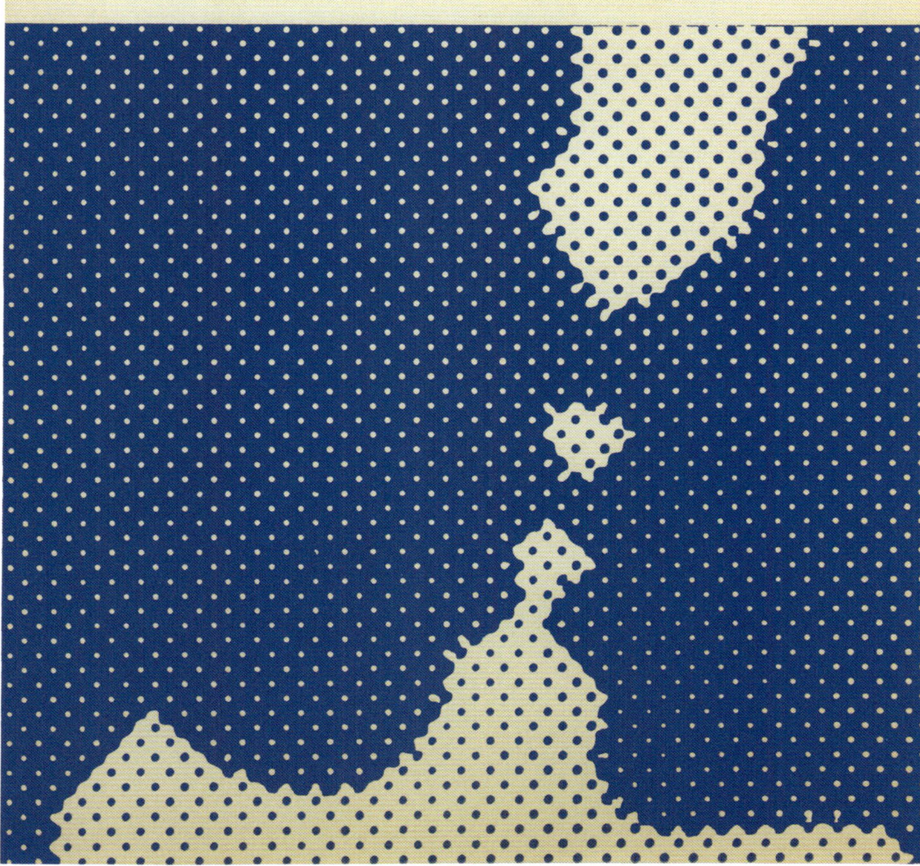

OBJECTS OF MY AFFECTION

1. *Self-Portrait*, reflected in a flexible mirror, is capable of infinite variations simply by the pressure of a finger to the surface of the mirror, permitting as many modifications as does the application of a brush to canvas, with the advantage of attaining that instantaneous quality felt in a work realized by more laborious means.

2. *Equivalents*, are the results of tensile strengths and weaknesses which by creating a stalemate, produce an illusion of perpetual motion.

3. *Life Saver*, like a picture with a handle, must be met half-way with equal buoyancy and outstretched hand; it has no means of self-propulsion.

4. *Domesticated Egg*, no more improbable than preserved egg, though admittedly less edible.

5. *Silent Harp*, is the *Violin d'Ingres* of a frustrated musician. He can hear color as easily as he can see sound.

6. *Mirage*, transplanted to the home, reflects numbers, projects shadows, turns and oscillates without departing from its base.

7. *Table for Two*, casseroles in the role of personages.

8. *Last Object*, or object of destruction. It is still my earnest desire, some day while the eye is ticking away during a conversation, to lift my hammer and with one well-aimed blow to completely demolish the metronome.

9. *Monogram*, on a pedestal, slightly adjustable and movable.

10. *Contraption* one of the elements in the inspiration for the title; it cannot be condemned as a pun any more than the first syllable in punctuation.

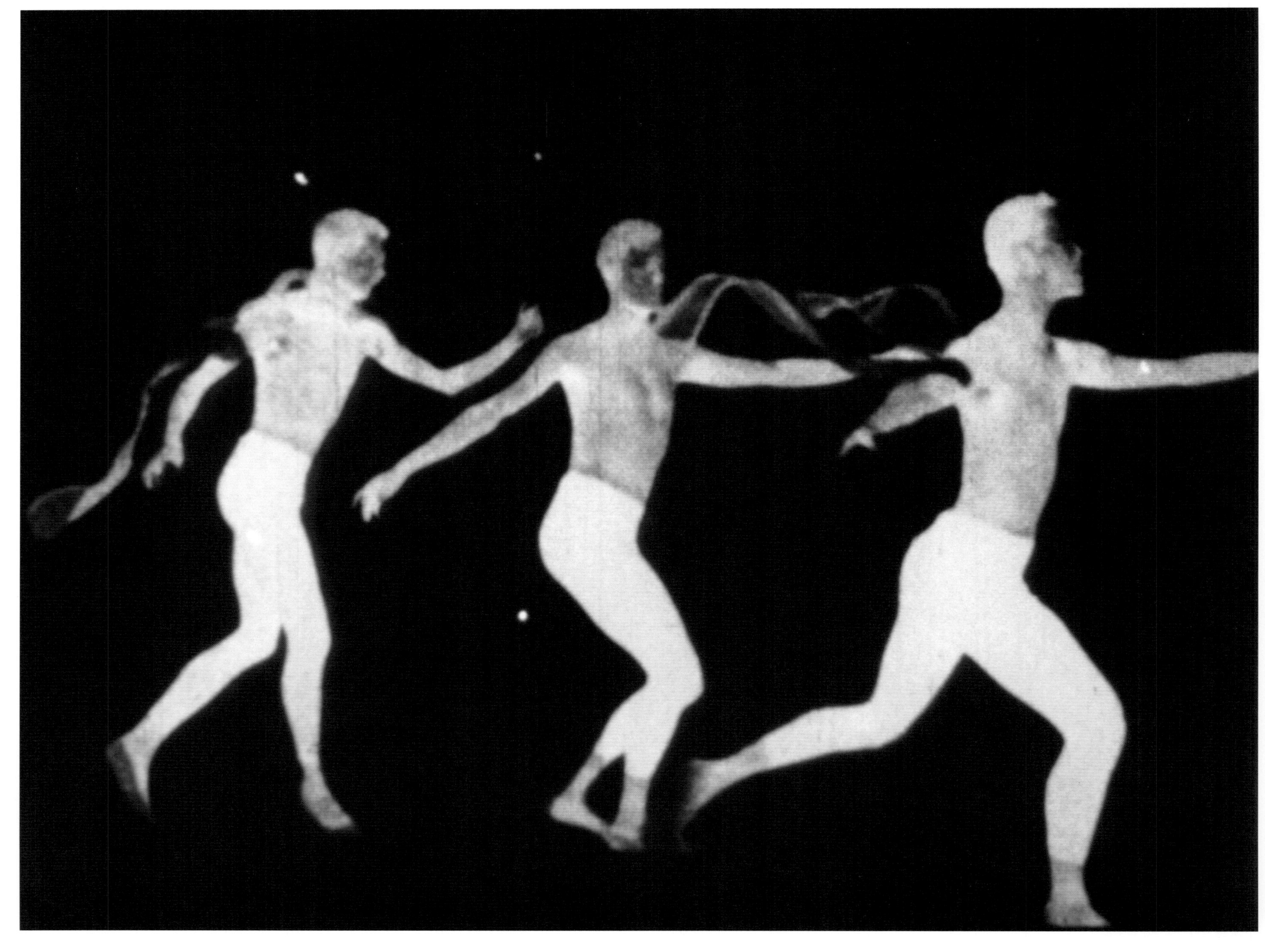

Opposite and below:
Stills from Maya Deren,
The Very Eye of Night,
1958. 16 mm film (black-
and-white, sound), 15 min.

Maya Deren thought of her films as "dances choreographed for and performed by the camera and by human beings together." Indebted to the tutelage of dancer and academic anthropologist Katherine Dunham, Deren pursued interests in ritual forms and the connections between dance, "possession," and anthropology. She made her final completed film, *The Very Eye of Night* (1958), which she called her "ballet of night," with choreographer Antony Tudor and his students at the Metropolitan Opera Ballet School in the early 1950s. Set to a soundtrack by Teiji Ito and projected in negative, the film features formations of dancers, who represent nocturnal states of mind and signs of the zodiac, floating against a black background pierced with stars.

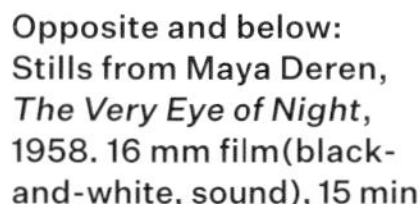

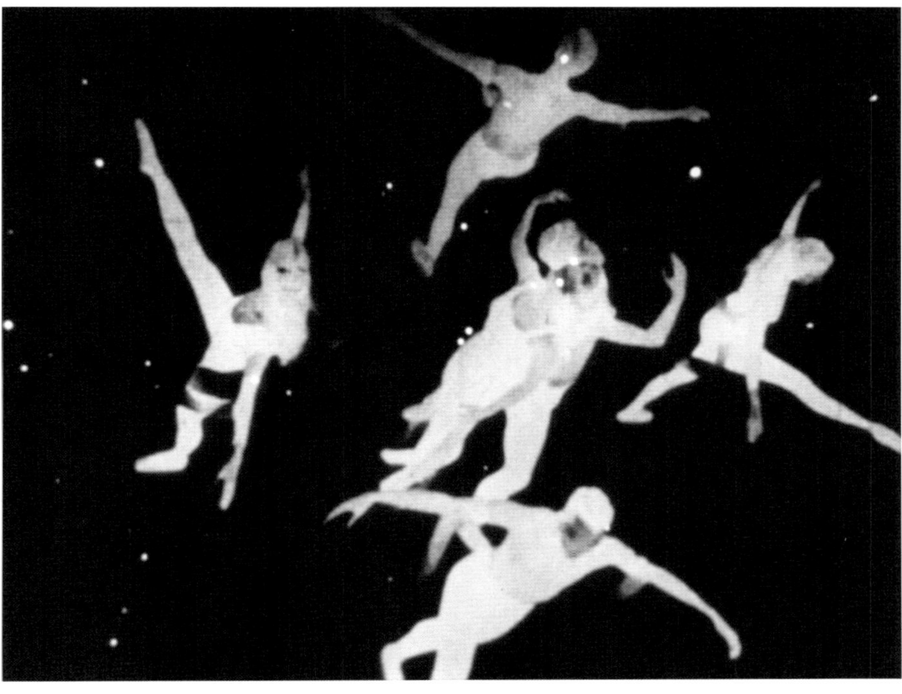

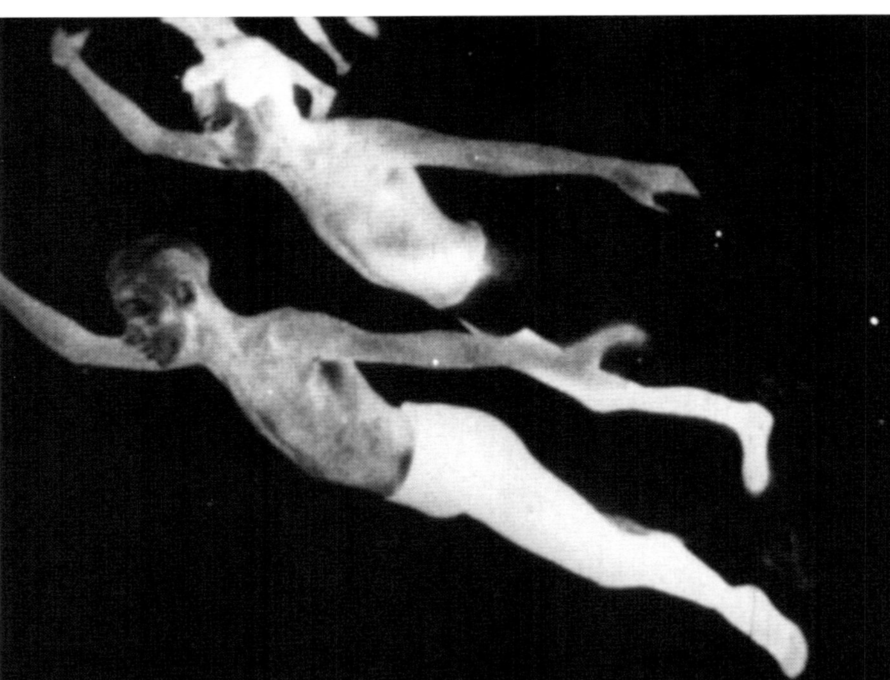

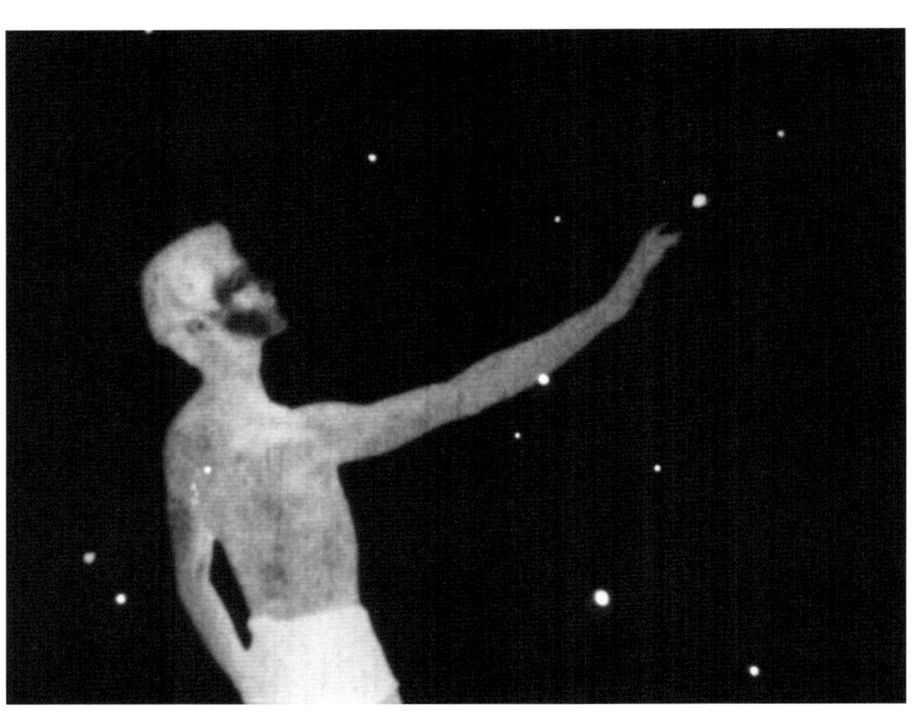

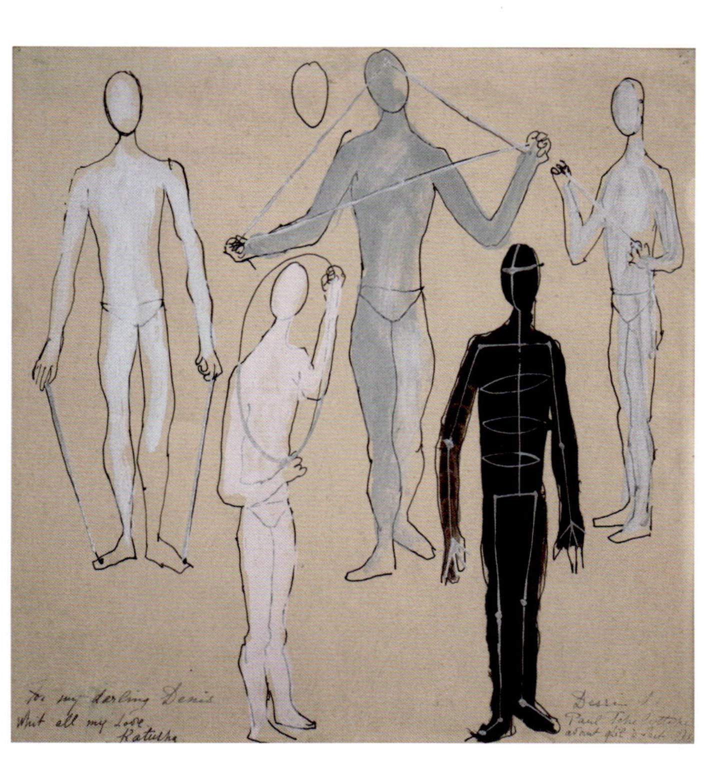

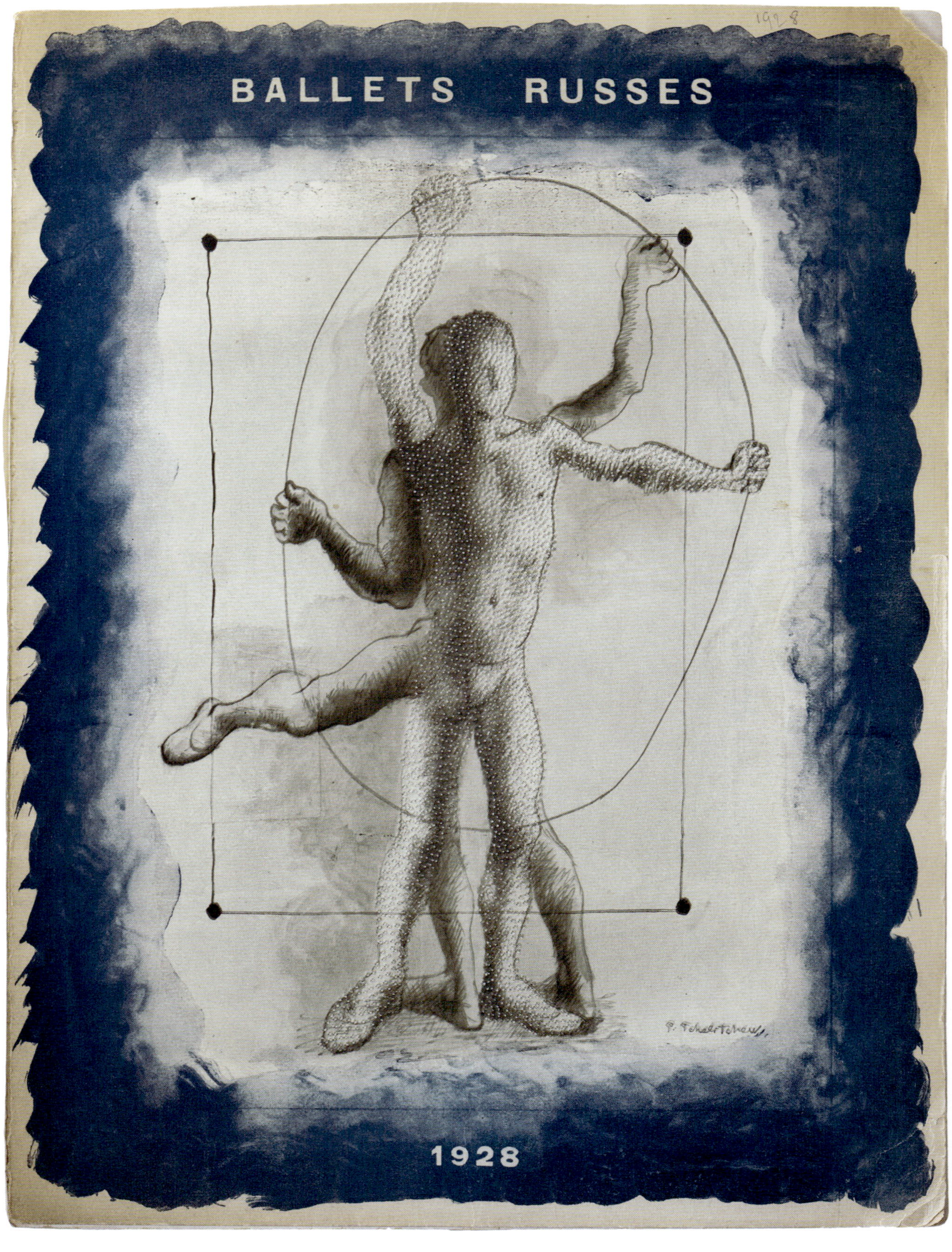

Surrealist painter Pavel Tchelitchew designed visionary multimedia sets and costumes for Serge Diaghilev's Ballets Russes and Boris Kochno and George Balanchine's short-lived European company, Les Ballets 1933. In New York, Tchelitchew continued to design sets for Balanchine ballets, as well as for choreographer Ruth Page's *Variations on Euclid* (1932), a ballet indebted to German artist Oskar Schlemmer. *Variations on Euclid* included a sack-like costume designed by Japanese American artist Isamu Noguchi, in which Page embodied Miss Expanding Universe, nodding to Edwin Hubble's recent discovery of the expansion of our universe.

Of all the American artists who collaborated with modernist dance makers, Noguchi cut the widest swath, working with Page, Balanchine, Martha Graham and her partner Erick Hawkins, and Merce Cunningham. Noguchi's sets, costumes, and props are distinctive in that they remain intrinsic to and interdependent with each production; they cannot be stripped away, replaced, or stylistically updated.

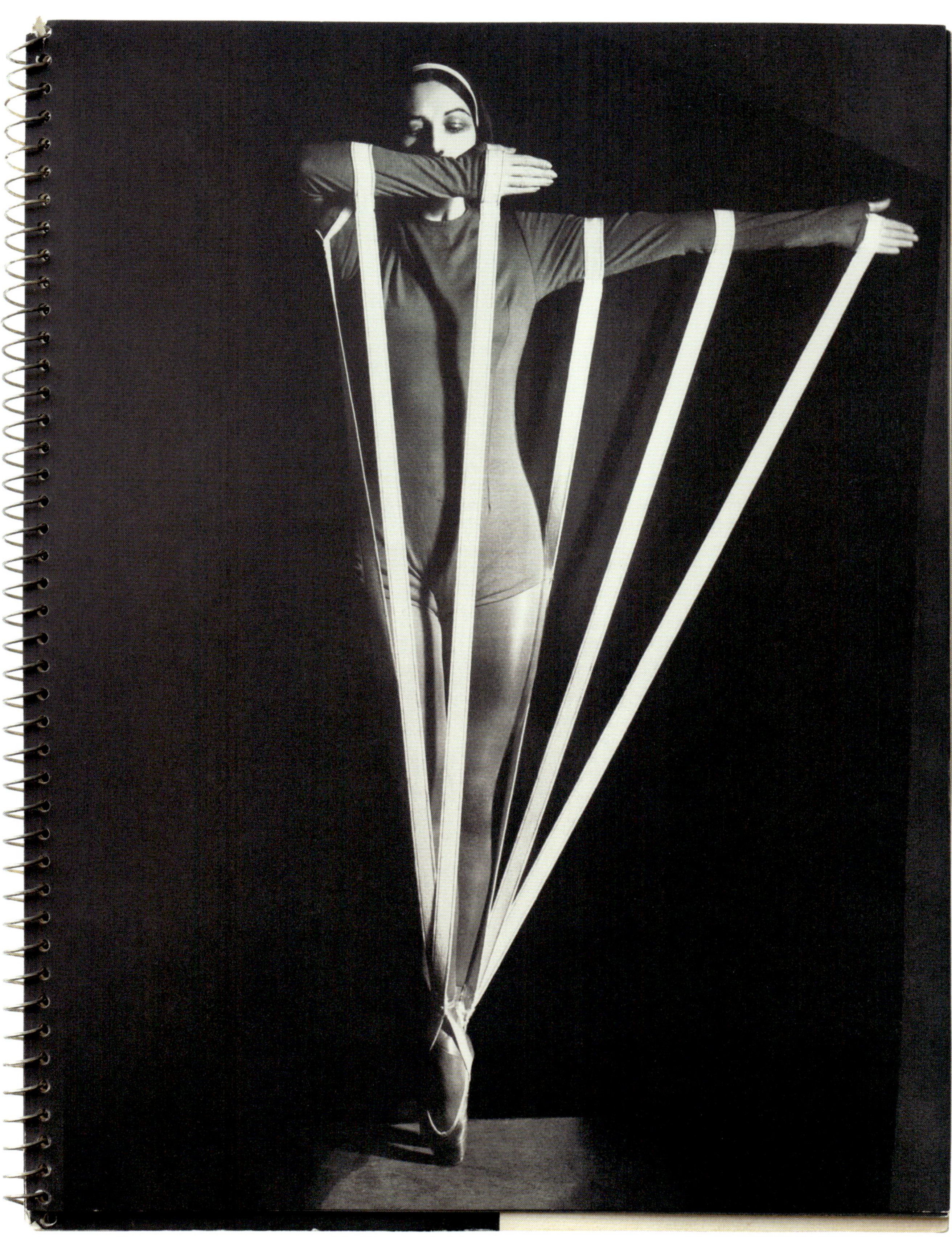

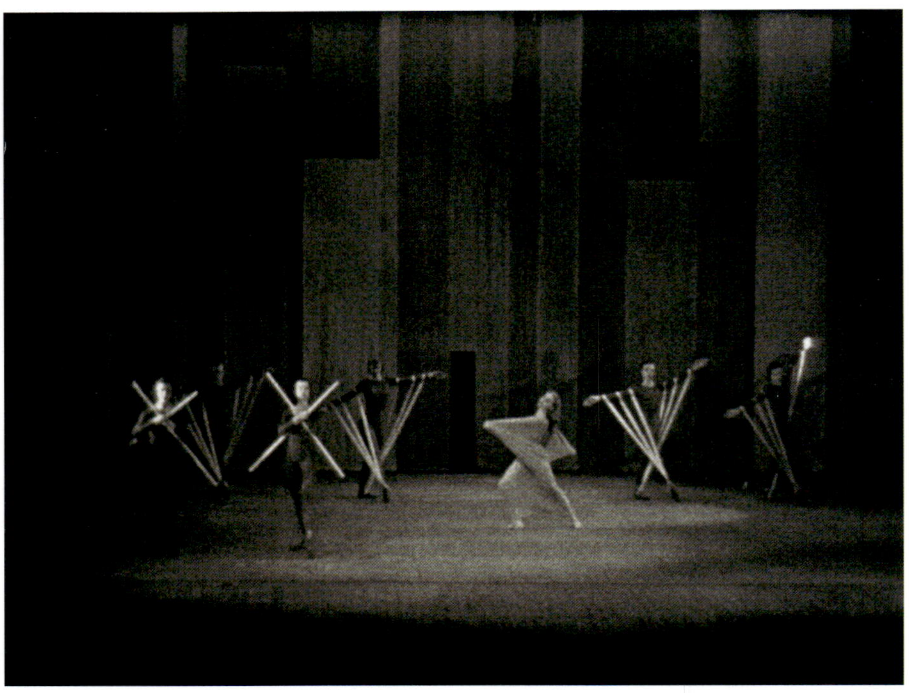

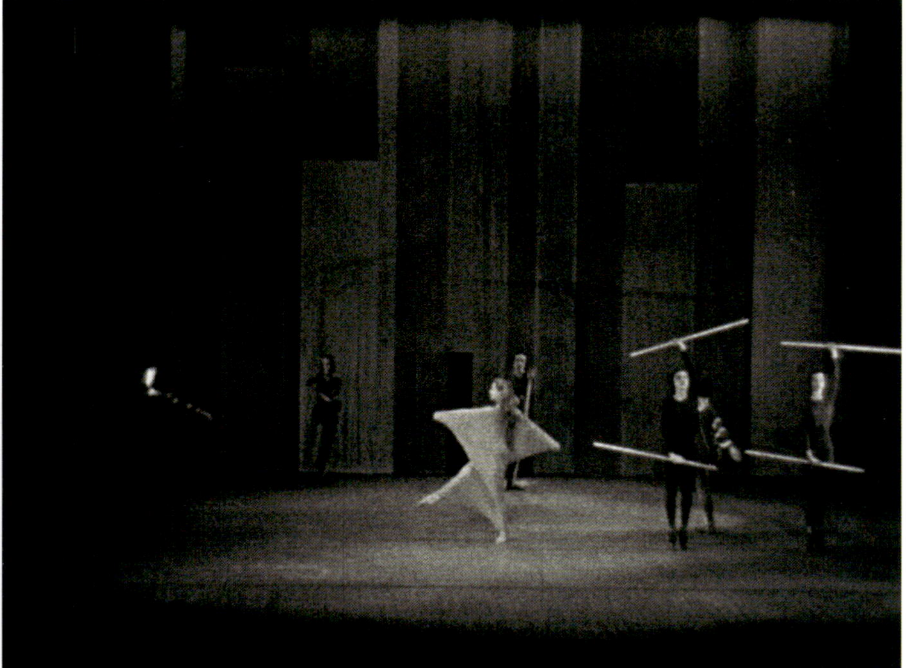

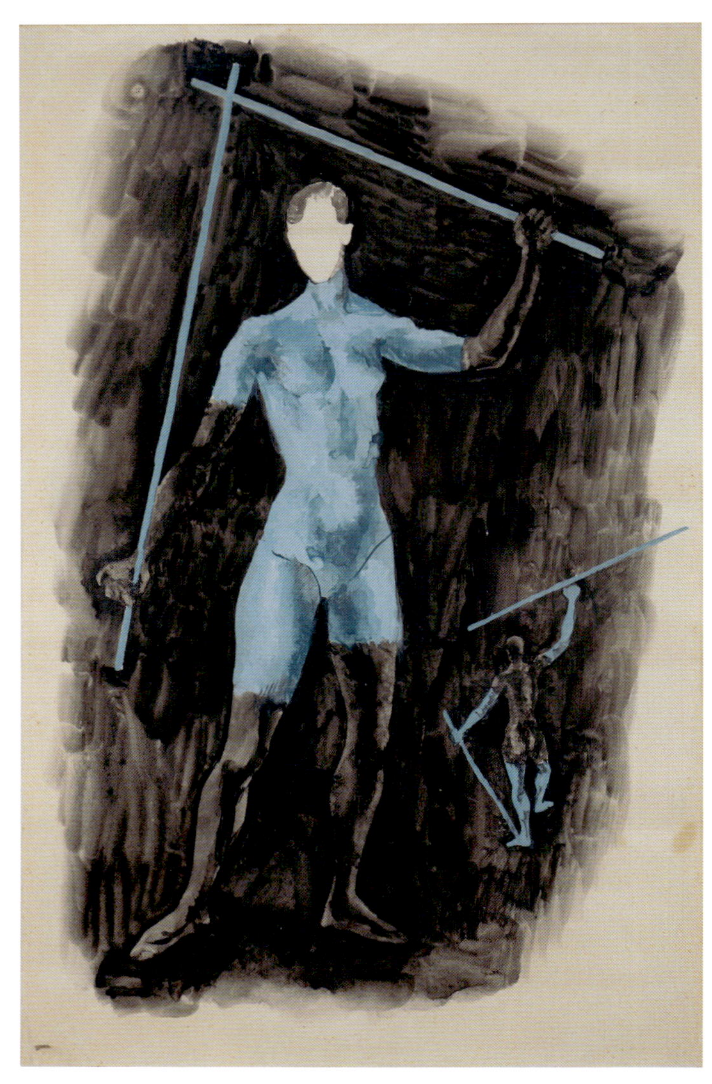

Left: Film stills of *Variations on Euclid* (aka *Expanding Universe*), choreographed by Ruth Page, c. 1938, with costumes by Isamu Noguchi and Pavel Tchelitchew

Above: Pavel Tchelitchew, costume design for *Variations on Euclid*, choreographed by Ruth Page, 1932. Gouache on paper, 19¾ × 12⅞ inches (50.2 × 32.7 cm). Jerome Robbins Dance Division, The New York Public Library for the Performing Arts, Astor, Lenox and Tilden Foundations

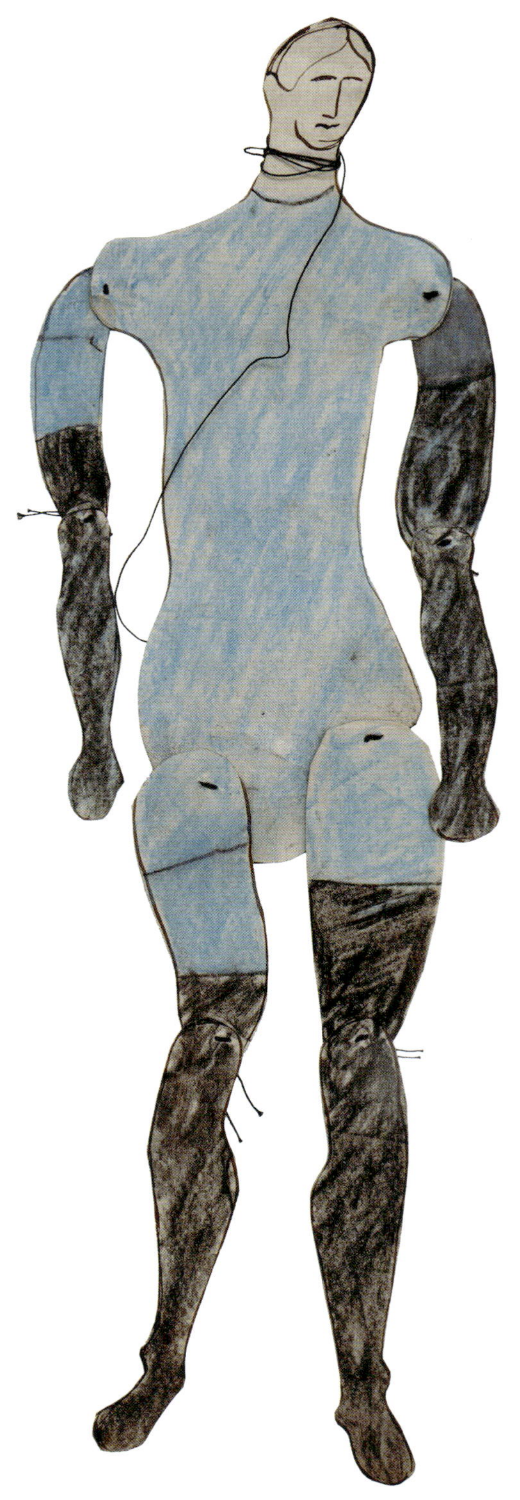

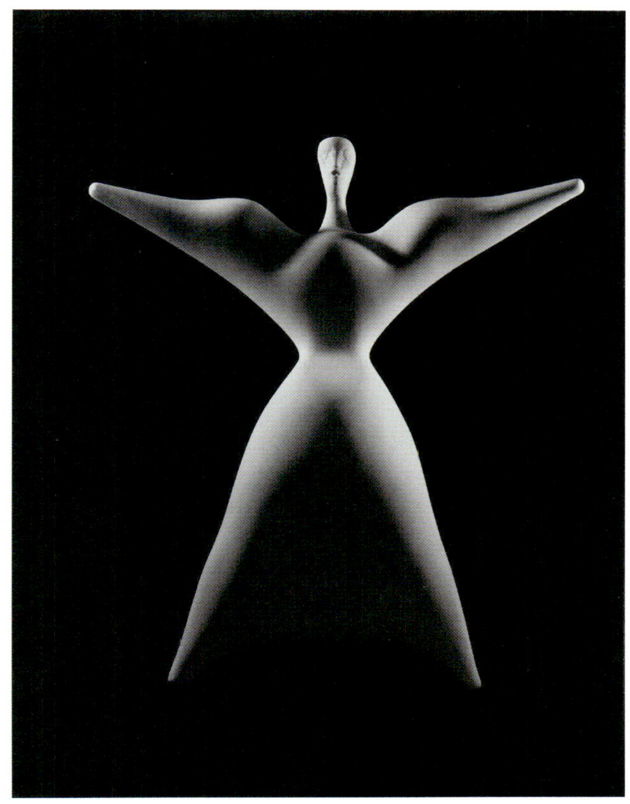

Left: Pavel Tchelitchew, costume design for *Variations on Euclid*, choreographed by Ruth Page, c. 1932. Paper, crayon, ink, and string, 28 × 22 × ¼ inches (71.1 × 55.9 × 0.6 cm). Jerome Robbins Dance Division, The New York Public Library for the Performing Arts, Astor, Lenox and Tilden Foundations

Above: Isamu Noguchi, *Miss Expanding Universe*, 1932. Plaster, 40⅞ × 34⅞ × 9 inches (113.9 × 88.6 × 15.2 cm). The Isamu Noguchi Foundation and Garden Museum, New York. Photo: F. S. Lincoln

Left: Isamu Noguchi, *Jungle Gym* (scaffold), 1947, set element of Erick Hawkins's dance *Stephen Acrobat* (1947). Steel, plastic, paint. The Isamu Noguchi Foundation and Garden Museum, New York

Right: Eric Hawkins in *Stephen Acrobat* (1947), with set by Isamu Noguchi, 1946. Photo: Philippe Halsman

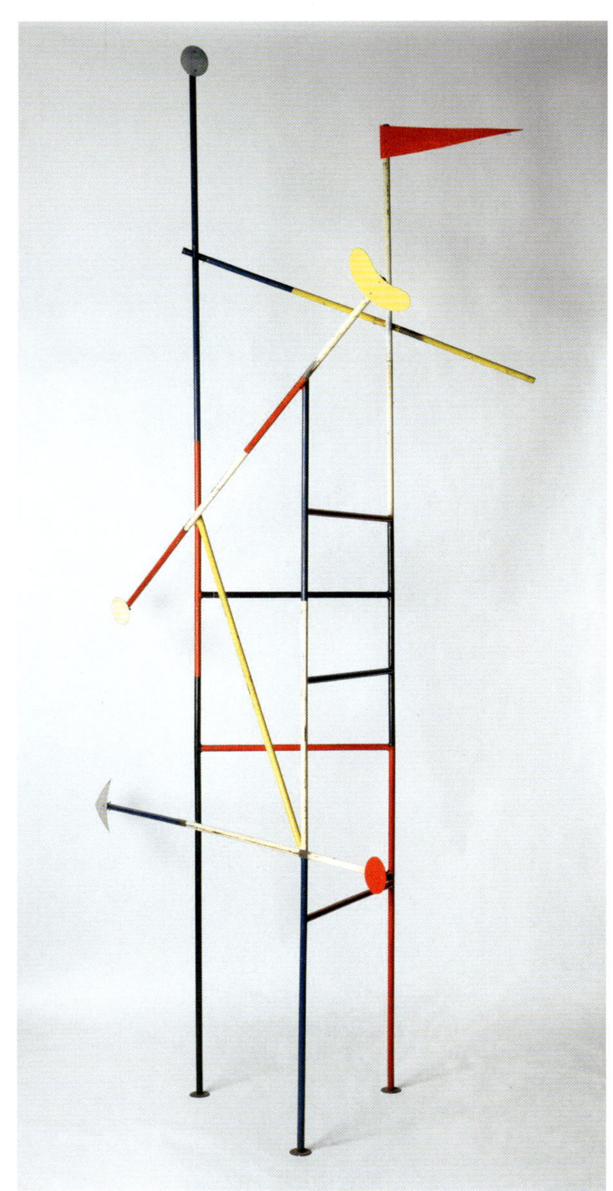

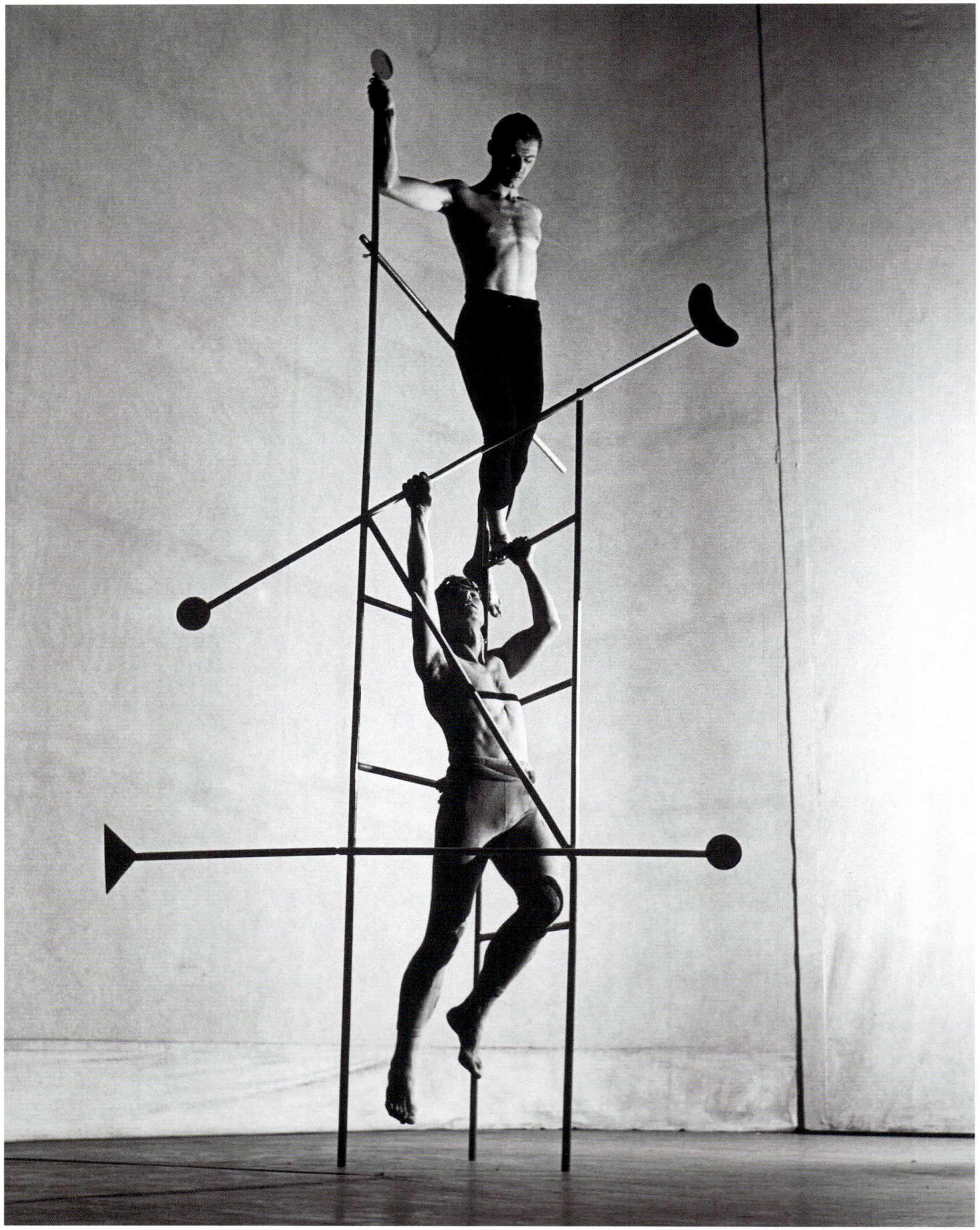

Left: Nicholas Magallanes and Francisco Moncion in New York City Ballet's *Orpheus*, 1950. Photograph by George Platt Lynes. Gelatin silver print on board with pencil, 10 × 8 inches (25.4 × 20.3 cm). Collections of the Kinsey Institute, Indiana University

Below: Isamu Noguchi, *Lyre*, 1948. Prop element of George Balanchine and New York City Ballet's dance *Orpheus* (1948, set design by Noguchi). Resin, balsa wood, wood, paint. The Isamu Noguchi Foundation and Garden Museum, New York

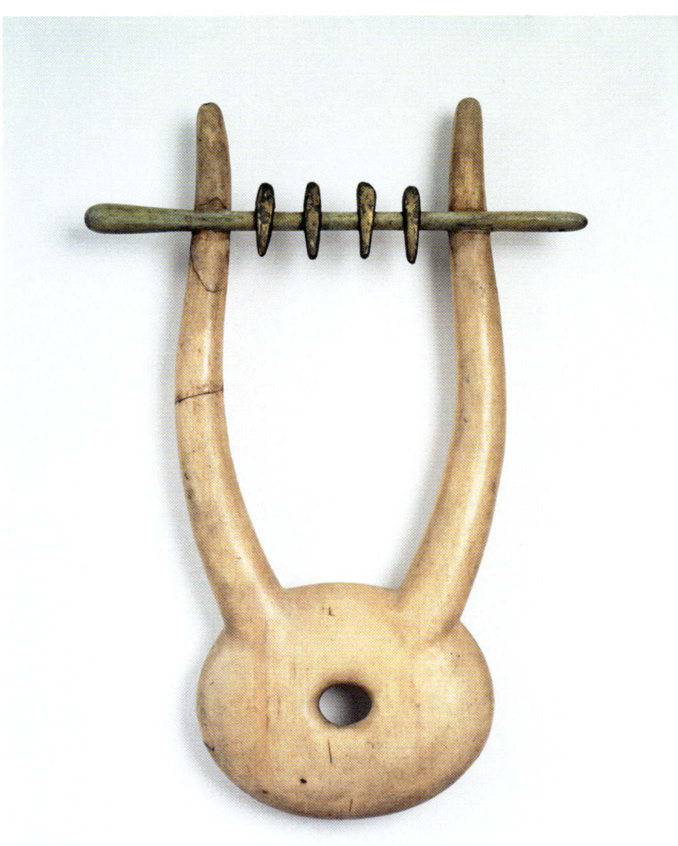

The artist and musician Xenia Cage presented a solo exhibition of her balsa-wood and rice-paper mobiles at Julien Levy's gallery in 1944. (None have survived.) Levy recalls the young artist in his memoir *Portrait of an Art Gallery*: "At this time I came to know John Cage and his fixed and silent sound at the home of Jean and Schuyler Watts. Cage, his wife Xenia, and the dancer Merce Cunningham were an inseparable triangle at that one moment, at the next Xenia and John were separated." Following her split with John, Xenia found work assembling Marcel Duchamp's elaborate retrospective edition in miniature, *Boîte-en-valise* (a few were made by Joseph Cornell), and later as a conservator at various institutions, including the Metropolitan Museum of Art, New York; and the Whitney Museum of American Art, New York. Cage and Cunningham became life partners and together forged a radical new model of collaboration for the stage, in which music, choreography, costume, and scenography coexist as if despite one another.

Xenia (Kashevaroff) Cage, untitled, 1954. Gouache on postcard. Private collection

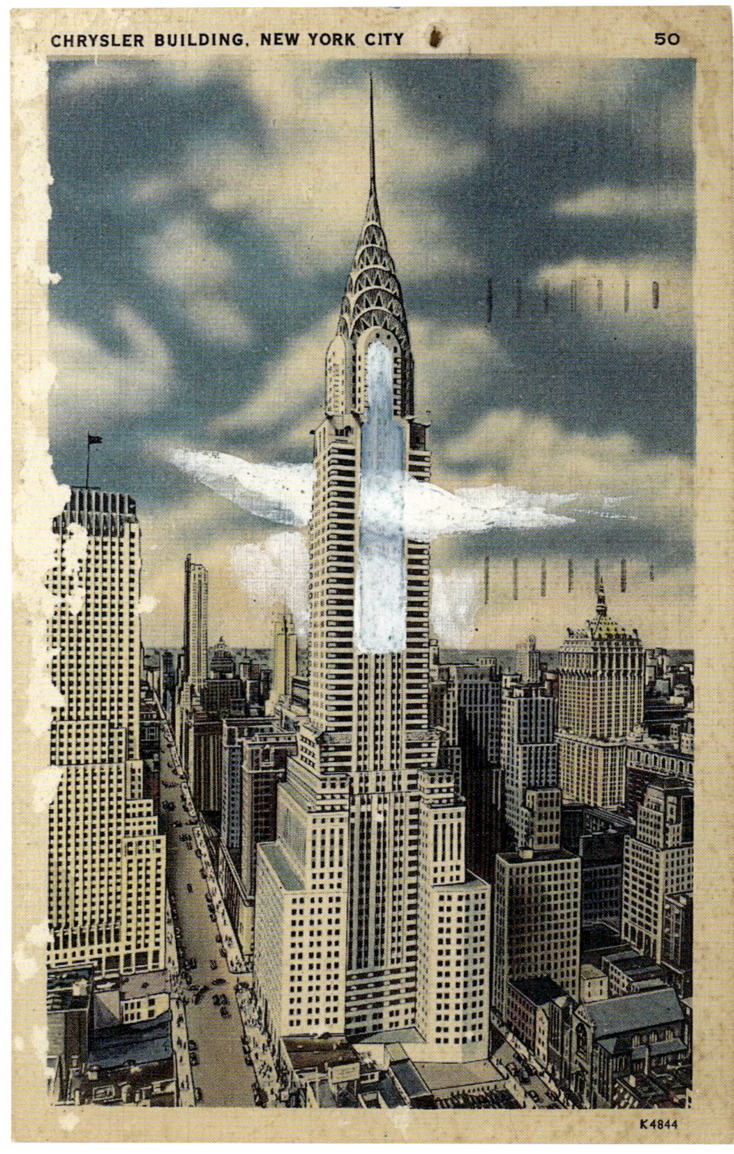

EVERY SOUL IS A CIRCUS

Despite her preoccupation with psychological subjects, Martha Graham is a comedienne with a deft, sly, humorous touch. *Every Soul Is a Circus*, her best comedy, is a study of the fantastic ideas that occupy the mind of a rather silly woman who imagines herself Empress of the Arena.

In the scene above she fancies herself enamored of an Acrobat (*left*) who carries a delicate flower to symbolize romantic, but harmless, flirtation. She is held back by the Ringmaster (Erick Hawkins) who represents the serious, inexorable, but rather stodgy logic of masculinity.

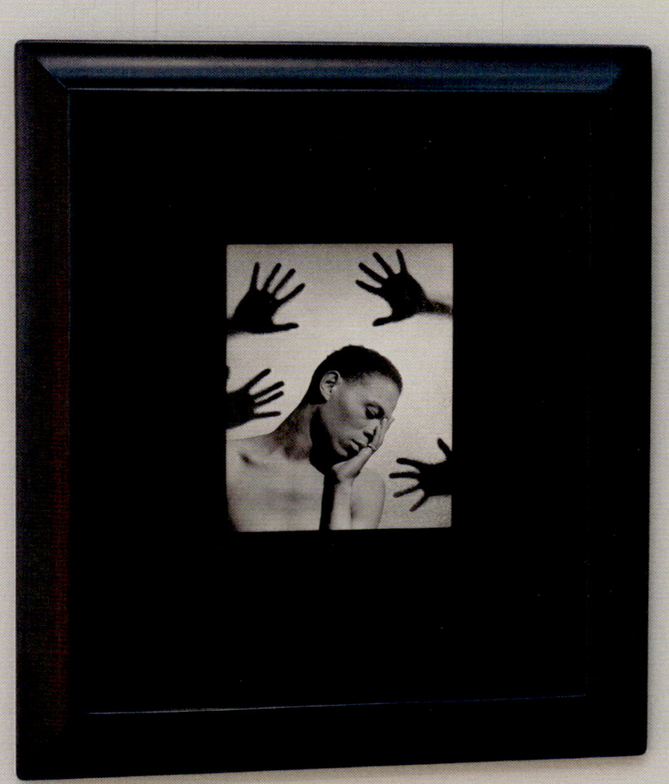

George Platt Lynes
b. 1907; East Orange, NJ
d. 1955; New York, NY

Cabaret performer James Leslie Daniels, c. 1937
Gelatin silver print

Collection of Beth Rudin DeWoody

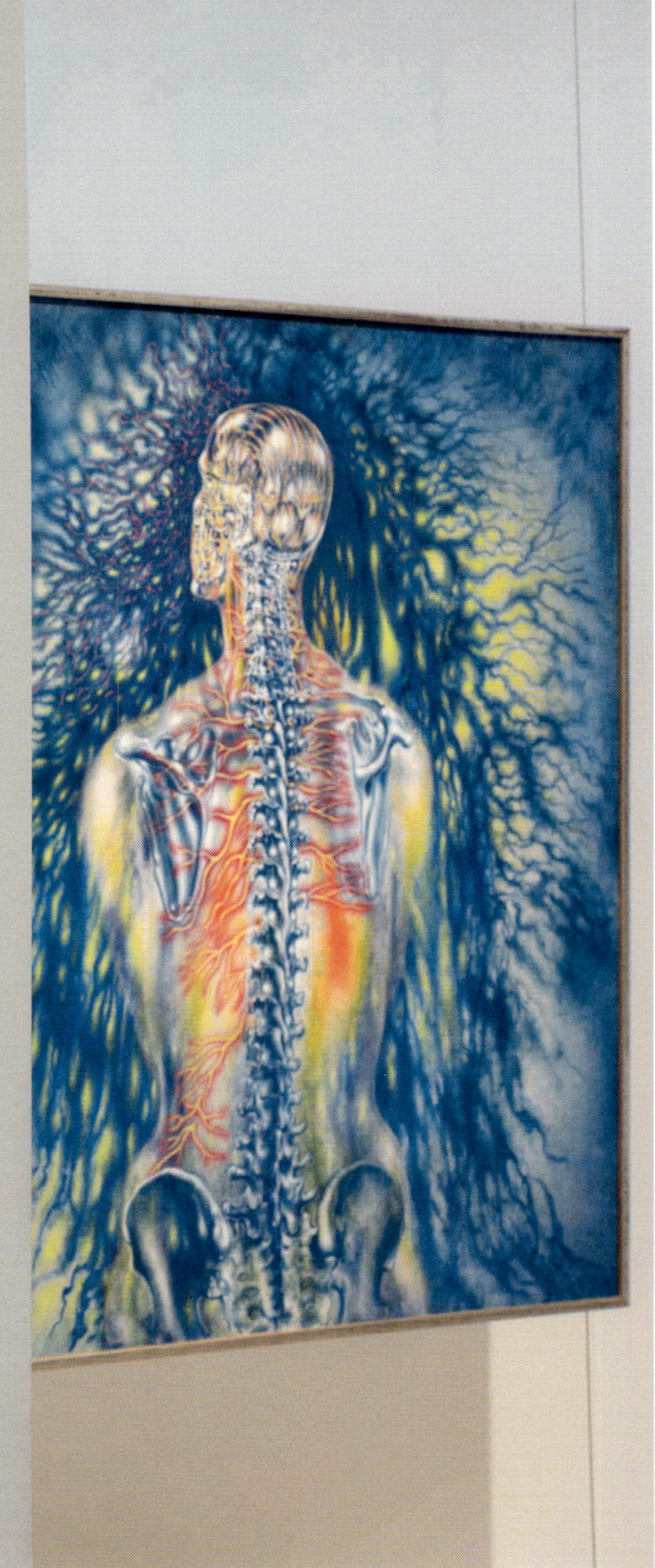

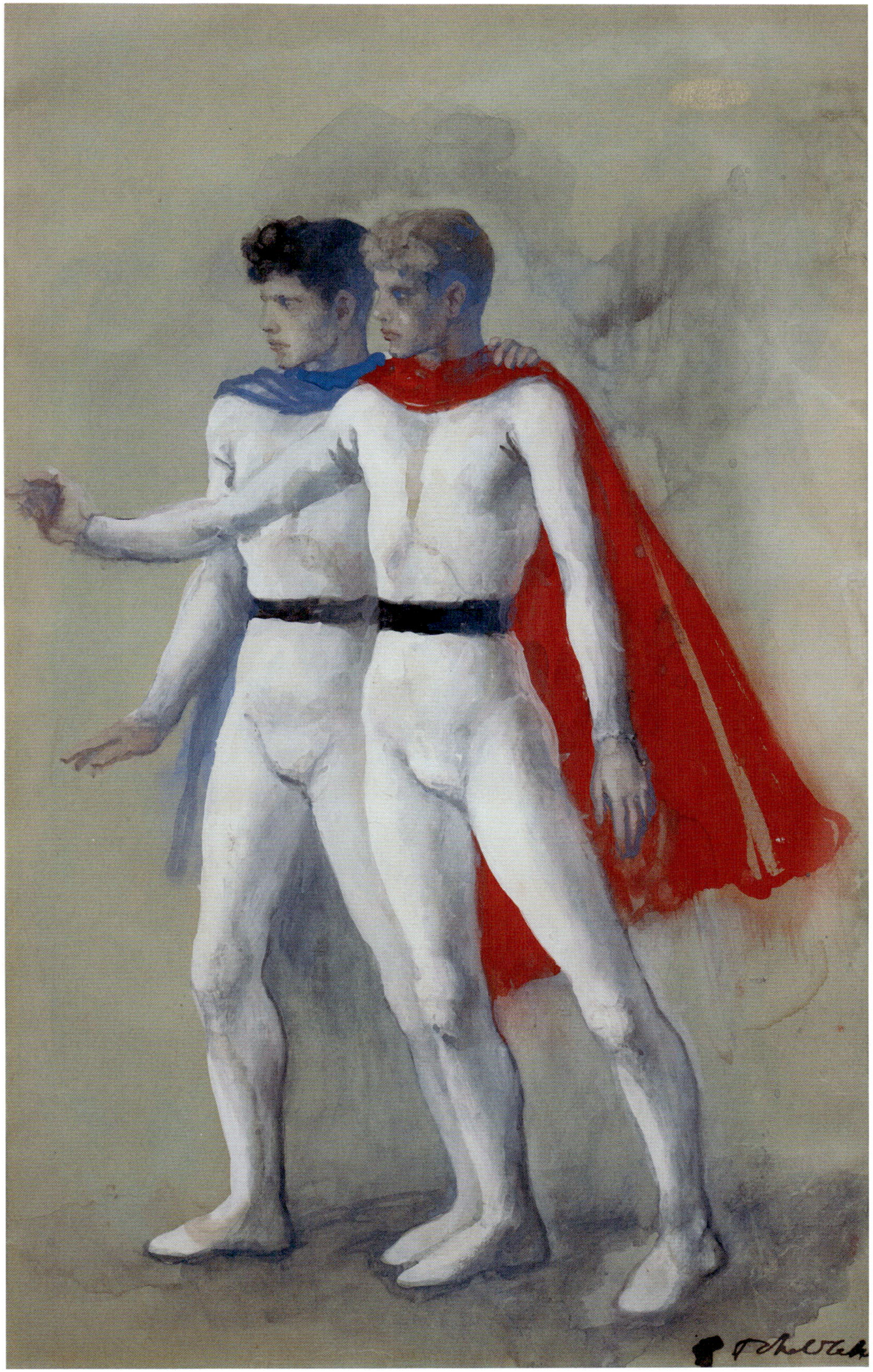

Opposite: Installation view of *Transmissions*, with (left to right) photograph by George Platt Lynes of cabaret performer James Leslie Daniels, c. 1937; and Pavel Tchelitchew, *Anatomical Painting*, 1946

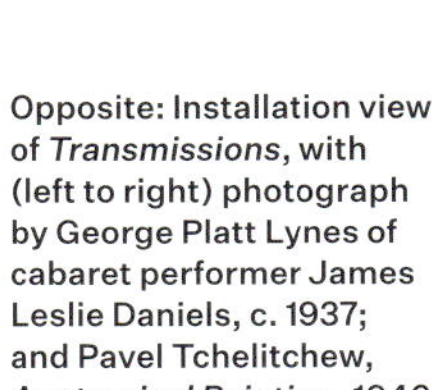

Pavel Tchelitchew, costume designs for *Errante*, choreographed by George Balanchine for Les Ballets 1933, 1933. Gouache on paper, 17 ⅞ × 11 ⅛ inches (45.4 × 28.3 cm). Jerome Robbins Dance Division, The New York Public Library for the Performing Arts, Astor, Lenox and Tilden Foundations

Pavel Tchelitchew commissioned the German photographer Ilse Bing to capture *Errante*, a "choreographic fantasy" he devised for Les Ballets 1933, his first collaboration with George Balanchine. Apart from photographs and written accounts, *Errante* is a "lost" ballet. Donald Windham described its sets, costumes, and pioneering lighting effects in an issue of *Dance Index* devoted to Tchelitchew's "ballet designs":

The stage of L'Errante was a semicircular cone of white muslin strips lighted from behind, as crystal and virginal as a mirror into which no image has yet been reflected. Swept into this universe upon a storm of wind, a woman appears, wet and green as Venus on her scallop shell. As she runs her great train of lacquered green silk ripples behind her like the waves of the sea. Men, creatures of earth, enter the mirror, and the difference in their elements, wet and dry, is expressed clearly in the stuffs of the costumes which are correspondingly and dull. As the drama progresses, the nacreous strips of muslin which compose the semicircle of the stage are saturated from behind with lights of sunset colors which reflect each shade and nuance of the action as well as do the music and choreography. Violent red storms of revolutionary banner flags, advancing from Tchelitchew's memory of Russia even into this ballet, cross the stage as the woman and her lover are parted. Blue-grey moonlight bathes the scene following the funeral. The mirror of the stage is penetrated by dancers costumed as imaginary figures, hermaphroditic angels, feathery maidens of spring, a child leading a man, such figures as boys and girls pictured in white clouds moving across a summer sky. Two images stand out at the climax of the ballet—a writhing shadow of man ascends the shadow of a rope ladder into the sky, and a great wet cloud of white Chinese silk cascades from heaven and obliterates the woman, leaving the mirror again crystal, white and empty.

Right and opposite: Ilse Bing, *Errante*, 1933. Gelatin silver print, 11⅛ × 8¾ inches (28.3 × 22.2 cm). Private collection

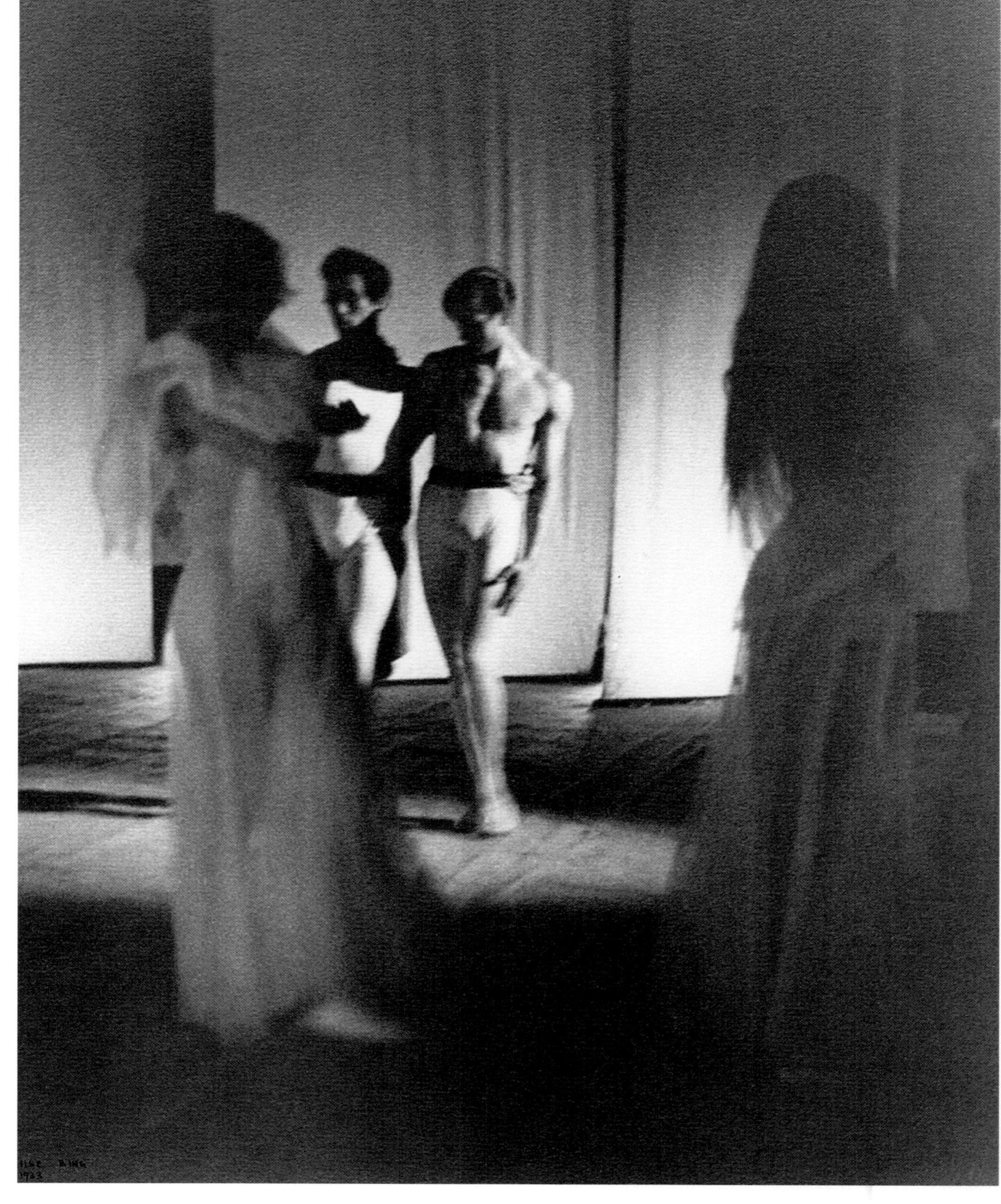

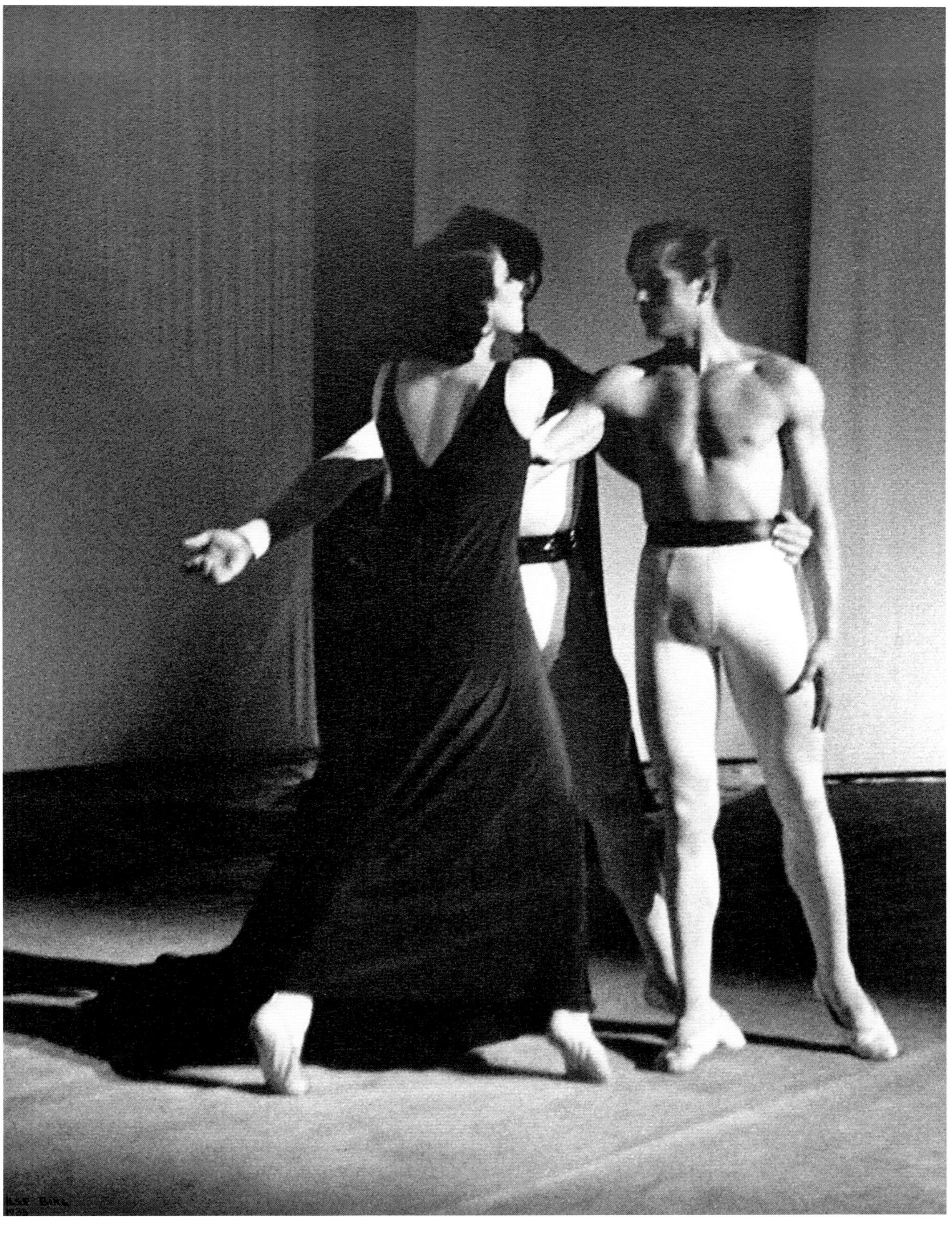

Ilse Bing, *Errante*, 1933.
Gelatin silver prints, 11⅛ ×
8¾ inches (28.3 × 22.2 cm)
each. National Gallery of
Art, Washington, DC

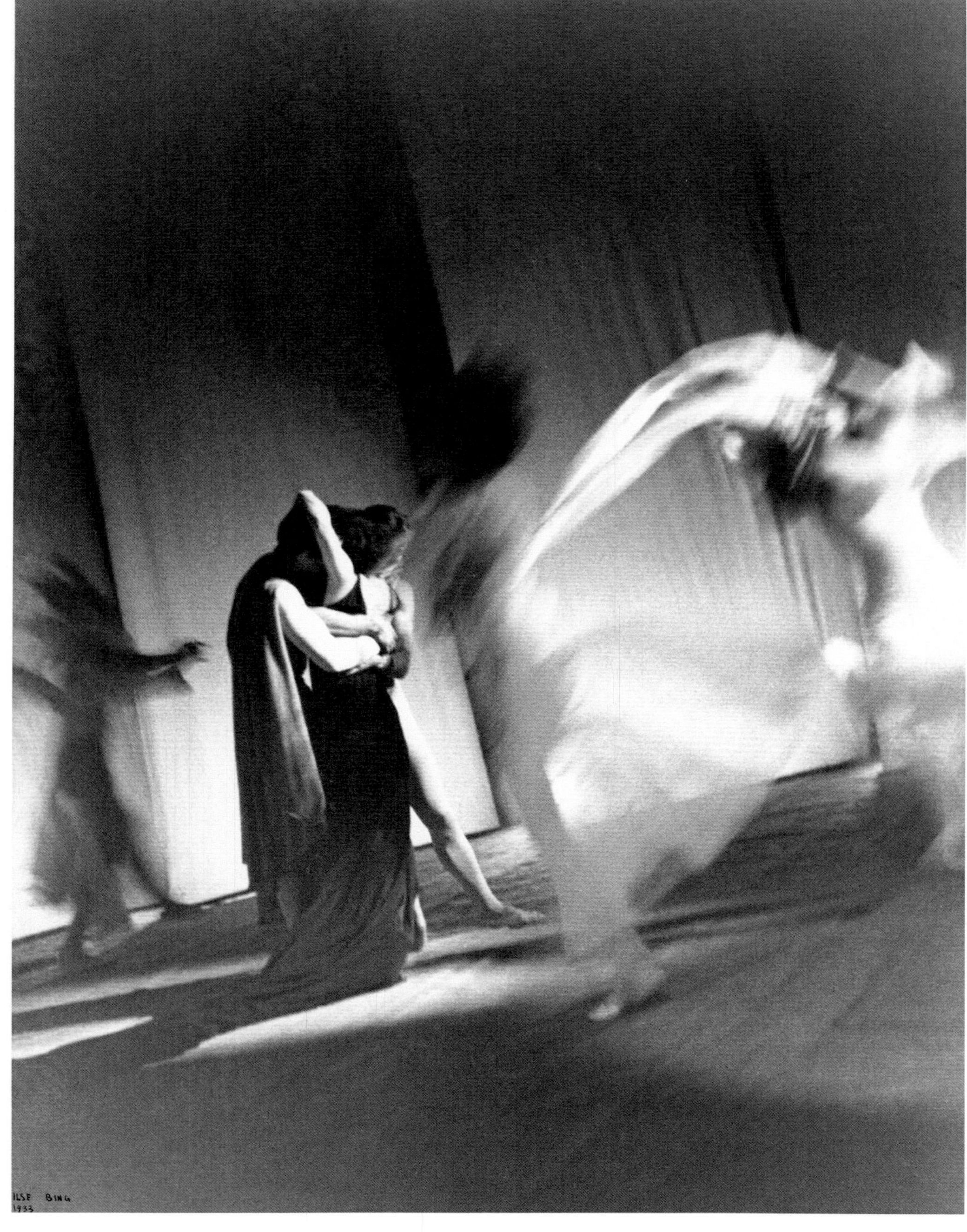
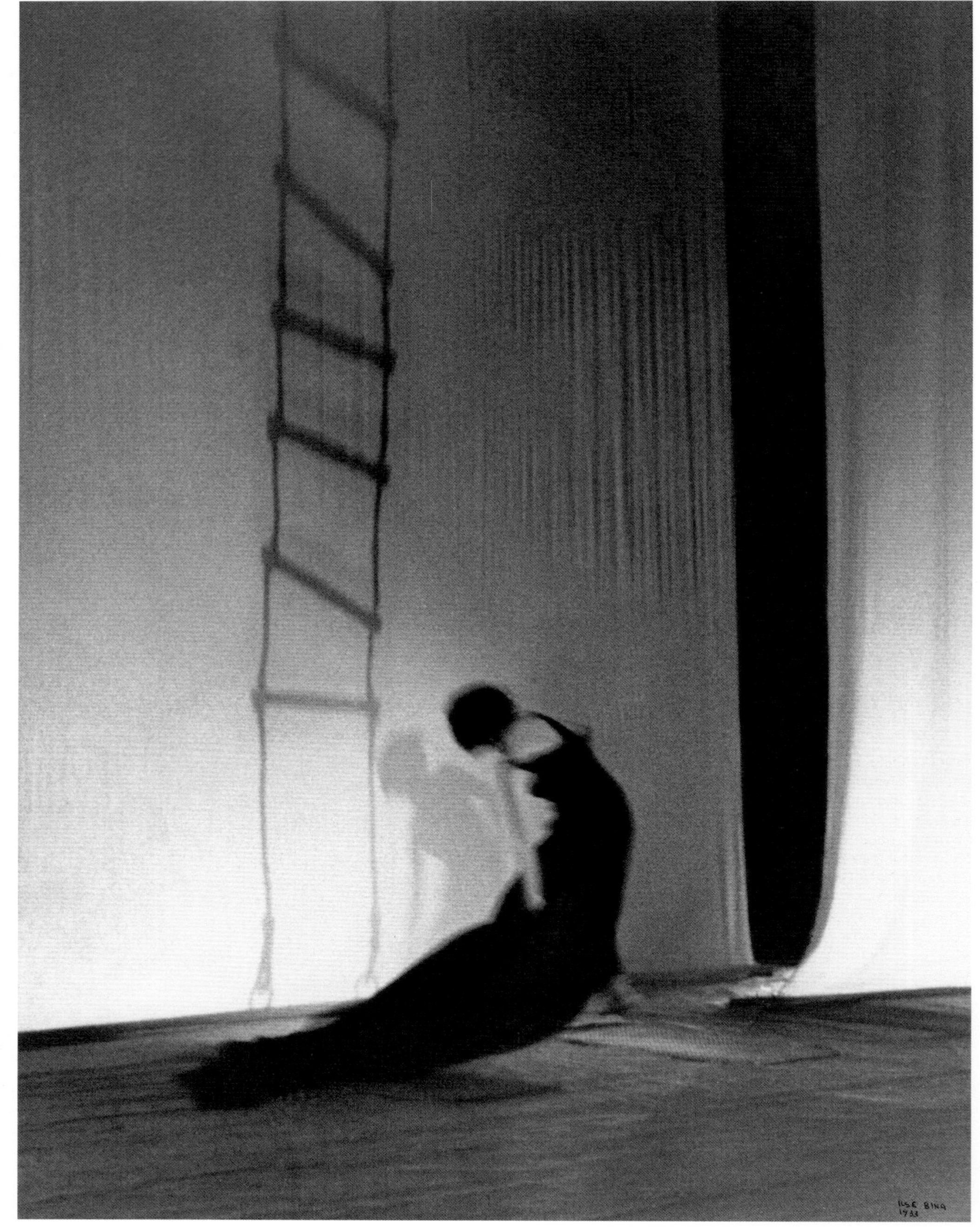

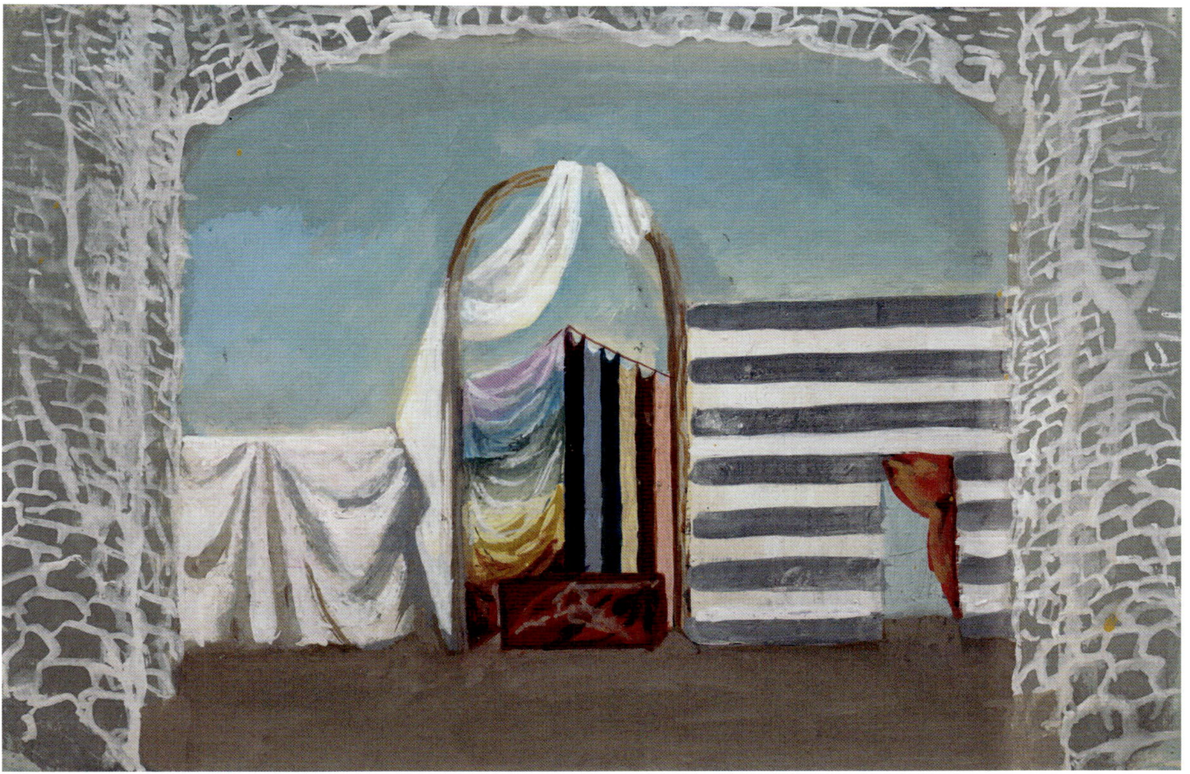

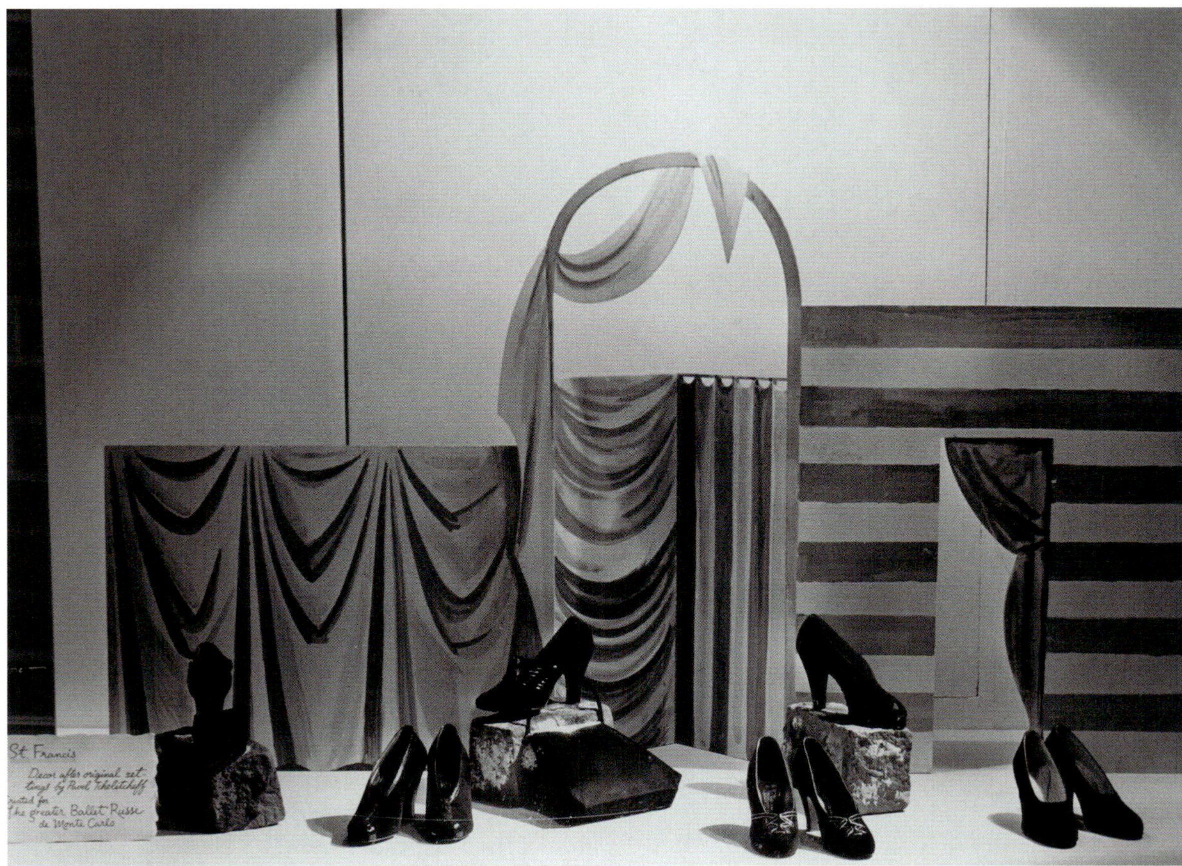

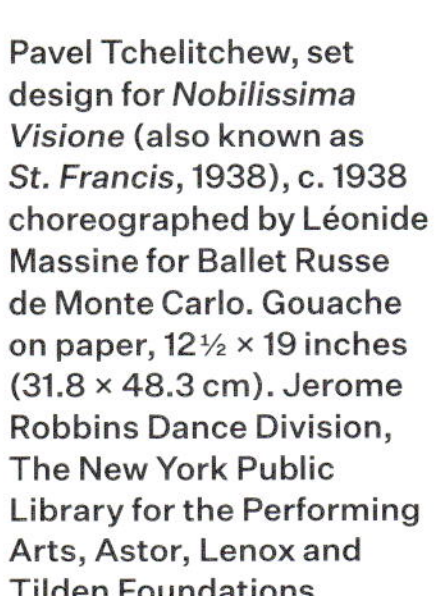

Pavel Tchelitchew, set design for *Nobilissima Visione* (also known as *St. Francis*, 1938), c. 1938 choreographed by Léonide Massine for Ballet Russe de Monte Carlo. Gouache on paper, 12½ × 19 inches (31.8 × 48.3 cm). Jerome Robbins Dance Division, The New York Public Library for the Performing Arts, Astor, Lenox and Tilden Foundations

Window display after set design by Pavel Tchelitchew for *Nobilissima Visione* (1938), c. 1938. Jerome Robbins Dance Division, The New York Public Library for the Performing Arts, Astor, Lenox and Tilden Foundations

A decoupaged changing screen made by Eugene Berman for his wife, Hollywood actress Ona Munson, doubles as a folding retrospective of the artist's motifs and trademark aesthetic: maudlin and tattered, the folding panels bring together desolate Surrealist vistas, architectural confabulations by Giovanni Battista Piranesi, and the Neo-Romantic trope of *Rückenfiguren* (figures from behind). Trompe l'oeil pins appear to affix to the screen not only these ragged-edged and stained drawings but also singed doilies and envelopes, festooned with invented stamps and elaborate inscriptions. The right panel of the screen features a study for Berman's set for *Concerto Barocco* (1941), which revised Renaissance stage perspective through the melodrama of a cult of ruin. (See the delicate corresponding stage model for this now-quintessential Balanchine ballet on pages 80–81.) Since midcentury, *Concerto Barocco* has been performed without sets or costumes, in practice clothes, to allow for total focus on the work's musicality and dancing. Julien Levy once noted that "though [Berman] is primarily an easel painter, stage design is not a minor incidental occupation, to be taken up as opportunity offers, but a major creative field having its own validity."

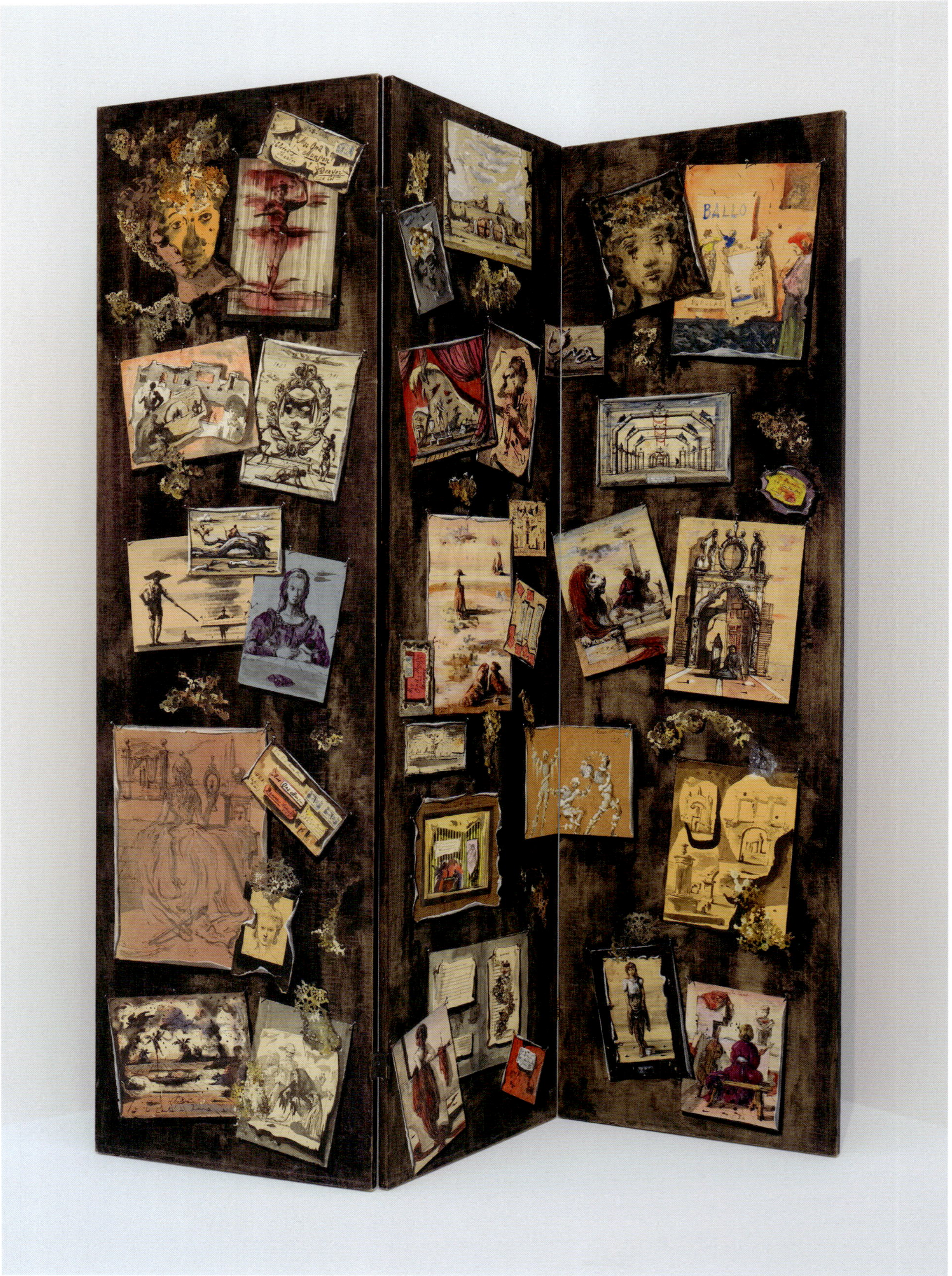

Right and opposite: Eugene Berman, painted three-fold screen with watercolor sketches (1937–42), 1944. Watercolor, pen-and-ink, and collage on painted paper-covered fabric, panels 80 × 23½ inches (203.2 × 59.7 cm) each. Philadelphia Museum of Art; gift of the artist in memory of his wife, Ona Munson, 1958

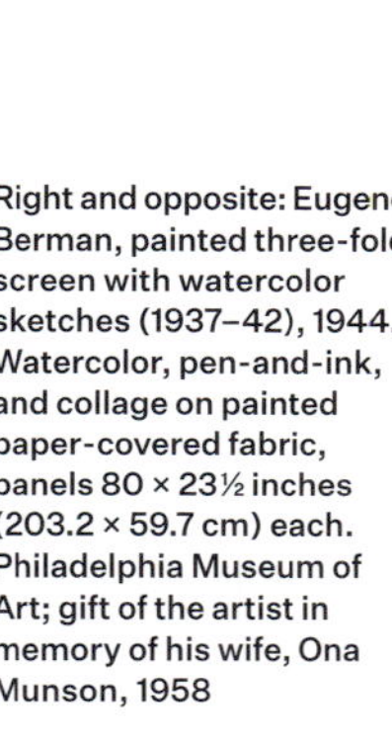

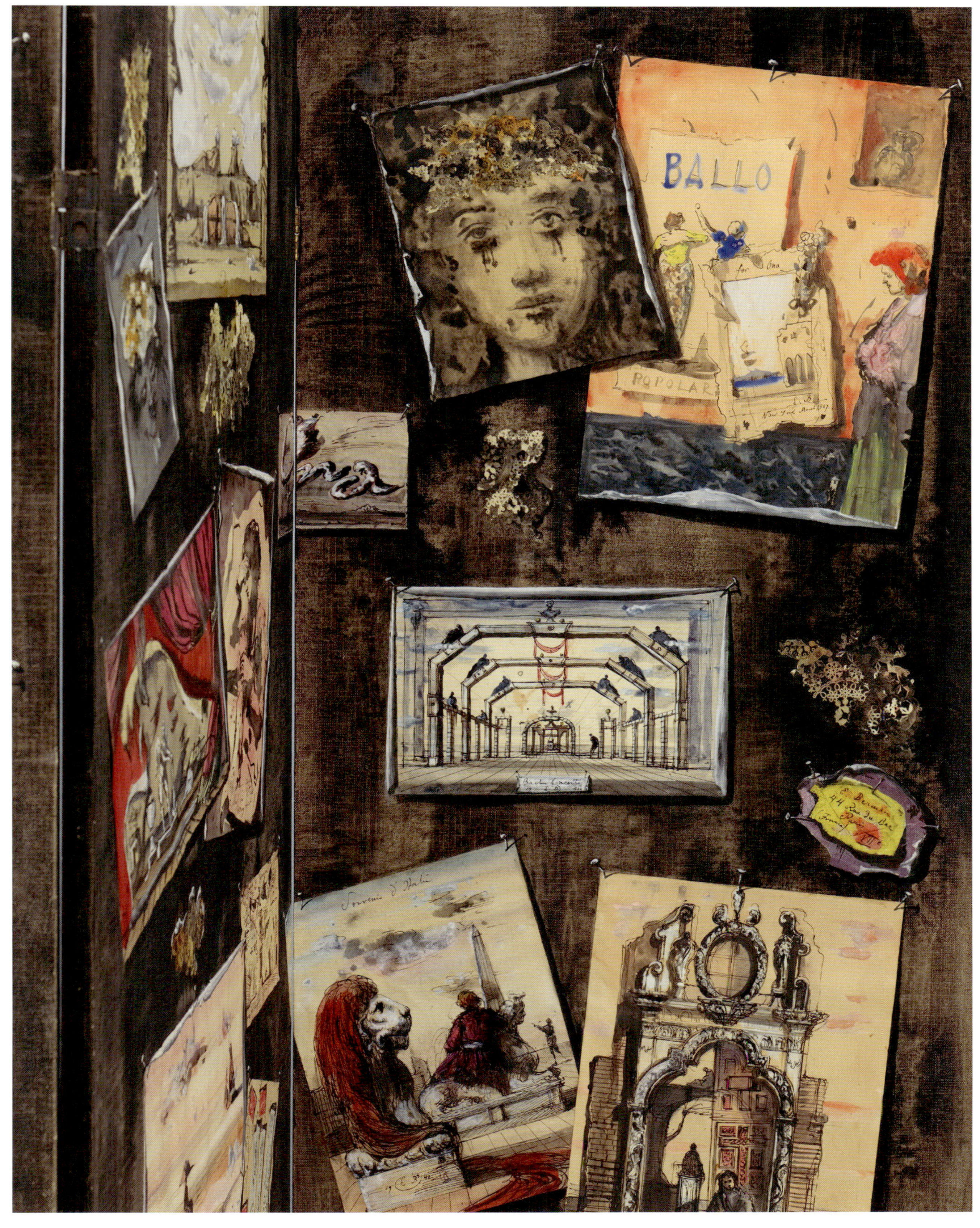

BALLO
POPOLAR

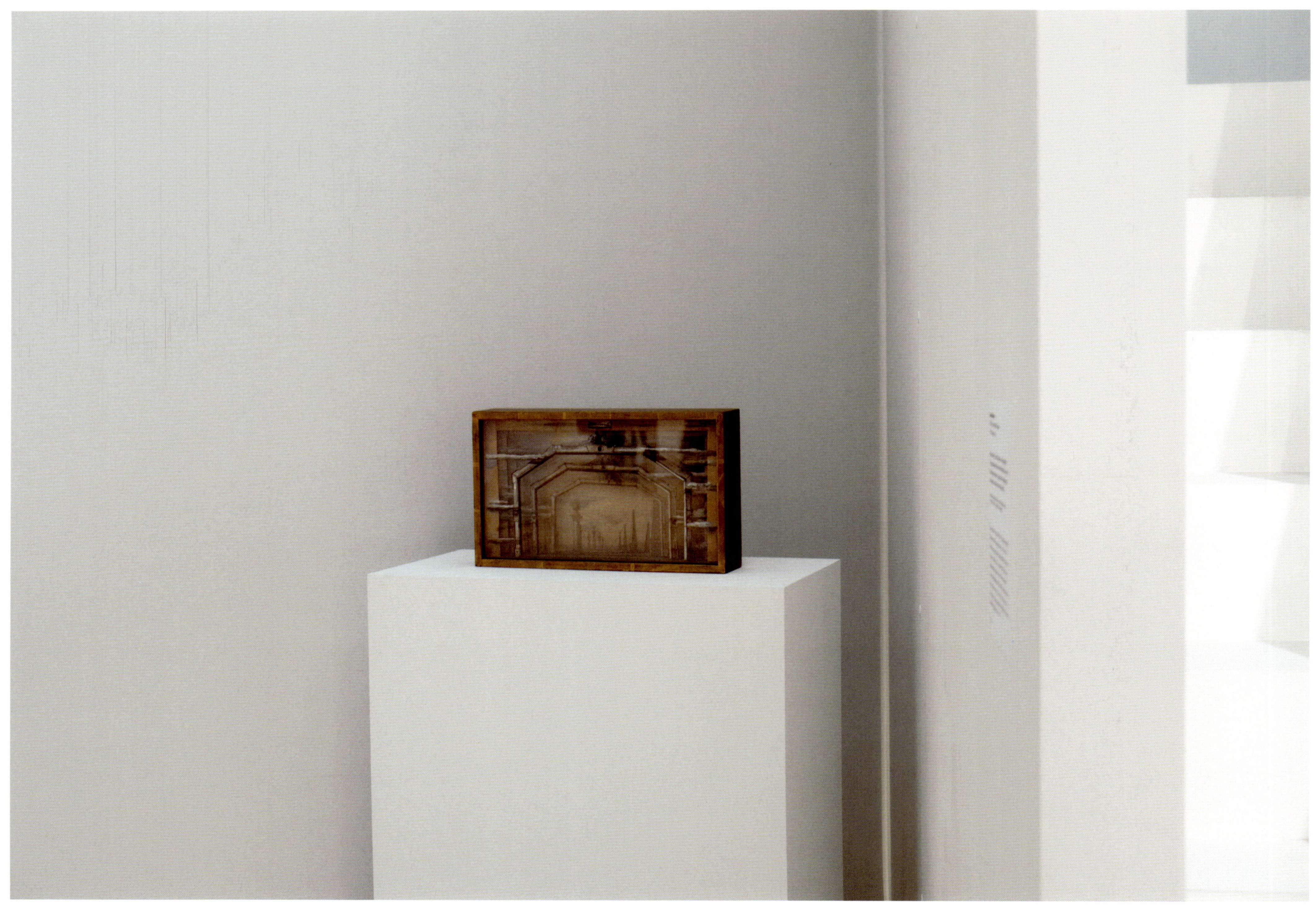

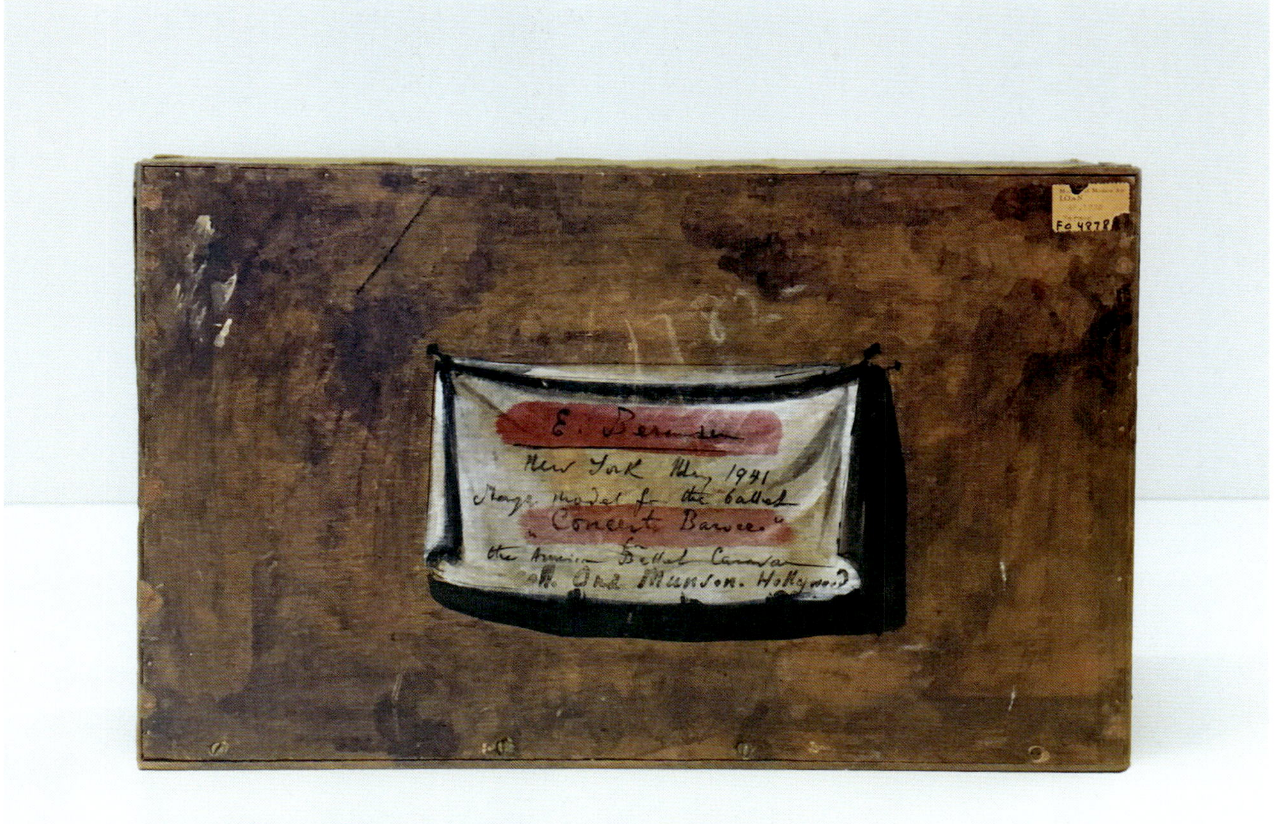

Opposite and left: Eugene Berman, stage model for *Concerto Barocco* (1941), choreographed by George Balanchine for American Ballet Caravan, 1941. Colored paper, water-color, gouache, metallic pigment, and graphite, in wooden box with glass front, 10 × 16⅞ × 3⅝ inches (25.4 × 42.9 × 9.2 cm). Jerome Robbins Dance Division, The New York Public Library for the Performing Arts, Astor, Lenox and Tilden Foundations

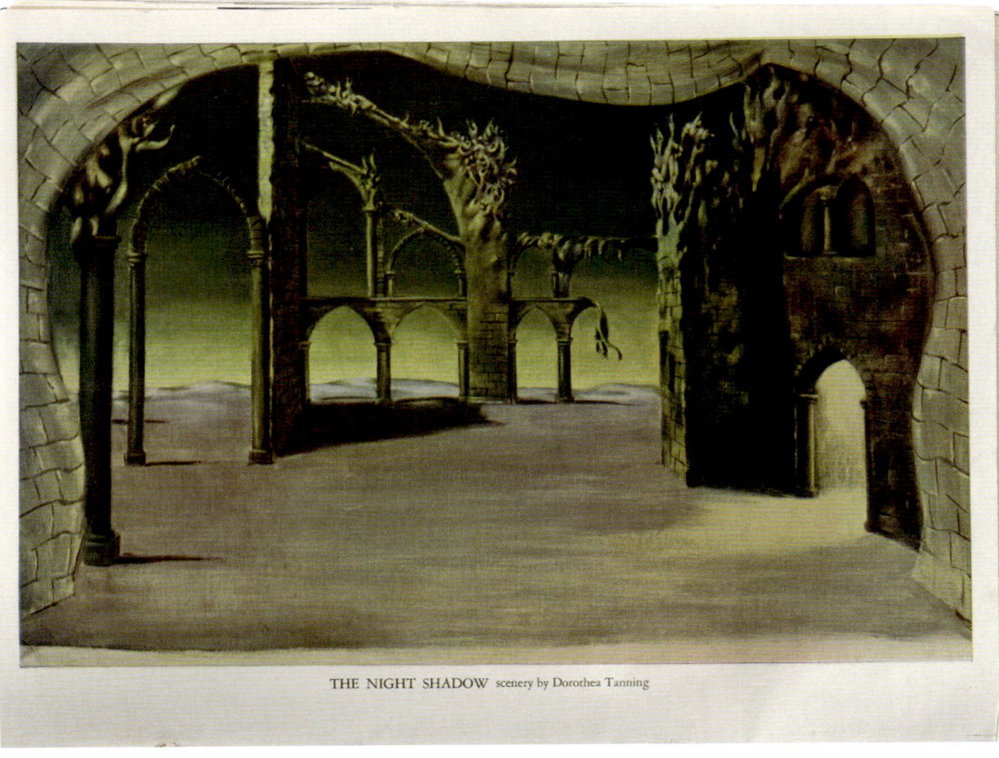

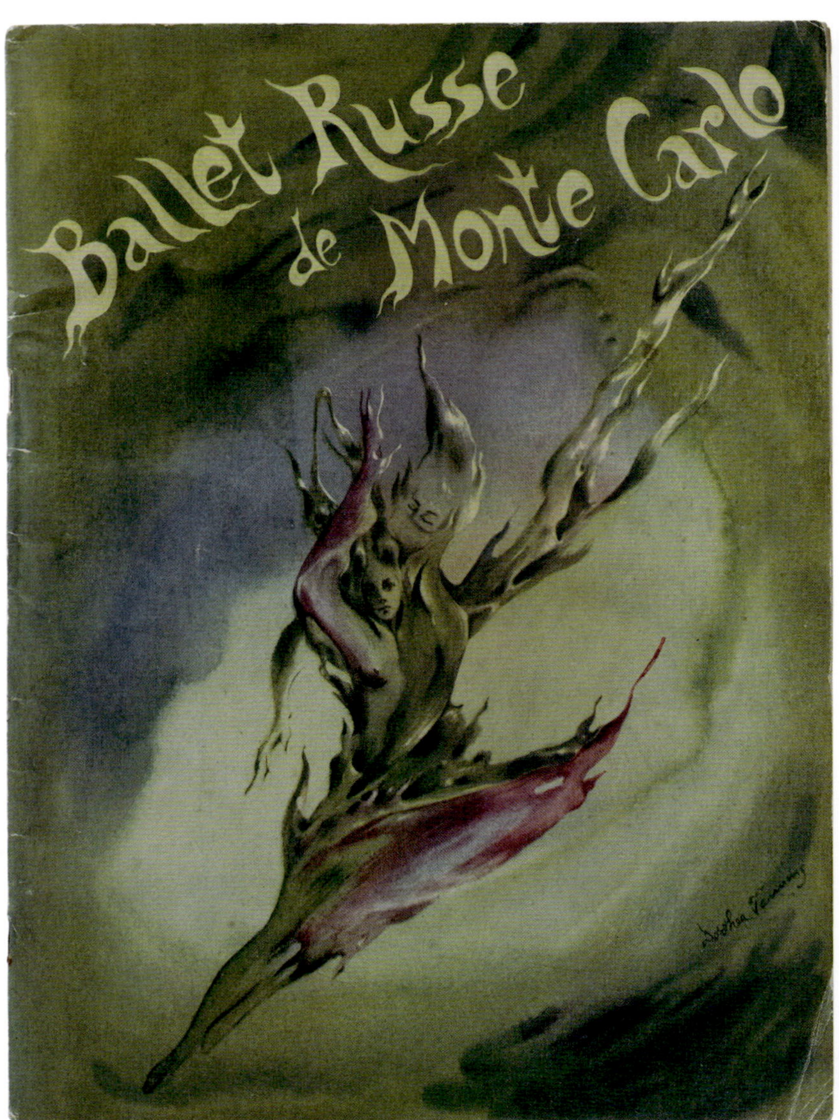

Above: Dorothea Tanning, scenery design for *The Night Shadow* (1946), reproduced in Ballet Russe de Monte Carlo's 1945–46 season program

Right: Dorothea Tanning, cover of Ballet Russe de Monte Carlo's 1945–46 season program

"I had discovered the work of a beautiful girl, Dorothea Tanning, who was creating a whole world from her subconscious, precisely painted, authentic as Dalí must have wished when he asked for a camera to take colored photographs of the interior of his mind. The interior of Dorothea's mind was of a very different sort, and erotic in another way, than Dalí's. Her paintings were utterly fascinating," Julien Levy reported in his memoir. It was at his gallery that Pavel Tchelitchew first introduced Tanning to George Balanchine. Tanning subsequently designed costumes for several Balanchine ballets, including those for *Night Shadow* (1946), which was derided by critic John Martin as "a rather foolish little piece of pseudo-surrealism." It is a goal of *Transmissions* to redress such flippant derision.

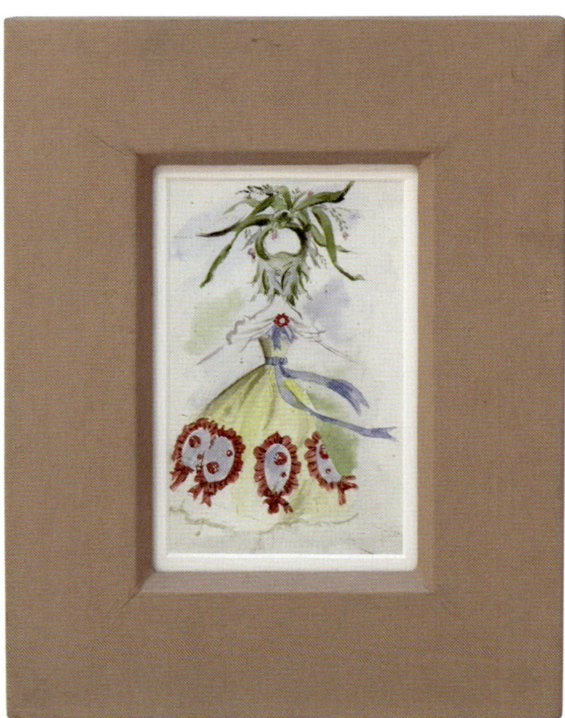
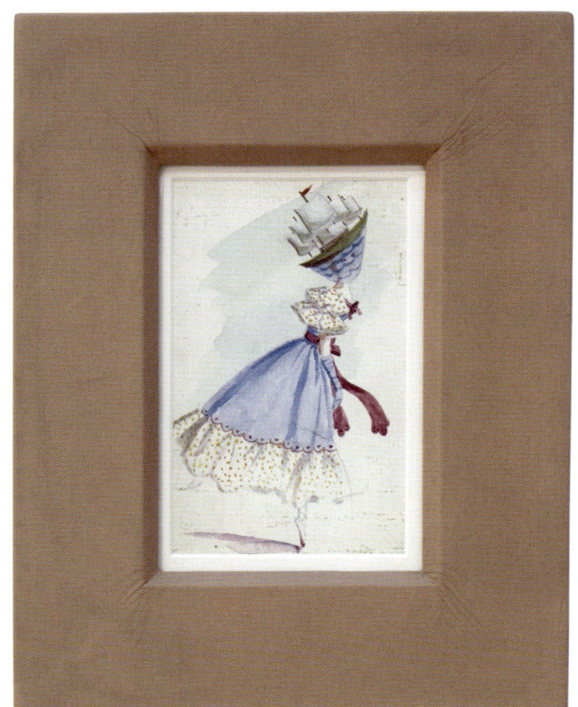
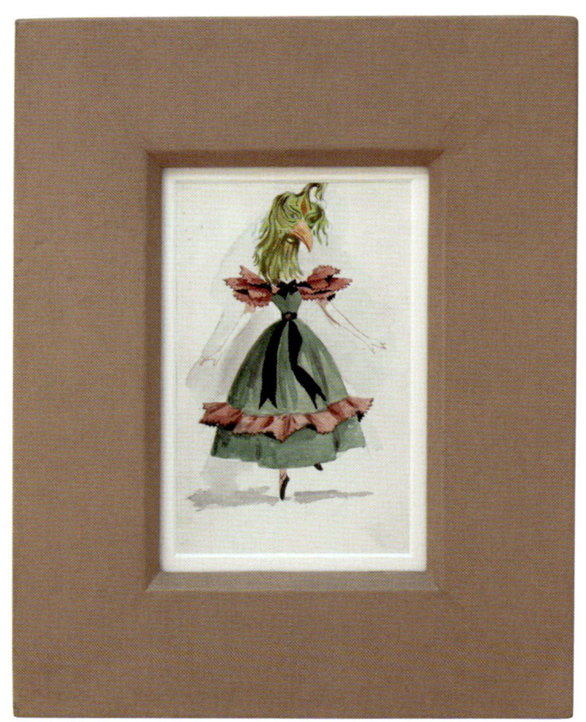

Above, left: Dorothea Tanning, costume design for dancer Shirley Weaver in *The Night Shadow* (1946), choreographed by George Balanchine for Ballet Russe de Monte Carlo, 1945. Watercolor over graphite on paper, sheet: 9 × 6 inches (22.9 × 15.2 cm). Philadelphia Museum of Art; gift of Judith Young-Mallin, 2015

Above, middle: Dorothea Tanning, costume design for *The Night Shadow* (1946), choreographed by George Balanchine for Ballet Russe de Monte Carlo, 1945. Watercolor over graphite on paper, sheet: 9 × 6 inches (22.9 × 15.2 cm). Philadelphia Museum of Art; gift of Judith Young-Mallin, 2015

Above, right: Dorothea Tanning, costume design for dancer Beatrice Tompkins in *The Night Shadow* (1946), choreographed by George Balanchine for Ballet Russe de Monte Carlo, 1945. Watercolor over graphite on paper, sheet: 9 × 6 inches (22.9 × 15.2 cm). Philadelphia Museum of Art; gift of Judith Young-Mallin, 2015

Right: Dancers wearing costumes based on Dorothea Tanning's designs for *The Night Shadow* (1946), c. 1946–48. Gelatin silver print, 10 × 8 inches (25.4 × 20.3 cm) sheet. Jerome Robbins Dance Division, The New York Public Library for the Performing Arts, Astor, Lenox and Tilden Foundations

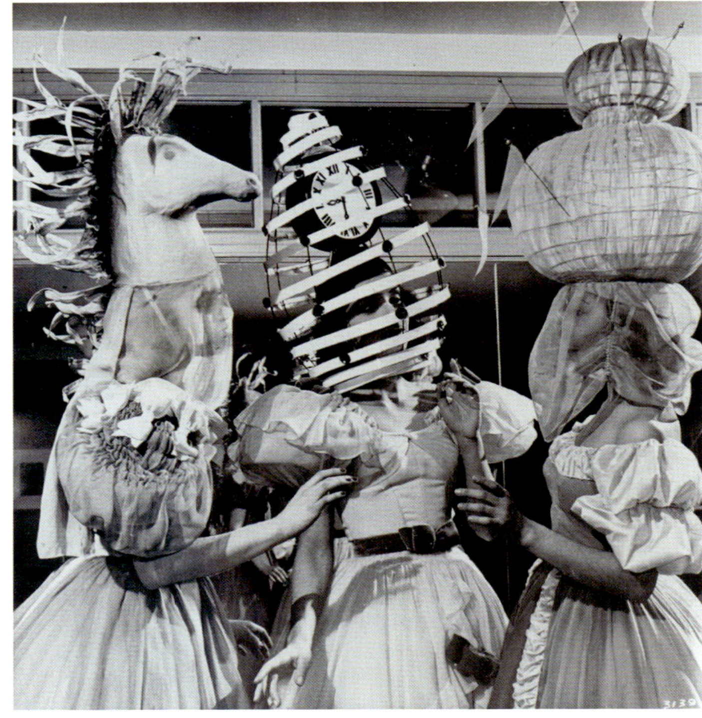

Martha Swope, a ballet student turned photographer, documented Jerome Robbins's work on Broadway's *West Side Story* (1957) and soon after became the official New York City Ballet photographer. This iconic photograph captures a rehearsal for *Agon* (1957)—a New York City Ballet production in George Balanchine's brilliantly stripped-down mature style—that shows Arthur Mitchell and Diana Adams rehearsing a pas de deux as the composer Igor Stravinsky and Balanchine look on. Balanchine made the dance specifically for Mitchell, the first African American principal dancer in a major American ballet company, and Adams, a white, Southern ballerina. Their pairing was deemed controversial, and until 1968 television stations refused to air recordings of their pas de deux in *Agon*. Following the assassination of Martin Luther King Jr. that same year, Mitchell cofounded the Dance Theatre of Harlem with Karel Shook.

Agon's choreography riffs on a French manual of courtly dance intended to educate dancing nobility in "the science of behavior towards others." About *Agon*, Lincoln Kirstein wrote: "It presents the traditional classic idiom, without stylistic deformation, in the language of a humane computer. Bodies are digits." And the dance critic Edwin Denby wrote: "The subject of *Agon*, as the poet Frank O'Hara said, is pride."

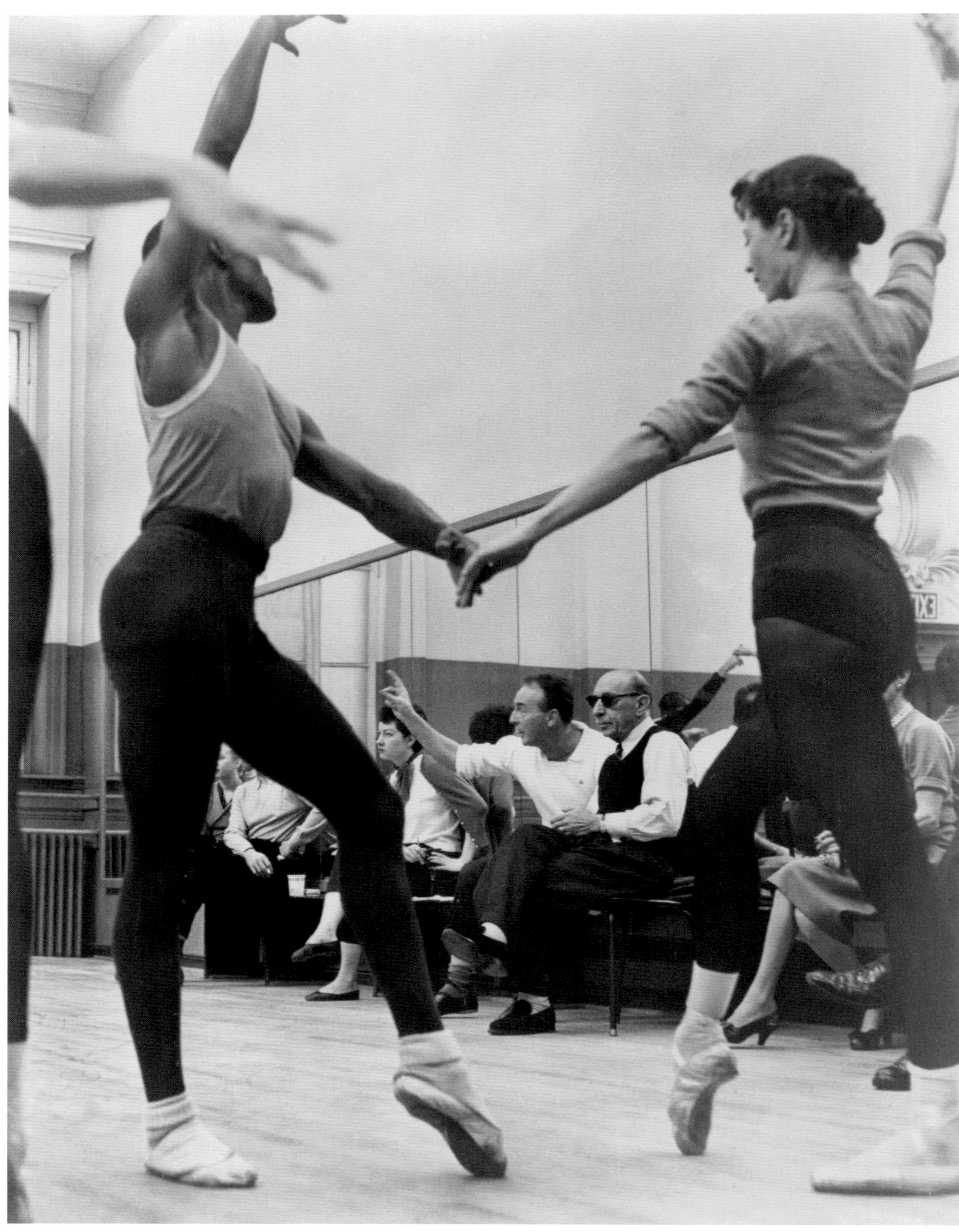

Martha Swope, dancers Arthur Mitchell and Diana Adams with George Balanchine and Igor Stravinsky during rehearsals for *Agon* (1957), choreographed by Balanchine for New York City Ballet, 1957. Gelatin silver print, 10 × 8 inches (25.4 × 20.3 cm). Jerome Robbins Dance Division, The New York Public Library for the Performing Arts, Astor, Lenox and Tilden Foundations

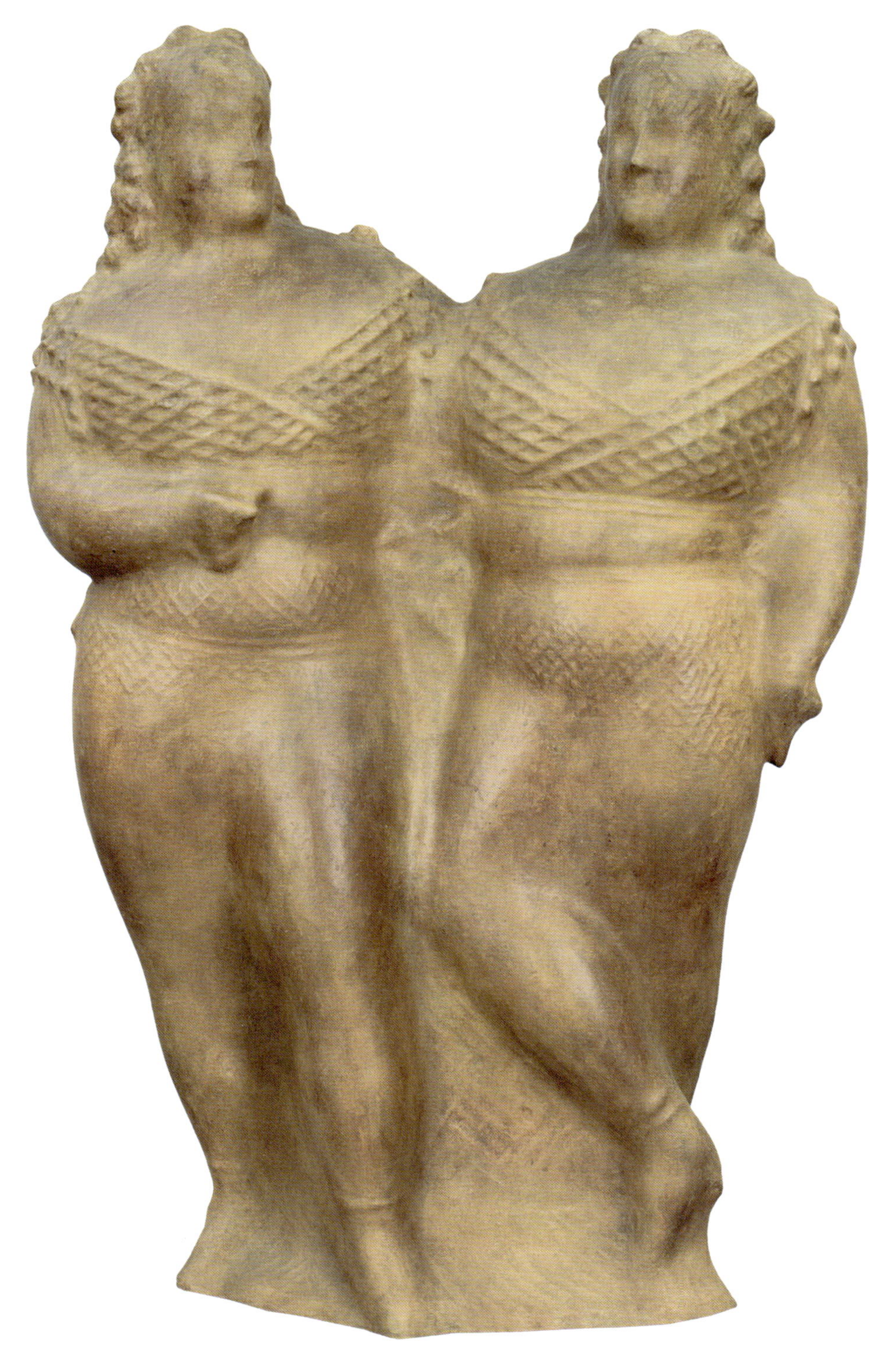

Elie Nadelman, *Two Circus Women*, c. 1928–29. Plaster and paper, 62 × 40⅞ × 17½ inches (157.5 × 103.8 × 44.5 cm). Whitney Museum of American Art, New York; purchase with funds from The Lauder Foundation, Evelyn and Leonard Lauder Fund

One of two identical sculptures, *Two Circus Women* is a monumental papier-mâché sculpture by Elie Nadelman; its twin inhabits Philip Johnson's iconic Glass House in New Canaan, Connecticut. *Two Circus Women* was used in 1964 as a model for the 19-foot-high copy in Carrara marble that Johnson commissioned for the New York State Theater at Lincoln Center, home of New York City Ballet.

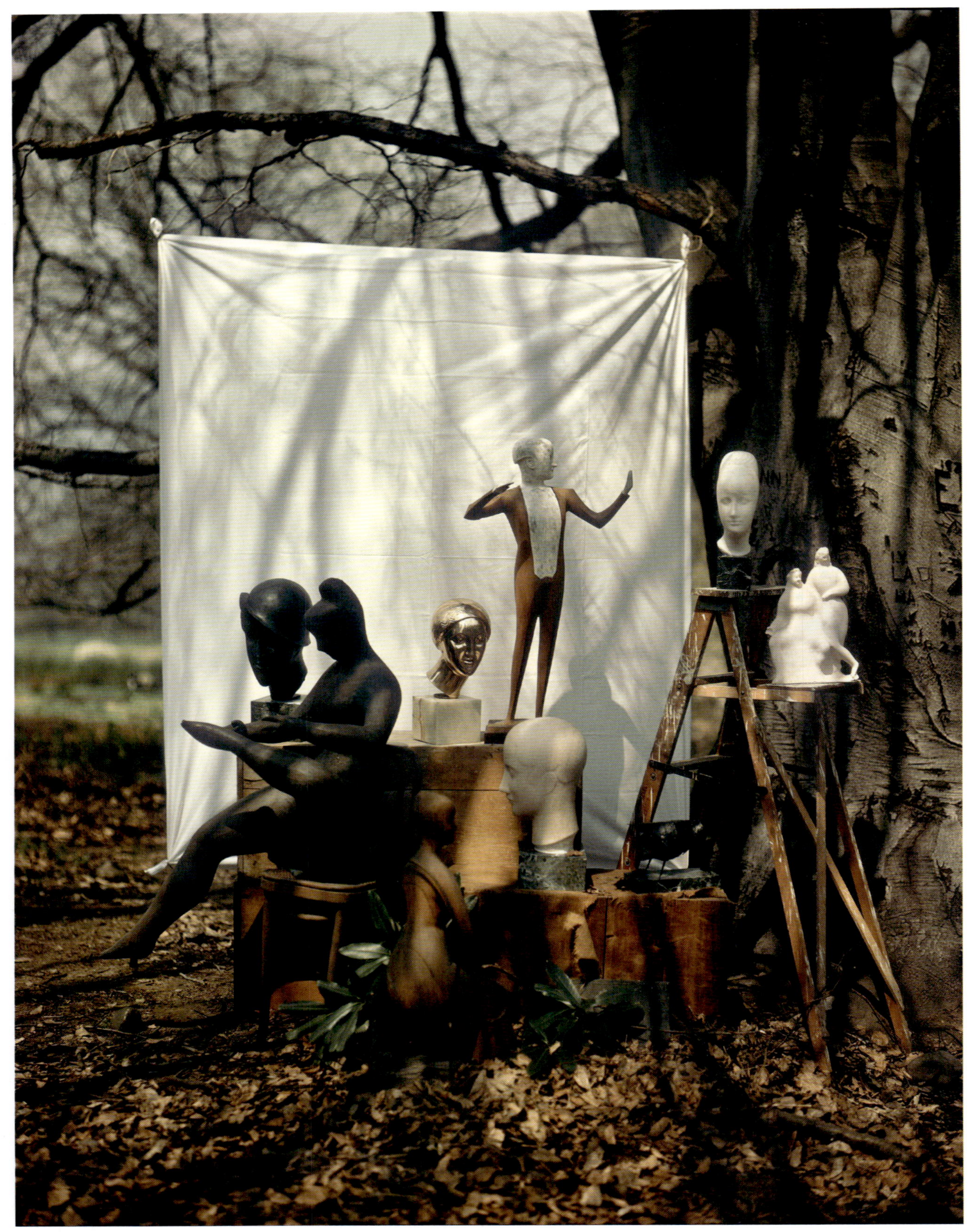

Leslie Gill, *Garden of the Sculptor Elie Nadelman, New York*, 1948. Scan from original transparency. Estate of Leslie Gill

Photographer Leslie Gill pictured an assembly of Nadelman's sculptures in the garden of the artist's house in the Bronx neighborhood of Riverdale after his death. A play on the artifice of "the studio," Gill's ad hoc setup on a floor of autumn leaves conjures a group of models posed for a fashion spread or a distracted family gathered for a portrait. Another, if less obvious, portrait, Man Ray's sculpture *New York* is a biting take on the modern city. Held together by a clamp, the sculpture reads like a chrome-coated joke.

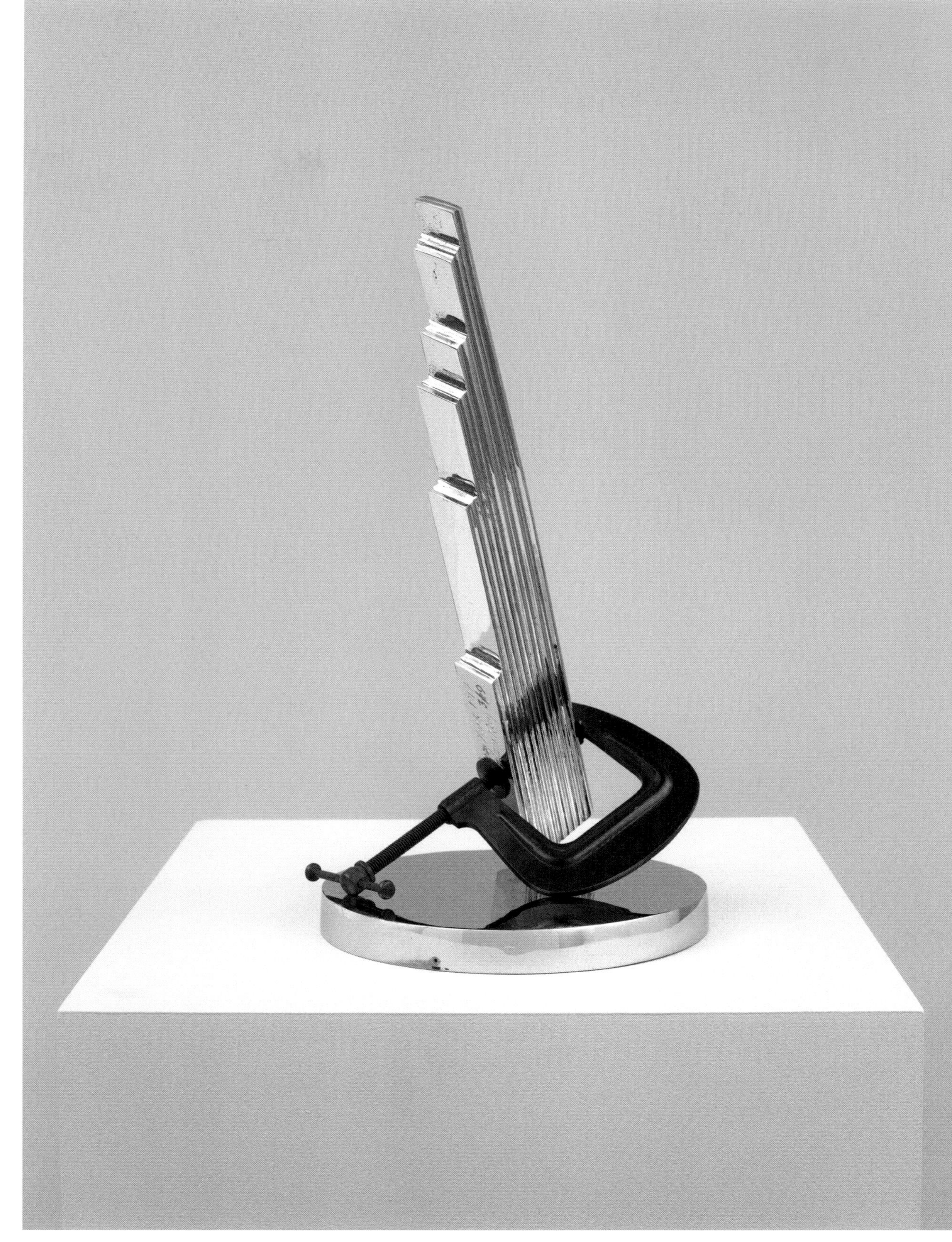

Man Ray, *New York*, 1917/1966. Nickel-plated and painted bronze, 17 × 9⁵⁄₁₆ × 9⁵⁄₁₆ inches (43.2 × 23.7 × 23.7 cm). Whitney Museum of American Art, New York; purchase with funds from the Modern Painting and Sculpture Committee

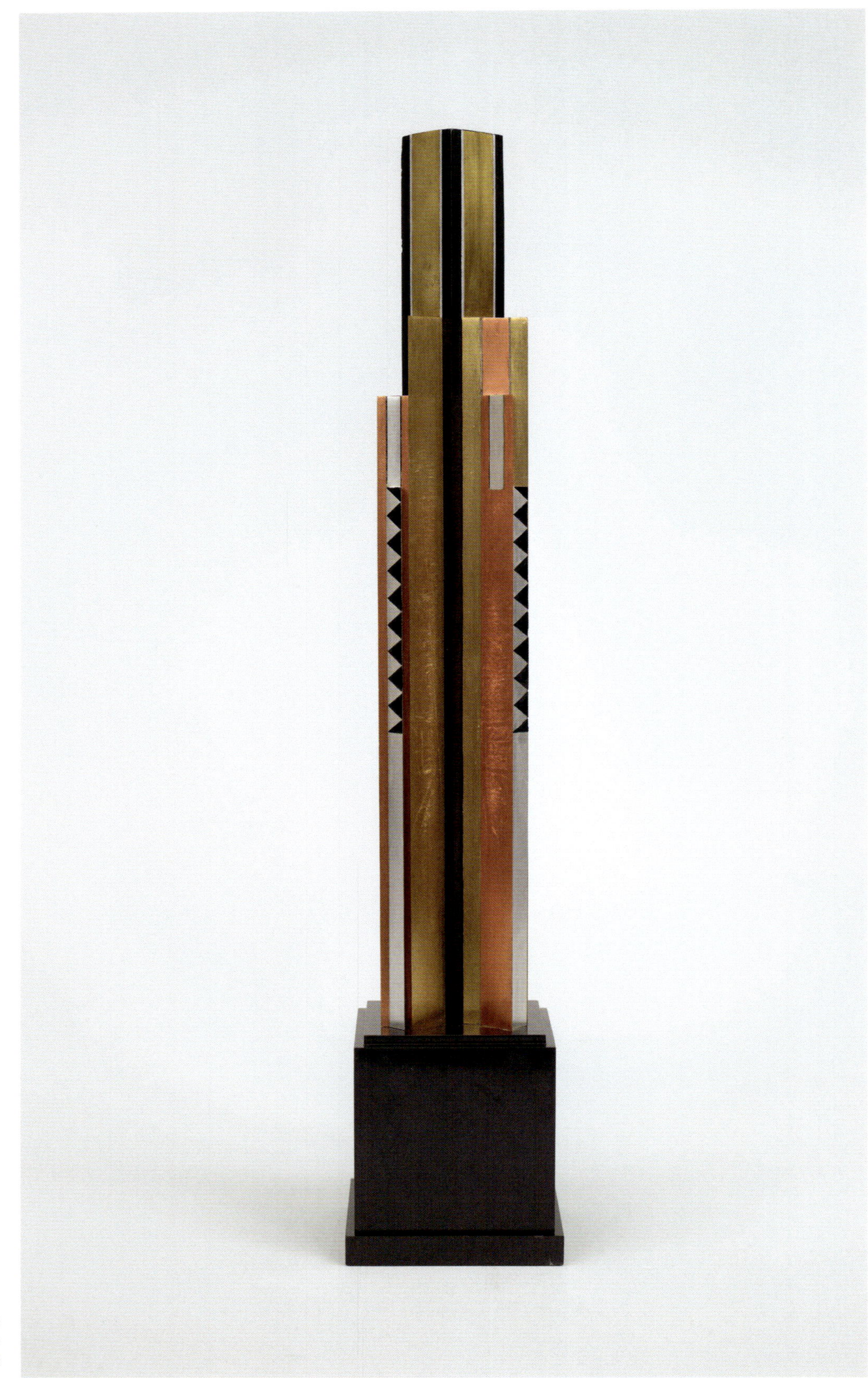

John Storrs, *Forms in Space*, c. 1924. Aluminum, brass, copper, and wood on marble base, 28⅛ × 5½ × 5¼ inches (71.4 × 14 × 13.3 cm). Whitney Museum of American Art, New York; gift of Charles Simon

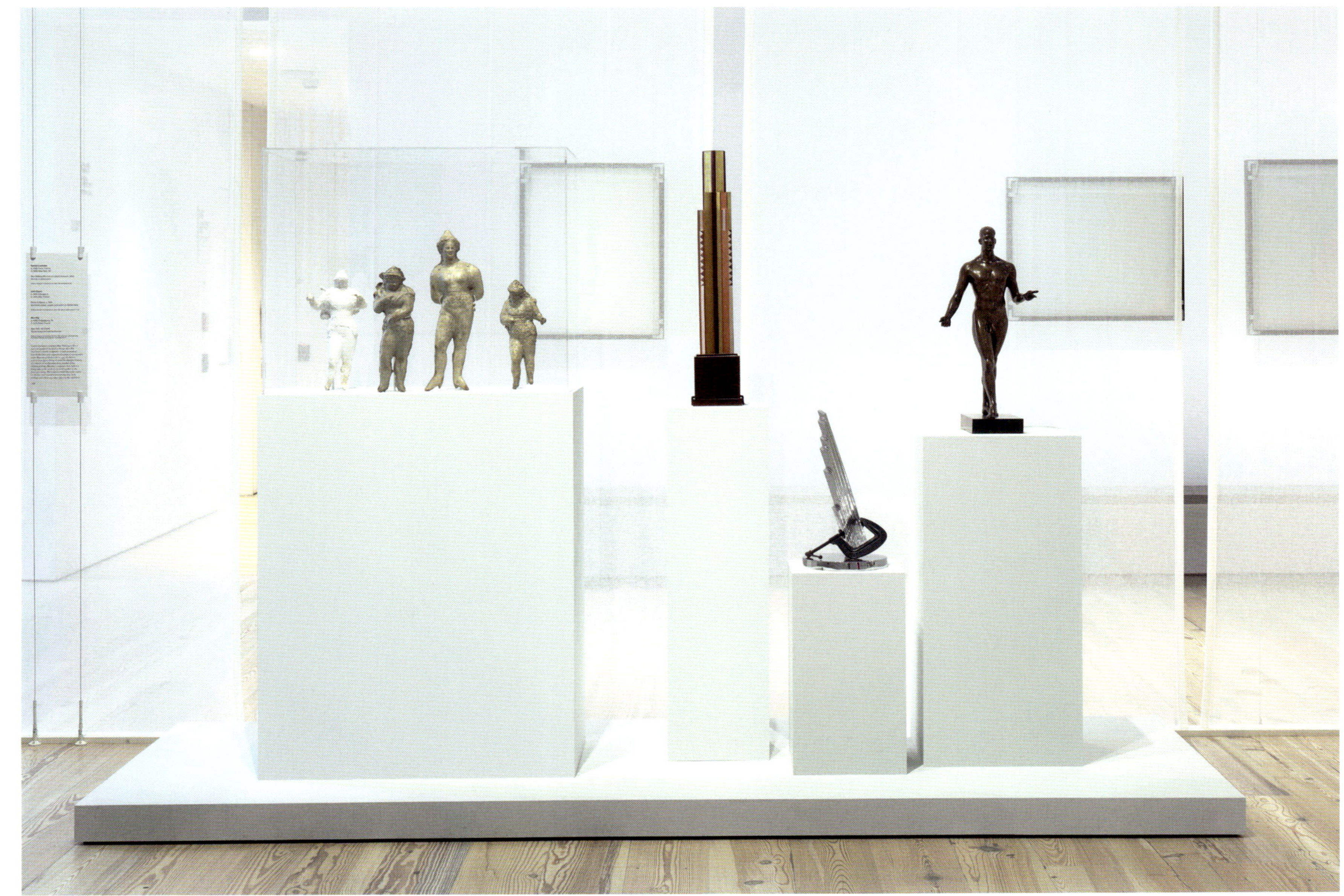

Installation view of *Transmissions*, with (left to right) four untitled works by Elie Nadelman, c. 1938–46; John Storrs, *Forms in Space*, c. 1924; Man Ray, *New York*, 1917/1966; and Gaston Lachaise, *Man Walking (Portrait of Lincoln Kirstein)*, 1933. Photo: Ron Amstutz

Gaston Lachaise, *Man Walking (Portrait of Lincoln Kirstein)*, 1933. Bronze on stone base, 21¼ × 11 × 8¼ inches (54 × 27.9 × 21 cm). Whitney Museum of American Art, New York; purchase

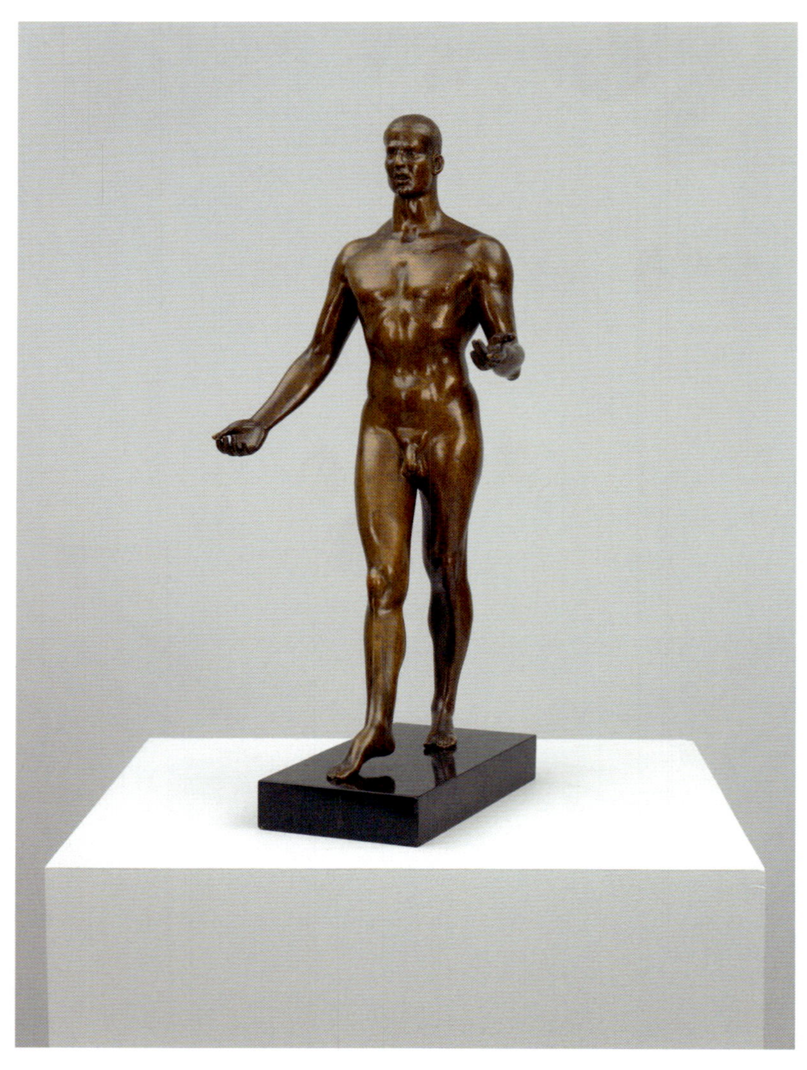

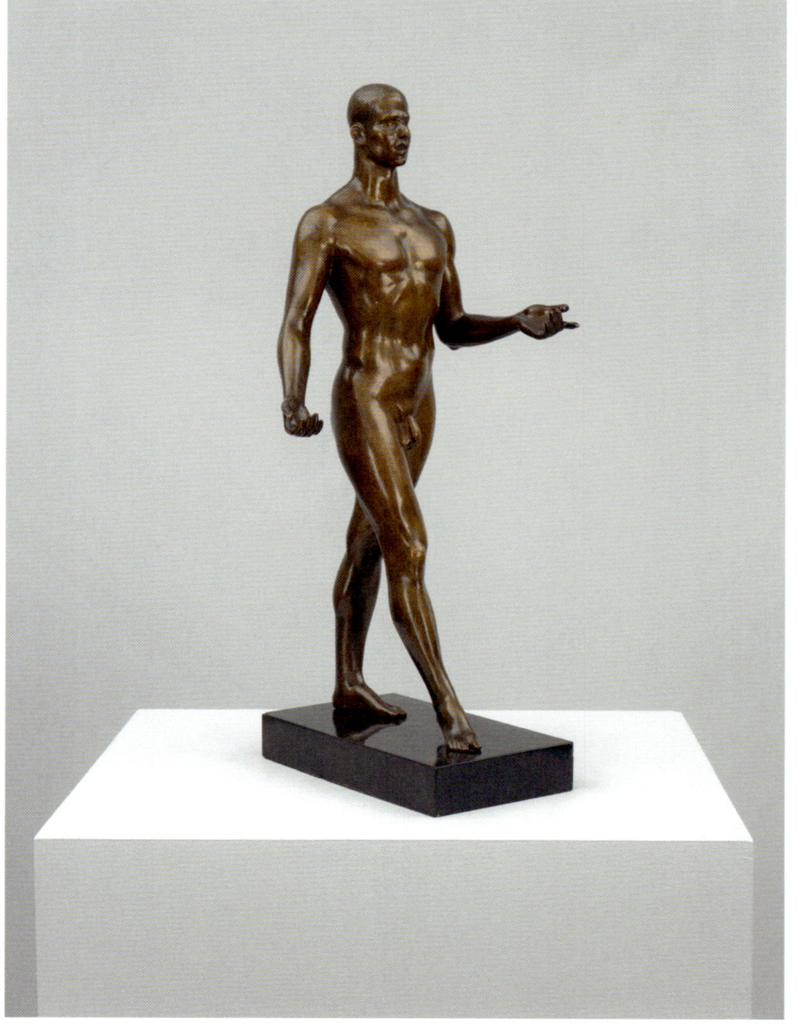

Gaston Lachaise's small-scale sculpture *Man Walking* portrays a nude Lincoln Kirstein (organizer of the artist's retrospective at the Museum of Modern Art in 1935) as a streamlined classical archetype, exhibiting the dignified bearing of a dancer or an Egyptian deity.

Pages 91–98: *Nick Mauss: Transmissions*, 2018. Photographs by Paula Court

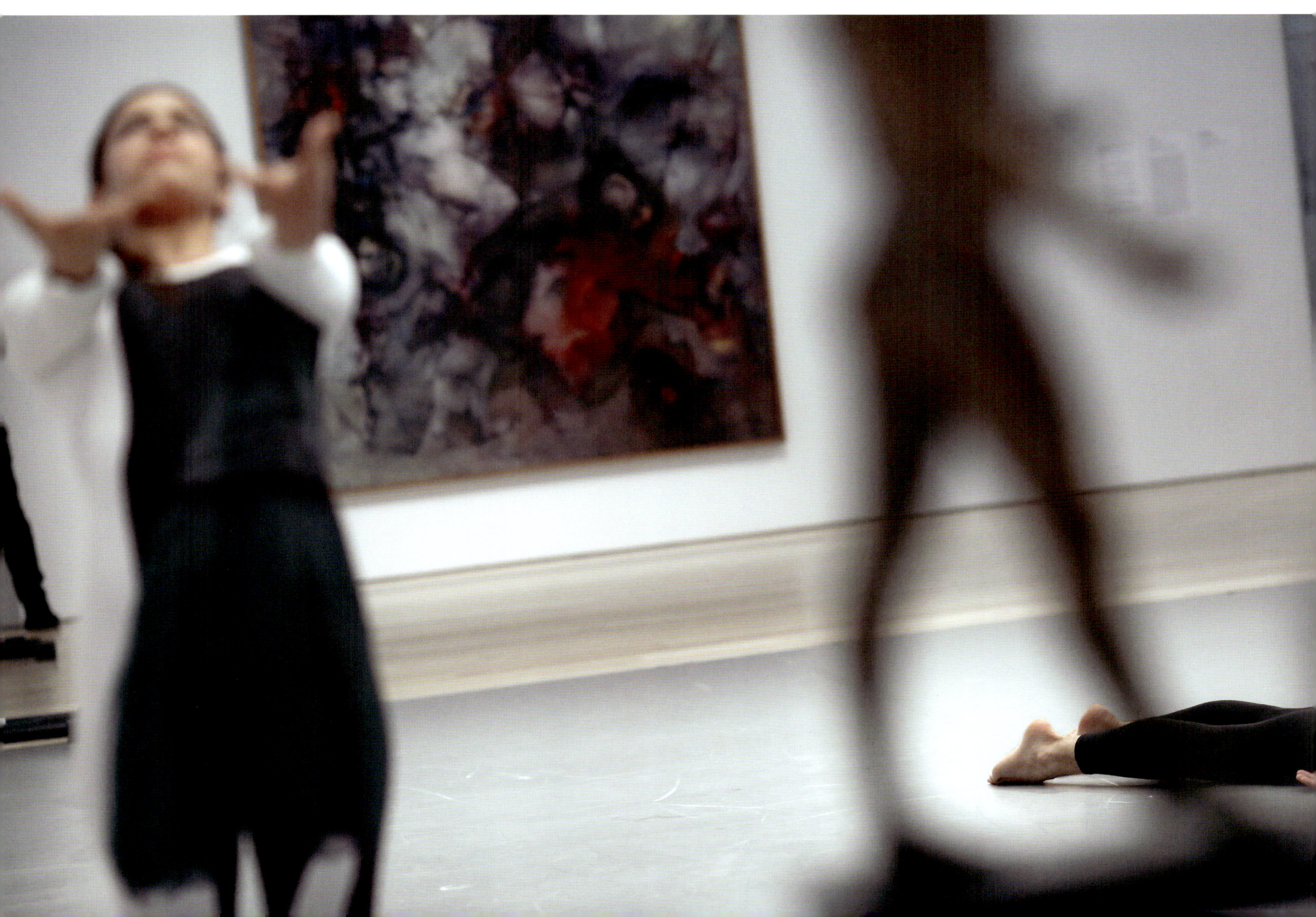

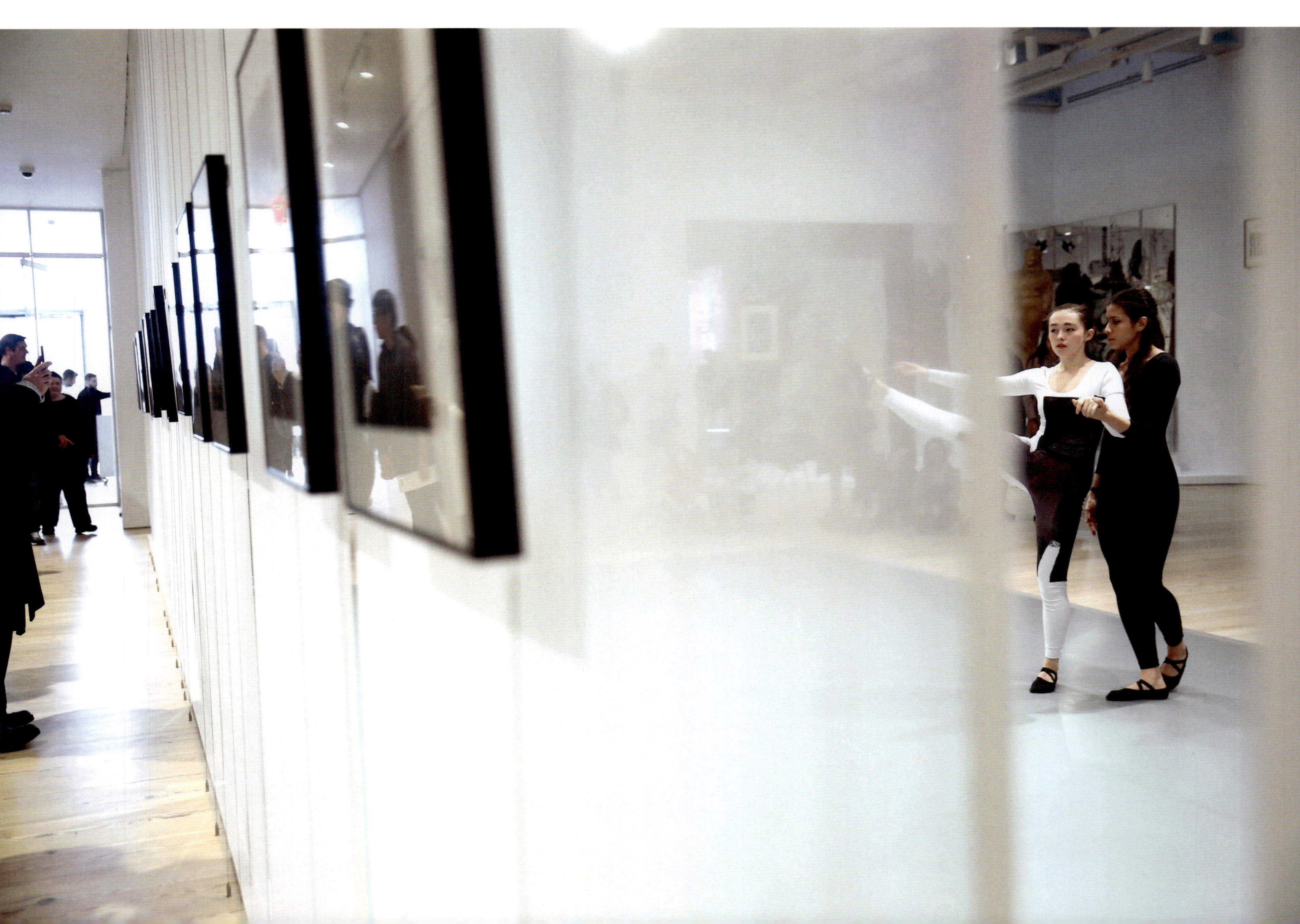

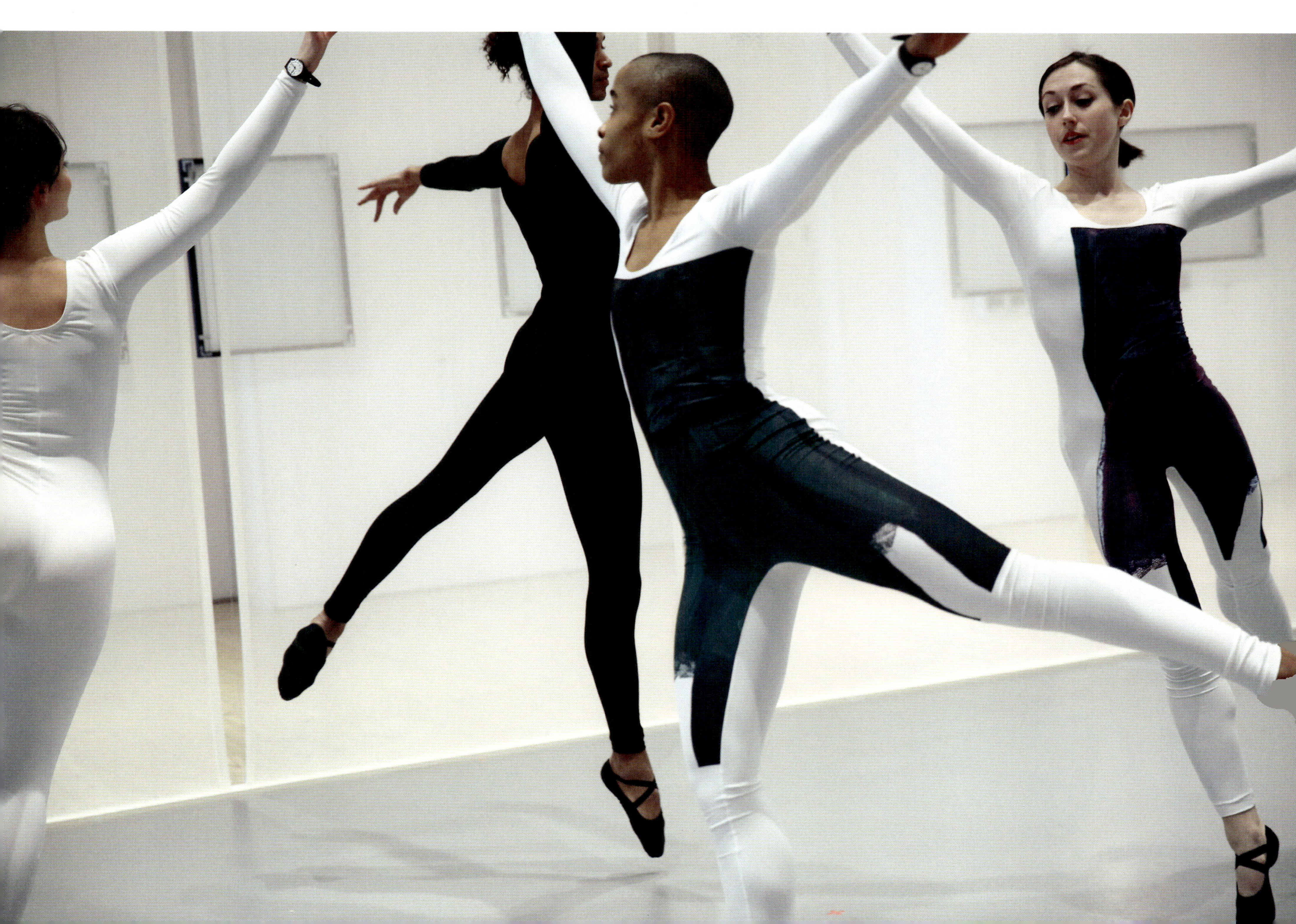

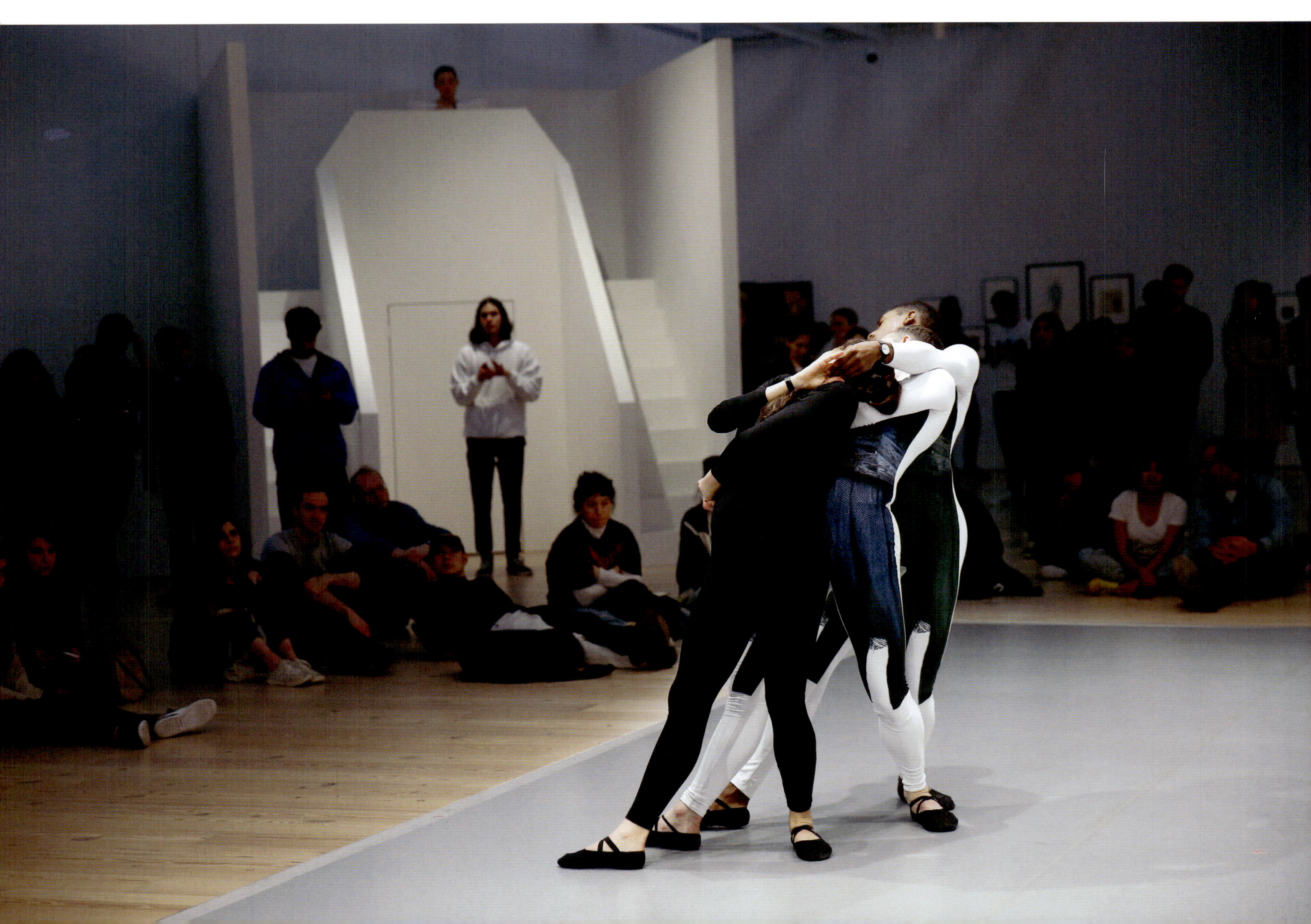

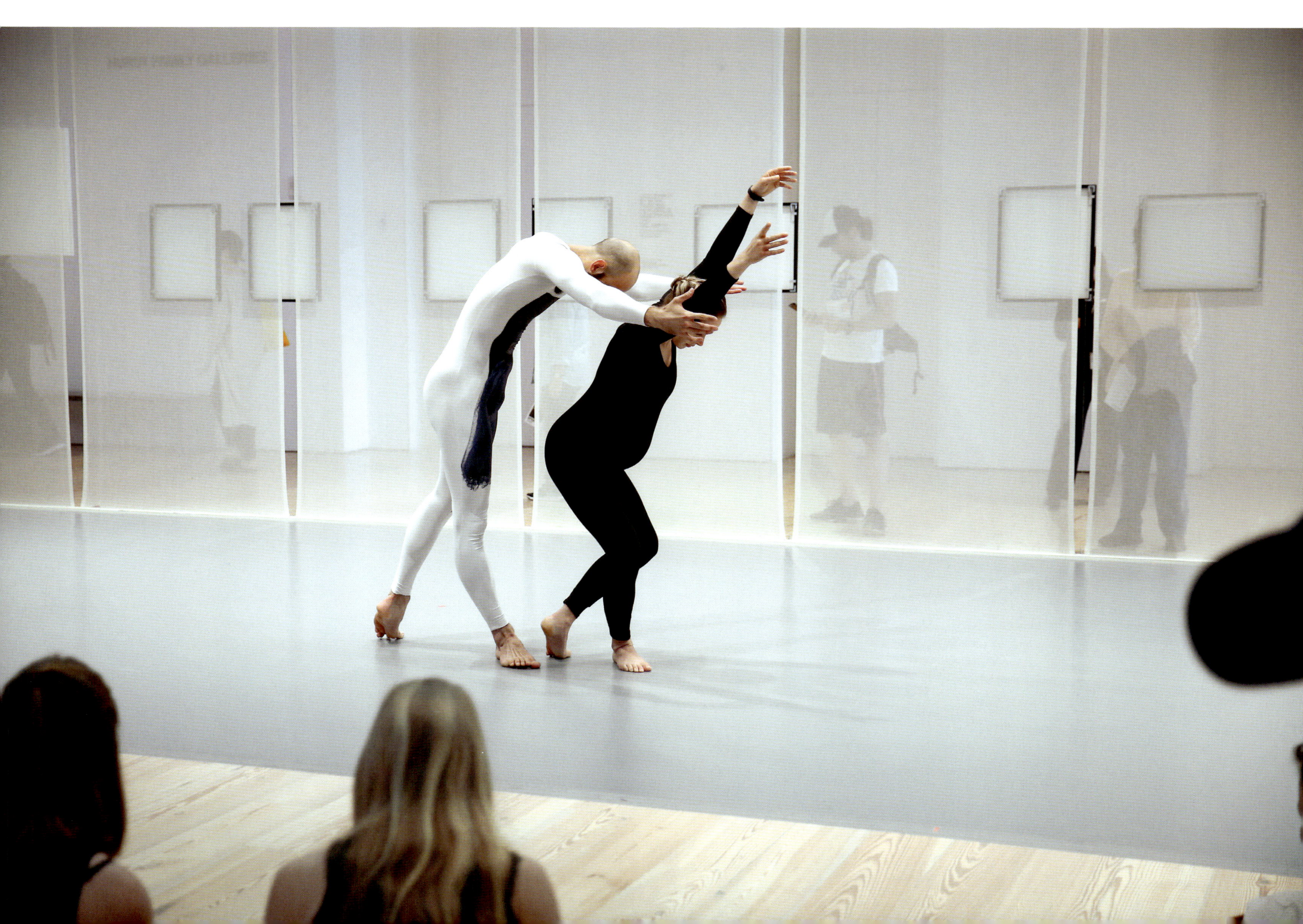

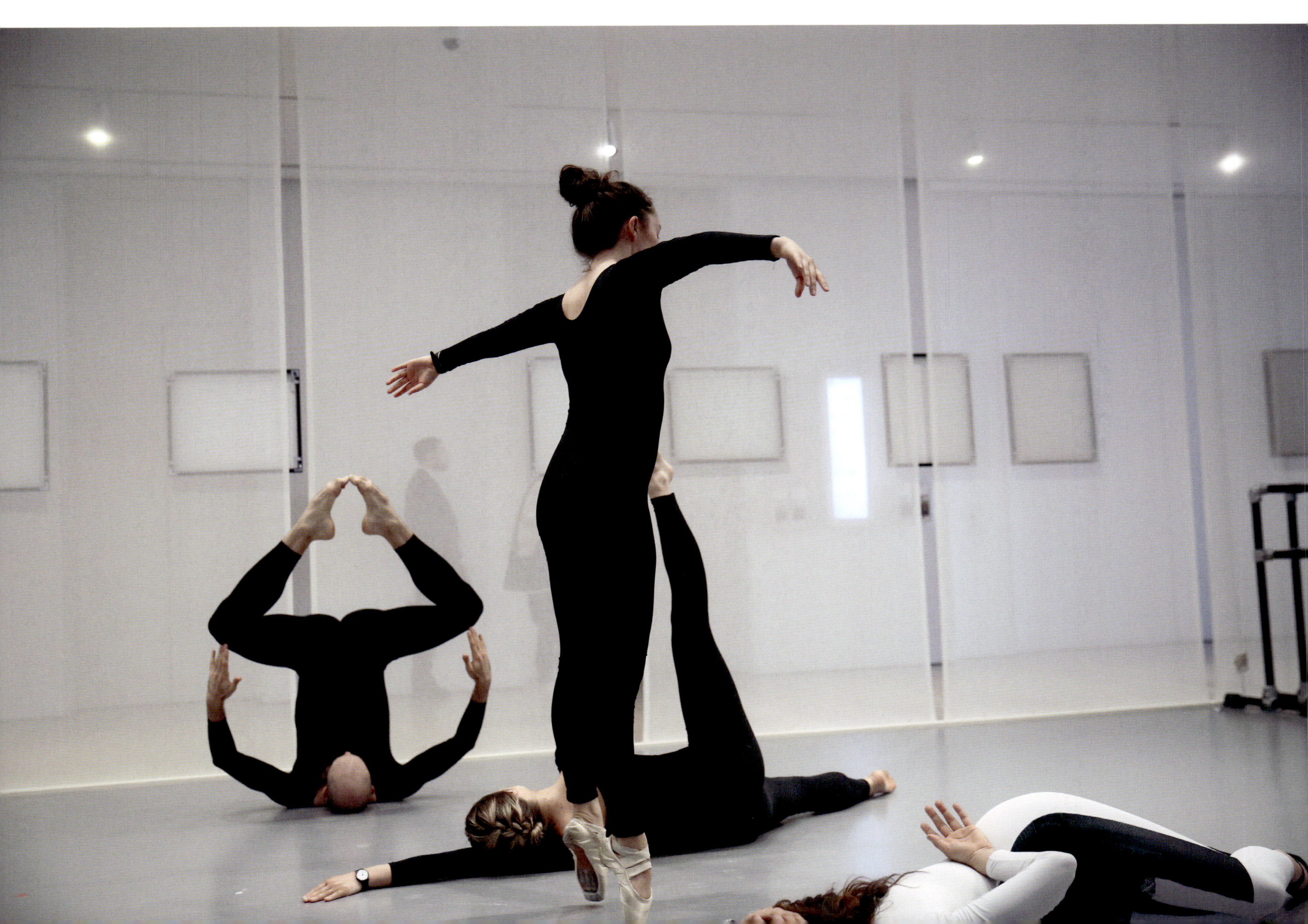

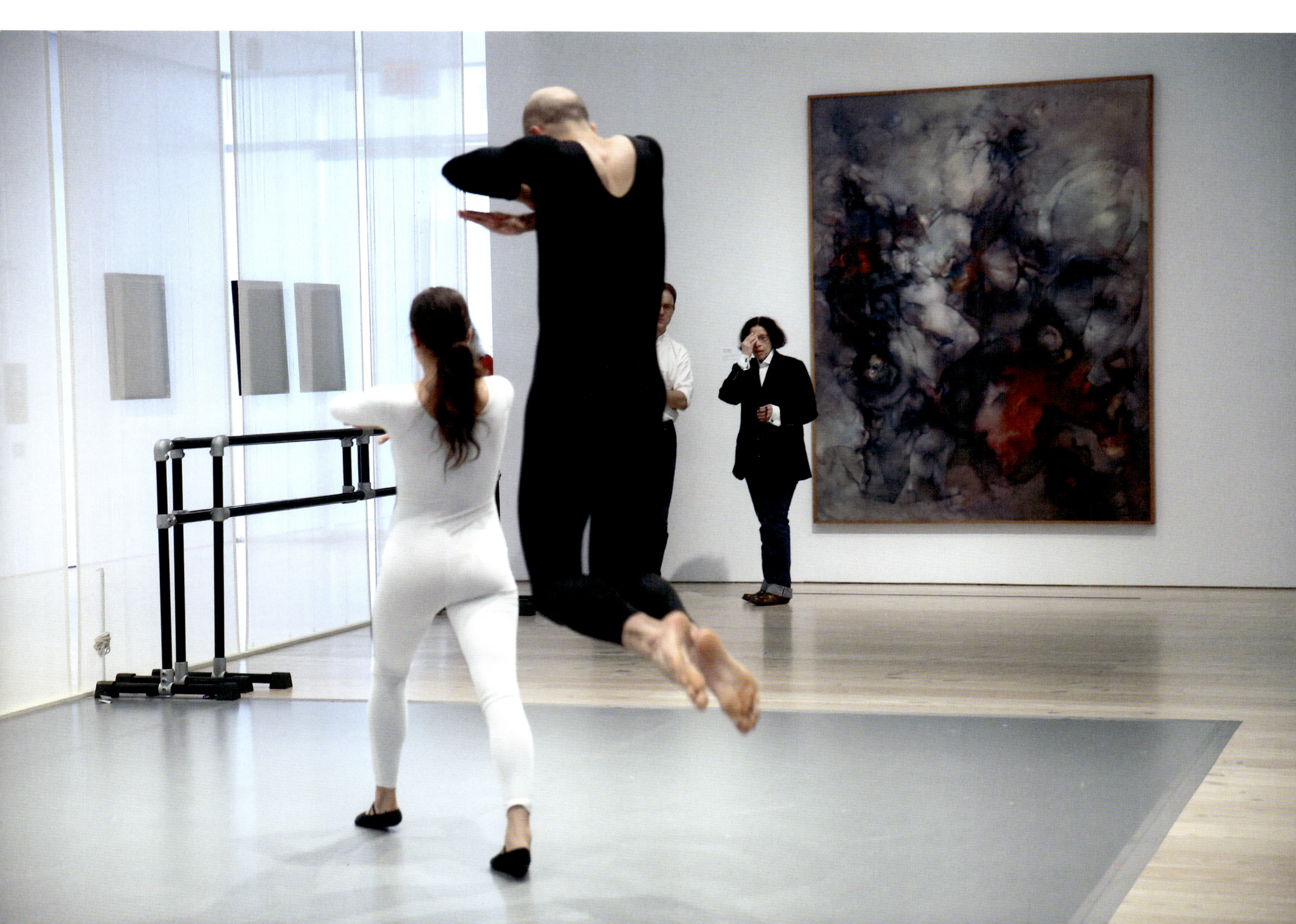

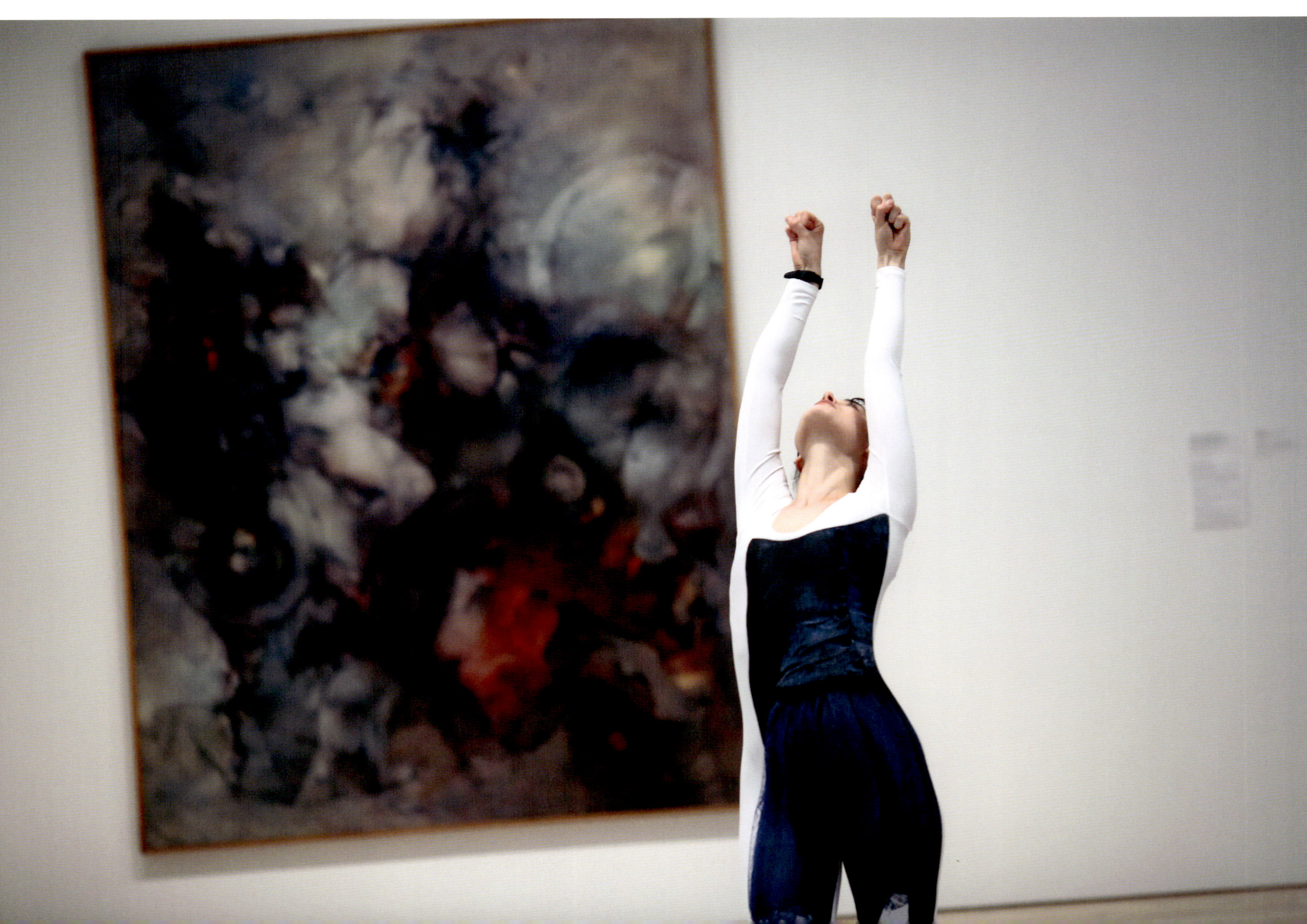

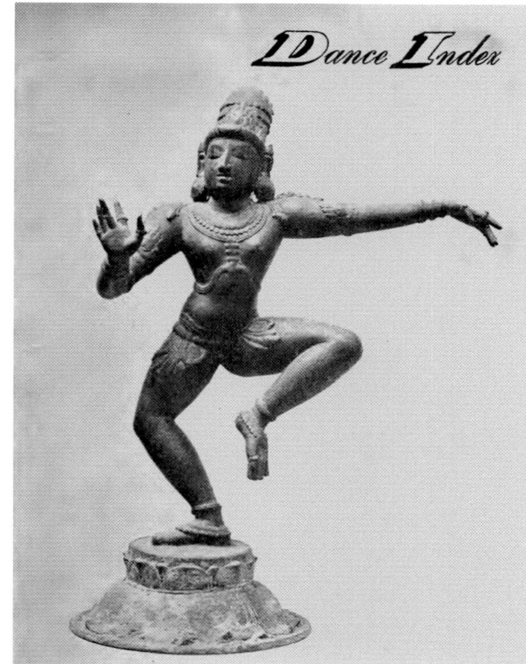

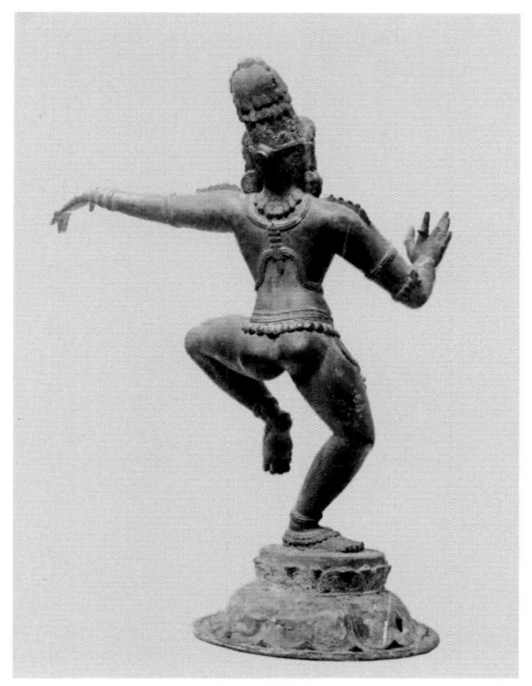

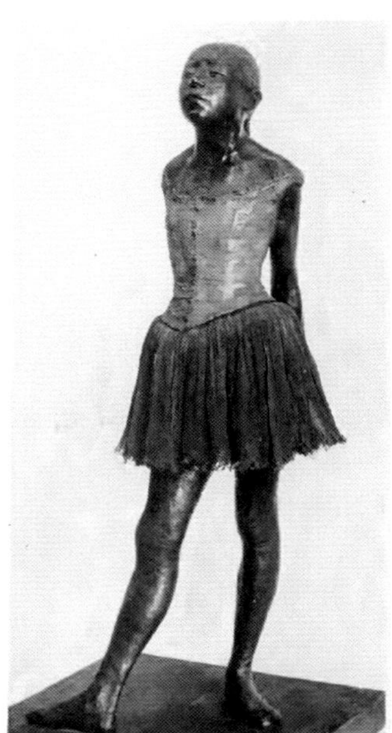

Ballet girl. Bronze (tarlatan skirt). Edgar Degas, 1865-81. Museum of Fine Arts, Boston

True dancing, like true wit, is best express'd
By nature only to advantage dress'd;
'Tis not a nimble bound, or caper high,
That can pretend to please a curious eye;
Good judges no such tumblers tricks regard,
Or think them beautiful because they're hard.

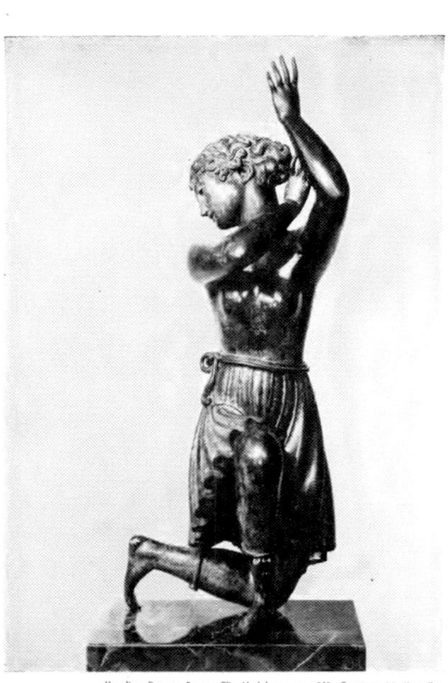

Kneeling Dancer. Bronze. Elie Nadelman, ca. 1922. Courtesy, M. Knoedler

'Tis not enough that ev'ry stander-by
No glaring errors in your steps can spy;
The dance and music must so nicely meet,
Each note should seem an echo to your feet;
A nameless grace must in each movement dwell,
Which words can ne'er express, or precepts tell;
(from "The Art of Dancing" by Soame Jenyns, 1729)

Front and back covers of and interior spread from "Dance in Sculpture," the April 1947 issue of *Dance Index*

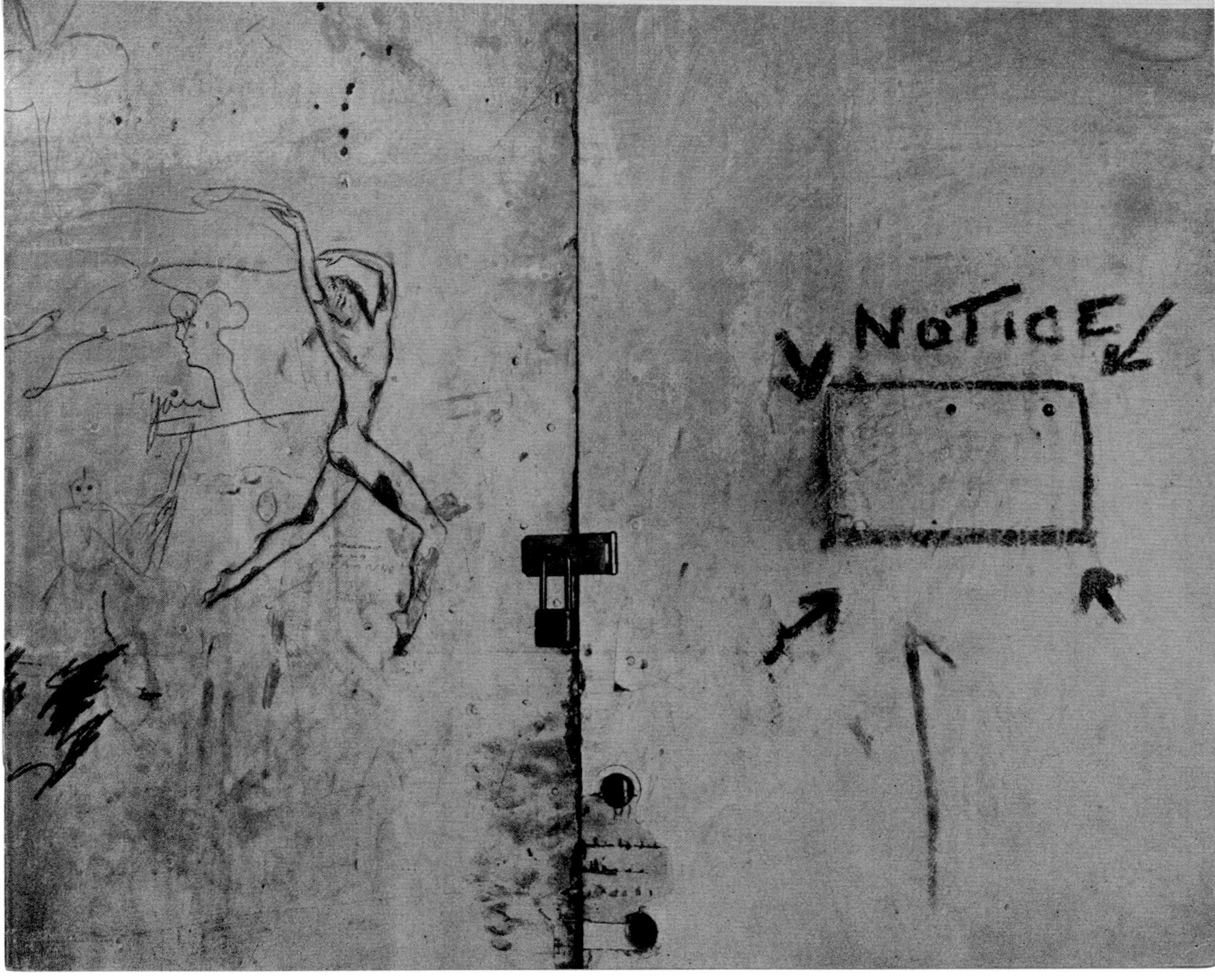

Cover of "The Criticism of Edwin Denby, Photographs by Walker Evans," the February 1946 issue of *Dance Index*

In 1942 Lincoln Kirstein founded the journal *Dance Index* to provide American audiences with a rigorous expository context for dance. In an eclectic array of thematic issues, whose covers often featured montages by artist and balletomane Joseph Cornell, *Dance Index* showcased the images dance produced and the language of its critics and faithful recorders. Its subjects spanned ancient, modern, cross-cultural, popular, obscure, political, museological, and antiquarian concerns, and entire issues were devoted to pioneers of avant-garde dance, including Isadora Duncan and Loie Fuller, as well as the dance writing of Carl Van Vechten and Edwin Denby.

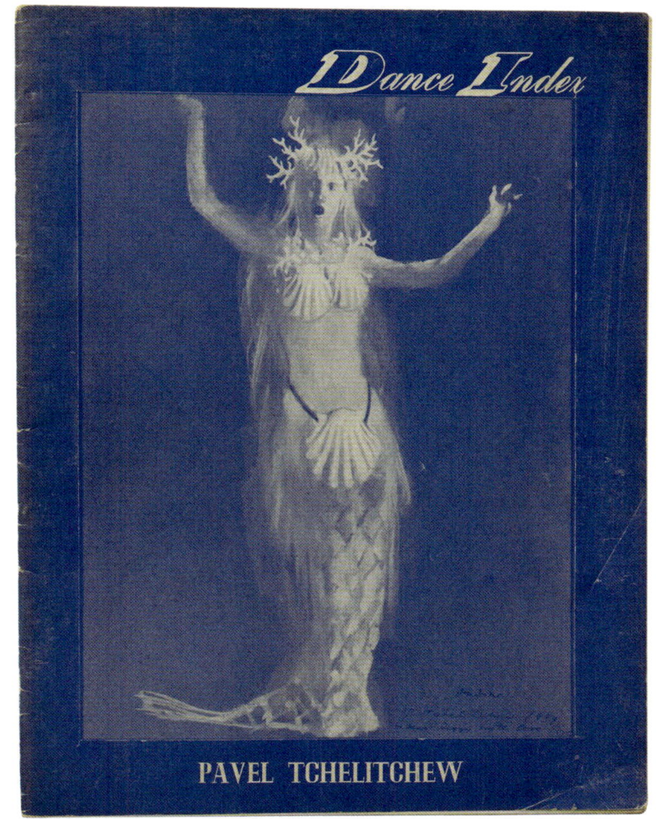

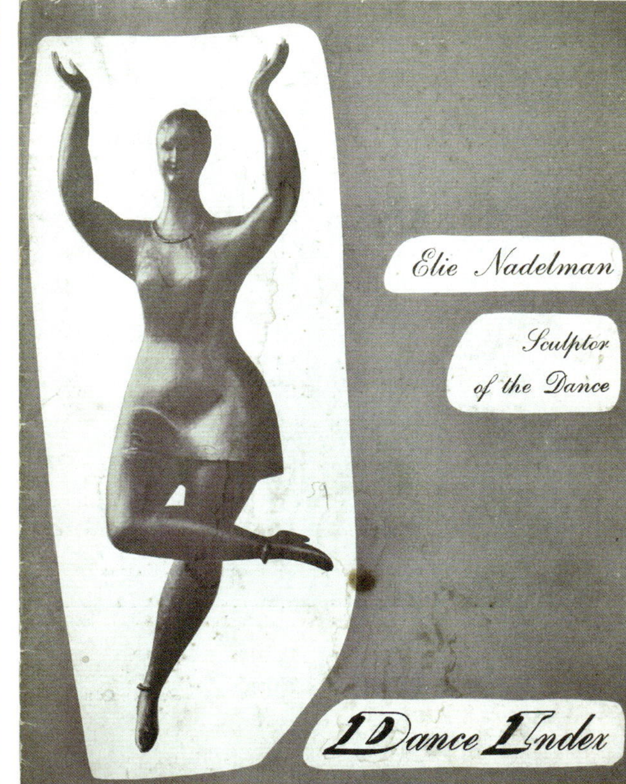

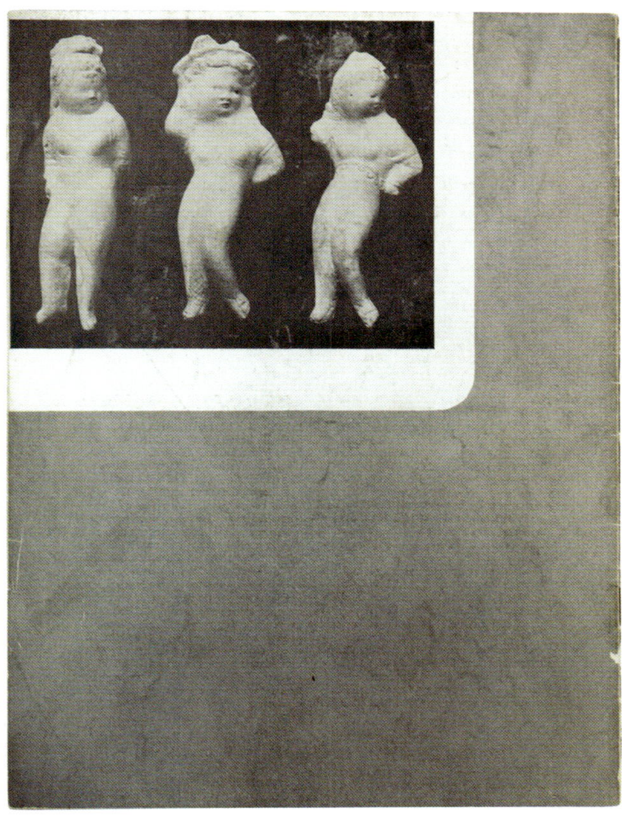

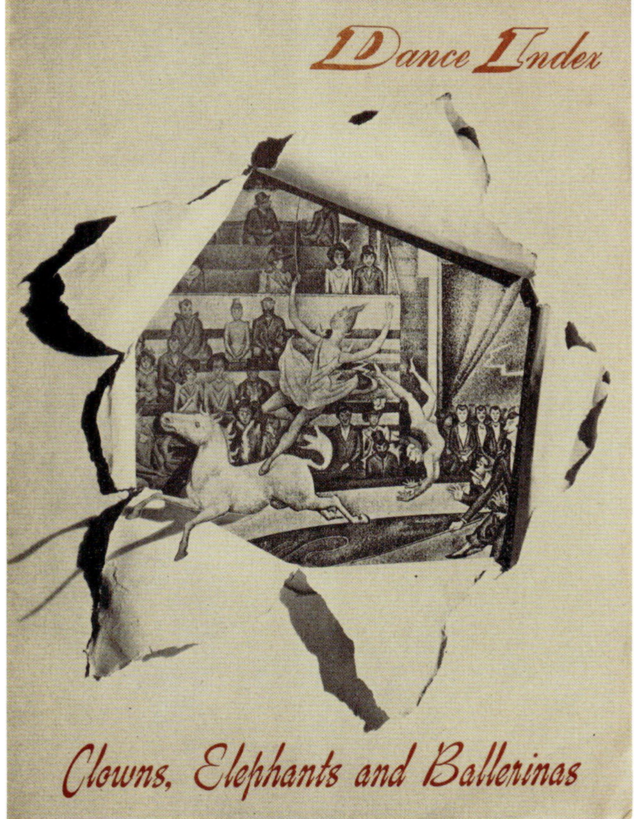

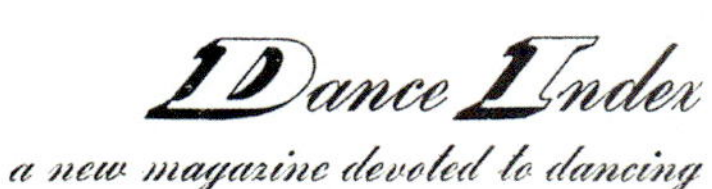

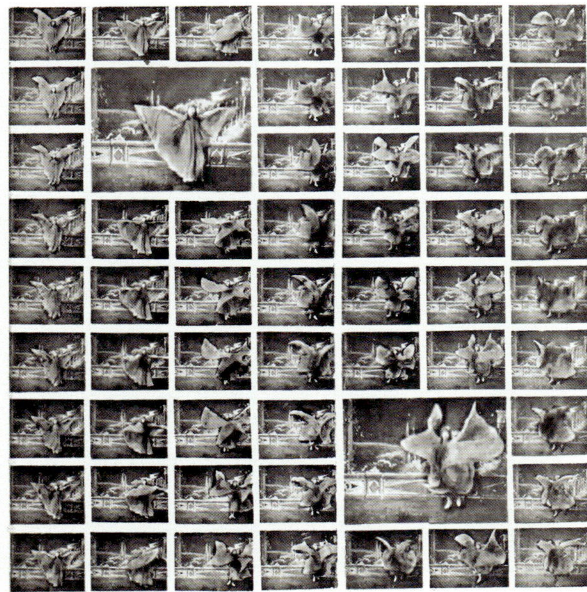

Clockwise: Cover of "Ballet Designs of Pavel Tchelitchew," the January–February 1944 issue of *Dance Index*; front and back covers of "Elie Nadelman: Sculptor of the Dance," *Dance Index* 7, no. 6 (1948); cover of "Clowns, Elephants, and Ballerinas," the June 1946 issue of *Dance Index*, designed by Joseph Cornell; cover of "Loie Fuller," the March 1942 issue of *Dance Index*, designed by Joseph Cornell

Below, left: Cover of the souvenir program for Gertrude Hoffmann's 1911 presentation of the Ballets Russes, with art by Léon Bakst

Below, right: Cover of the souvenir program for Colonel W. de Basil's Ballets Russes's 1936–37 season, with art by Natalia Goncharova

Opposite, left: Cover of the souvenir program for Ballet Russe de Monte Carlo's 1939–40 season, with art by Henri Matisse

Opposite, right: Cover of the souvenir program for Ballet Russe de Monte Carlo's 1941–42 season, with art by Salvador Dalí

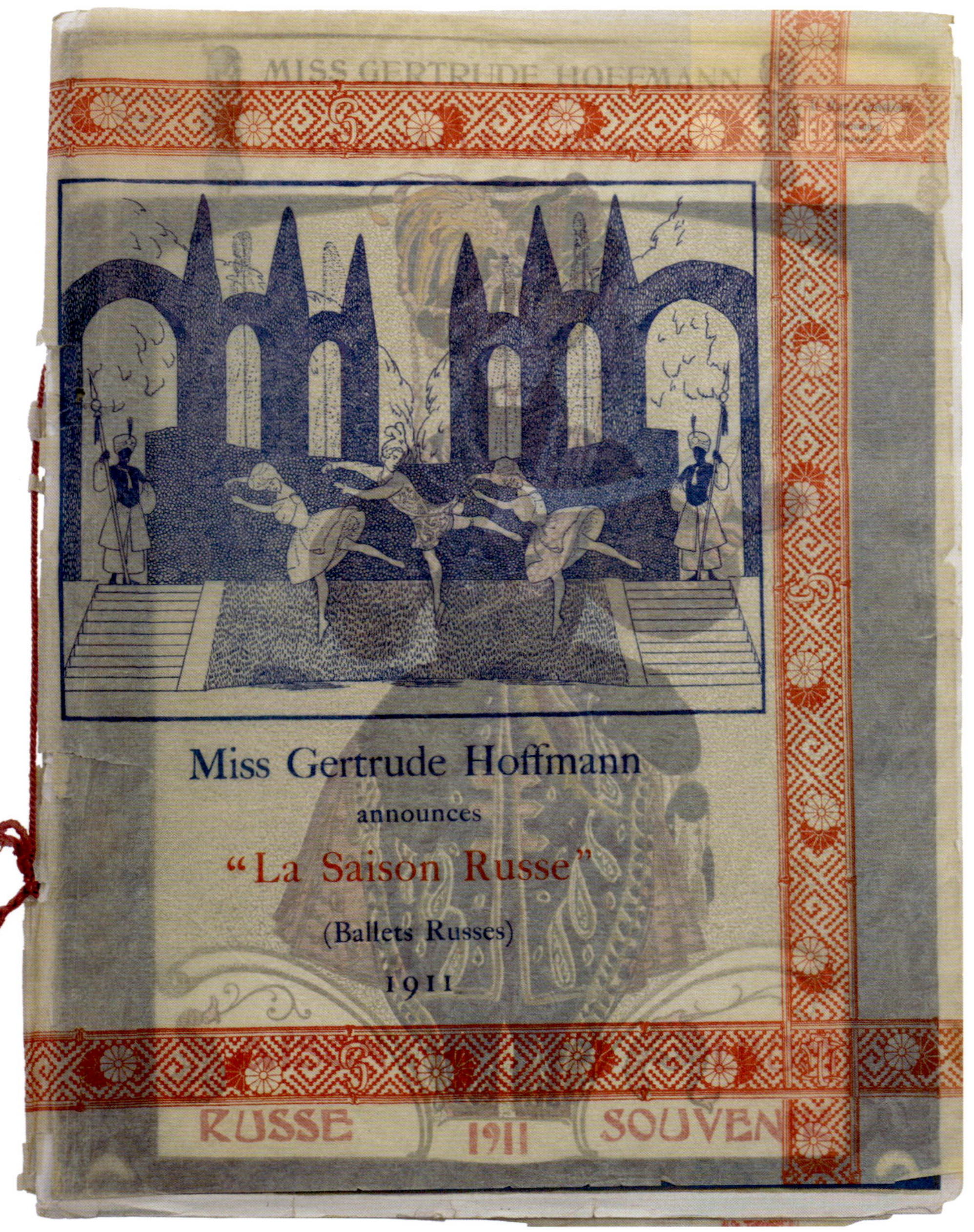

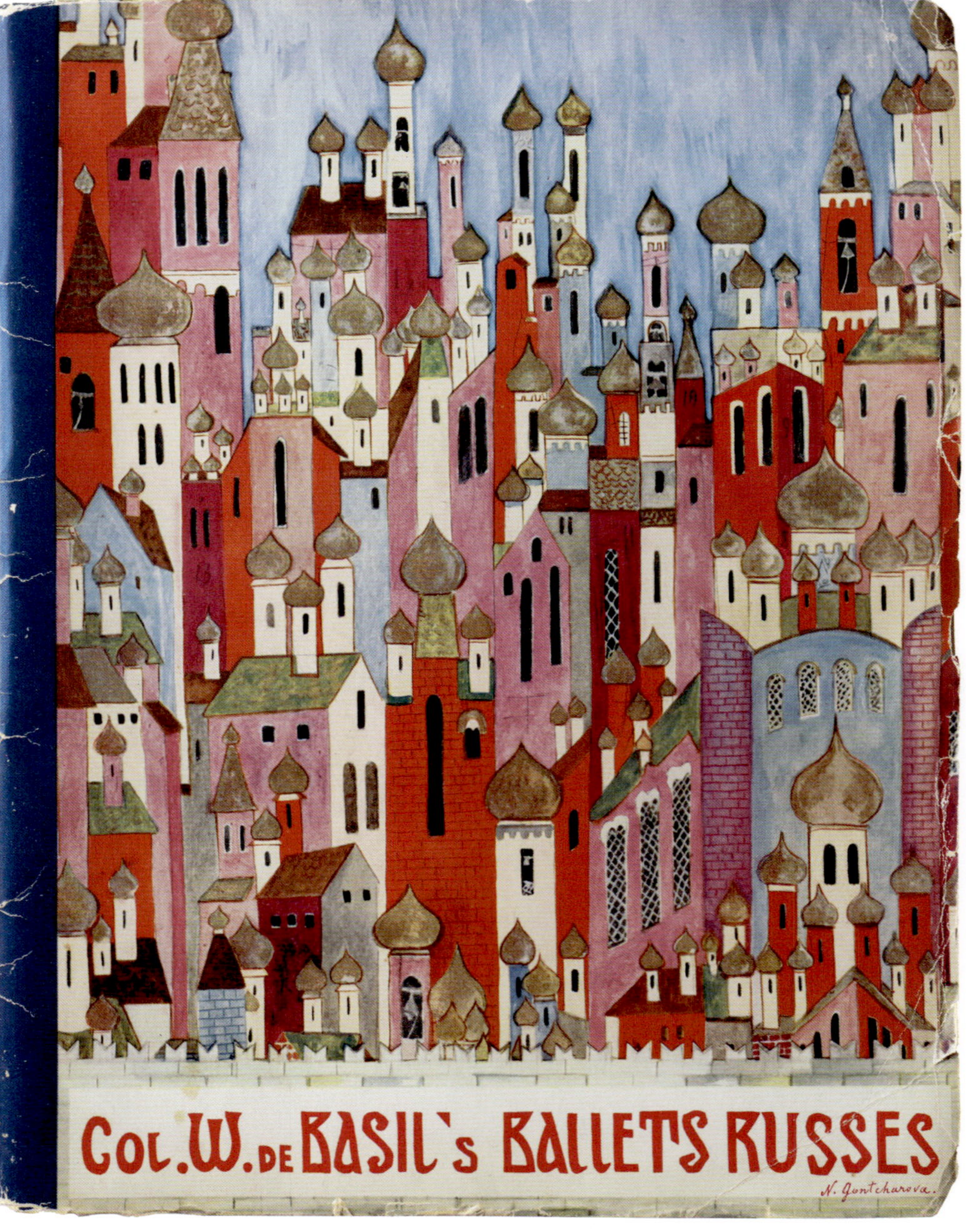

What looks like a 1911 Ballets Russes souvenir program, adapted for an American audience with the addition of a printed translucent jacket, is in fact a program for a production of Russian dance by Gertrude Hoffmann, vaudeville dancer and mimic often credited as the first female American practitioner of "art dance." This illegitimate appropriation of the design of Ballets Russes ephemera signals an historic juncture, the introduction of ballet to America as a product of Russia. Nearly five years before Serge Diaghilev's company arrived, Hoffmann toured her imitation of the Ballets Russes throughout the United States, albeit with the inclusion of American elements such as vaudeville numbers.

Even after Diaghilev's death in 1929, the influence of his inimitable Ballets Russes lived on, not least in the rival companies that splintered off from his legacy and competed over the company's trademark heritage. Featuring dancers and choreographers shaped under Diaghilev's tutelage, these companies included Colonel W. de Basil's Ballets Russes (later named the Original Ballet Russe) and Serge Denham and René Blum's Ballet Russe de Monte Carlo, which toured the United States extensively from the late 1930s until the early 1950s and contributed to the growing mania for dance in America.

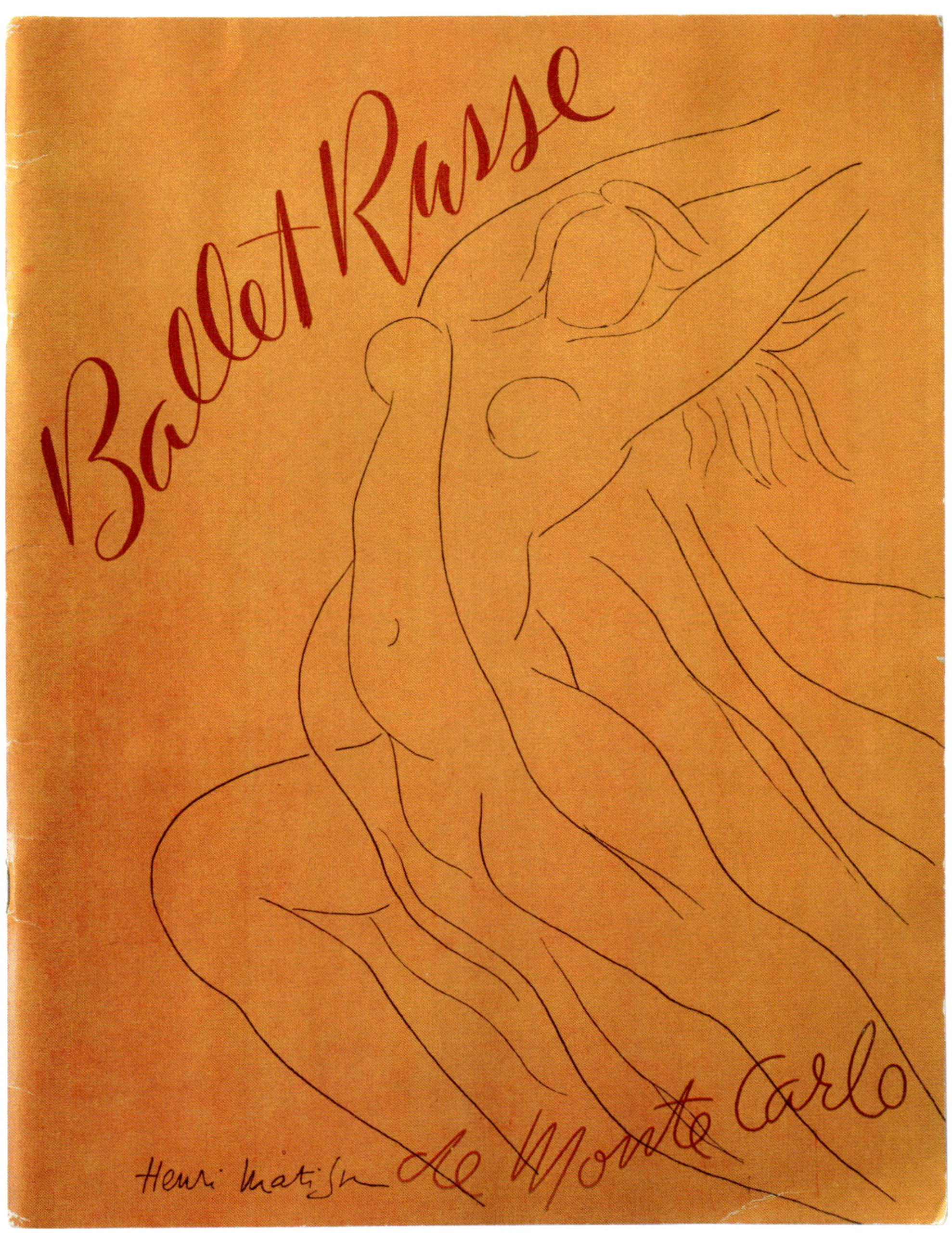

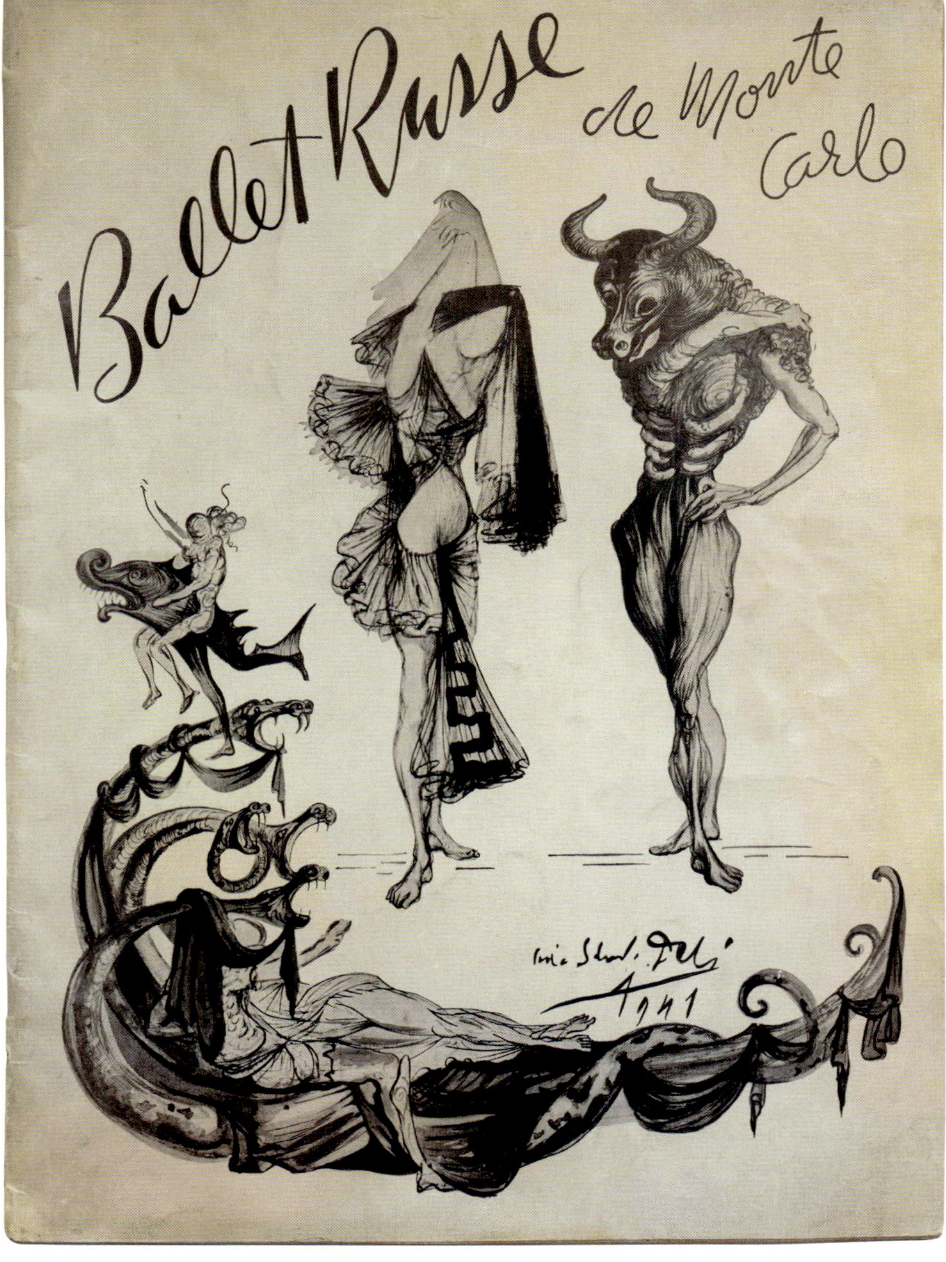

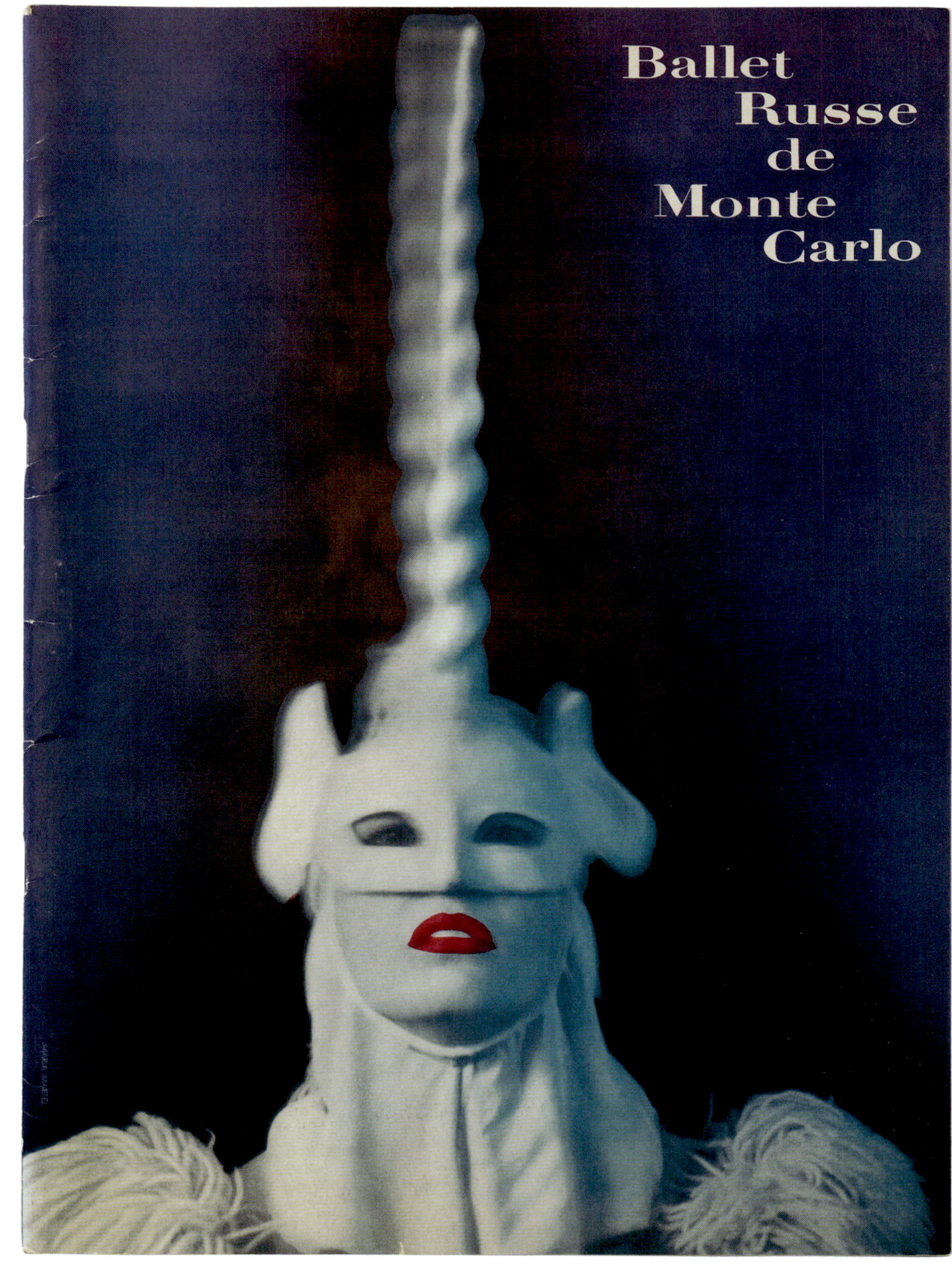

Cover of the souvenir
program for Ballet Russe
de Monte Carlo's 1956–57
season, designed by
Alexei Brodovitch

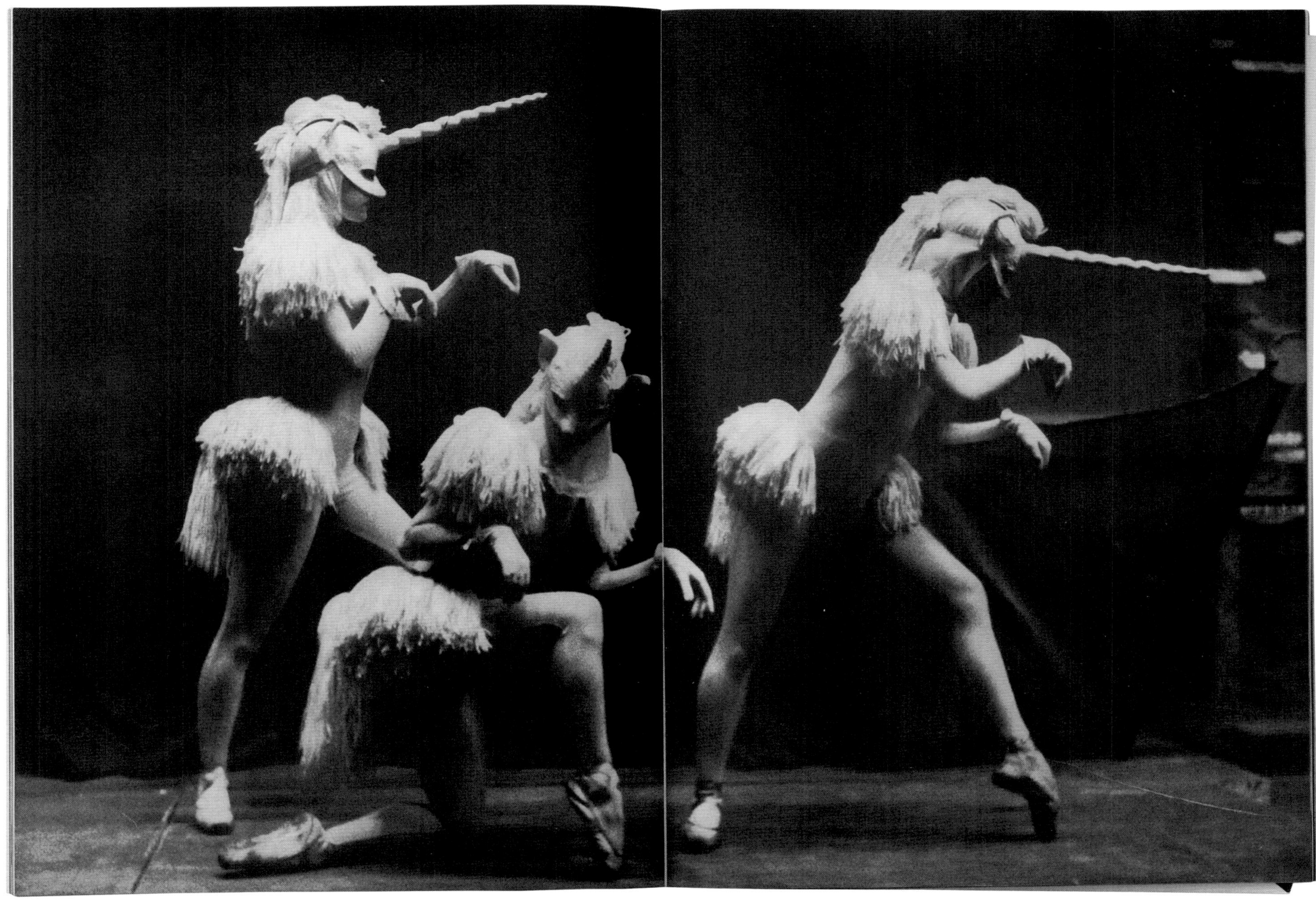

Interior spread from the souvenir program for Ballet Russe de Monte Carlo's 1956–57 season, featuring dancers posing in costumes from Jean Cocteau's *La Dame à la licorne* (1953)

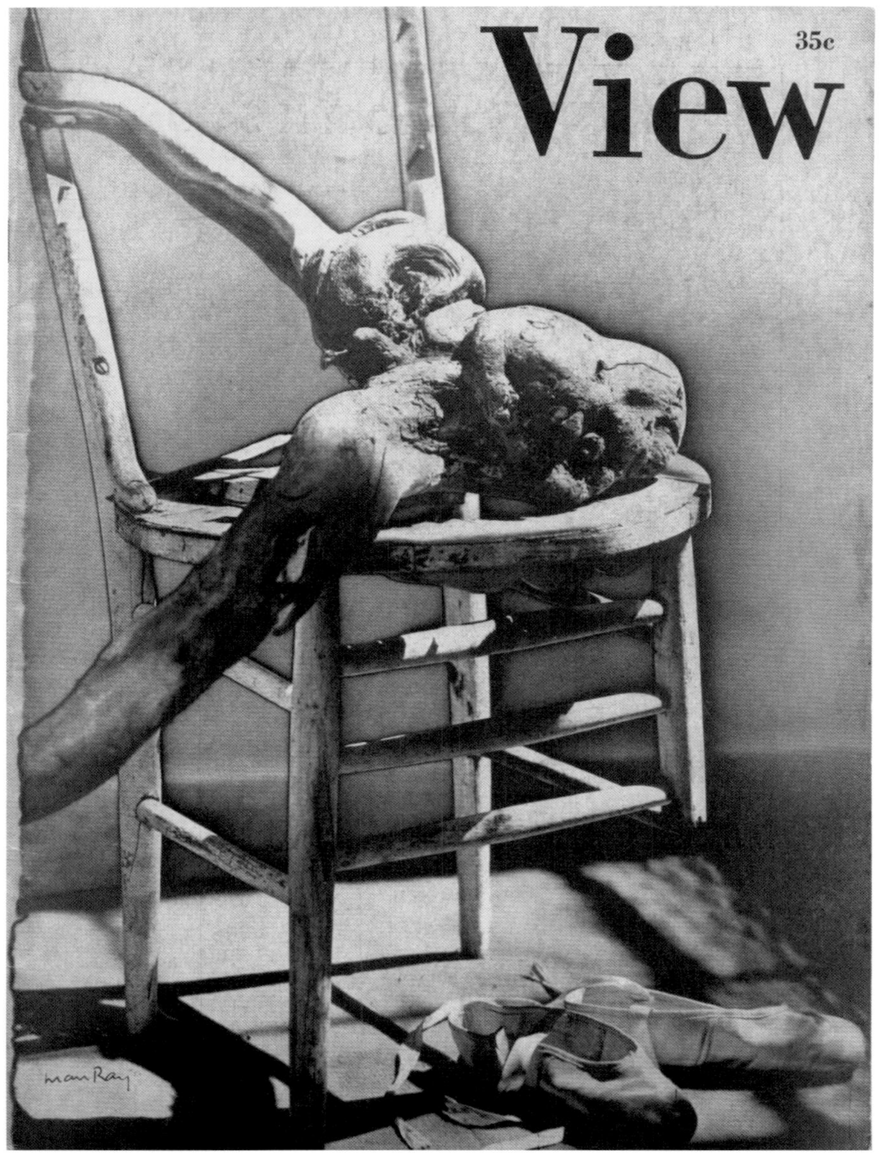

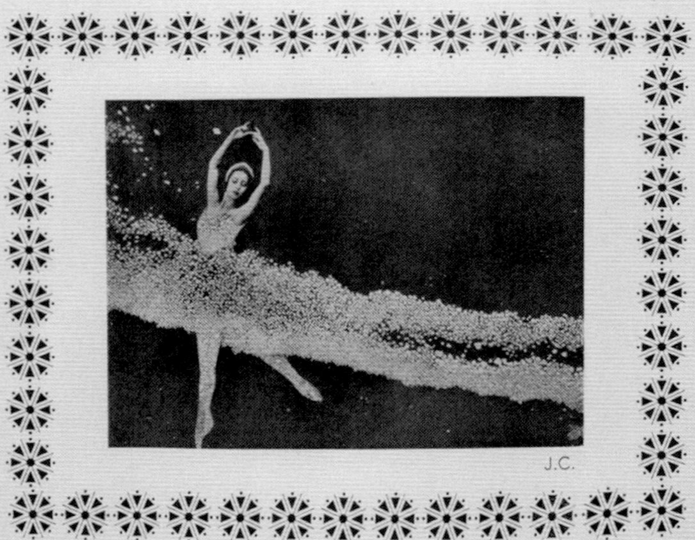

J.C.

TAMARA on her toes goes through snowflakes,
Large and white as little butterflies
Which never light on the same place twice
And never quite lie down.

Tamara's toes, too, seem to skim the ground
As though the green grass were greenest water,
As it to touch it she would drown.
Yes, the slow grass would turn to quick water
If only to hold Tamara all around!

But a house is being built for her
With tiger-tooth nails and rugs of bees' fur,
The front doorknob is a swarming tear
Wept by a giant the first time he saw
A piouette! ('Twas Tamara in the snow.)

The sun with tongue of softest gold
Carves the windows in the walls of mist
And windowpanes are tears of joy
Brought by boys who heard Tamara's name
Spoken in their dreams! Ah, Tamara's

Heart gives a leap and leaps with her
To the shimmering door where she knocks and listens.
Although the door is a wide-open rose
(Its doorknob core a great dewdrop)
The rose must close before the door will open. . .

Tamara with her black hair warm as summer honey
Asks a pretty orphan if he will keep her company
Until the roof is ready. Doves and flowers
Scatter plumes and petals on the spiderweb rafters
And fishes hold hands to make a shiny chimney
More wonderful than any in China or India.

But Tamara! Who is that in a hood as black
As your hair, dark hair as sweet as night's honey?
Tamara turns her great green eyes
On his eyes, green too, as only eyes can be.

He holds out a key, she holds out her hand,
But the snowflakes, hard as diamond butterflies,
Have stopped in midair, like a net of stars
That no one, nor the melancholy man
Nor even Tamara can move among!

The good giant looking for his missing tear
(For giants always save their rare tears)
Passed his hand like a headless beast
With five legs and five sharp teeth
(Somewhere the tear was trembling, waiting,
Someday the tear would shiver with cold,
For tears, like hearts whose sweat they are,
As quick as hearts, may change from hot to cold)
Over the sleeping mountain's armpit,
There where the constellation's prisoners
(Still as the photograph of a dream)
Had lost all hope of ever touching
Hand or lip, skin or hair again!

But warm as a tongue or cool as the shadow
A bee designs on breast or shoulder,
The giant longed for the touch of a tear
He could call his own. . . The tear lay there
In the heart of the rose, then tumbled in his palm
As though the rose shed its first drop of grief.
The butterfly stars cut the giant fingers
But the hand stayed on its back like a beast
While the monster's eyes were fixed on Tamara.

Tamara didn't care now, if the door were open,
Reading her future in the crystal tear
Of the animal's belly. . . The fish broke the chimney,
Frantic as birds, they whispered, speechless,
Warnings in the shells of Tamara's ears;
The orphans awoke and their dream disappeared;
Only the man in the hood was happy.

The twisting key put its head in his pocket,
He shook his cloak and the claws of his feet
Left the ground to find a branch to fit.
Ah, Tamara, your beautiful neck is the tree!

But what she sees is stronger than feeling. . .
Riding a horse on the edge of the world,
The world is flat as fortune's wheel,
The horse's tail is an old man's beard,
Tamara's face is a frozen place
Where two birds live in the ice of her eyes
And the flame of her mouth is colder than the sky.

Tamara! can't you feel the startled blood
That jewels your breast and makes your skin more white?
But Tamara's eyes, green as hummingbirds,
Plunge their beaks in the tear and beat
Their wings against that other ice,

And her hand, as if hypnotized, has touched
The horse and herself on the edge of the world,
And they fall! — from the edge of the world like a tear
From the world's closing eyelid. . . Tamara, crying,
Fades from the light to follow her image

From the light of day, but the man of night
With wings like hair is taking her away. . .
The giant hurls his tear like a moon
And it bursts like sun around Tamara
As he plucks the black wings from her shoulders,

But where is Tamara? . . .
                    The giant's tears
Make a fountain, now, in his melancholy garden
And he always watches the black statue there
Catching the snow like melting butterflies,
Butterflies melting on her hand and dark hair.

by

Charles

Henri

Ford

Man Ray's composition, on the cover of *View* magazine, of a splayed driftwood trunk, a three-legged chair, and a pair of empty, unlaced pointe shoes evokes a transfigured ballerina. A poem by Charles Henri Ford, illustrated by Joseph Cornell, in another issue of *View* imagines the scenario for an unrealizable dream ballet dedicated to both the poet's and the artist's favorite dancer, Tamara Toumanova.

Several issues of *View* were likely backed by the wealthy Marquis George de Cuevas, who took out a number of full-page ads for his Ballet International. Cuevas's company prided itself on collaborations "with the foremost American and European artists: composers, painters, poets, choreographers and dancers." Ballet International's cast included the young Greek dancer Alexander Iolas, who later became legendary as a gallerist, presenting Andy Warhol's first exhibition *15 Drawings Based on the Writings of Truman Capote* in 1952. Iolas founded the Jackson/Iolas Gallery in 1955 with another former dancer, Brooks Jackson, and went on to open galleries around the world, exhibiting works by Cornell, Ray Johnson, René Magritte, Dorothea Tanning, and Paul Thek, among others.

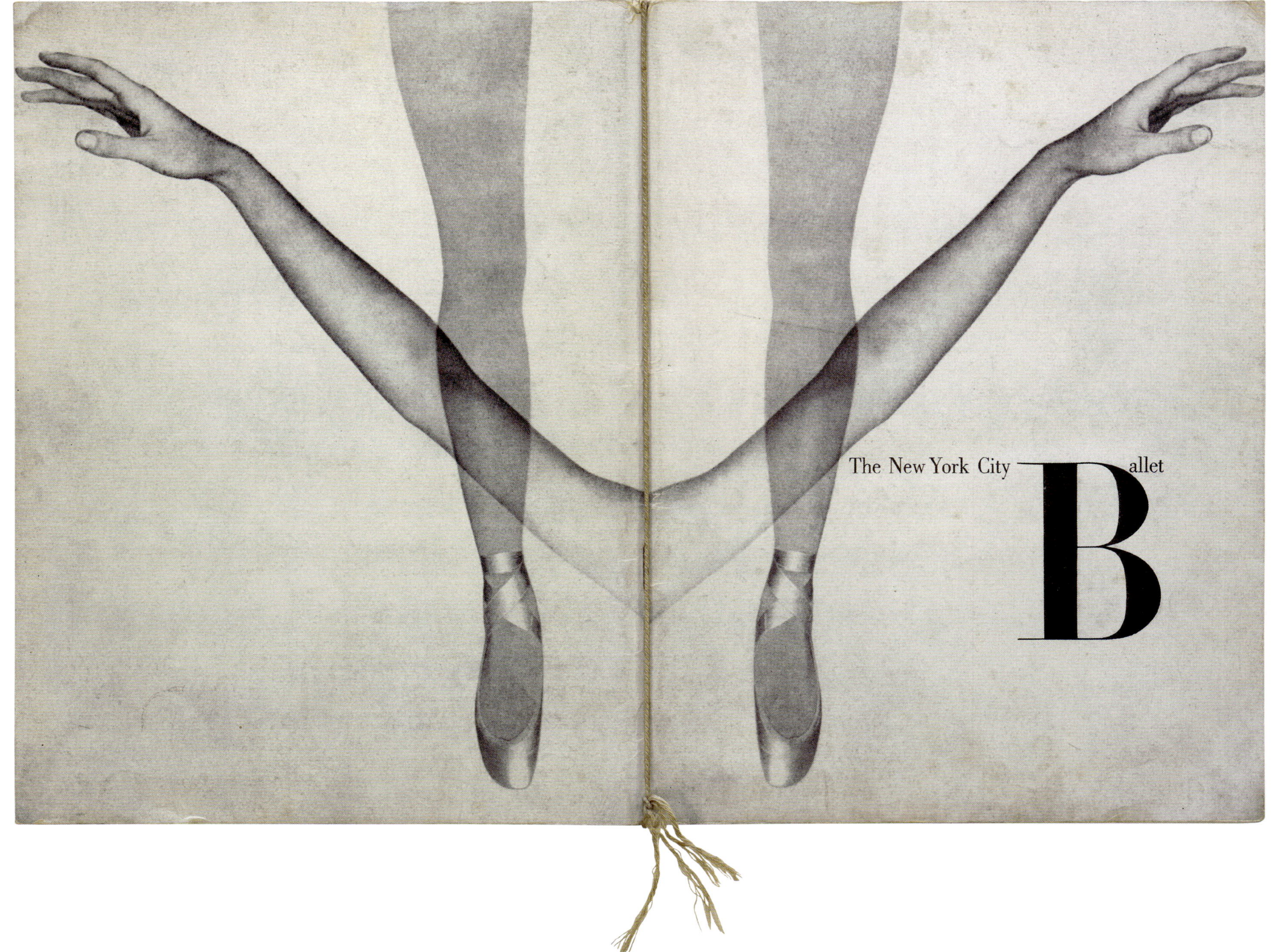

The New York City
B
allet

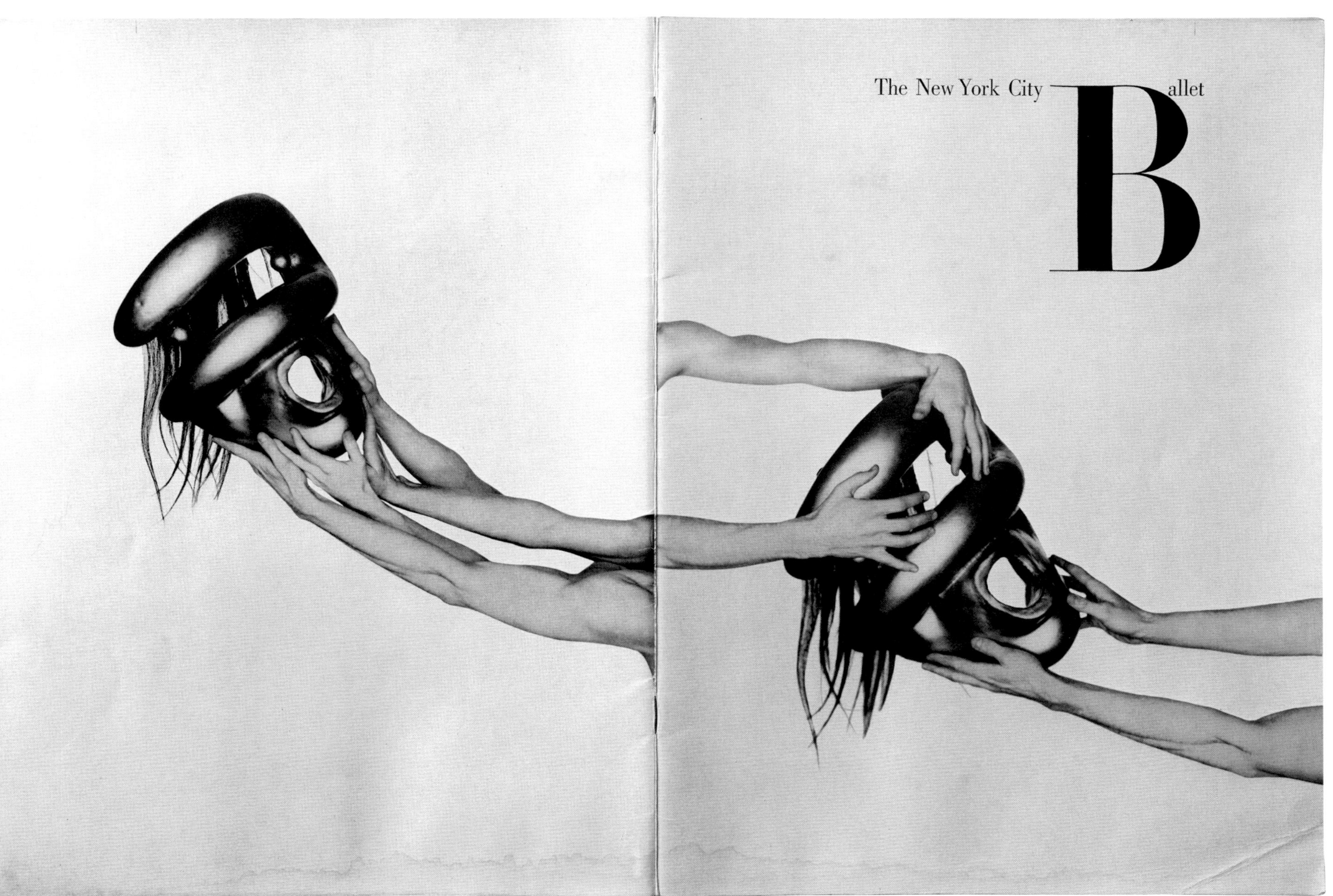

Opposite: Back and front cover of the souvenir program for New York City Ballet's second European tour, 1952

Back and front cover of New York City Ballet's 1951 souvenir program

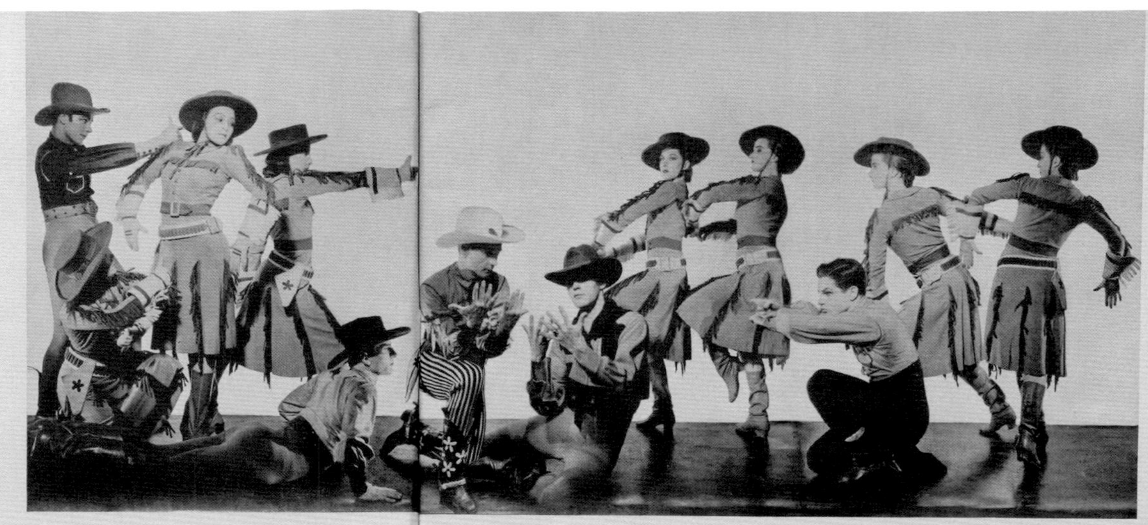

Back and front cover of the souvenir program for American Ballet's first Latin American tour, 1941

Opposite: Interior spread from the souvenir program for American Ballet's first Latin American tour, 1941

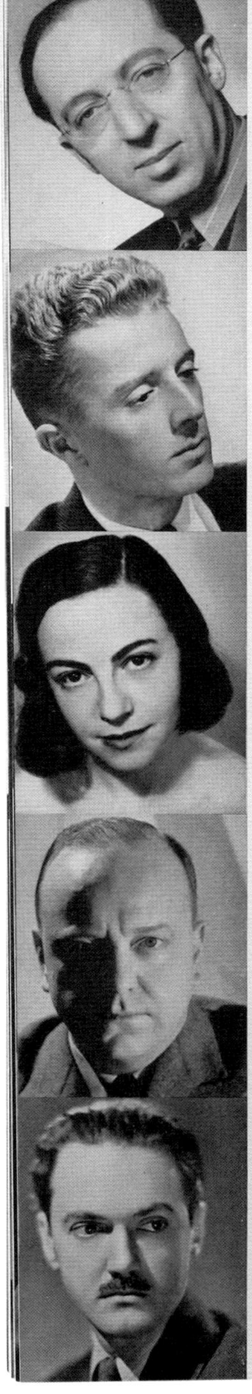

Compositores

Aaron Copland

Nació el año 1900. Es uno de los tres compositores norteamericanos más ilustres. Estudió en los Estados Unidos y en París con Nadia Boulanger. *Despedida* fué escrita en 1925, habiéndose convertido ya en la obra clásica de la primera época del jazz, formando desde entonces parte del repertorio de la *Boston Symphony Orchestra* que dirige el maestro Serge Koussevitzky. *Billy the Kid* fué escrito por encargo del *American Ballet* en 1938. Ha escrito los temas musicales para las películas *Of Mice and Men* y *Our Town*, así como varias sinfonías y una ópera.

Paul Bowles

Nació en Brooklyn, Nueva York, en 1909. Como músico casi se educó a sí mismo y ha sentido un especial interés hacia la música indígena de rasgos exóticos. Ha vivido en España, en el Norte de Africa y en México. Entre sus obras musicales se encuentra música para el teatro, especialmente para las producciones de Orson Welles *Faustus* y *El Sombrero de Palma*. Compuso *el Clíper Yanqui* para el *American Ballet* en 1937. Completó en Taxco, estado de Guerrero, México, la música para *Pastorela*. También ha escrito canciones, una ópera y música para películas.

Trude Rittmann

Nació en Mannheim, Alemania, en 1907. Empezó a estudiar con Ernst Toch, matriculándose más tarde en la *Hochschule für Musik* de Colonia. Después de recibir diplomas del Estado por sus conciertos, emprendió jiras de conciertos por Alemania, Suiza, Francia, Holanda e Inglaterra. Al mismo tiempo sus composiciones para orquesta y voz y sus arreglos musicales obtuvieron éxitos notables. Por algún tiempo estuvo en Inglaterra, trabajando en colaboración con Kurt Jooss y después, en 1937, se incorporó a la compañía del *American Ballet*. Creó su ballet *Charade* en 1939.

Virgil Thomson

Nació en Kansas City el año 1900. Se educó en la universidad de Harvard en donde tocaba el órgano de la capilla. Estuvo en París y allí compuso su ópera *Cuatro Santos en Tres Actos*, con libreto de Gertrude Stein, la cual causó una gran sensación en Nueva York. Ha preparado acompañamientos musicales para películas del Gobierno de los Estados Unidos, para Orson Welles, para *Hamlet*, *Macbeth* y *La Duquesa de Malfi*. Es ahora crítico musical del diario neoyorquino *Herald Tribune* y sus artículos son famosos por su perspicacia y su sinceridad.

Alec Wilder

Nació en Rochester, estado de Nueva York, en 1907. Se graduó en la escuela de música *Eastman* donde había cursado estudios académicos de música. Abandonó la carrera de compositor académico para aprender todo un repertorio de orquesta popular de jazz y de *swing*. Ha hecho numerosos arreglos para orquestas de baile. Ha organizado su propio conjunto musical, utilizando solamente el clavicordio e instrumentos de viento. Los discos que ha impresionado han obtenido gran fama por su delicadeza y equilibrio.

Escenógrafos

Paul Cadmus

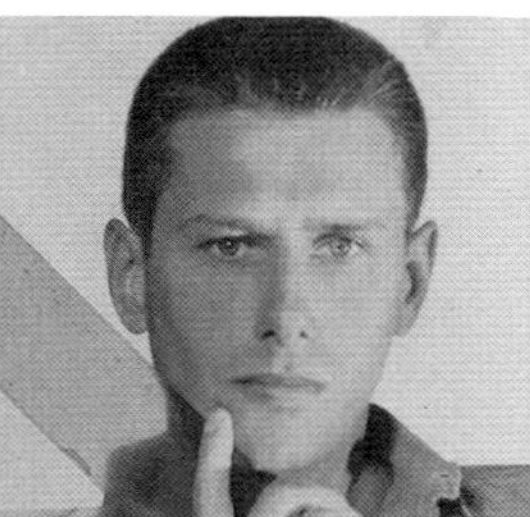

Nació en la ciudad de Nueva York en 1906. Sus padres también fueron pintores, habiéndose educado en la *National Academy of Design*. Ha sido Paul Cadmus el *enfant terrible* entre los pintores norteamericanos por el talento satírico y mordaz de su pincel. Es un excelente dibujante y ha realizado pinturas murales de grandes dimensiones. Es también retratista, grabador, interesado en hacer revivir la técnica medioeval italiana de pintar sobre madera solamente con colores hechos de tierra mezclada con yemas de huevo. También es autor de ilustraciones.

Alvin Colt

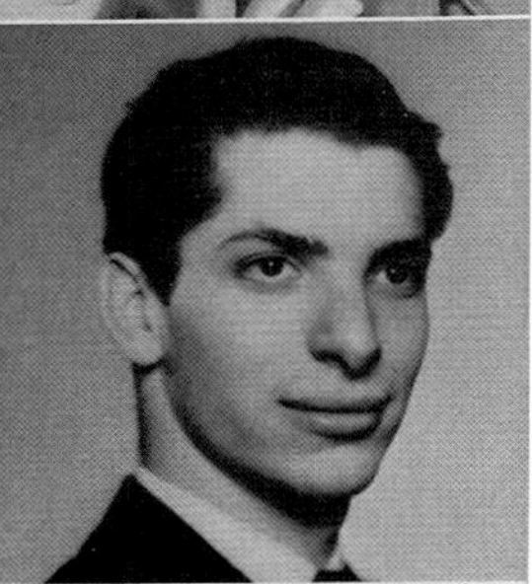

Nació en Charlottesville, estado de Virginia, en 1916. Fué alumno de la Escuela de Drama de la universidad de Yale donde se especializó en decorados para el teatro y en vestuario. En sus trabajos para los teatros de verano llegó a conocer a la compañía del *American Ballet* en una de sus jiras. Desde entonces ha hecho los diseños para *Pastorela*, *Charade* y *La Vida del Caballo* para la Feria Mundial de Nueva York en 1940. Es pintor, decorador de escaparates y autor de los decorados para la radio televisión.

Jared French

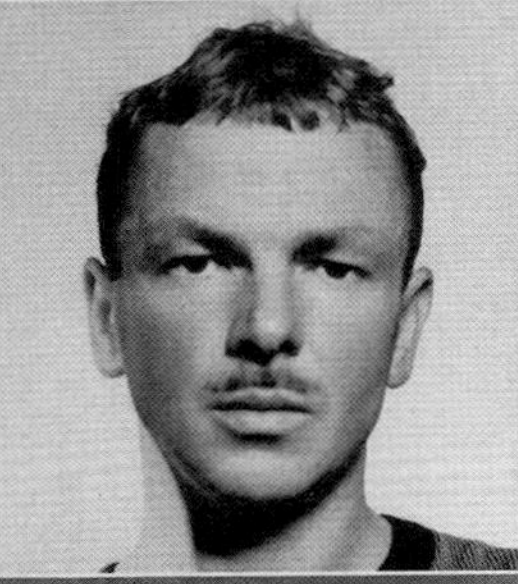

Nació en Nueva York en 1907. Estudió en la universidad de Amherst y no tenía propósito alguno de ser pintor hasta que después de haber vivido dos años en España y en la isla de Mallorca (España), se dedicó a aprender dibujo. Se ha hecho un artista conocido por sus pinturas murales, siendo notable entre éstas, su decoración de la casa de correos de Richmond, Virginia, que consiste en la representación pictórica de un poema de Walt Whitman sobre el tema de la guerra civil norteamericana. Pinta con preferencia la figura humana.

Tom Lee

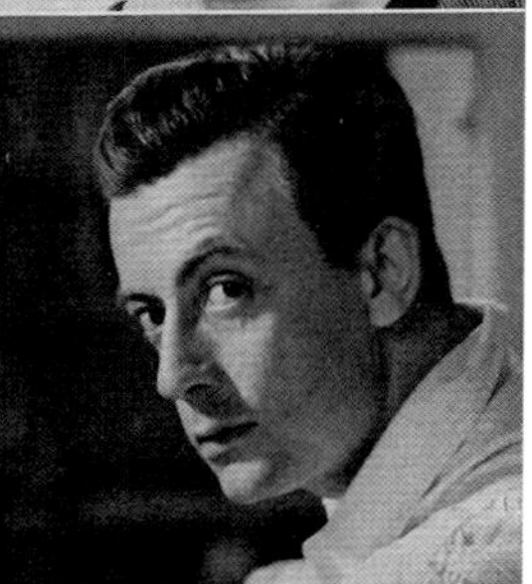

Nació en 1909 en Costa Rica, donde su padre era cónsul de los Estados Unidos. Pasó cinco años en Porto Alegre y Rio Grande do Sul. Hizo sus estudios en Portugal y en Inglaterra continuándolos en Nueva York en la Academia Nacional de Dibujo. Sus trabajos han sido de carácter comercial —anuncios para propaganda de películas y cubiertas de libros. Sus decorados para escaparates de tienda son de una gran imaginación y de un carácter tan llamativo que le han dado a conocer desde Australia hasta la Quinta Avenida de Nueva York.

Pavel Tchelitchev

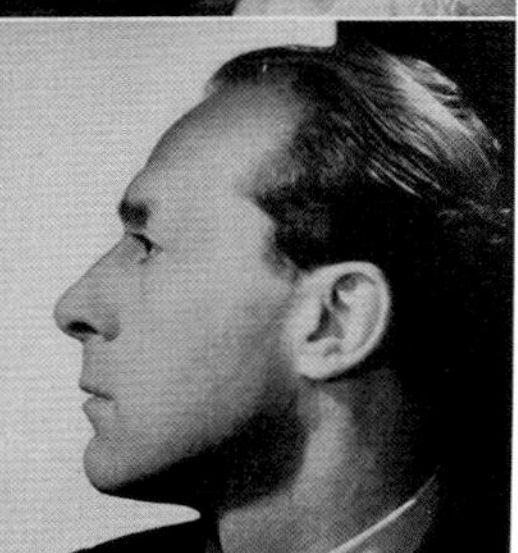

Pintor del ballet *Alma Errante*, es de origen ruso. Salió de su país natal en 1921 y dió a conocer sus obras en los teatros de Turquía, Berlín, París y Londres. En Norteamérica ha logrado fama con una composición de gran tamaño, *Phenomena*, síntesis del mundo actual. Creó el ballet *Oda* para Serge Diaghilev, *Nobilísima Visione* para el *Ballet de Monte Carlo* y el *Orfeo* de Gluck para la Metropolitan Opera de Nueva York.

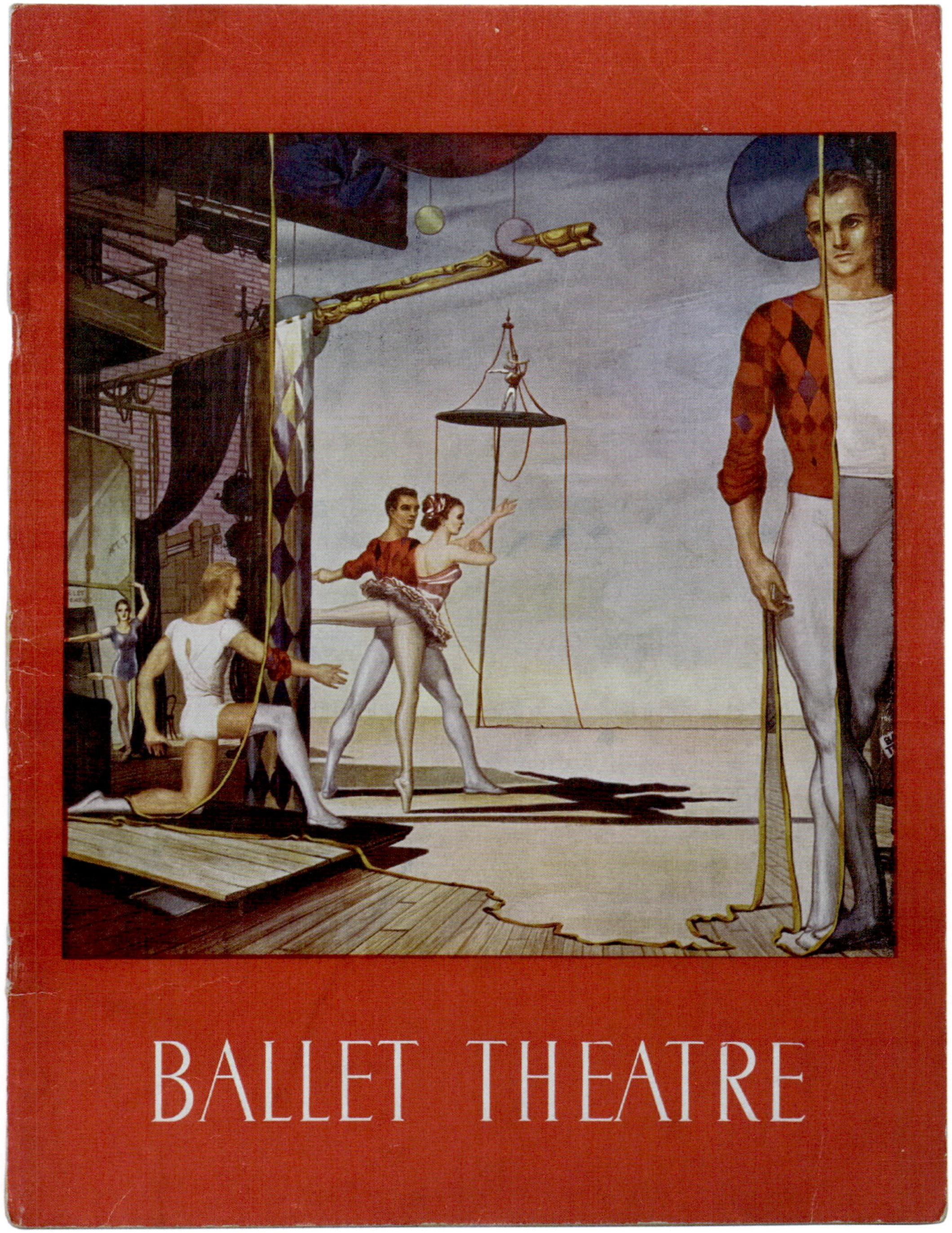

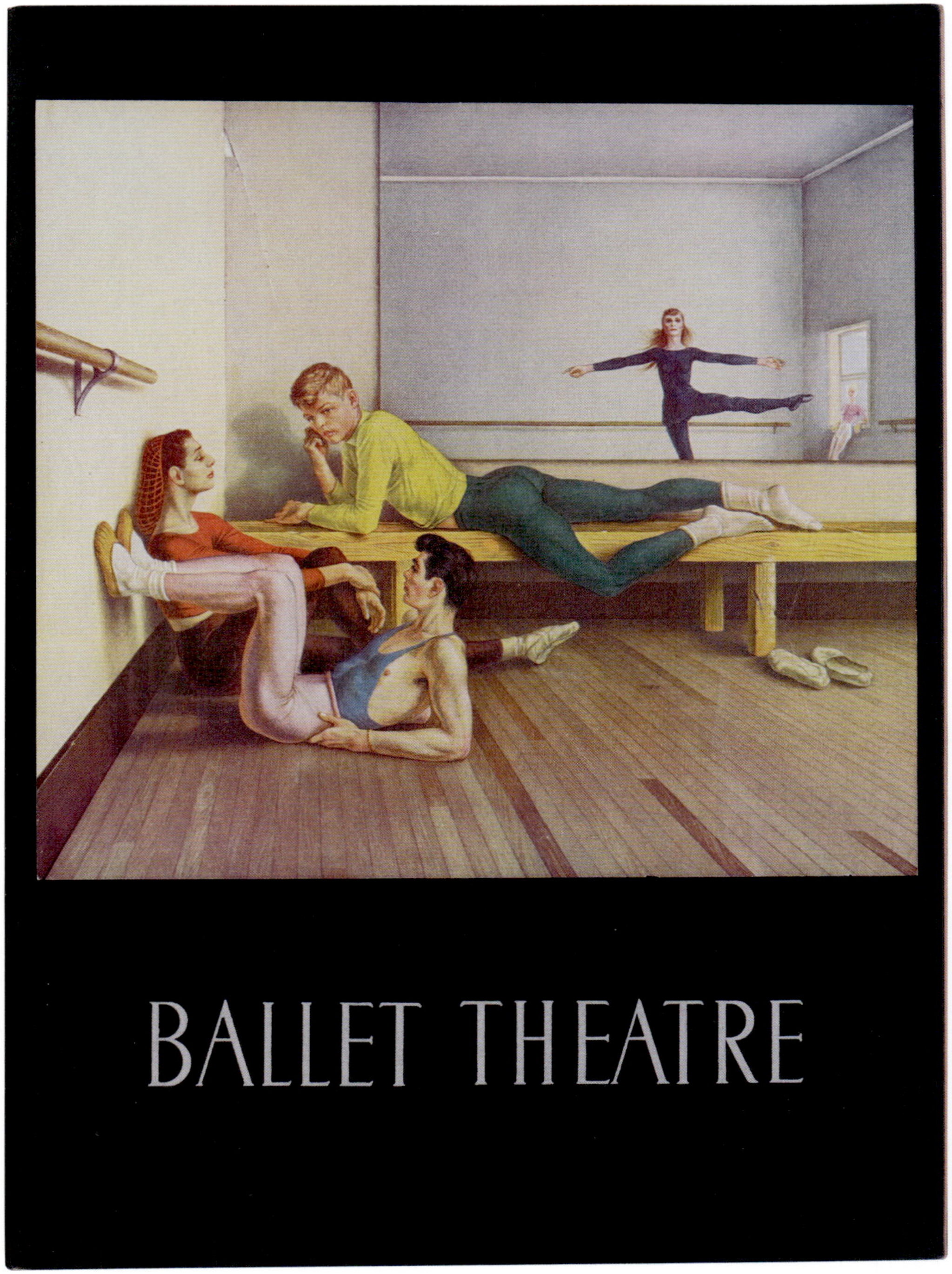

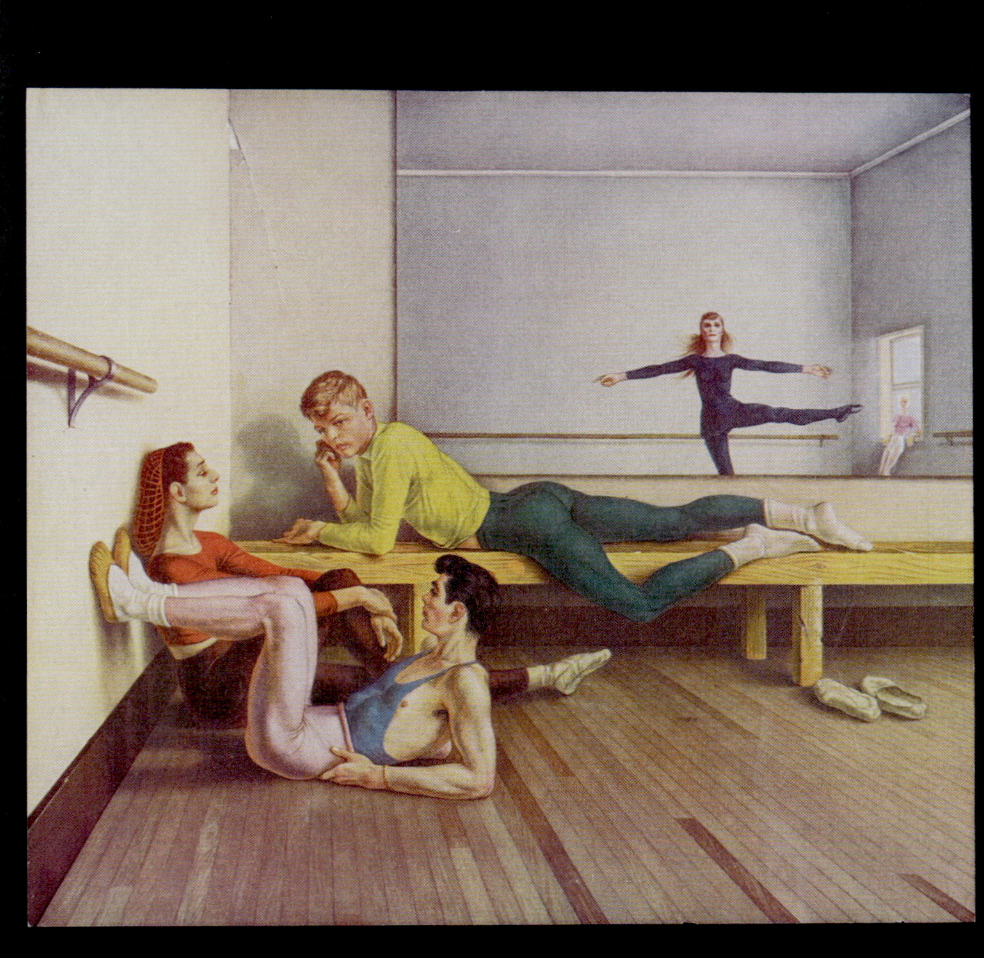
BALLET THEATRE

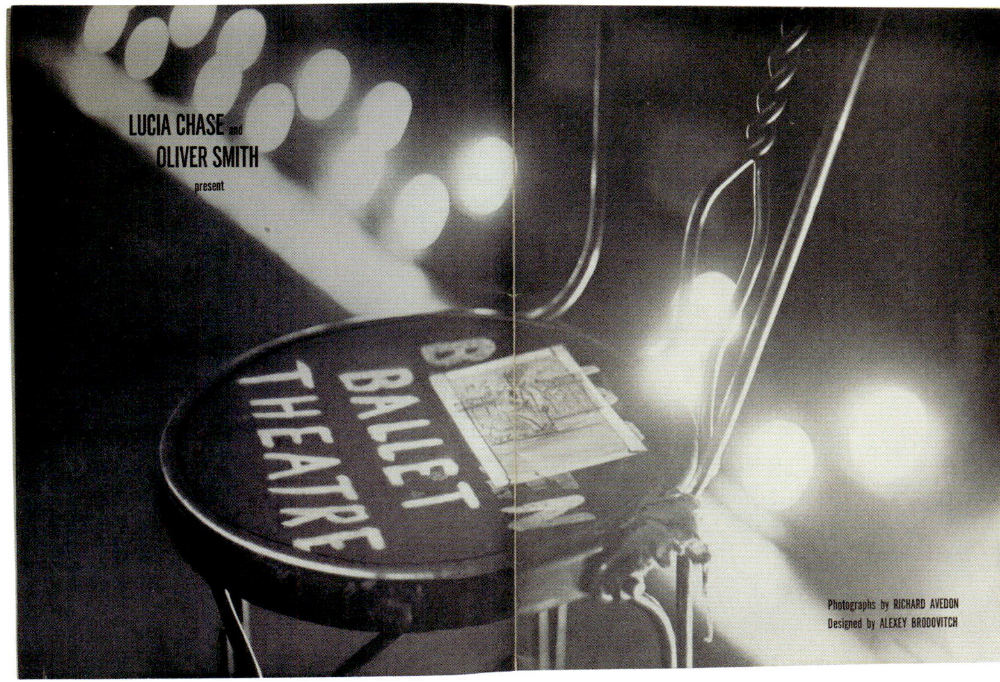

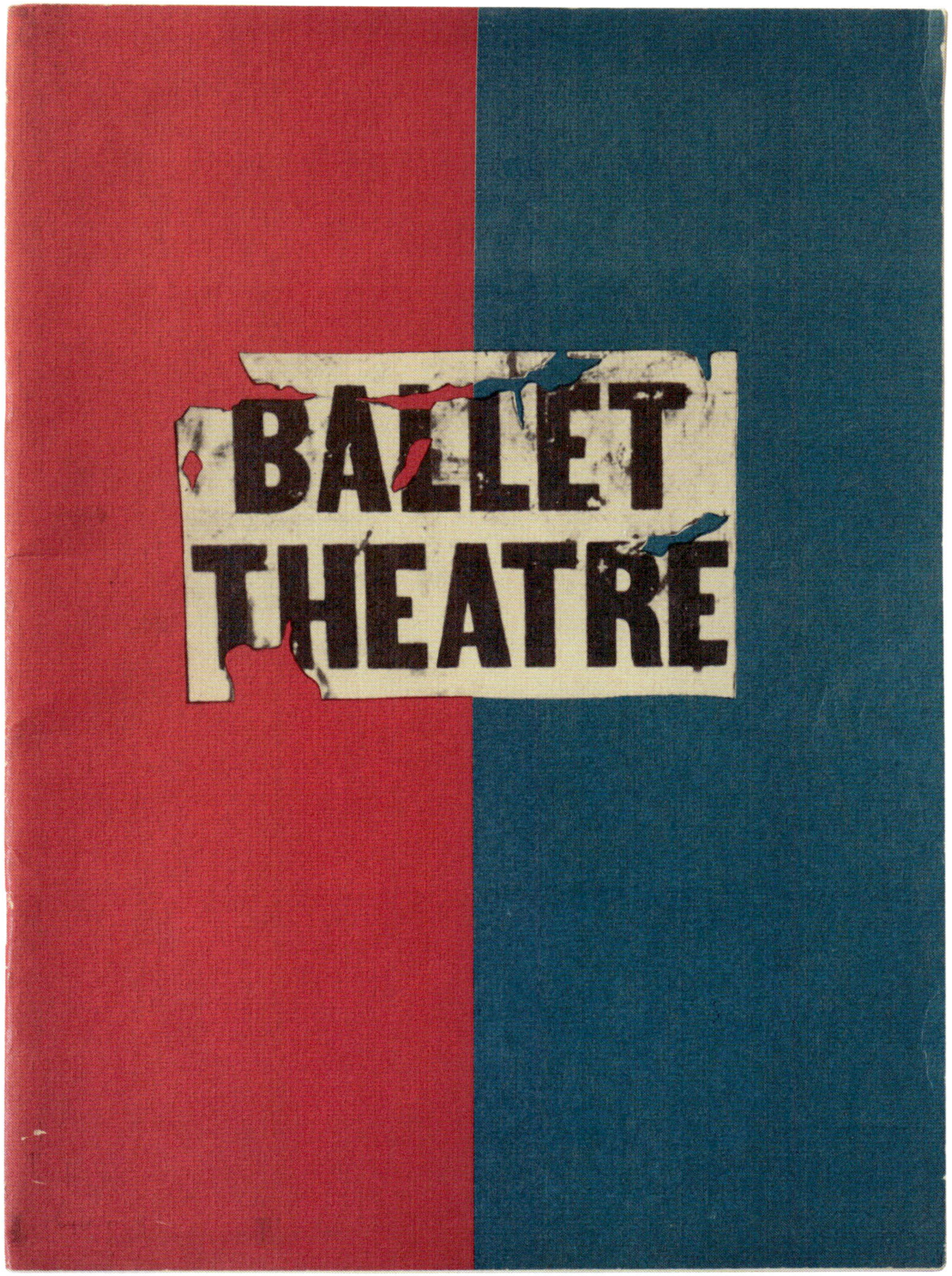

Opposite, left: Cover of
Ballet Theatre's 1953
souvenir program, with
art by John Lear

Opposite, right: Cover
of the souvenir program
for Ballet Theatre's
1951–52 season, with
art by Paul Cadmus

Above: Interior spread
from Ballet Theatre's 1949
program, with photograph
by Richard Avedon

Right: Cover of Ballet
Theatre's 1949 program,
designed by Alexei
Brodovitch

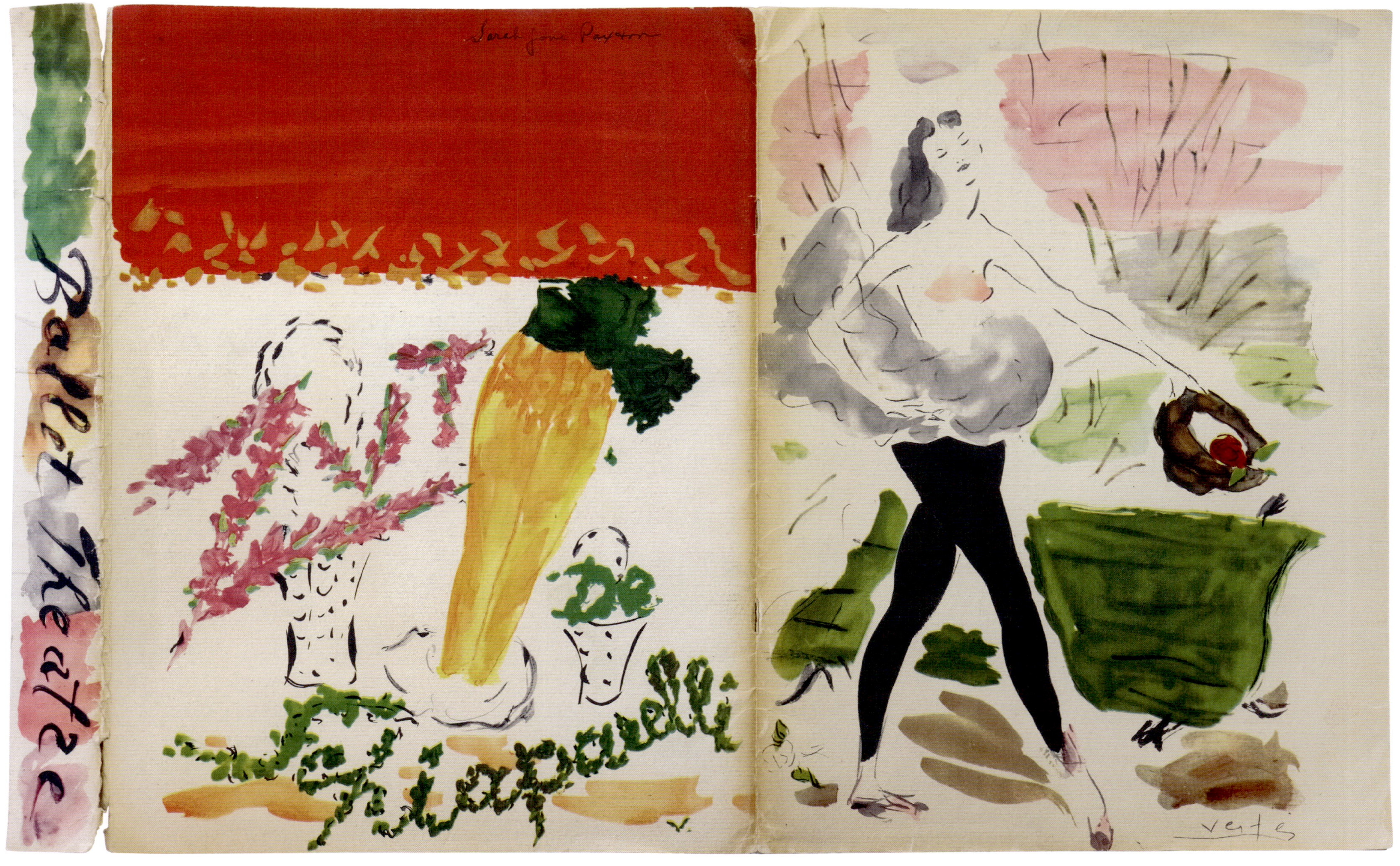
Sarah Jane Paxton
Ballet Theatre
Schiaparelli
vertes

Interior spread from
Ballet Russe de Monte
Carlo's 1946–47 program,
featuring costume designs
by Isamu Noguchi and
Henri Matisse

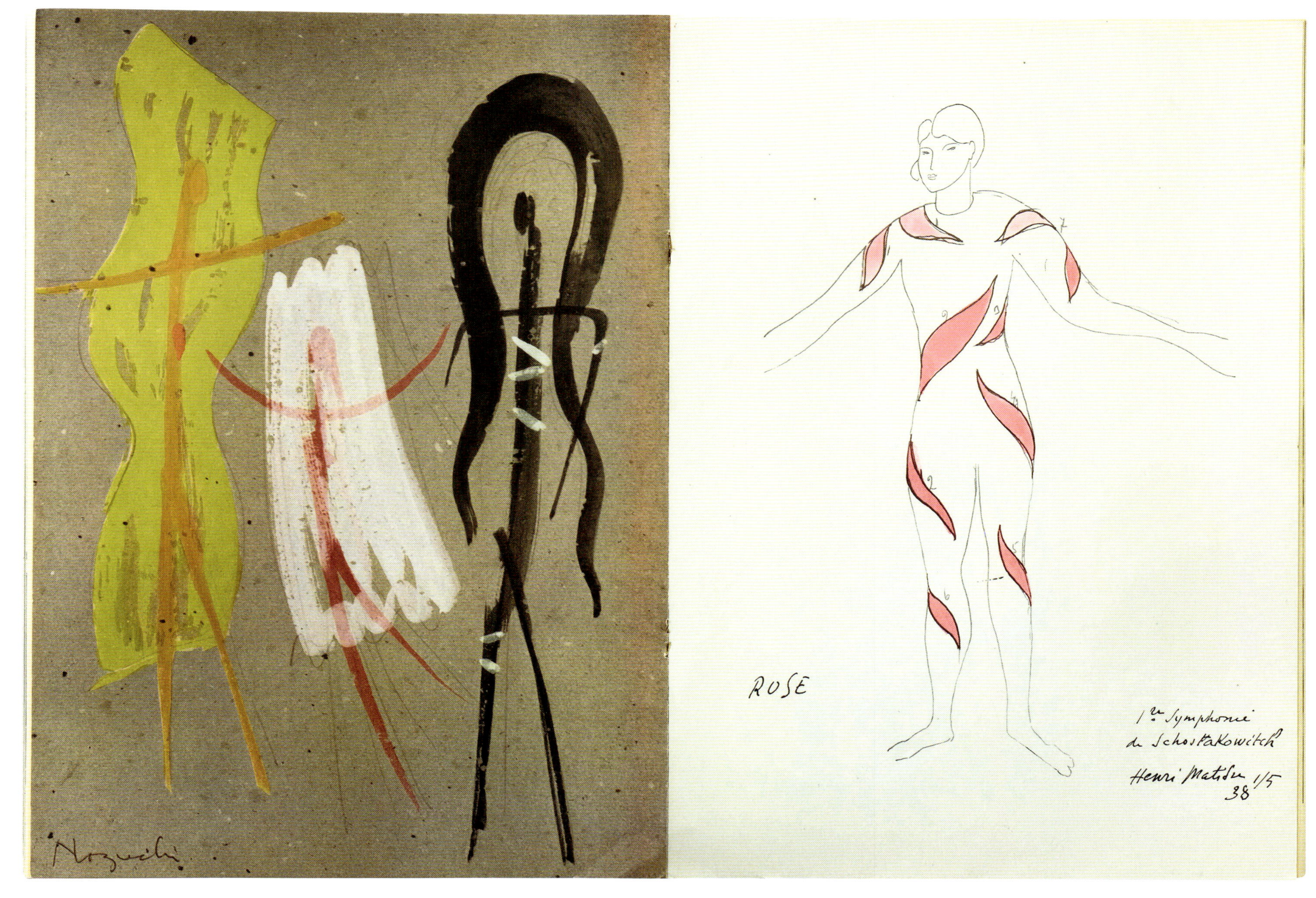

116

This parodic array of nominees for a Hall of Fame in *Vanity Fair* includes an image from a series of portraits of dancer-choreographer Bronislava Nijinska by Man Ray. Avant-garde artist Mikhail Larionov painted Nijinska's face makeup for her role as Kikimora in the ballet *Contes Russes*. The same page features two subversive *poupée* (puppet) portraits of Henri Matisse and Pablo Picasso by artist Marie Vassilieff.

In his scenario *A Room in a Sea-Shell*, commissioned for the pages of *Vogue*, Pavel Tchelitchew stages a "painting for the camera" (termed *photo-painting* by the magazine), a new expressive form based on an artist's sketch that might be described as falling somewhere between a fashion shoot and a proto-Happening. The artist drew his materials and effects from the same arsenal as for his designs for the stage; diaphanous fabrics and celestial lighting emphasize such qualities as transparency, weightlessness, arrested movement, and interiority.

Page from the November 1922 issue of *Vanity Fair*, with portrait of Bronislava Nijinska by Man Ray (bottom center)

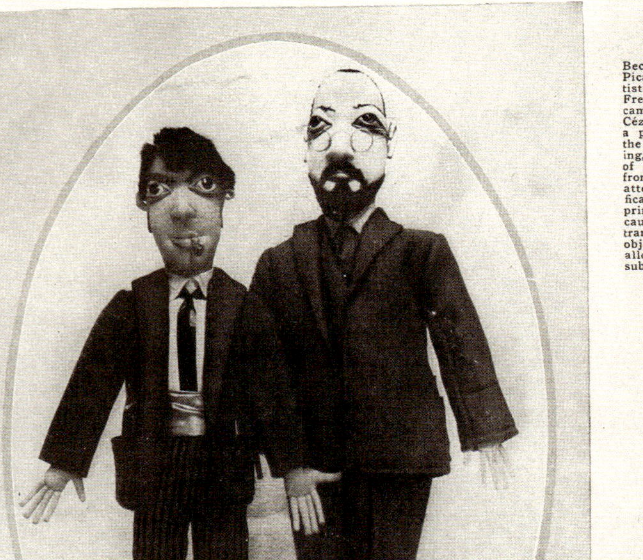

PABLO PICASSO

Because he is the creator of Cubism; because he has been called the most inventive of modern artists and has excelled, not only as a Cubist, but as an experimenter with and master of half a dozen other artistic methods; because he is a great aesthetic theorist as well as a creator and, though a Spaniard, the undisputed intellectual leader of contemporary French art; and, finally, because he has sat for his portrait to Mlle. Marie Vassilieff, the incomparable maker of puppets

HENRI MATISSE

Because he has a place with Picasso and Derain in the artistic trinity which dominates French art; because he early came under the influence of Cézanne and with Cézanne as a point of departure launched the new French school of painting, because he was thus one of the first to depart entirely from literal representation and attempt to restore the simplifications and distortions of primitive art and finally, because, having simplified and transformed so many persons and objects himself, he has finally allowed Mlle. Vassilieff to subject him to the same ordeal

AMY LOWELL

Because she was one of the earliest leaders in the new awakening of an interest in poetry in America; because, though commonly supposed to be the prophet of revolutionary artistic doctrines, she is really only a belated theorist of the epoch of Leconte de Lisle, who believed, like her, that poetry should exclude emotion and confine itself to objective description; because she smokes excellent cigars; and finally, because she presents so genial an appearance in this wood carving by John Held

LA NIJINSKA

Because she is a sister of the great Nijinski; because, like Fokine a decade ago, she is the chief choreographer of the Diaghilev ballet and directed brilliantly the work of Stravinsky at the Paris Opera last season; because she contemplates coming soon to America and opening a school of dancing; and finally, because she has not been afraid to put on this horrifying make-up to appear in Paris in a modernisitic ballet designed by Larionov

HENRY FORD

Because he has changed the whole rural life of America by lowering the price of motor cars; because in his assertions that he would not give ten cents for all the works of art ever created, that "history is bunk", and that the Jews have banded together in a sinister conspiracy to control the United States, he has made some of the most ludicrous statements ever conceived by a public man; because the benevolent paternalism prevailing in his factories is enormously applauded and admired by everyone except his employees; and, finally, because this bust of him by John Held throws a new light on his character

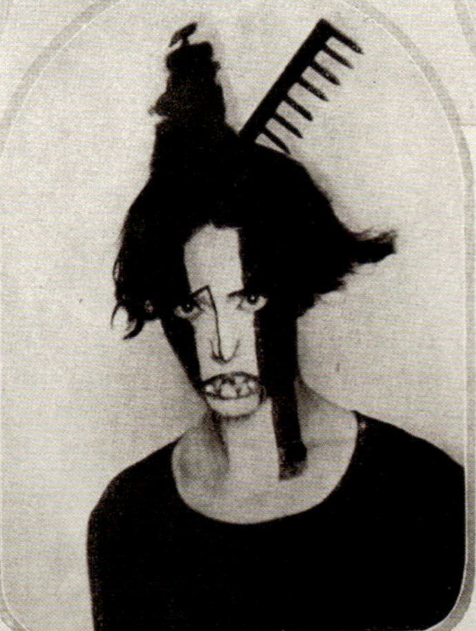

We Nominate for the Hall of Fame:

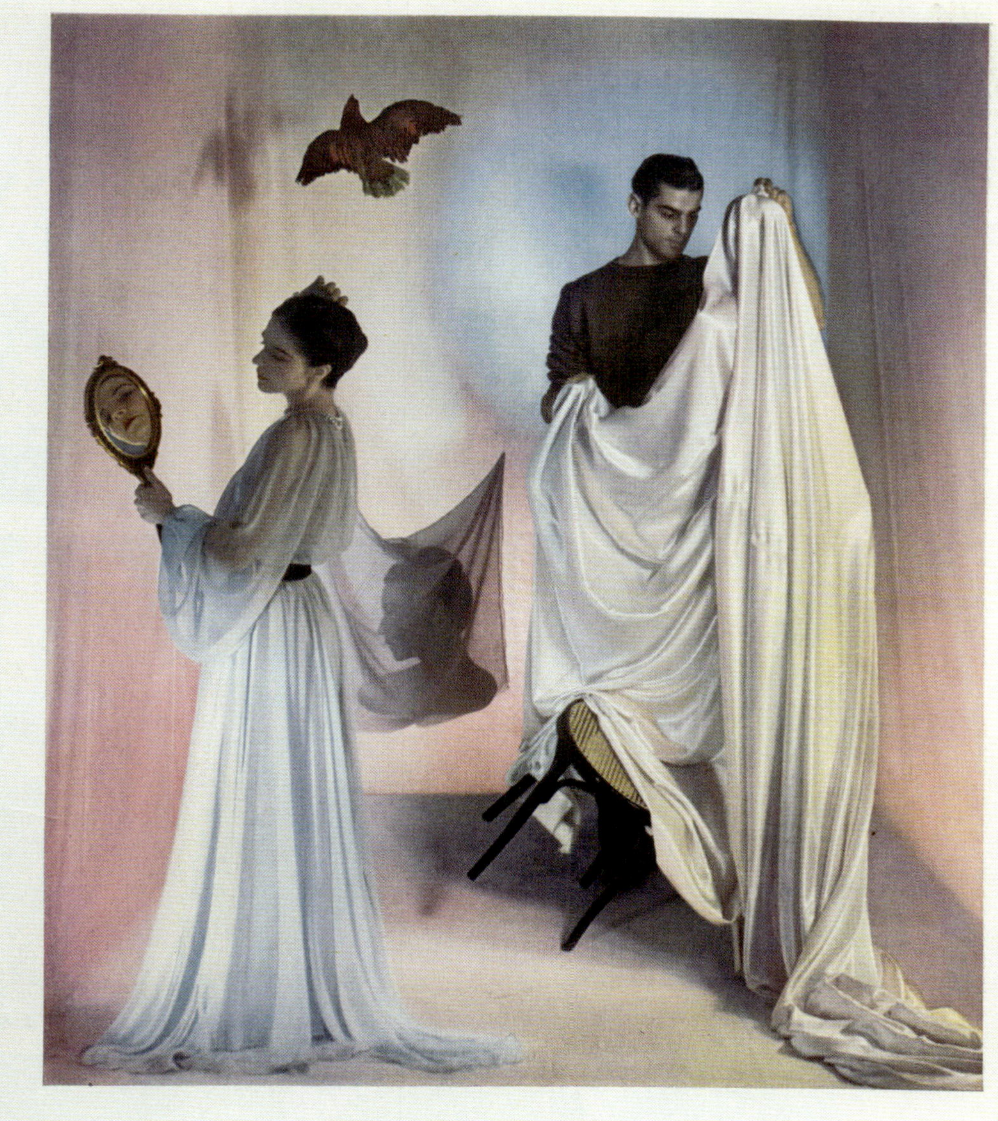

Page from the March
1937 issue of *Vogue*, with
A Room in a Sea-Shell,
a "photo-painting," by
Pavel Tchelitchew

During the 1940s, *Vogue* magazine commissioned renowned avant-garde artists to make works for the magazine's covers, bringing them to wide visibility—literally, to newsstands on every urban street corner. The magazine described them as follows:

COVER: Vogue's spring cover is painted by Eugene Berman, Russian-born romantic painter, who has designed the costumes and décor for many ballets, the greatest of which, perhaps, is "Romeo and Juliet." Here he paints a little figure with a sweet neck, and sprinkles her with a collage of sentimentalia: pink paper lace and blue birds; has Spring turn [sic] her back on this long winter, and face a rosier set of tomorrows.
(*Vogue*, April 1, 1945, cover by Eugene Berman)

With the unerring instinct of the true artist, Pavel Tchelitchew has made the intangible spirit of New York a tangible design on the cover of this issue. Through the enchanted forest of sky-scrapers, pricked with light in the early dusk, walks a woman, heroically graceful, inexorably forward-moving. The long, voluminous cape she wraps around her echoes, in the glitter of its sequins, the galaxy of city lights against the sky-line.
(*Vogue*, April 1, 1935, cover by Pavel Tchelitchew)

Cover of the April 1, 1945, issue of *Vogue*, by Eugene Berman

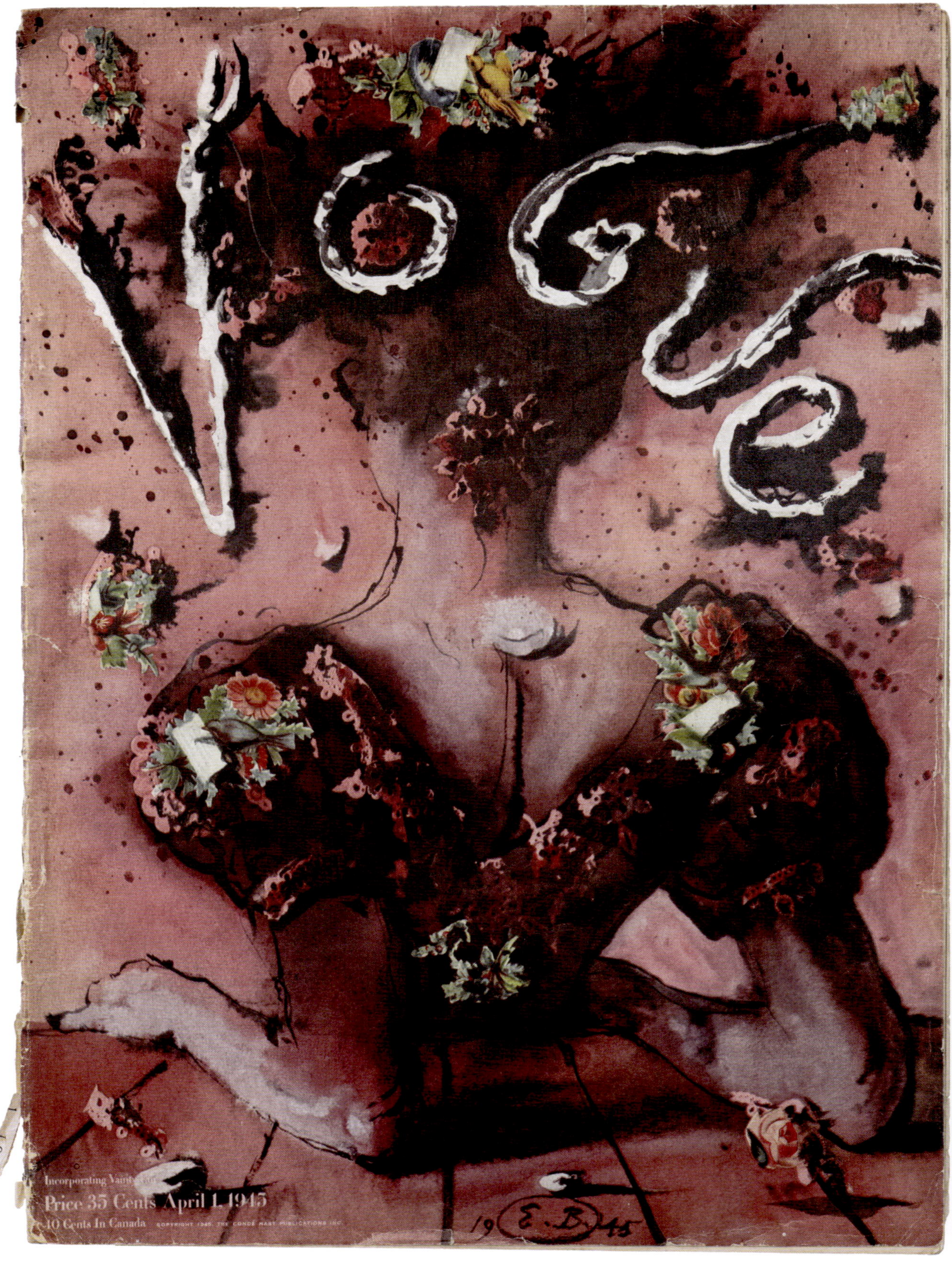

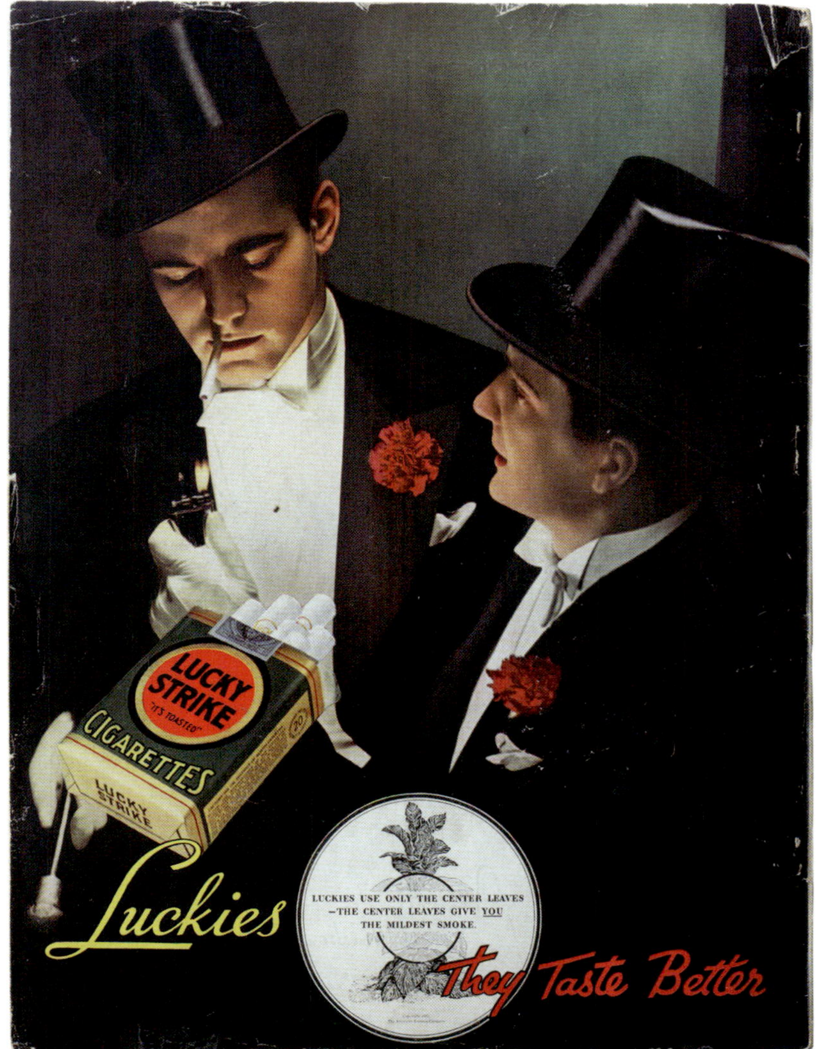

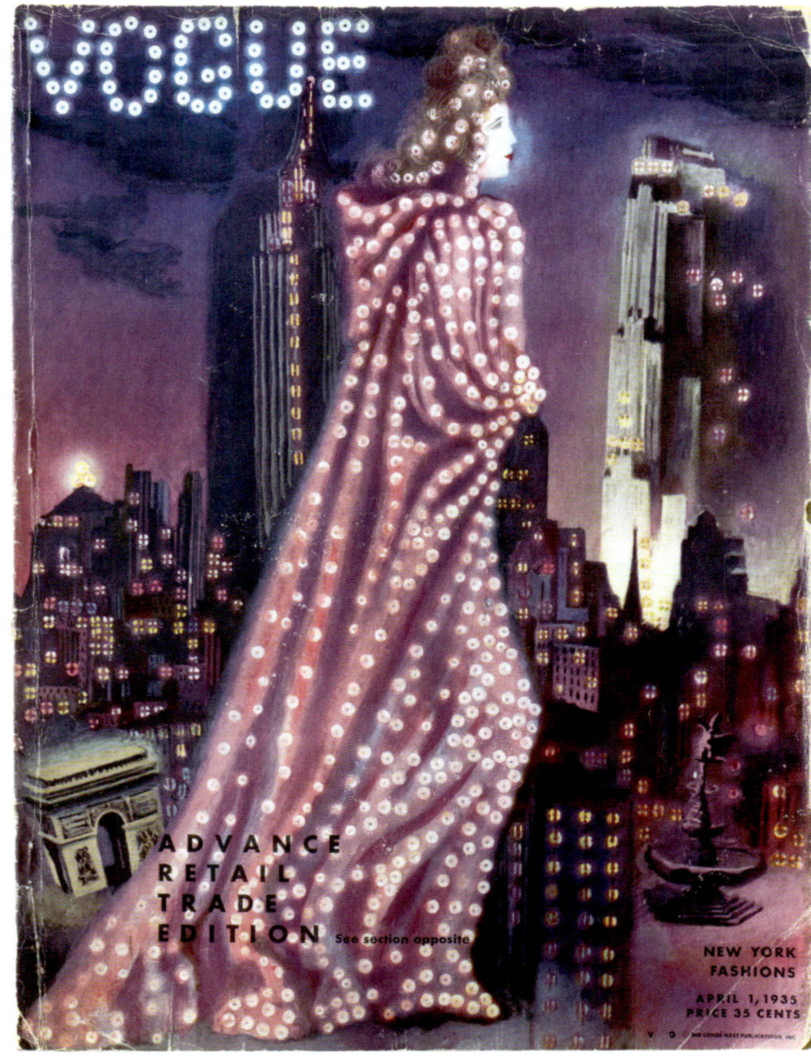

Back and front covers of
the April 1, 1935, issue
of *Vogue*, front cover by
Pavel Tchelitchew

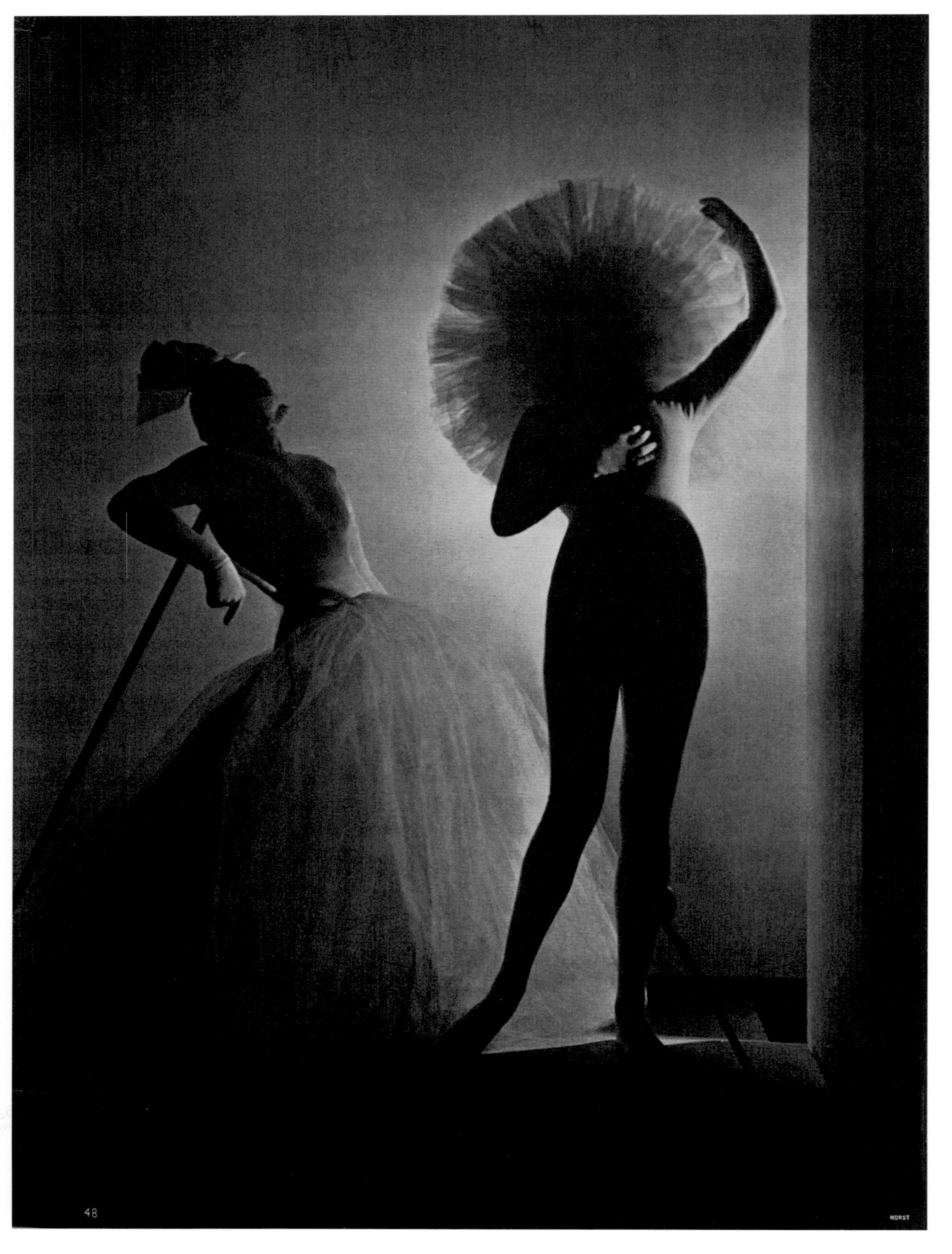

Models in Salvador Dalí–designed costumes fabricated by Chanel for the ballet *Bacchanale* (1931), choreographed by Léonide Massine, in the October 15, 1939, issue of *Vogue*, photograph by Horst P. Horst

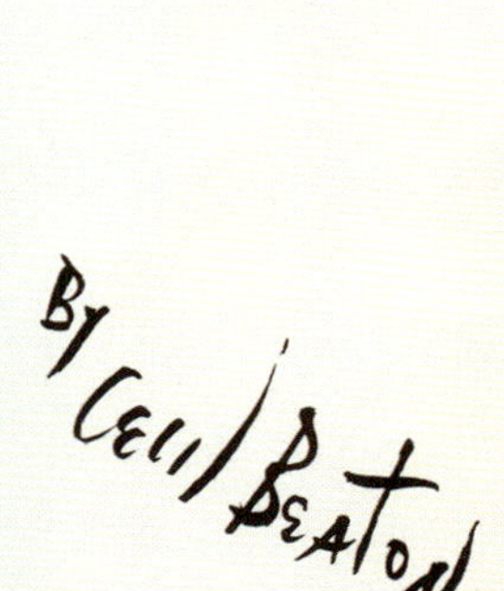

WHY do you go to a fancy-dress party as Pierrot and Pierrette? Why do you go as Charlie Chaplin? As a comic clergyman? Why do you go as a nun in the bed-sheets? Why do you put make-up on only underneath the eyes? Why do you wear a shapeless white cotton wig? Your own hair, powdered and set, is infinitely more becoming and authentically eighteenth century.

"What about putting your head into a bag of gold net? What about pinning roses from your great-aunt's hat all over your cherry-coloured velvet evening jacket, and cutting white kid leggings above the knees, to go as a garden boy? What about taking all your coloured handkerchiefs and bandaging your entire body? Or, with a necklace of thread spools, going as a *gitane?* What about hanging a gold frame around your shoulders and calling yourself a portrait? What about taking last year's tulle ball dress and singeing it? (Bérard introduced burnt ballerinas into the last act of the 'Symphonie Fantastique.')"

Fancy-dress fashions are ever-changing. To-day, at no cost must the costume cost much. It is embarrassing to appear in anything elaborate. To appear effective as the result of a last-minute brain-wave is the great achievement, for the slight and unpretentious gesture is necessary. Beggars in rags, sweepers with wicker baskets and birch brooms, window-glaziers who carry on their backs large sheets of plate glass in a wire frame (thick mica will do for the glass), chimney-sweeps (they bring luck), mechanics in overalls, and millers with neck, hair, and lashes covered with flour are fashionable to-day. Catherine of Russia and the Pompadour, in all seriousness, are unpardonable.

Mrs. Mencken has monopolized the Queen of Sheba, and a former Mrs. Hutton is unsurpassable as Marie Antoinette, so that now an effective grandeur can only be legitimately achieved with every-day utensils, and materials being used for purposes for which they were not meant. Steel wool pot-cleaners, egg-beaters, egg-separators, dish-cloths, tin moulds, and patent hangers all make excellent costume trimming. Even Queen Elizabeth is permissible if her farthingale is made of cane matting, her crinoline of the stuff that is hung up around the shower, and her jewellery of shells and cork covered with tinsel paper.

This is not perversity. An effect is created only by the unexpected and provocative. Anybody who can afford it, can hie himself to a hire shop, and at great expense in proportion to the effect which it will create, acquire still another fancy-dress costume. By taking a tour throughout the variegated counters of any big store, with fancy dress written on the mind and five dollars in the pocket, it is possible to find innumerable materials that can be misused with effect. The successful costumes have frequently been the result of an idea rather than the handiwork of a hundred embroiderers. (Continued on page 116)

By Cecil Beaton.

Interior spread from the article "Suggestions for Fancy Dress," in the December 15, 1937, issue of *Vogue*, with photograph of Charles Henri Ford in Salvador Dalí–designed costume and illustration by Cecil Beaton

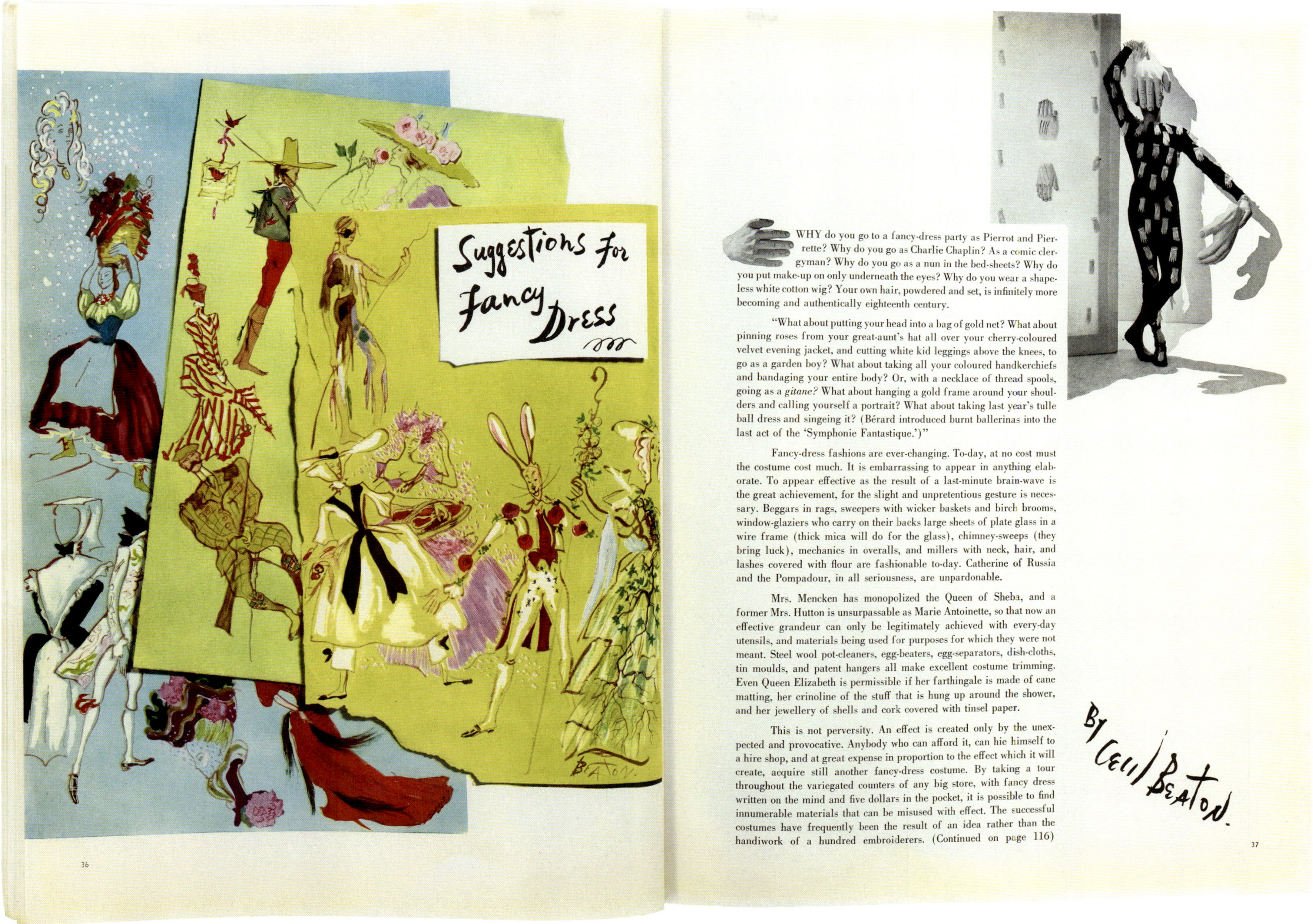

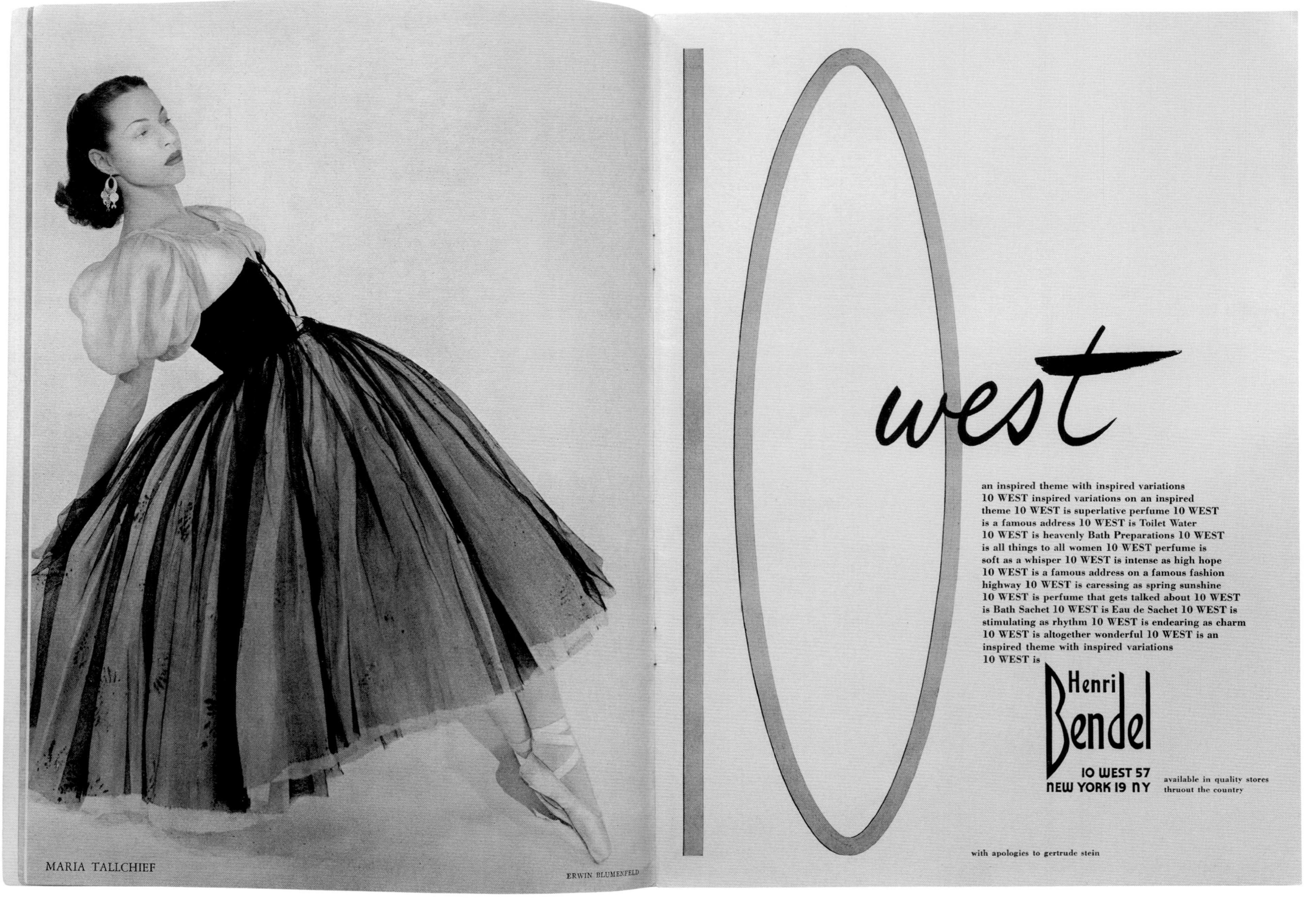

MARIA TALLCHIEF
ERWIN BLUMENFELD
west
an inspired theme with inspired variations
10 WEST inspired variations on an inspired
theme 10 WEST is superlative perfume 10 WEST
is a famous address 10 WEST is Toilet Water
10 WEST is heavenly Bath Preparations 10 WEST
is all things to all women 10 WEST perfume is
soft as a whisper 10 WEST is intense as high hope
10 WEST is a famous address on a famous fashion
highway 10 WEST is caressing as spring sunshine
10 WEST is perfume that gets talked about 10 WEST
is Bath Sachet 10 WEST is Eau de Sachet 10 WEST is
stimulating as rhythm 10 WEST is endearing as charm
10 WEST is altogether wonderful 10 WEST is an
inspired theme with inspired variations
10 WEST is
Henri
Bendel
10 WEST 57
NEW YORK 19 N Y
available in quality stores
thruout the country
with apologies to gertrude stein

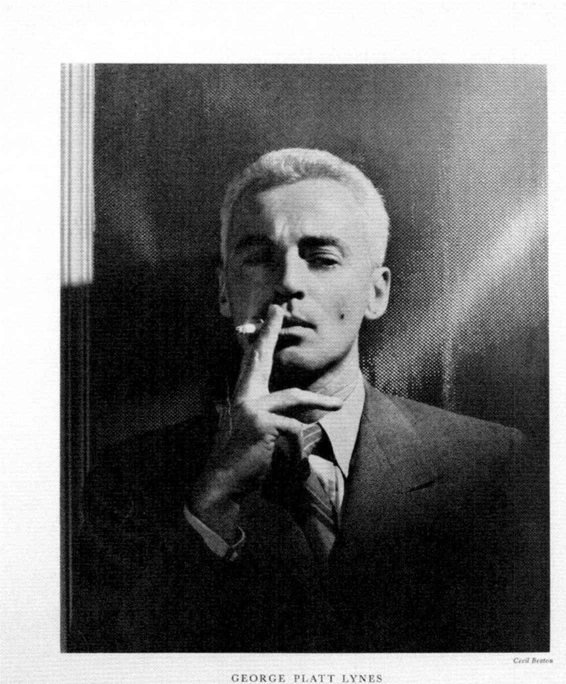

Opposite: Interior spread from Ballet Russe de Monte Carlo's 1946–47 program, featuring a portrait of Maria Tallchief by Erwin Blumenfeld and an advertisement for Henri Bendel, presumably by George Platt Lynes

Right, top: Portrait of George Platt Lynes by Cecil Beaton, reproduced in New York City Ballet's commemorative album of photographs by George Platt Lynes, 1957

Right, bottom: Advertisement for Henri Bendel in Ballet Russe de Monte Carlo's 1945–46 souvenir program, with photograph by Cecil Beaton signed by George Platt Lynes

Shuttling between dance and fashion (which frequently intersected with advertising), George Platt Lynes forged his own artistic terrain, inhabiting several worlds at once. In his work as art director and photographer for the print campaigns of the luxury retailer Henri Bendel—which were featured in not only fashion magazines but also ballet programs—Lynes's unmistakable wit comes to the forefront: an exclusively typographic advertisement for Bendel's lightly mocks Gertrude Stein by stylistically ventriloquizing her work. Here, Lynes's insouciance is a veiled homage to his early mentor as much as a flirtation with an astute audience that might pride itself on catching on to his gag. A portrait of an urbane, smoking Lynes taken by Cecil Beaton is inserted into another Bendel's advertisement—the appropriated image is radically cropped; peddling cologne, Lynes has insinuated himself as the advertisement's anonymous object of desire, intoning, "Men, too, may enjoy fine toiletries."

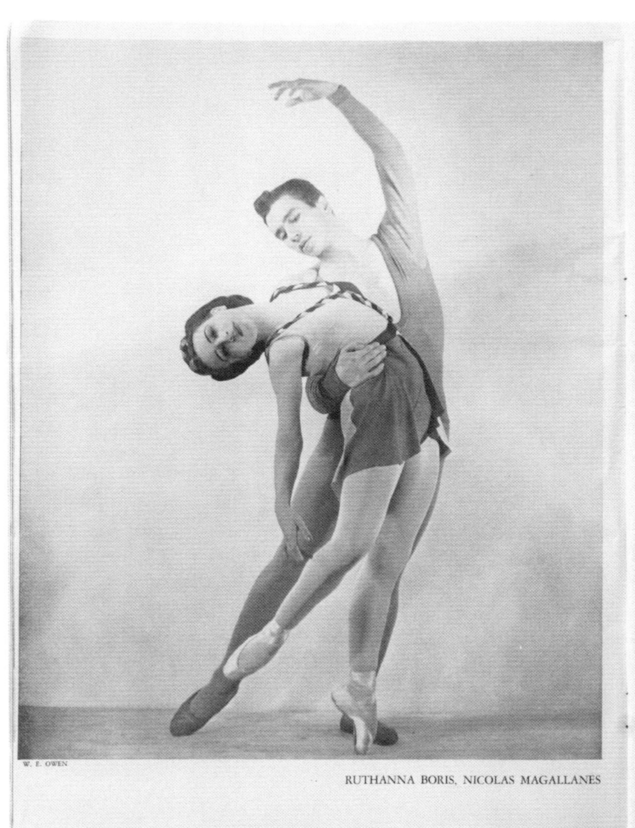

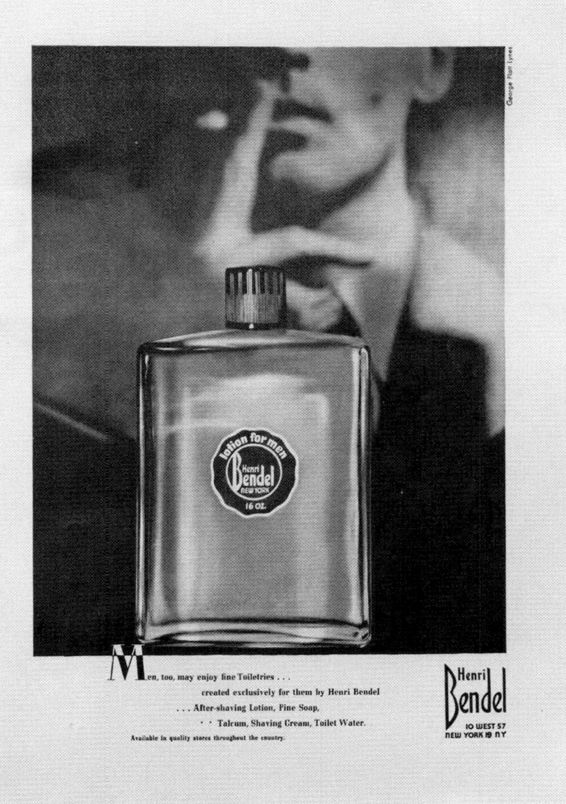

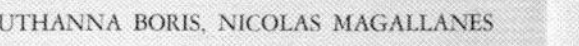

Cover of the first issue of *Bachelor* magazine (April 1937), with Bronzino's portrait of Cosimo I de' Medici (c. 1520)

Opposite: Interior spread from the article "A Portfolio of Bachelors of the Arts," in the April 1937 issue of *Bachelor*, featuring photographs of George Platt Lynes by Cecil Beaton and Jean Cocteau by George Platt Lynes

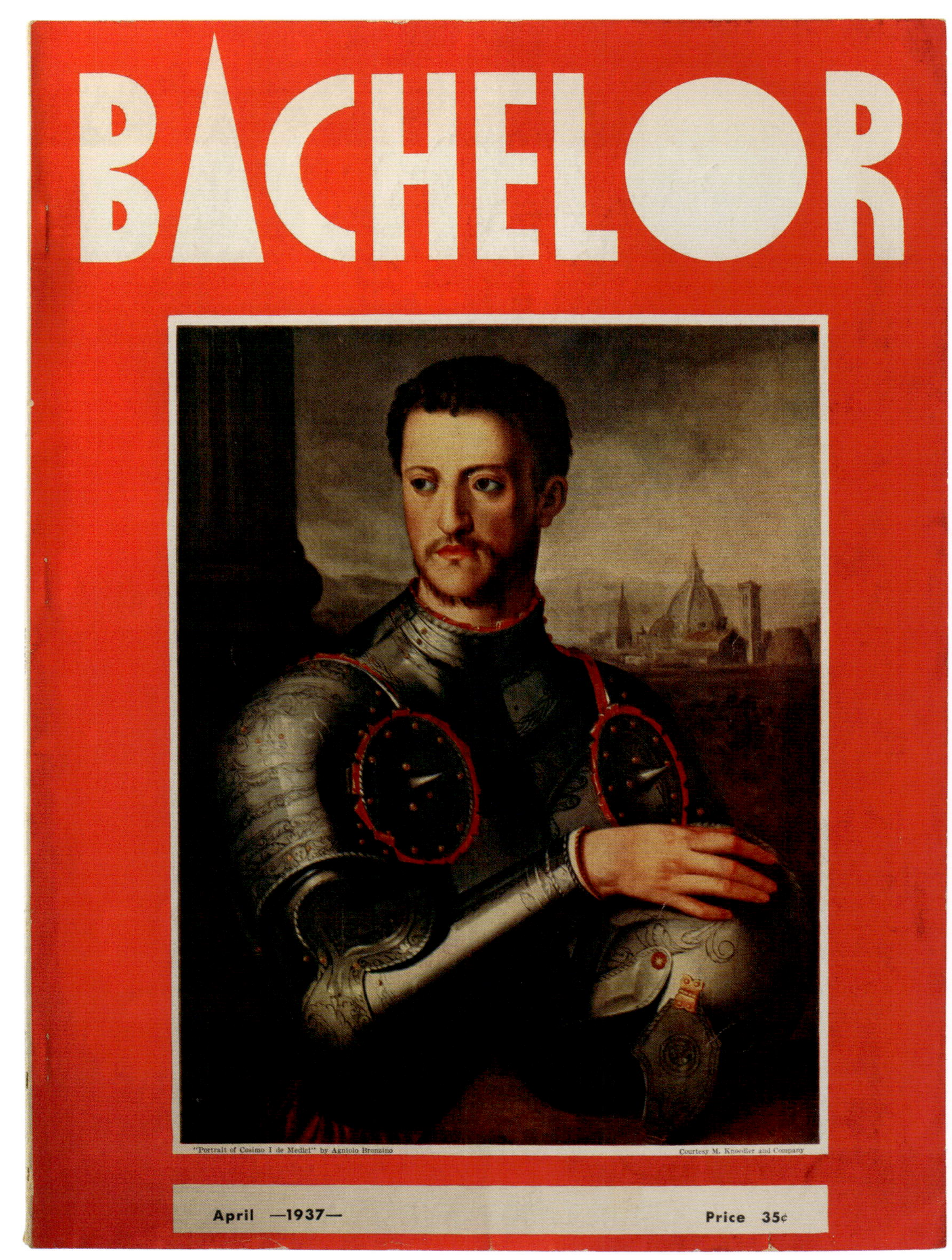

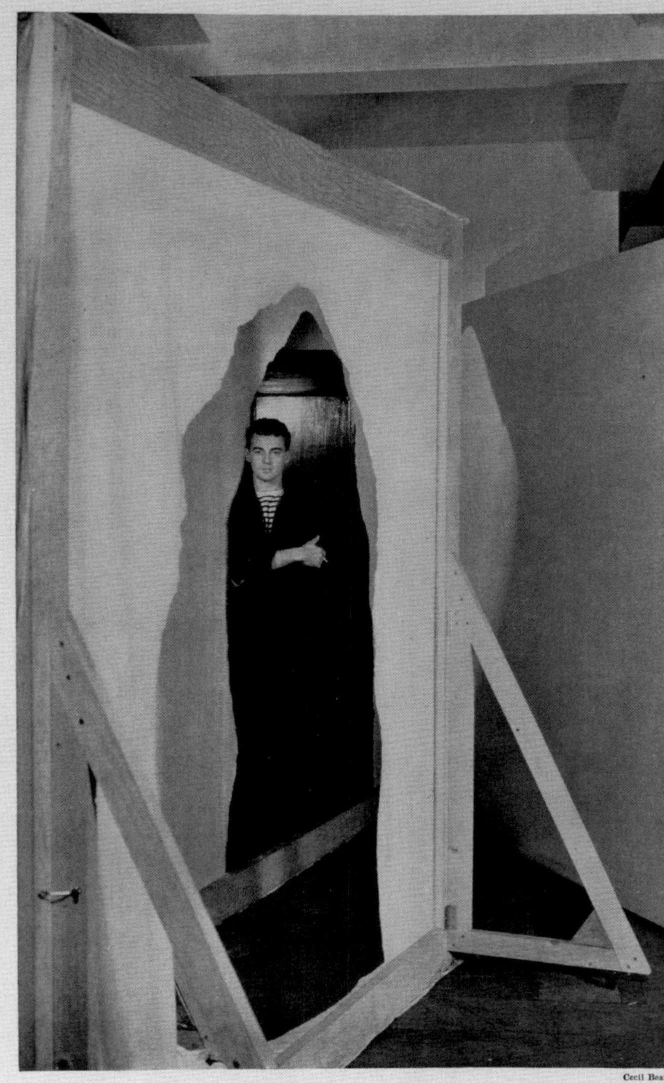

Cecil Beaton

George Platt Lynes

"Fantastic art" this photographer styled his contributions to the recent surrealist exhibition at the Museum of Modern Art. But that is not the summing up of his art. His especial forte is portraiture created through minute study of the sitter's character. By way of diversion he is fond of turning his camera toward the American Ballet. Born in East Orange in 1907, Mr. Lynes left Yale twenty years later to study photography in Paris. He has two hobbies: turning down Hollywood offers and pulling over sweaters—of which he has twenty

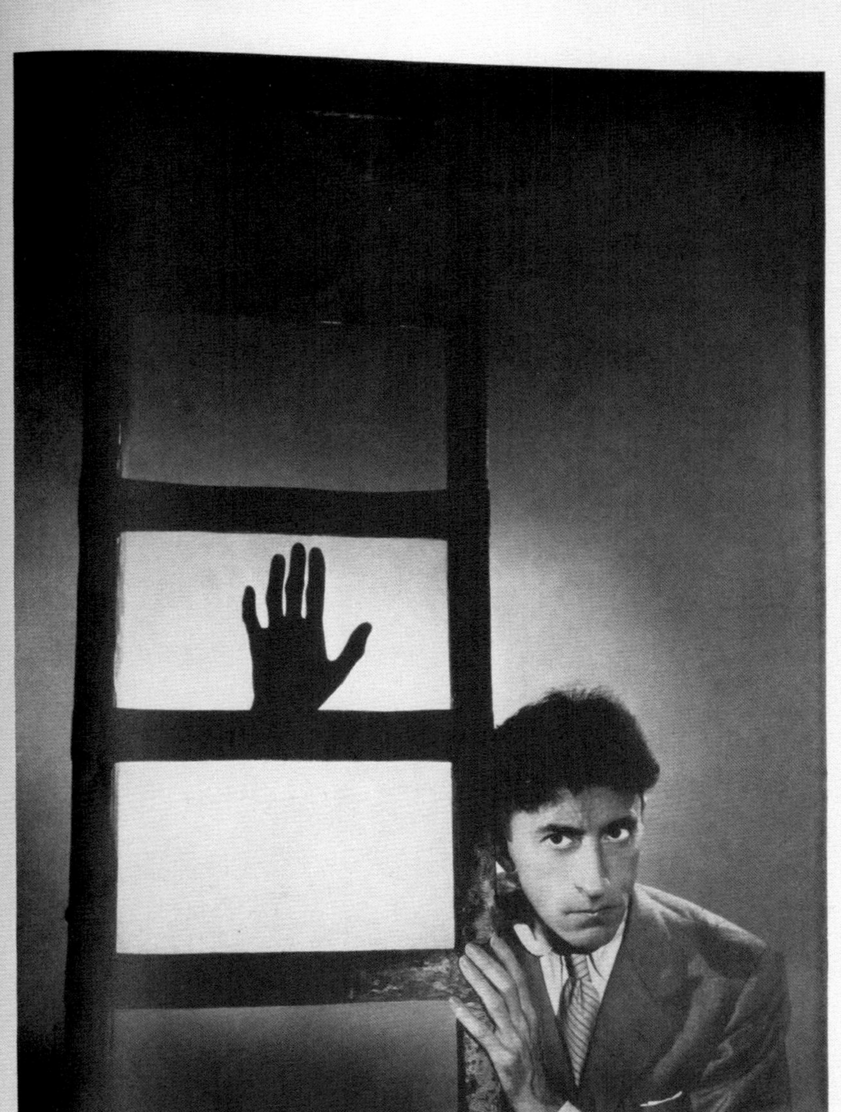

Geo. Platt Lynes

Jean Cocteau

Author of "Enfants Terribles," poet, playwright and artist, he is a patron of the younger French school of writers. An imaginative disciple of pagan pagentry, the decadent and macabre, this urbane bachelor once appeared, so Parisian legend has it, in a photographer's studio to have his picture taken, wearing red, white and black gloves

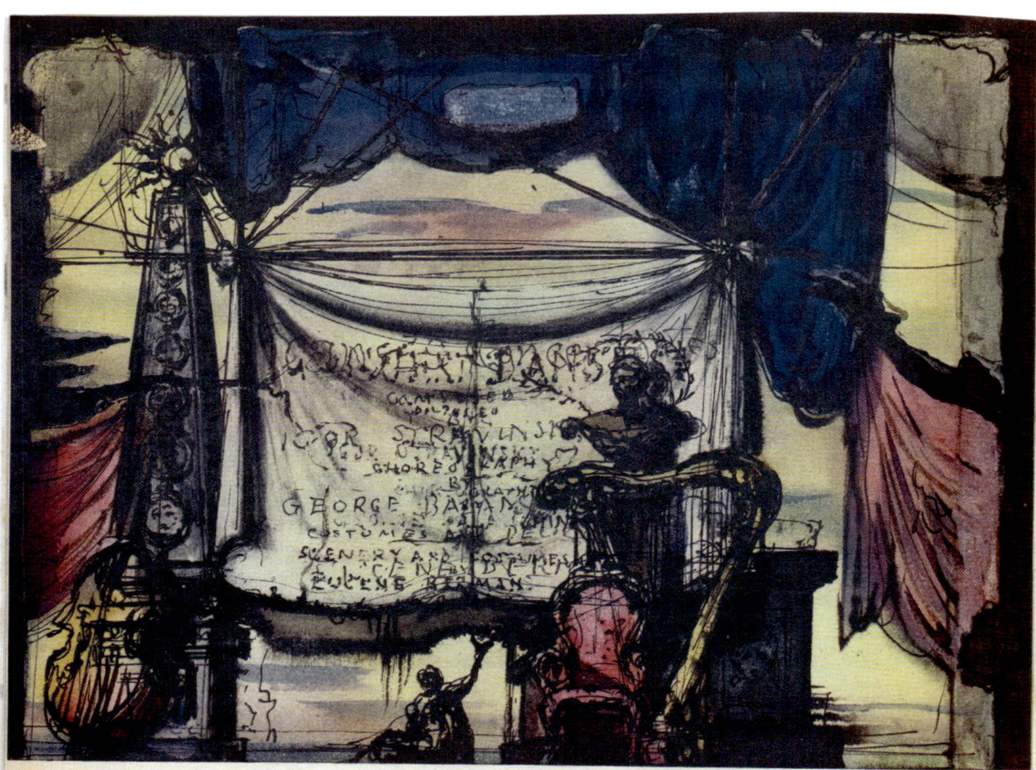

THE BOOM *in Ballet*

The dancers are gifted · the public response is superb · the bookkeeping is provocative

*T*HERE can be little doubt that the most striking artistic development of the past American decade has been the new popular success of ballet. Ten years ago this form of art was the arcane pleasure of a flight of esthetes. Today it is a busy branch of show business, with two main companies, the Ballet Theatre and the Ballet Russe de Monte Carlo, loudly acclaimed on nationwide annual tours of seventy-odd cities apiece. The total audience for these troupes may be estimated at over 1,500,000, and the gross take at $2 million. Moreover, in Broadway musical comedy, most famously in *Oklahoma!*, recent taste has called for ballet numbers rather than the traditional platoons of high kickers. Even Hollywood has been infected; some of the leading ballerinas have been seen along Wilshire Boulevard.

The reason for all this is not far to seek. The most obvious fact is, simply, that a large portion of the U.S. public has been catching up with the white art of Taglioni and Pavlova. The classic ballet, like the classic musical repertory, is always there. It is full of wonders, such as the shapes that float to the haunted oboes of *Swan Lake*. To be sure, like the finest music, it is a good deal of an acquired taste. Some people feel the magic at once. Others require considerable educating as to what they are supposed to see. But learning has been proceeding rapidly in the past decade. A whole new American audience has been discovering the fine art whose diaphanous graces have been rugged enough to withstand every world upheaval since 1700. Aside from the audiences on the road, it is estimated that at least half the ballet's metropolitan public are people who had never seen a pirouette ten years ago.

[*Continued on page 183*]

Ballet Russe's *Danses Concertantes* announces itself with Eugene Berman's subtly elegant curtain (left).

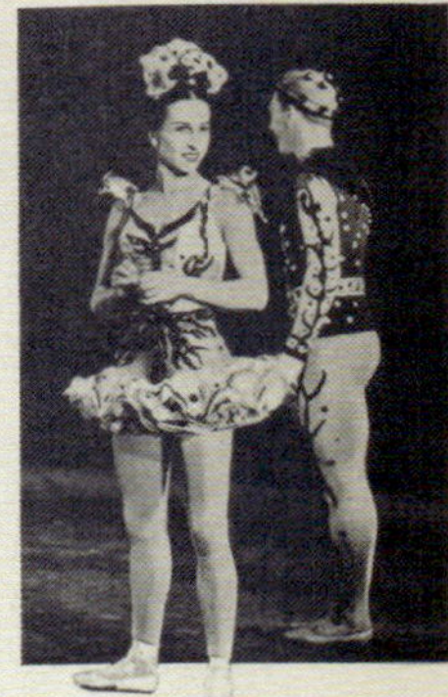

Berman's sharply patterned costumes point up Balanchine's exceedingly syncopated choreography.

The working sketches of many scene and costume designers in the great tradition of ballet are memorable in themselves. In this respect Berman resembles such figures as Bakst, Picasso, and Matisse.

Berman's *Servante de Mlle. Jourdain* in *Le Bourgeois Gentilhomme*.

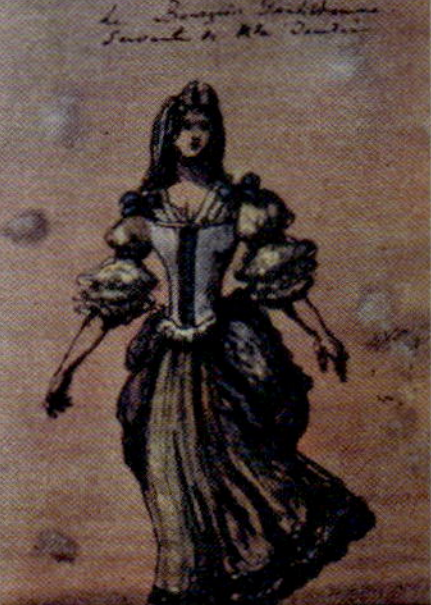

Cleonte's costume from the same Balanchine—Richard Strauss ballet.

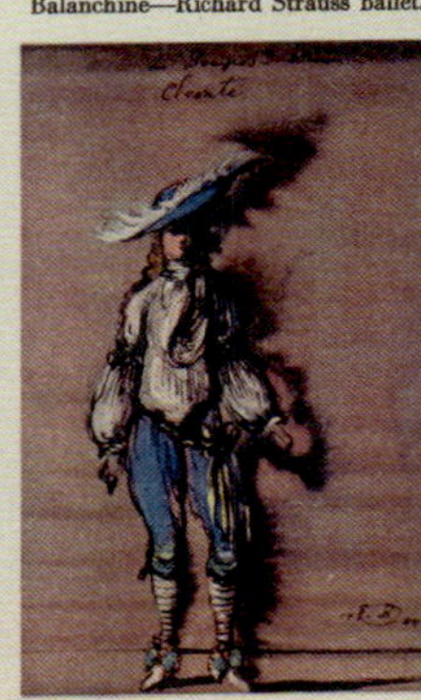

An Indian dancer joins in Molière's eighteenth-century vaudeville.

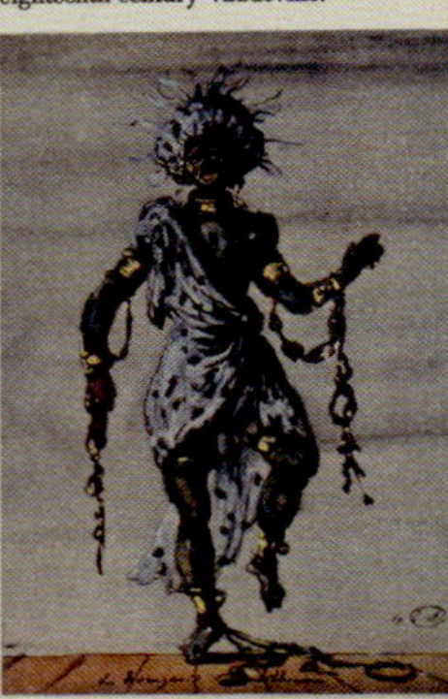

Interior spread from the article "The Boom in Ballet," in the December 1945 issue of *Fortune*, with photographs by Walker Evans

186

patronage, and no sound businessman, least of all the cautious Messrs. Hurok and Denham, will suppose that a millennium of popular support for the collaborative fine arts has suddenly arrived.

The public at large may never understand the ballet patron's apparent eagerness to take large losses. Many people have never come closer to the ballet than a liking for the ravishing pastels of Edgar Degas (Anna Pavlova didn't admire them; she said they depicted attitudes rather than motion). Even many lovers of dancing, in one form or another, seem incurably distressed by ballet's high formalism, agreeing with that distinguished music critic, George Bernard Shaw, that it is "the most punctilious, ceremonious, professor-ridden, pig-headed solemnity that exists. Talk of your fugues, canons, key relationships, single and double counterpoint, fifty orthodox resolutions of the chord of the minor ninth and the rest of it! What are they to the *entrechats, battements, ronds de jambes, arabesques, élévations* that are the stock in trade of the art of theatrical dancing? . . . an ordinary ballet is no more a true dance than an ordinary Church of England service is a true act of worship."

On the other hand, ballet is the one fine art whose addicts are habitually alluded to as being maniacal in their addiction. The balletomane's seething interest should not be too difficult for most people to understand, whether or not they can share it. Bear in mind, to begin with, that the ballet, which in-

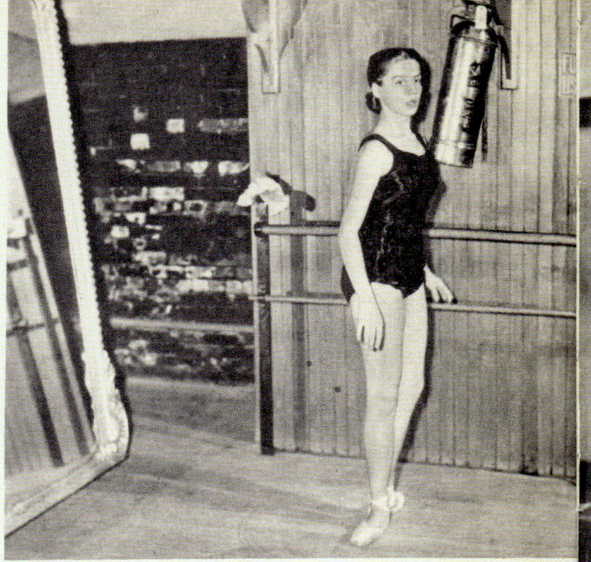

A Ballet Theatre youngster practices at the *barre*, or hand-rail, in the Metropolitan Opera rehearsal room.

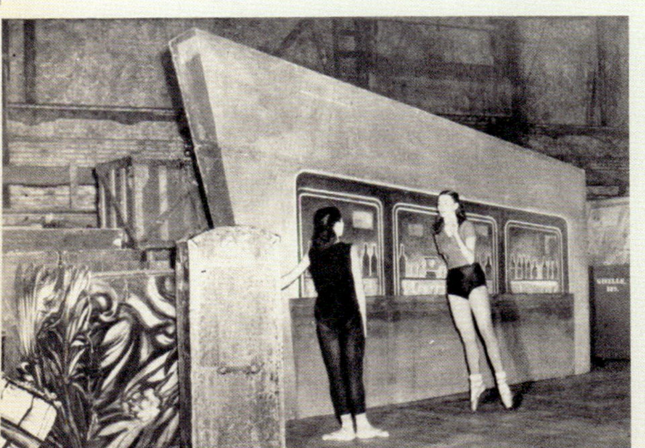

A backstage warm-up by Ballet Theatre girls, with sets and props for Jerome Robbins' *Fancy Free*.

cludes painting, music, and a literary element, is the only fine art centered on one of the most magnetic elements in human experience—the appeal of the human body in motion. Ballet exhibits superb bodies in subtle individual dancing and, as the English music critic W. J. Turner puts it, in an "inexhaustible richness of possible groupings . . . either as foreground, background, or as an integrated rhythmic complement to the action of the solo dancers." Now the balletomane contends that the highest formal beauty and expressiveness of human motion is obtained through, and only through, the classic ballet tradition as developed by three centuries of ballet masters.

In other words, an Isadora Duncan or a Martha Graham may create her own idiom of bodily motion, with its own values. But how can it hope to compare with the end product of three hundred years of balletic experience? Here is the point as made in *The Book of the Dance* by Lincoln Kirstein, the rousing amateur of the arts who easily merits the title of American ballet's No. 1 enthusiast and gadfly: "Mary Wigman [the famous German dance innovator] doubtless invented a new type of gesture.

187

That is, she evolved a particular quality of spasmic alternative of tension and relaxation . . . But a new type of gesture is no more remarkable than a private choice of colors by a painter . . . Anna Pavlova toured the world continually with an inferior company, no 'taste,' unworthy music, and inconsequent choreography. But somehow, neither carelessness nor vulgarity tainted her . . . She represented an artificial perfection so personally intense in reliance on tradition that her work became, even against odds, a new and remarkable force in itself."

The classic ballet tradition is a vast vocabulary of movement springing from five basic foot positions, all at right angles to the body (see below), and with numerous fixed usages in the handling of the limbs. It is this vocabulary, universally known among trained ballet dancers, that helps make possible the handing down of old or the teaching of new ballet formations. The choreographer conveys his ideas to his company by a mixed technique of dancing out patterns himself and describing them in terms of the classic vocabulary. The permutations and combinations possible on the basis of this vocabulary are, of course, without end; a limitless plastic literature is possible.

Ballet today falls into two broad general divisions—what may be called classic and narrative ballet. Classic ballet is that in which the emphasis falls strongly on the dancing as formal beauty, on

Food is of consuming interest to artists who depend on great physical energy; few ballet dancers worry about weight.

The five basic foot positions on which are founded the countless developments of classic ballet style.

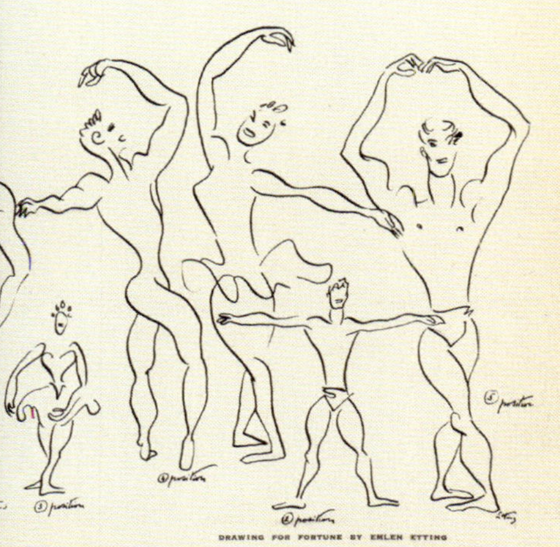

DRAWING FOR FORTUNE BY EMLEN ETTING

the plastic poetry of the art, while the literary interest, if any, is distinctly secondary. Narrative ballet is that which, while it may make extensive use of classic ballet technique, definitely stresses a story—the dancing being designed to express personal developments and dilemmas. As it happens, there is a general cleavage between the two leading U.S. ballet companies in the matter of these two forms. While both companies present the older classic works such as *Swan Lake* and *Les Sylphides*, the Ballet Russe de Monte Carlo is especially noteworthy for newer works in the classic spirit, and Ballet Theatre for a new repertory in the narrative spirit.

The difference is well illustrated by the two finest choreog-

raphers of the period, each chiefly associated with one of the companies mentioned, each a decided ornament to his calling. The forty-one-year-old Russian, George Balanchine, husband of Vera Zorina and resident choreographer to the Ballet Russe, is conceded by the critic John Martin of the New York *Times* to produce only "workmanlike pieces of pretty mathematics." But Martin is in a decided minority among the cognoscenti, who tend to see Balanchine as the greatest dance designer alive and one of the greatest of all time. It is a mere detail to his admirers that this former employee of the great Diaghilev Russian ballet has wowed Broadway with the dances for *I Married An Angel, On Your Toes, Louisiana Purchase, Rosalinda*, and others. That, in effect, was mere hack work. A superb musician, Balanchine's all-out efforts have included a series of ballets (*Danses Concertantes* to Stravinsky, *Concerto Barocco* to Bach, *Waltz*

[*Continued on page 220*]

Rehearsing *Giselle* at the Metropolitan Opera, Ballet Theatre's Alicia Markova commands the attention of the *corps de ballet* as easily as she does that of the most fervent members of the audience.

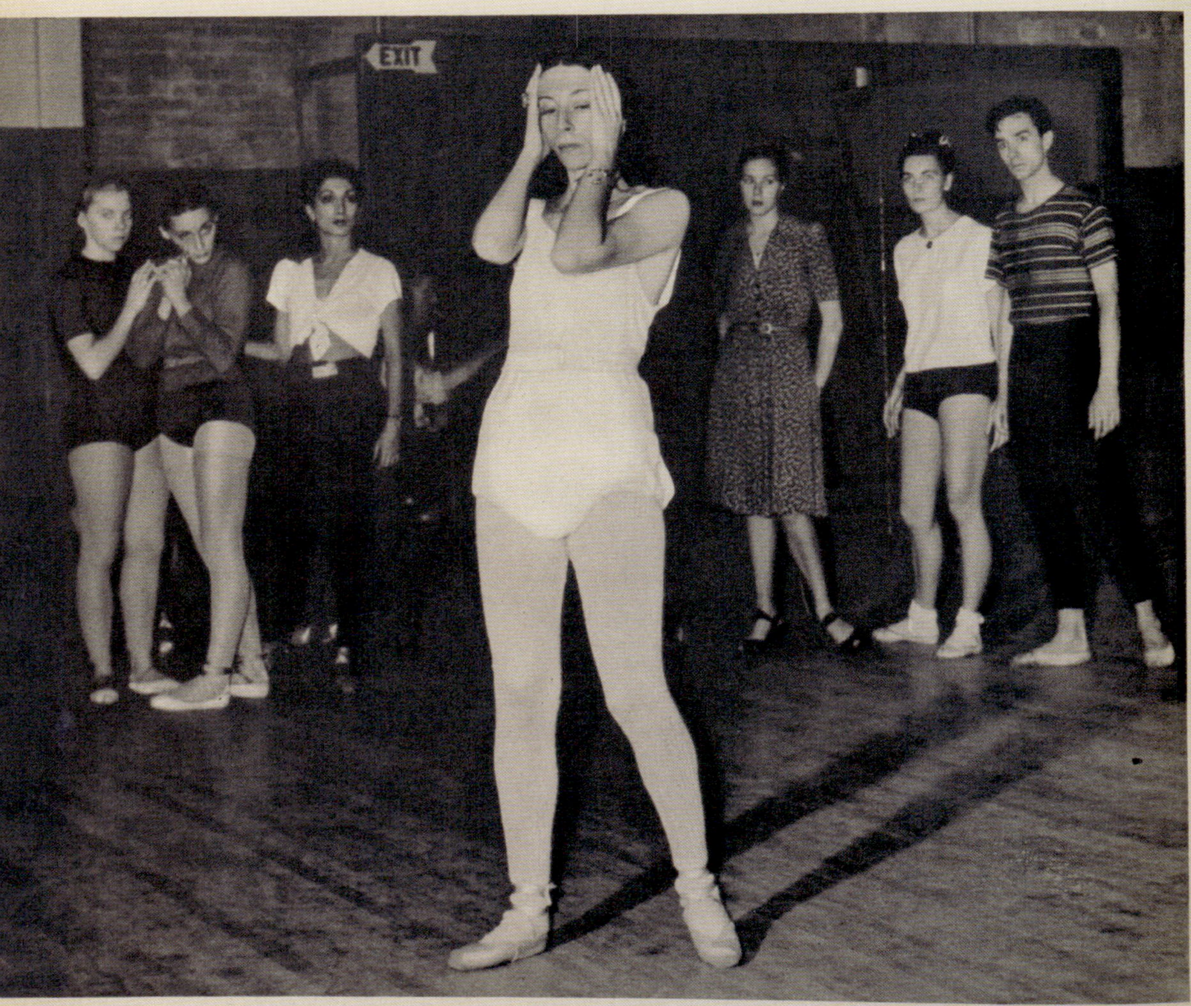

Interior spread from the article "The Boom in Ballet," in the December 1945 issue of *Fortune*, with photograph by Walker Evans

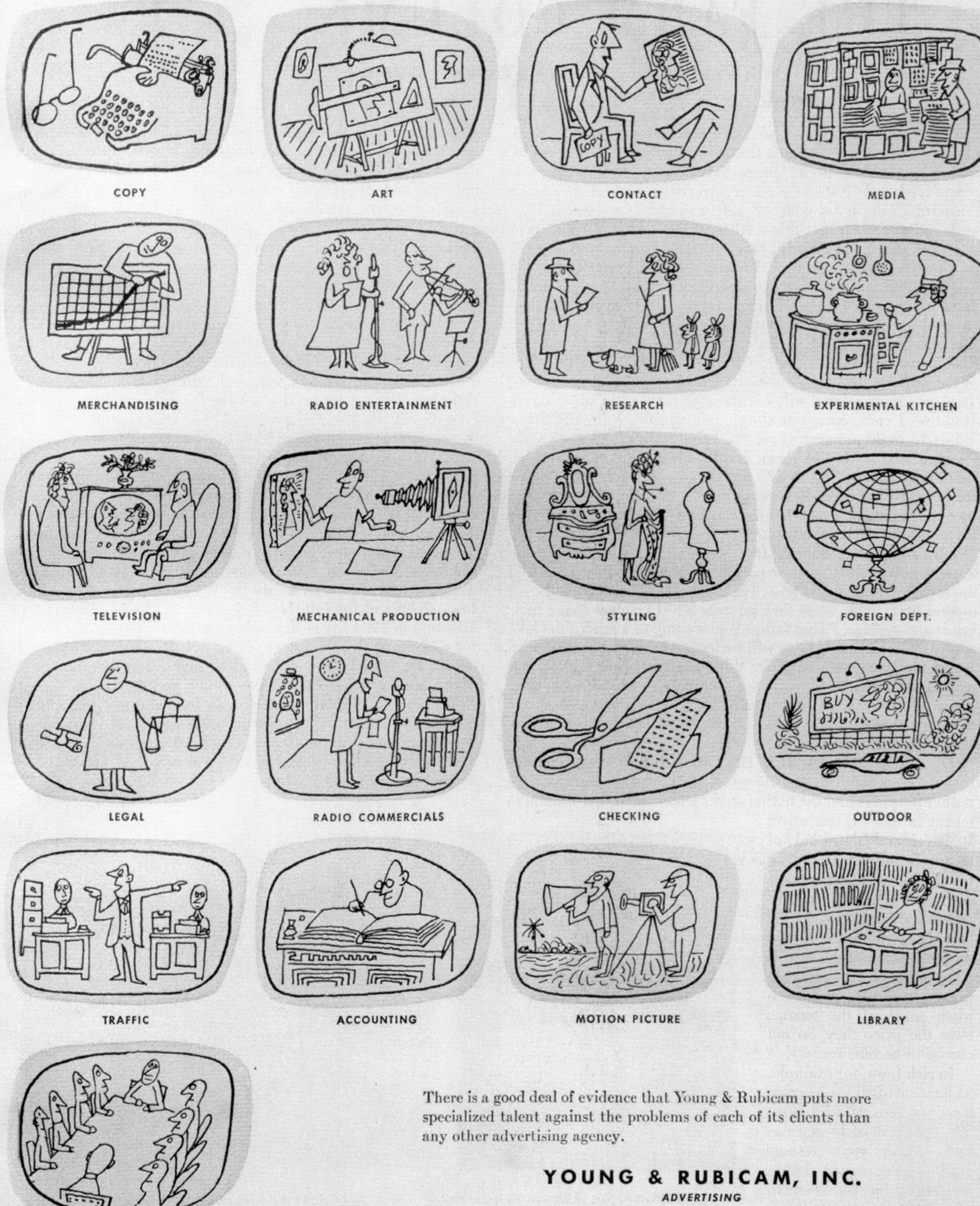

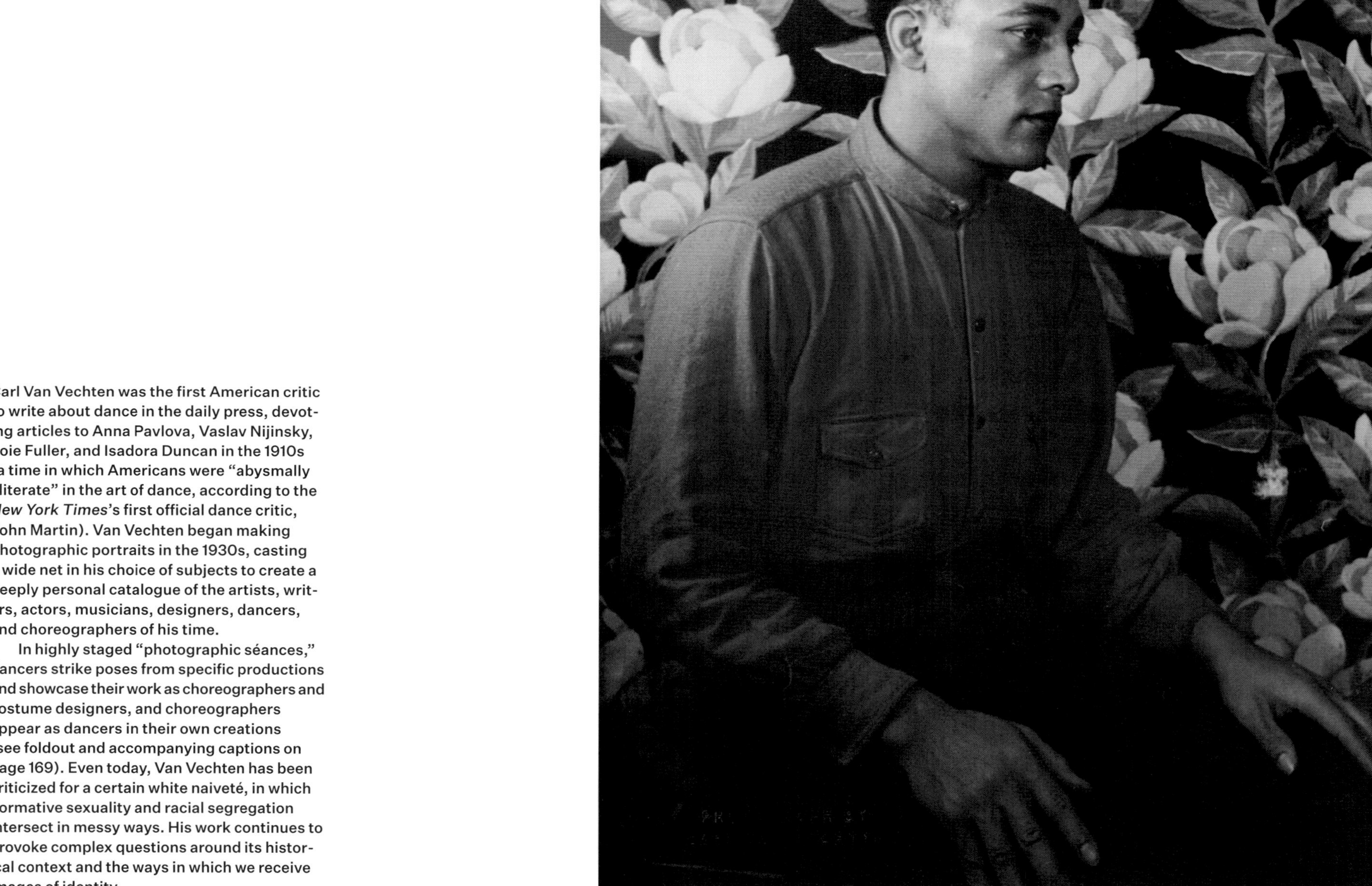

Carl Van Vechten was the first American critic to write about dance in the daily press, devoting articles to Anna Pavlova, Vaslav Nijinsky, Loie Fuller, and Isadora Duncan in the 1910s (a time in which Americans were "abysmally illiterate" in the art of dance, according to the *New York Times*'s first official dance critic, John Martin). Van Vechten began making photographic portraits in the 1930s, casting a wide net in his choice of subjects to create a deeply personal catalogue of the artists, writers, actors, musicians, designers, dancers, and choreographers of his time.

In highly staged "photographic séances," dancers strike poses from specific productions and showcase their work as choreographers and costume designers, and choreographers appear as dancers in their own creations (see foldout and accompanying captions on page 169). Even today, Van Vechten has been criticized for a certain white naiveté, in which normative sexuality and racial segregation intersect in messy ways. His work continues to provoke complex questions around its historical context and the ways in which we receive images of identity.

Right and opposite: Carl Van Vechten, *Dancer Al Bledger of the American Negro Ballet*, 1938. Gelatin silver print, 10 × 7½ inches (25.4 × 19 cm). Fania Marinoff Collection of Photographs of Dancers and Allied Artists, Jerome Robbins Dance Division, The New York Public Library for the Performing Arts

Early twentieth-century ballet in New York was unencumbered by genre boundaries—in fact, the term *ballet* was often used loosely in a dance scene defined by vaudeville, jazz dance, and Broadway. According to historian Jessica Zeller, "most ballet performances outside the opera houses featured a blend of Euro-Russian ballet with social and popular dances, many derived from Africanist movement aesthetics or the period's fascination with expressive movement."

Choreographers and dancers found various ways to negotiate the task of creating authentically American dance forms in a racially segregated country whose artistic heritage and popular culture were largely shaped by African Americans. A number of "all-black" dance companies emerged in the 1930s. The German dancer and choreographer Eugene Von Grona, a vaudeville dancer who had studied with the expressionist dancer Mary Wigman, founded the American Negro Ballet in 1937, teaching his dancers ballet technique as well as body relaxation exercises. The company's repertoire included dances set to music by such varied composers as J. S. Bach, Igor Stravinsky, and Duke Ellington but lasted only a year before being briefly reinvented as Von Grona's American Swing Ballet. Carl Van Vechten's two portraits of Al Bledger, a dancer in Von Grona's company who also performed on Broadway, are striking, direct, and unadorned in comparison to the fantasy tableaux of Van Vechten's color slide portraits. Ballet Theatre (later American Ballet Theatre) originally planned to have several "wings" in its company: "American," "Russian," "British," "Fokine" (after the Russian choreographer), "Negro," and "Spanish." In 1940, Agnes de Mille staged her first ballet for the company's short-lived "Negro Wing," titled *Black Ritual (Obeah)*, set to Darius Milhaud's *La Création du monde* (1922–23). De Mille's ballet featured an all-female cast of sixteen African American dancers with little or no classical training—"a complete novelty for any ballet company to sponsor, and, as it turned out, an extremely interesting one," in the words of dance critic John Martin.

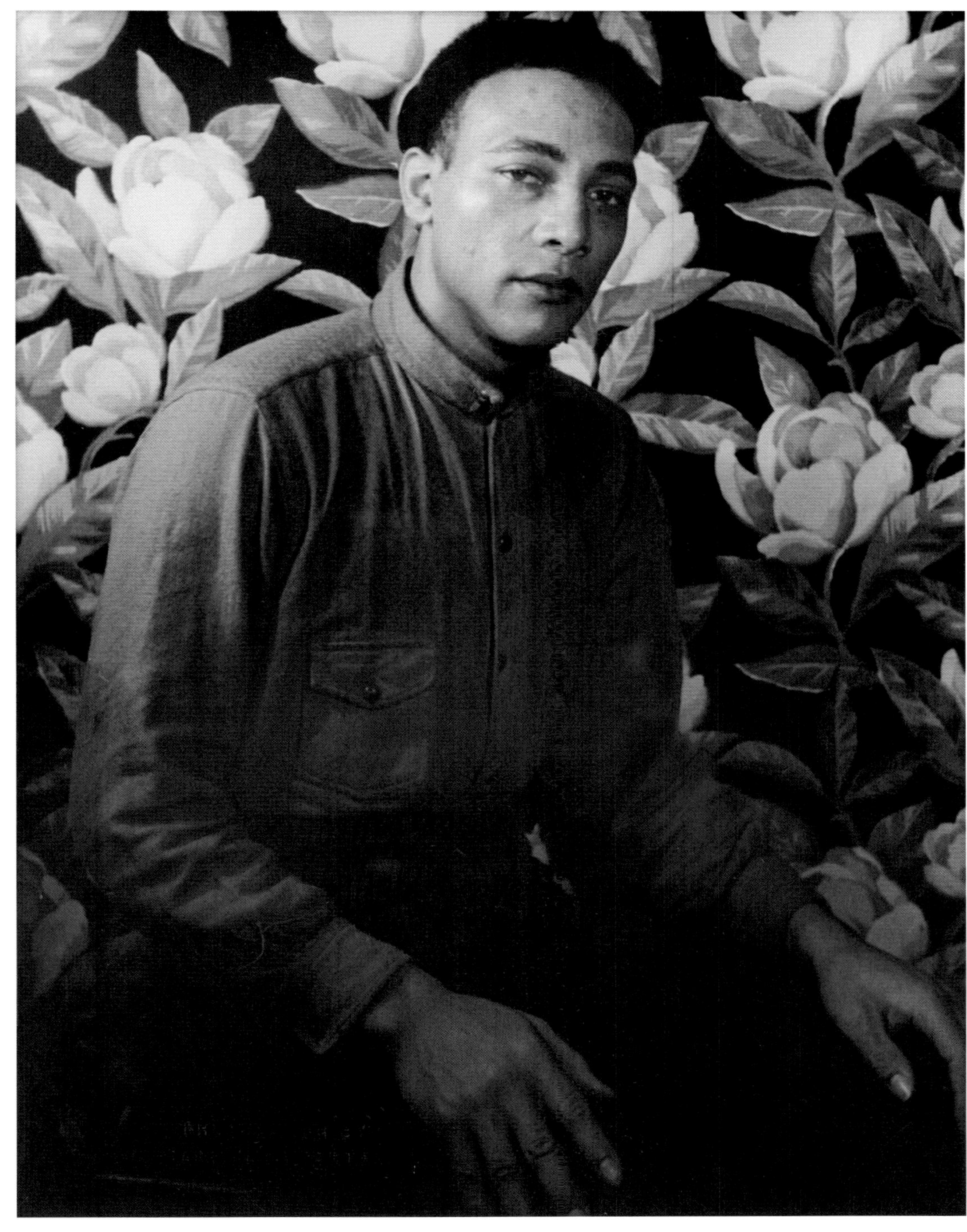

Ilse Bing's photographs of birds in the sky from 1936 index her transatlantic voyage from Paris to New York for an exhibition of her work at June Rhodes Gallery. In 1940, Bing and her husband returned to New York as refugees, making a home for themselves in a city that had become a haven for countless displaced European artists and intellectuals. By 1959, Bing had given up photography in favor of writing poems and scenarios that she called "snapshots without a camera."

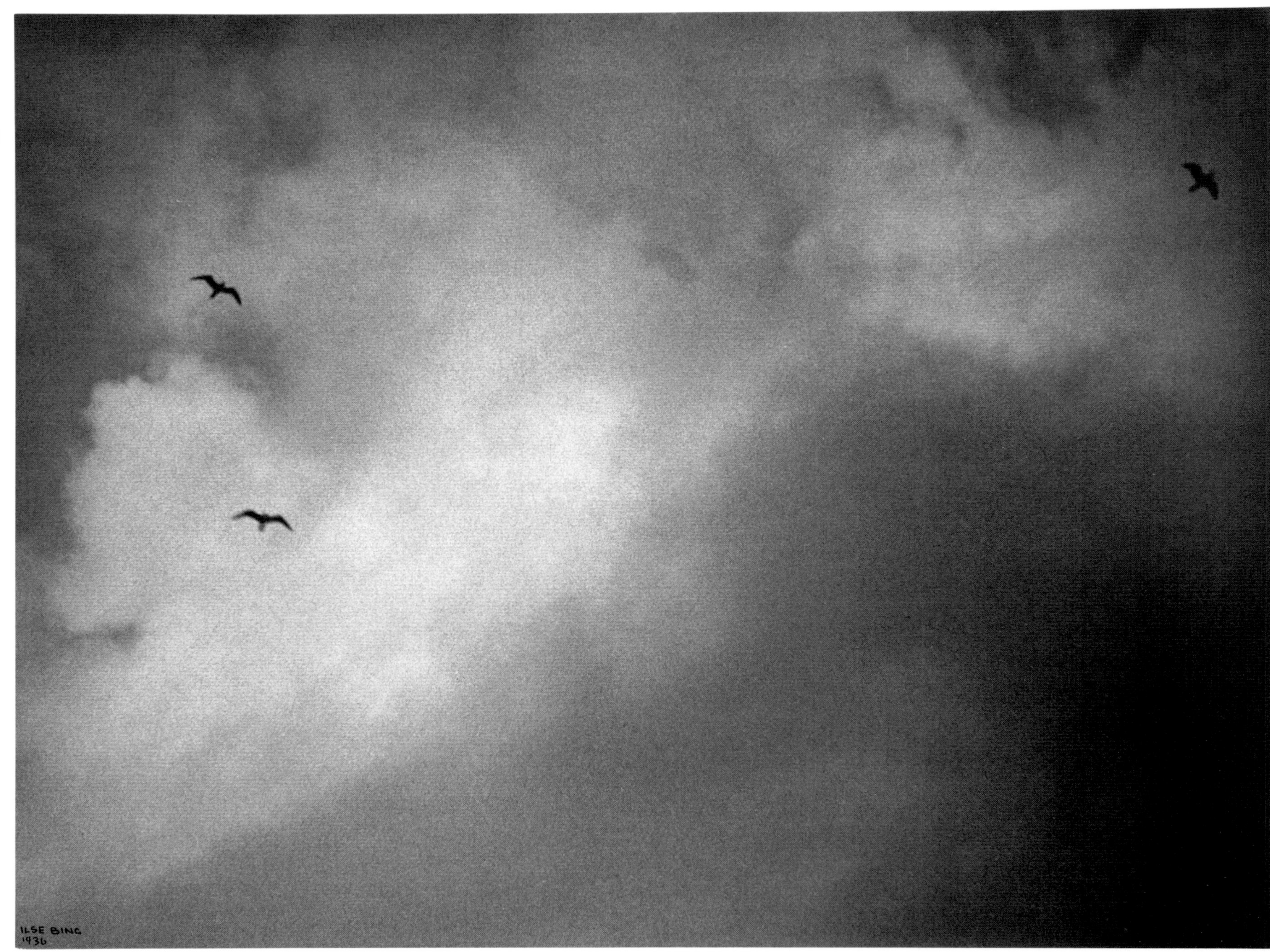

Ilse Bing, *Between France and U.S.A. (Seascapes)*, 1936. Gelatin silver print, 8⁵⁄₁₆ × 11³⁄₁₆ inches (21.1 × 28.4 cm). Whitney Museum of American Art, New York; bequest of Ilse Bing Wolff

Opposite: Ilse Bing, *Three Birds in the Sky, Paris*, 1936. Gelatin silver print, 8⅜ × 11⅛ inches (21.3 × 28.3 cm). Whitney Museum of American Art, New York; bequest of Ilse Bing Wolff

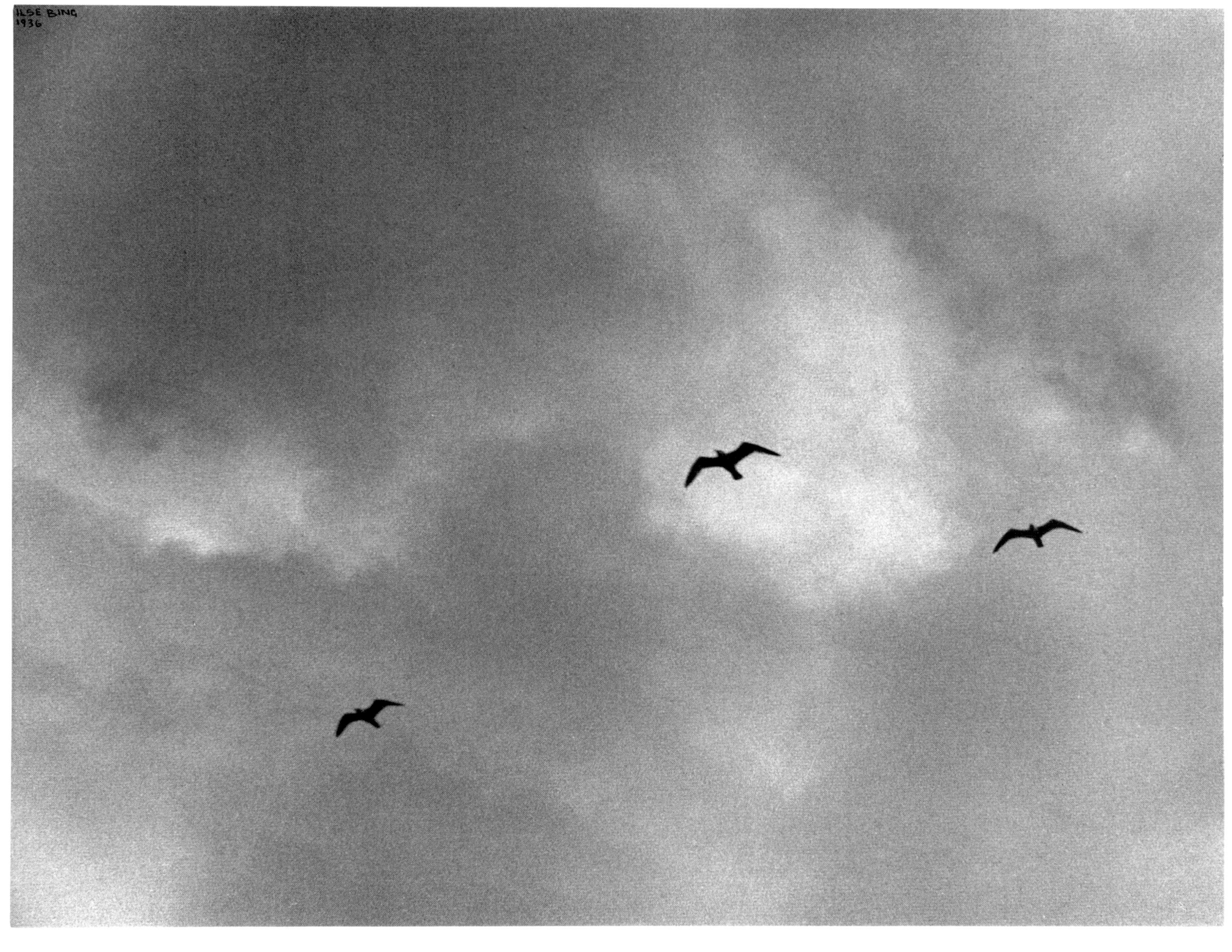
ILSE BING
1936

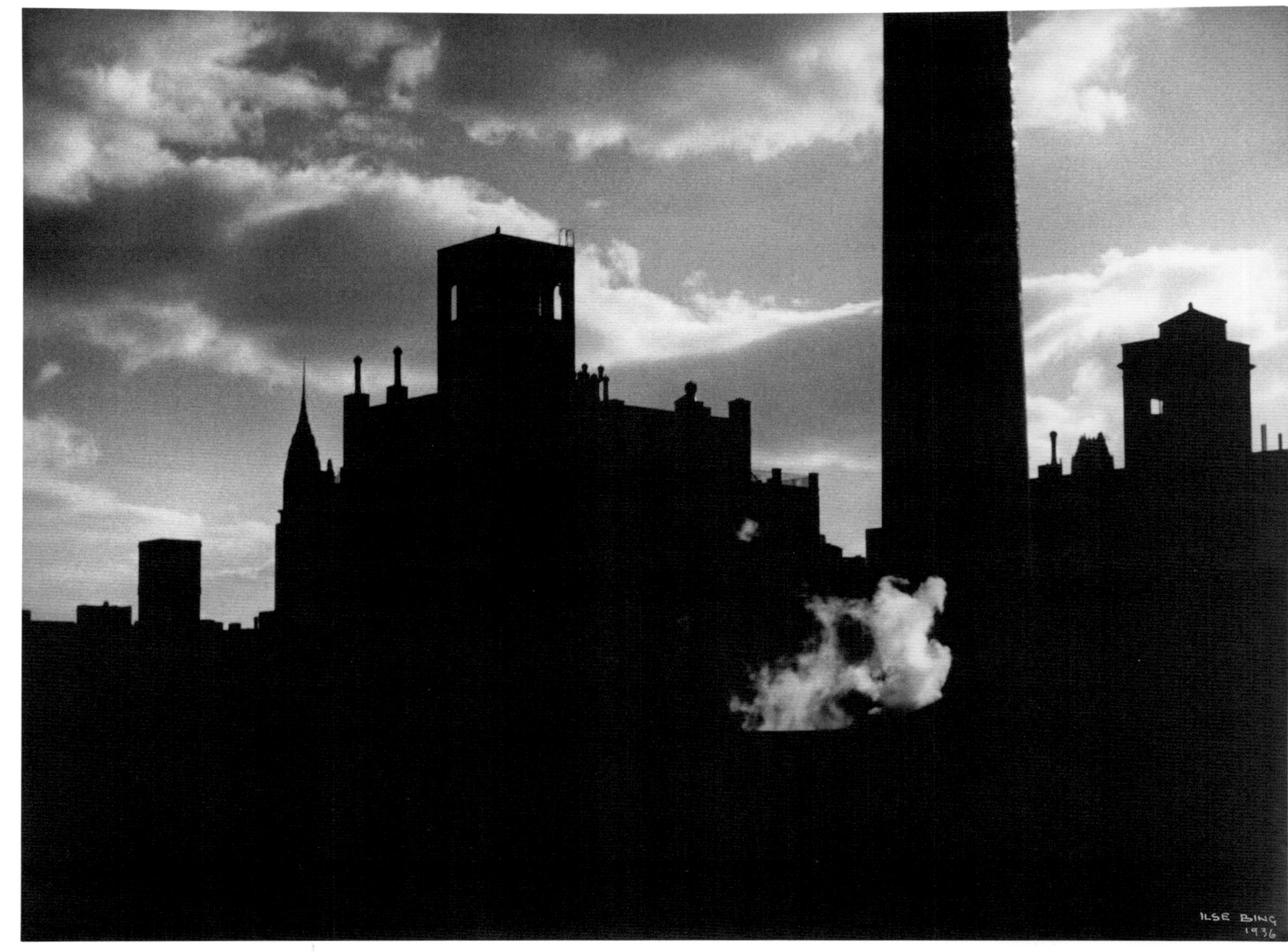

Ilse Bing, *Dead End II*, 1936. Gelatin silver print, 8 1/16 × 11 1/8 inches (20.5 × 28.3 cm). Whitney Museum of American Art, New York; bequest of Ilse Bing Wolff

Opposite: Ilse Bing, *Untitled (Skyscrapers, night, NY)*, 1936. Gelatin silver print, 8 3/4 × 11 1/8 inches (22.2 × 28.3 cm). Whitney Museum of American Art, New York; bequest of Ilse Bing Wolff

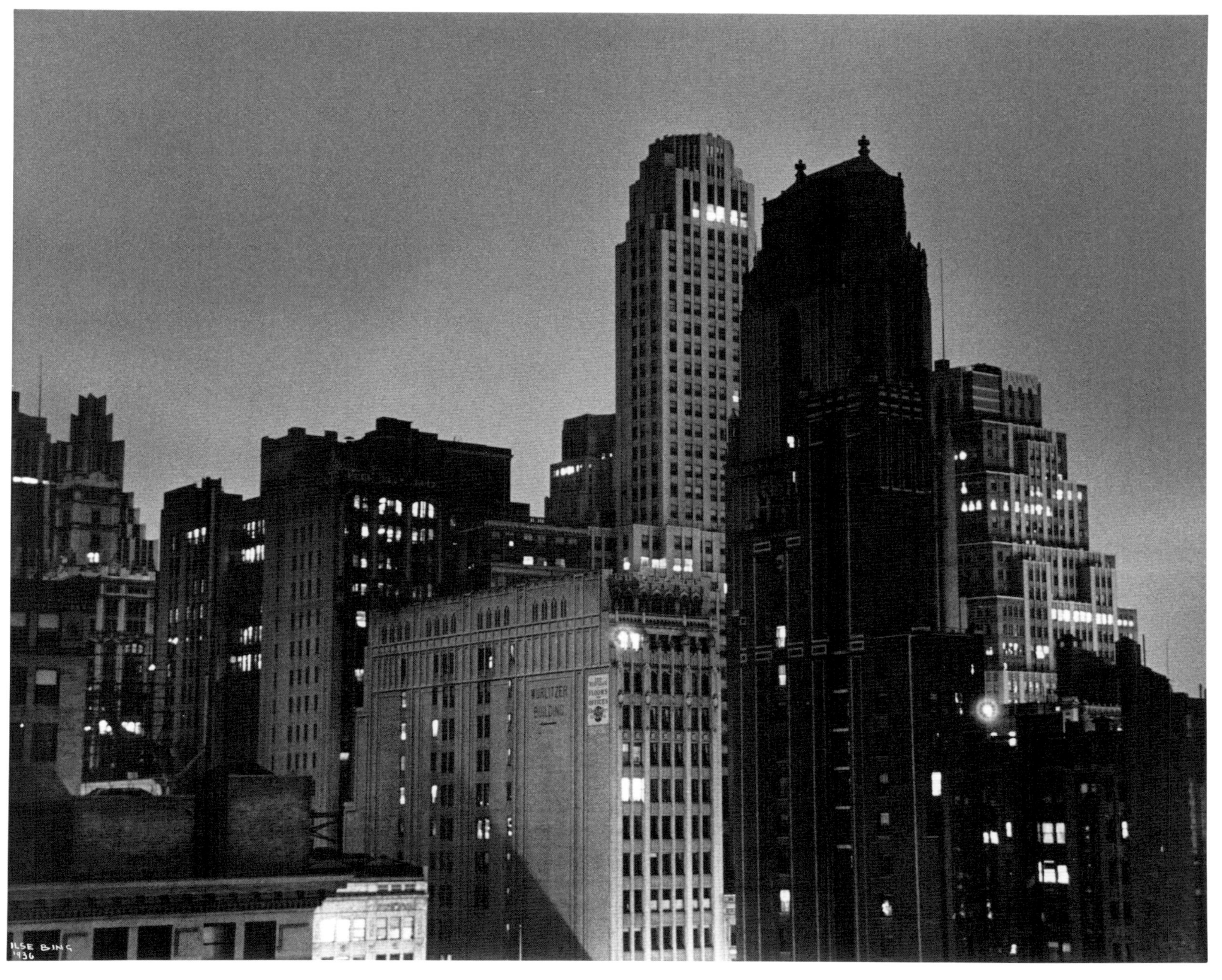

In 1967 the artist Sturtevant performed *Relâche*, a reiteration of a legendary incident in the history of European avant-garde ballet, at the School of Visual Arts in New York. The original *Relâche* was a Dadaist ballet, with sets by Francis Picabia, music by Erik Satie, and a filmic interlude by René Clair that included a sequence in which Picabia, Marcel Duchamp, and Erik Satie play chess on a Paris rooftop. On its opening night in Paris in 1924, the audience arrived at the theater to find the doors plastered with signs proclaiming *"relâche"* (canceled) and read them as echoing the title's provocation; in fact, the ballet's lead dancer-choreographer was ill. In the catalogue for Sturtevant's exhibition at White Columns in 1986, Douglas Davis and Eugene M. Schwartz described Sturtevant's "repetition" of the canceled ballet:

The audience finds the doors to the theater up on the second floor shut tight. As they mill about in the hall, Duchamp unexpectedly arrives. He walks through the crowd, hesitates long enough to inspect the poster nailed on the door, ("STURTEVANT'S RELÂCHE," it reads), turns around without a word and descends to the street below where his wife, Teeny, awaits him in a taxi with its meter running. A few days later, he invites Sturtevant to dinner. Not a word until the end, when the other guests leave. He asks her how the performance had gone. "Fine, thank you," she says. He asks if what happened was by intention. "Yes," she answers. He smiles and says, "That's quite beautiful."

Opposite: Installation view of *Transmissions*, with (left to right) monitor on folding chair playing films of George Balanchine and dancers during rehearsal into mirror; Pavel Tchelitchew, *Interior Landscape Skull*, 1949; John Storrs, *Forms in Space #1*, c. 1924; Elie Nadelman, *Two Circus Women*, c. 1928–29; figural stand by Gustav Natorp, 1898; Sturtevant, *Relâche*, 1967; Ilse Bing, *Untitled (Skyscrapers, night, NY)*, 1936; and Ilse Bing, *Dead End II*, 1936; arranged in front of Nick Mauss, *Images in Mind*, 2018. Photo: Ron Amstutz

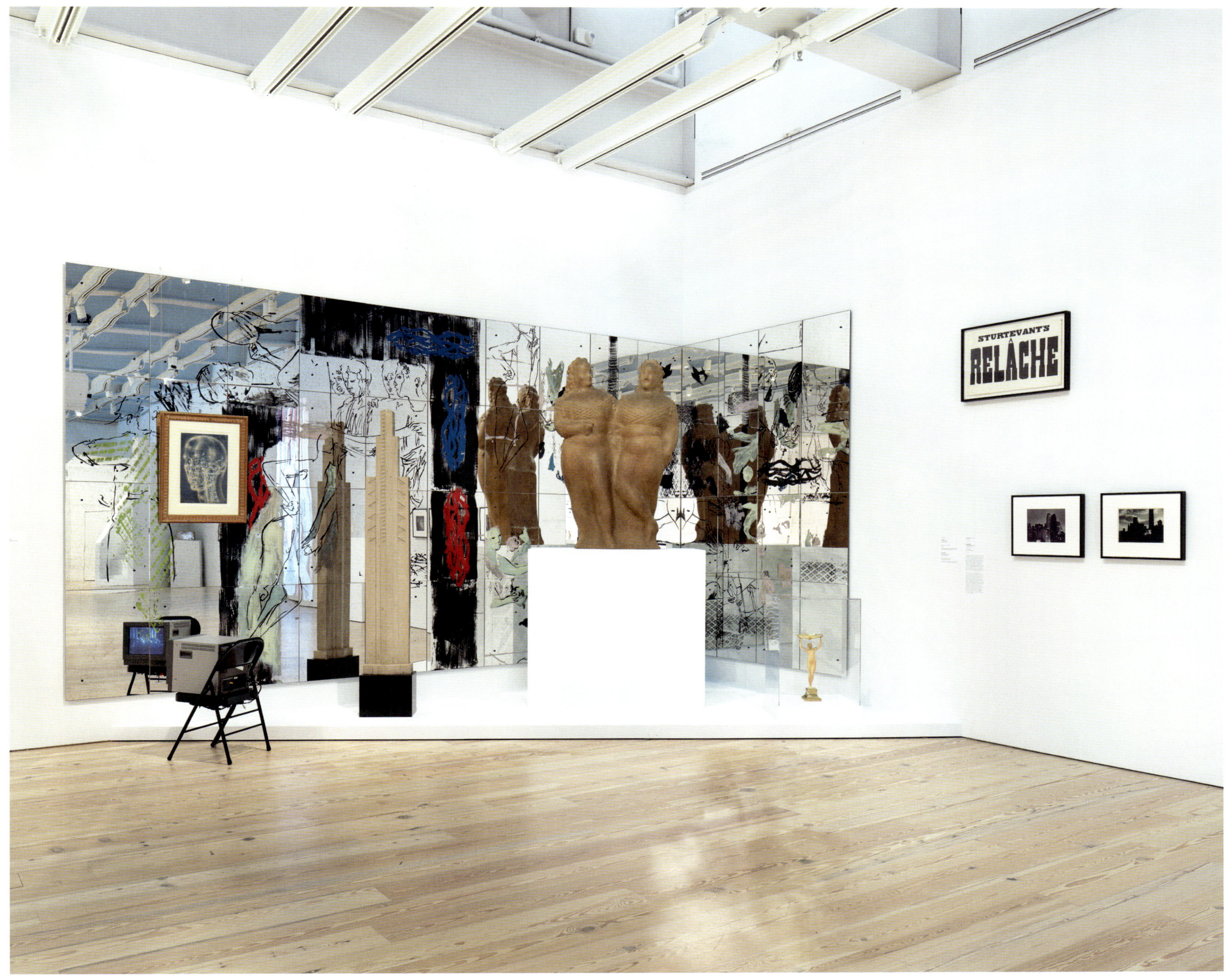

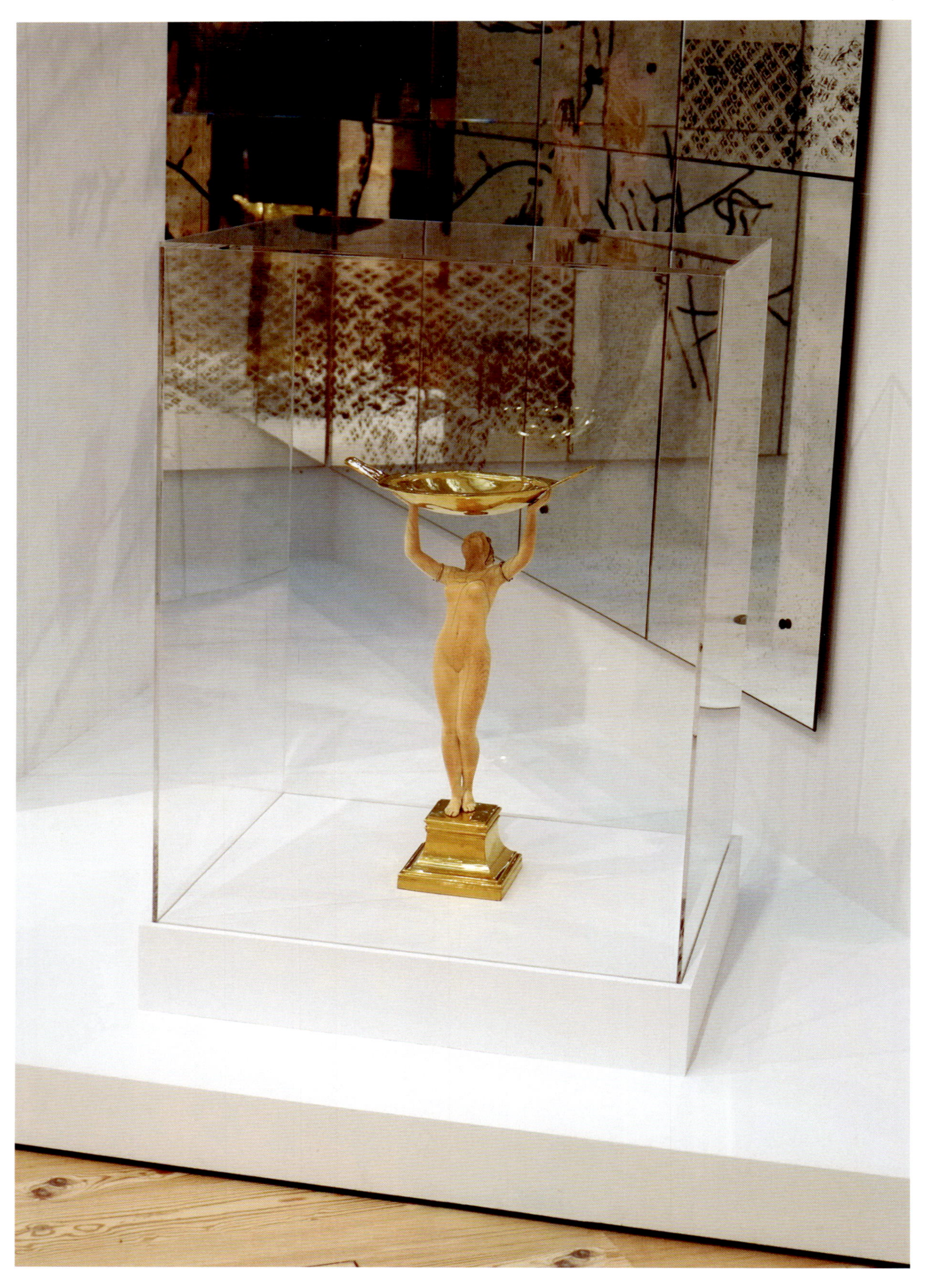

Left and opposite: Figural stand by Gustav Natorp (1898), holding Serge Diaghilev's calling card. Private collection

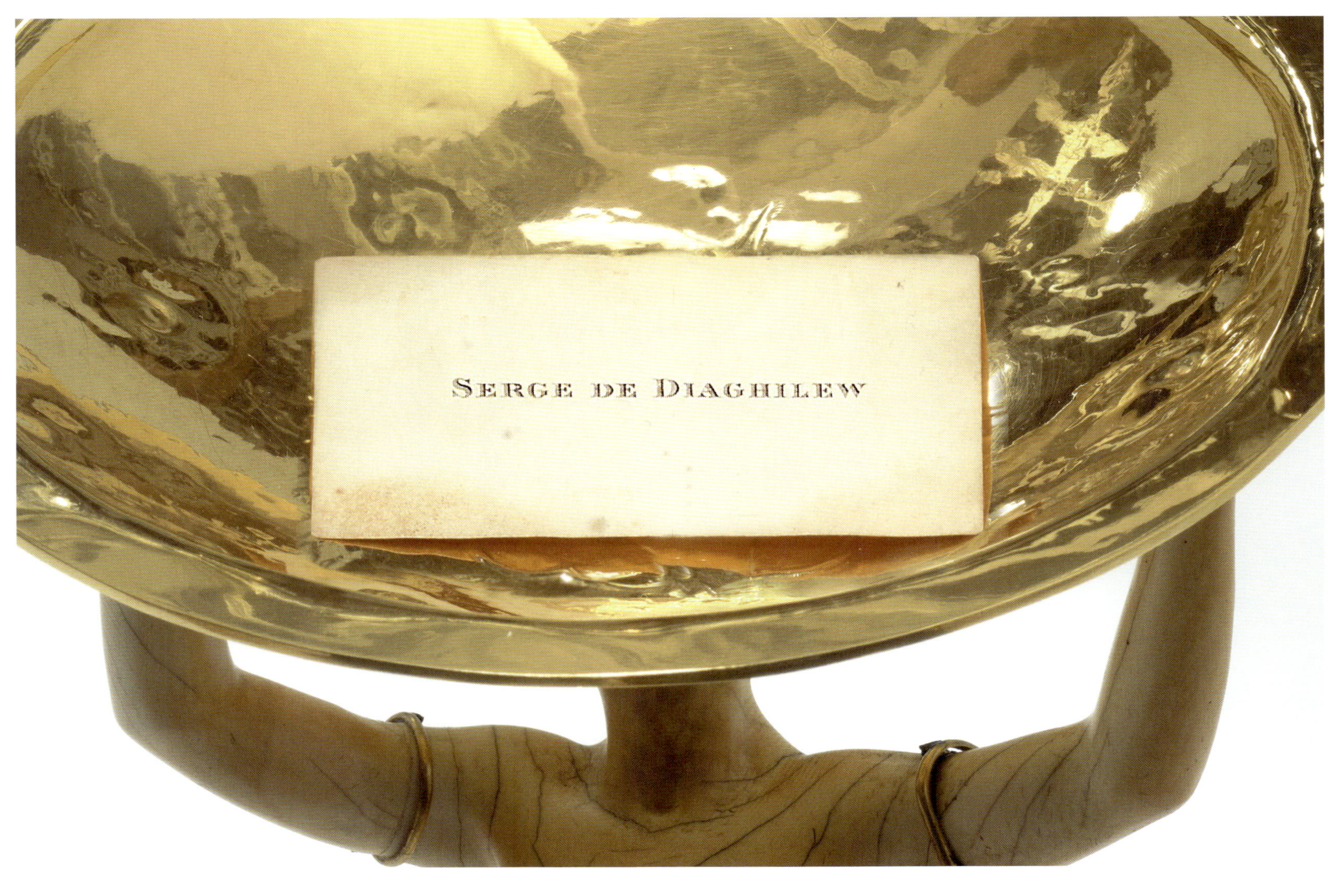

SERGE DE DIAGHILEW

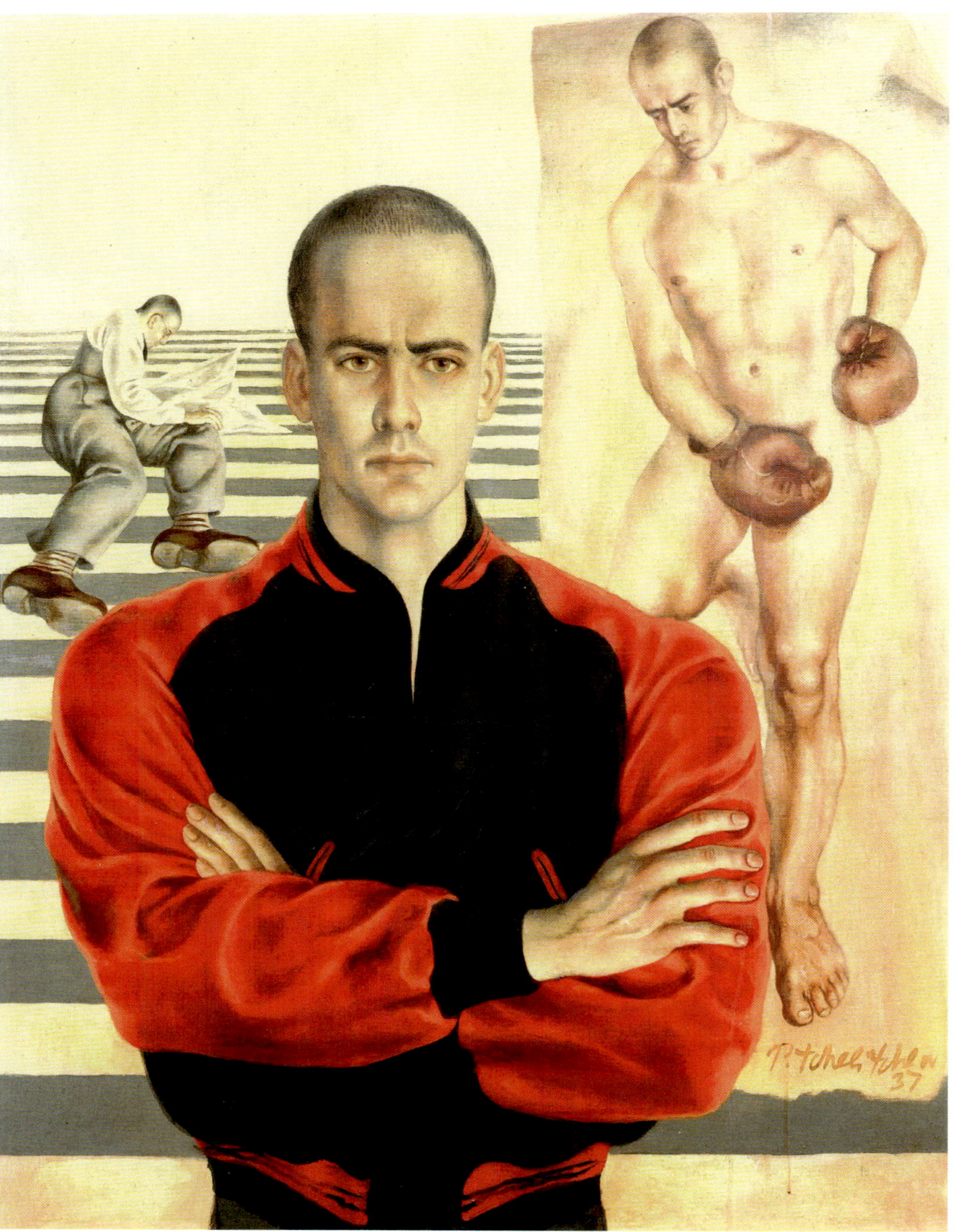

Pavel Tchelitchew, *Portrait of Lincoln Kirstein*, 1937. Oil on canvas, 48 × 36 inches (121.9 × 91.4 cm). Collection of the School of American Ballet

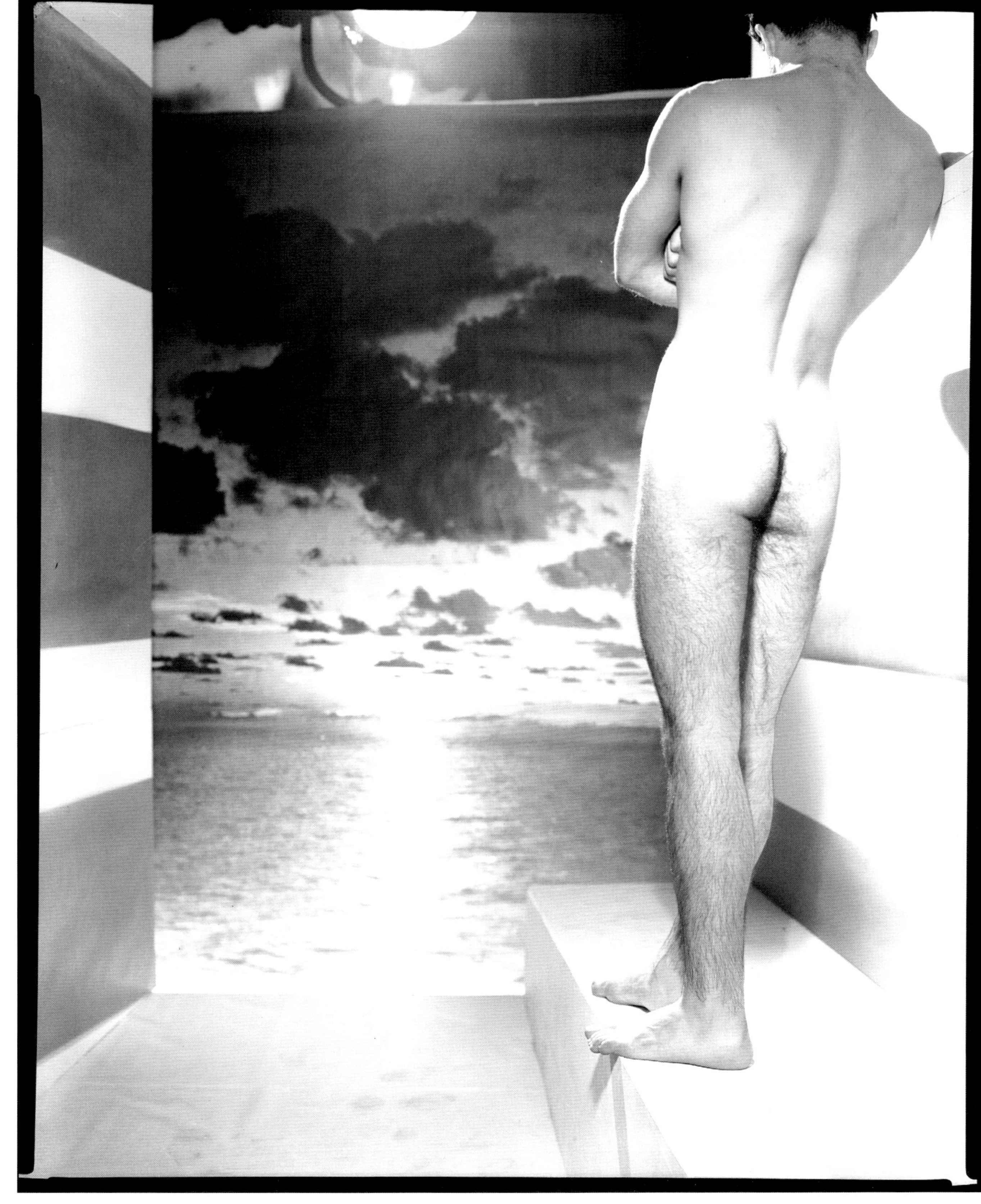

George Platt Lynes,
unidentified model in striped
set, n.d. Scan from original
negative. Collections
of the Kinsey Institute,
Indiana University

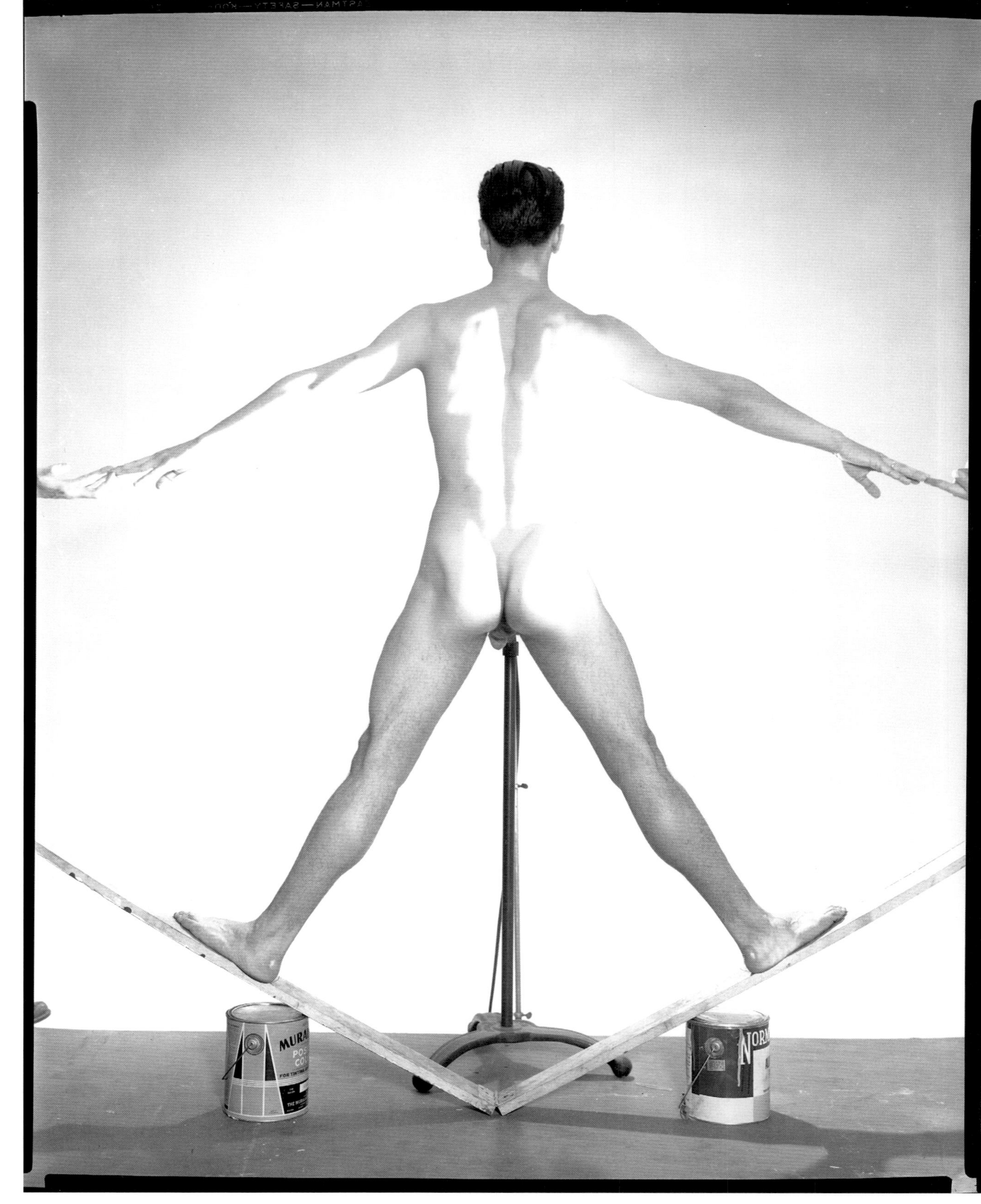

George Platt Lynes,
unidentified model, n.d.
Scan from original negative.
Collections of the Kinsey
Institute, Indiana University

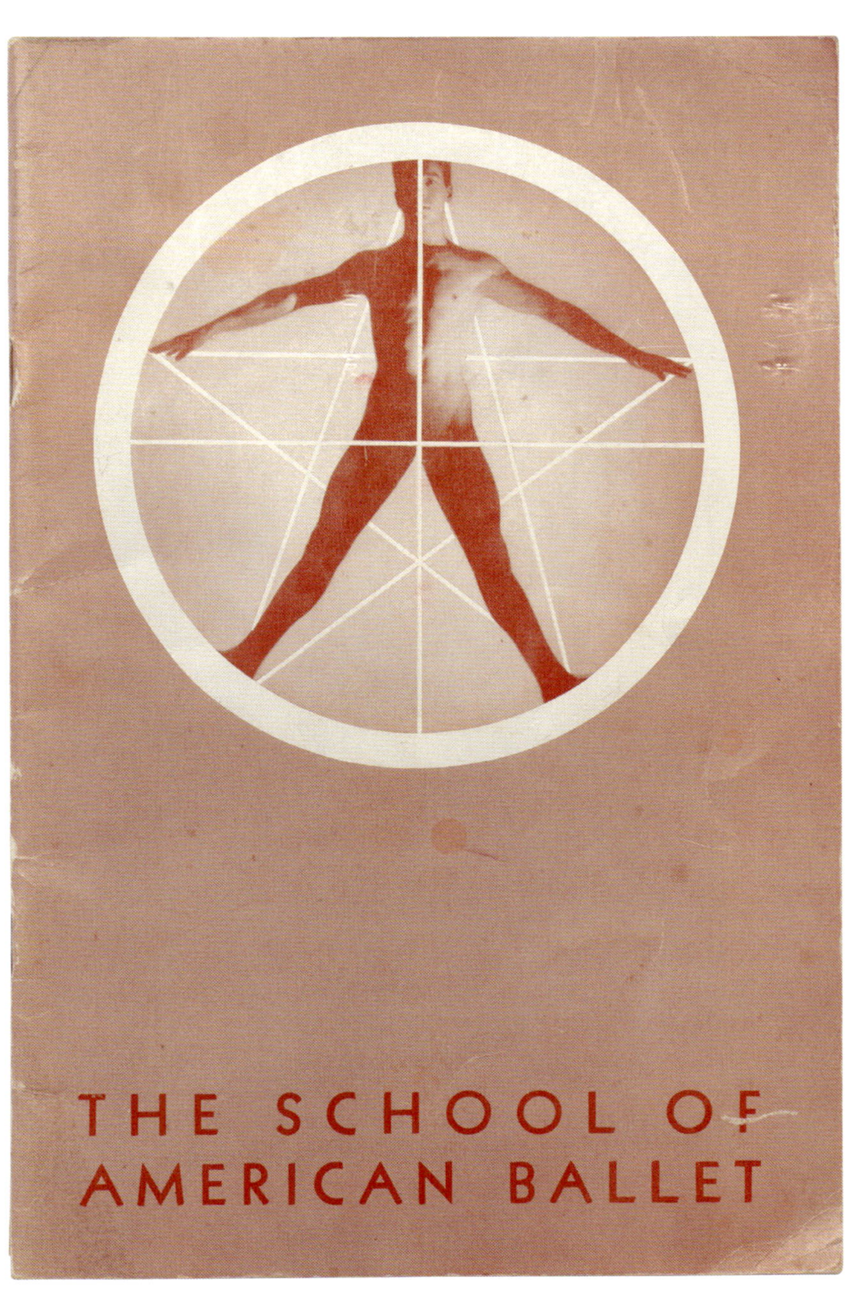

THE SCHOOL OF
AMERICAN BALLET

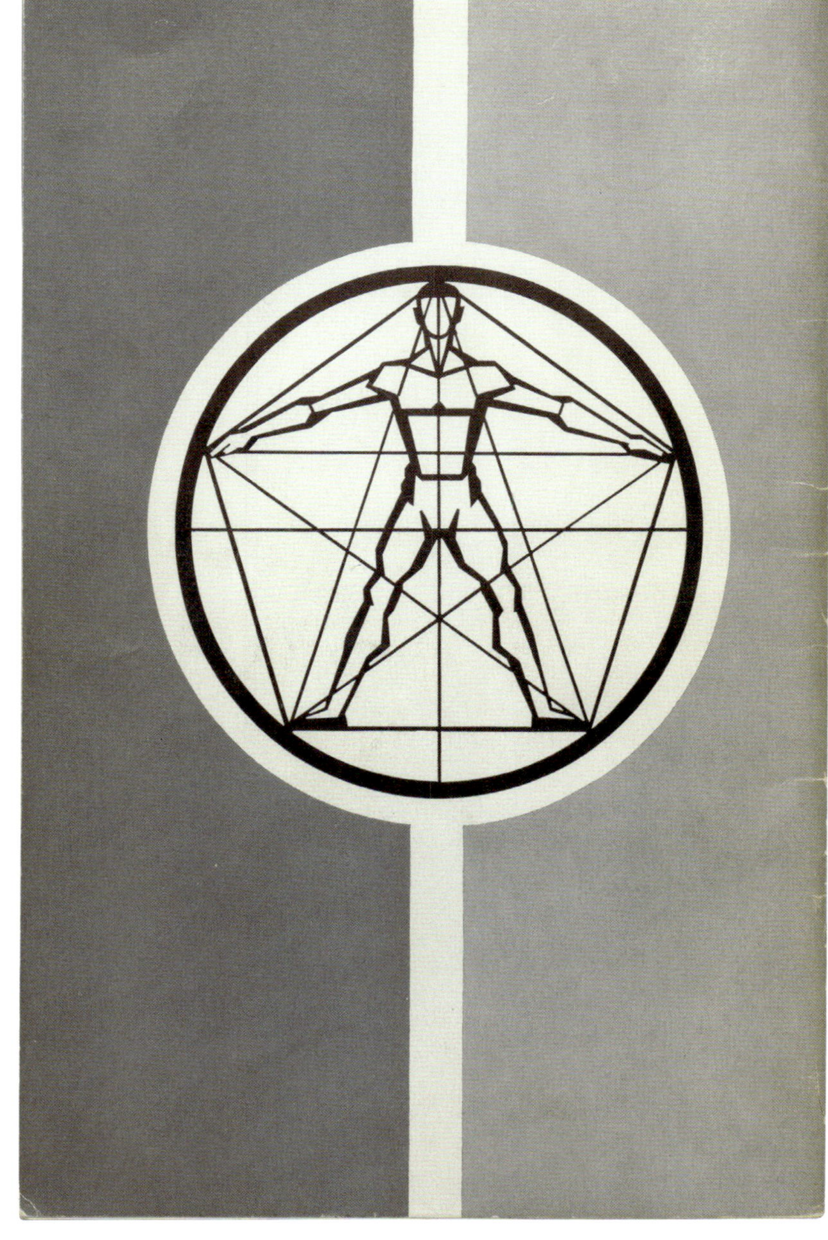

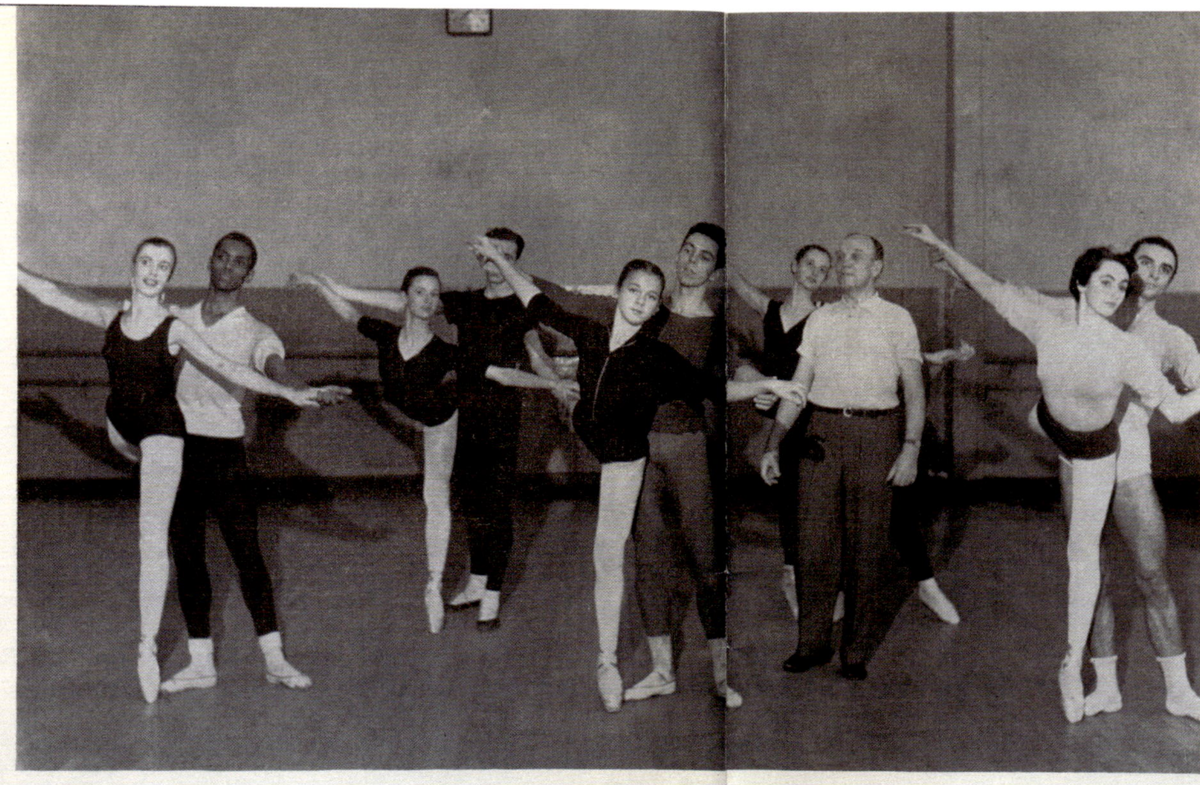

Adagio Class

Scholarships

The School of American Ballet is not endowed and depends on
income from tuition fees for its operating expenses. The School is
able therefore to give only a very limited number of
scholarships.* In awarding these the applicant's ability,
financial need and age are considered. (With few exceptions
scholarships are awarded to students under sixteen). All applicants
for scholarships are required to enroll for one trial month
as regular students and to fill out a questionnaire concerning
their financial status. No scholarships are given for the
summer courses.

*The School of American Ballet, a non-profit corporation,
welcomes contributions to its Scholarship Fund. These are
deductible from Income Tax.*

Summer Courses

The yearly summer courses at the School of American Ballet
are held primarily for the benefit of out-of-town students,
professional dancers and teachers who are unable to attend
during the school year. The schedule of courses is based on the
regular winter curriculum. It is planned with the aim of
condensing within a short period a maximum of sound technical
instruction. Members of the permanent faculty, as well as
guest teachers conduct the classes. The summer courses begin
early in July and continue for six weeks.
The dates, program and faculty of the summer courses are
announced in April of each year, and a
descriptive circular mailed upon request.

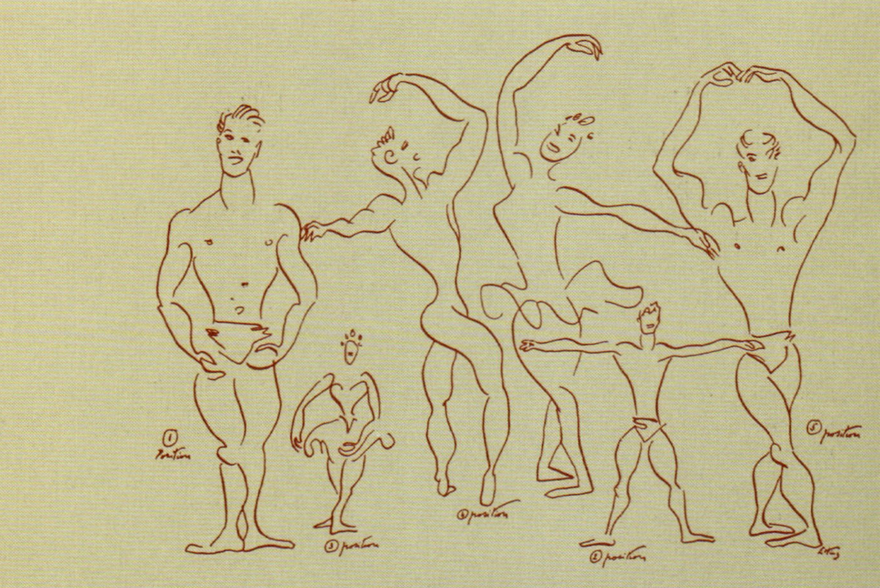

THE FIVE POSITIONS BY EMLEN ETTING

COURTESY OF THE MIDTOWN GALLERIES, NEW YORK

SCHOOL OF DANCE ARTS

Valentina Perejaslavec

leading faculty member since 1949

819 CARNEGIE HALL   CIRCLE 5-8636

OREST SERGIEVSKY
formerly with Ballet Theatre, Ballet Russe

THEATRE STUDIO OF DANCE
137 West 56th St., N. Y. C.   JU 6-9454

FAMOUS GUEST TEACHERS

Special classes for balletomanes
Ballet • Character • Modern

Children • Beginners • Intermediate • Advanced • Professionals

---

Advanced • Intermediate
Elementary
Ballet Lessons in the
Great Tradition

CAIRD LESLIE Classical Ballet School

129 W. 56th St., New York 19
Circle 5-9420

CELLI

Former Ballet Master — La Scala, Milan
Teacher of

ALICIA MARKOVA   ANTON DOLIN
MARY ELLEN MOYLAN   IGOR YOUSKEVITCH
MIA SLAVENSKA   ROYES FERNANDEZ
and many other world renowned dancers

1697 Broadway, Studio 607, CI 5-7358   New York City

BALLET SCHOOL

METROPOLITAN OPERA HOUSE STUDIO
BORIS NOVIKOFF, Director

Complete Education in Theatrical Dancing
Classes and Private Lessons for Professionals,
Advanced, Beginners and Children

Entrance 1425 BROADWAY, Studio 15, New York • Tel. LO 5-0864

---

603 *Carnegie Hall*
circle 6-9699

IRENE V. MAYO SCHOOL

of comparative dance techniques

*offers specialized training to meet the requirements of
Today's Theatre*

*ballet • modern
dance of India*

*professional classes daily
choreography • ballet repertoire*

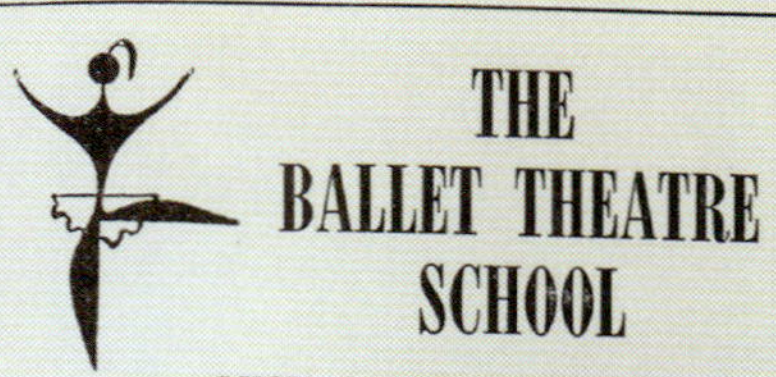

LUCIA CHASE — DIRECTOR

*offering a complete education in classic ballet
and related dance forms.*

FACULTY

EDWARD CATON

WILLIAM DOLLAR

YUREK LAZOWSKY

VALENTINA PEREYASLAVEC

LUDMILA SHOLLAR

ANATOLE VILZAK

Apply to Elena Balieff, Secretary
152 WEST 56th STREET, NEW YORK 19, NEW YORK
Telephone JUdson 6-1941

SCHOOL OF AMERICAN BALLET

Official School of the New York City Ballet

Faculty:

GEORGE BALANCHINE, FELIA DOUBROVSKA,

ANATOLE OBOUKHOFF, ELISE REIMAN,

MURIEL STUART, ANTONINA TUMKOVSKY,

PIERRE VLADIMIROFF.

Guest Teachers:

YUREK LAZOVSKY, ANNA SOKOLOW

Director: LINCOLN KIRSTEIN

Catalogue Upon Request

637 Madison Ave., New York 22, N. Y.   PLaza 5-1422

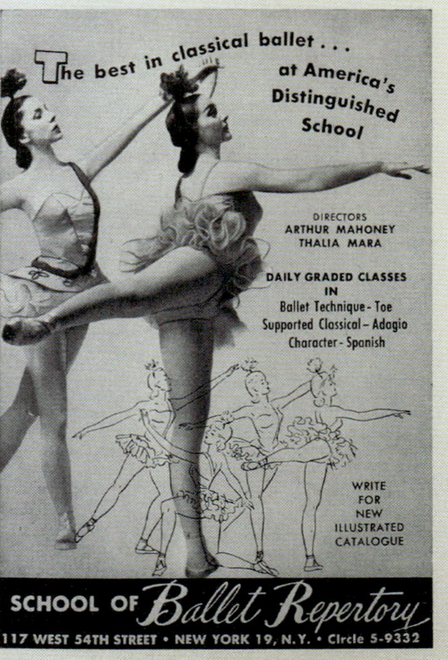

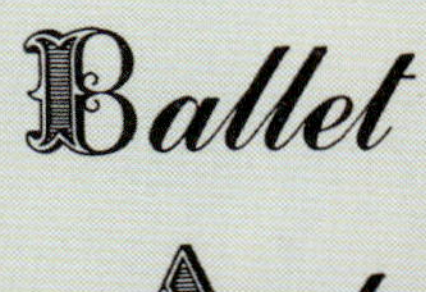

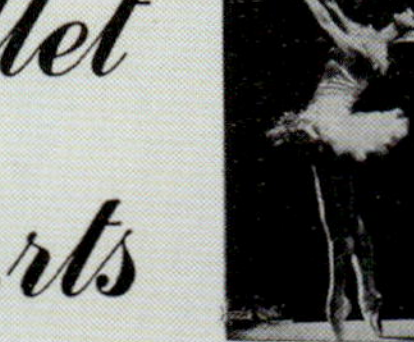

Ballet Arts

**INSTRUCTION UNDER WORLD
RENOWNED DANCERS**

AIDA ALVAREZ   VERA NEMTCHINOVA
AGNES DE MILLE   YEICHI NIMURA
VLADIMIR DOKOUDOVSKY   NINA STROGANOVA
LISAN KAY   PAUL SZILARD
VLADIMIR KONSTANTINOV ERIC VICTOR

GUEST INSTRUCTOR, ANTON DOLIN

Ballet Arts School CARNEGIE HALL
154 WEST 57th STREET, NEW YORK 19, N. Y.
COLUMBUS 5-9627

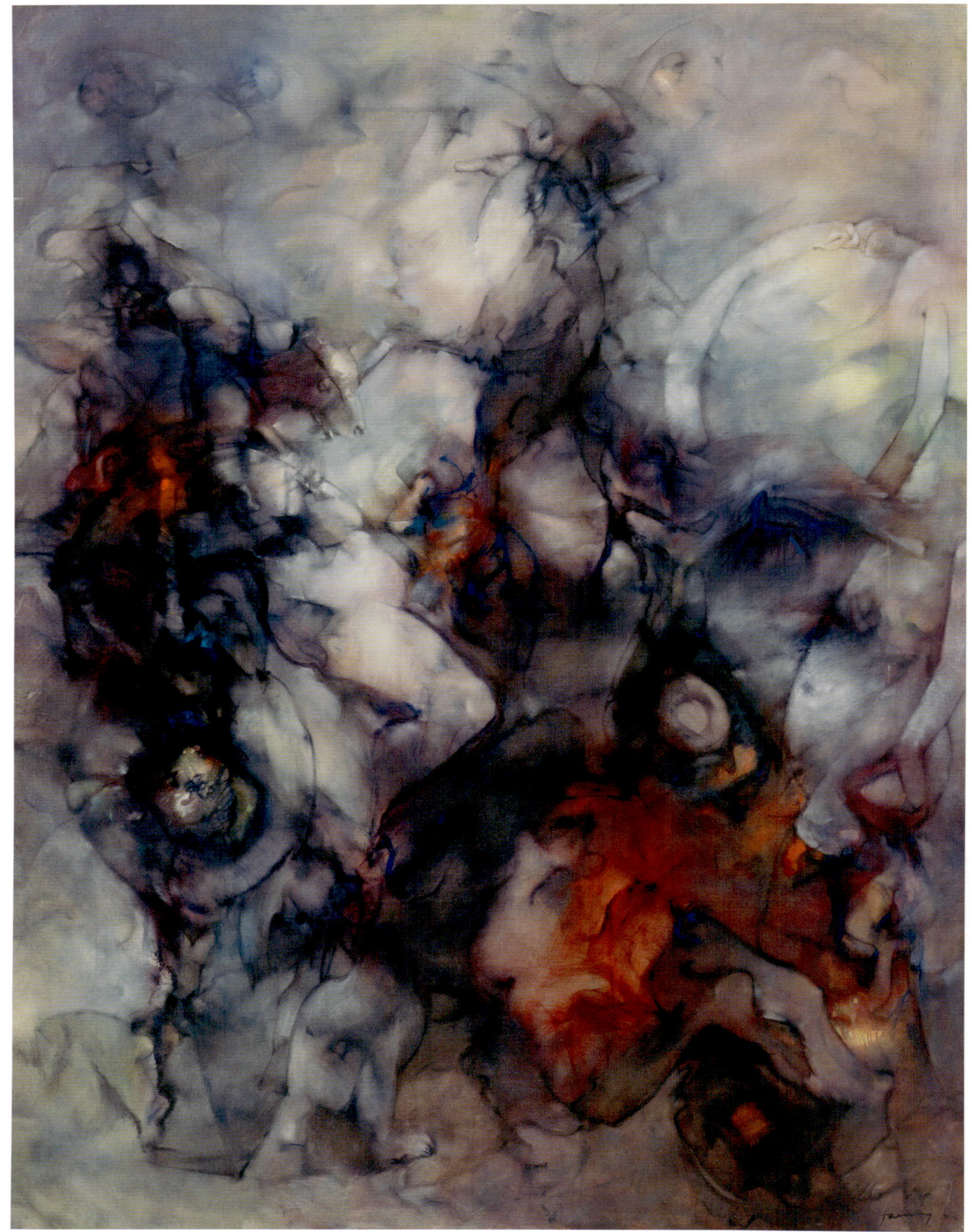

Dorothea Tanning, *Aux environs de Paris (Paris and Vicinity)*, 1962. Oil on linen, 100½ × 78⅝ inches (255.3 × 199.7 cm). Whitney Museum of American Art, New York; gift of the Alexander Iolas Gallery

Tanagra figurines, n.d.,
lithograph on paper
on cardboard, with
photograph by unknown
photographer, 9⅜ × 11½
inches (23.8 × 29.2 cm)

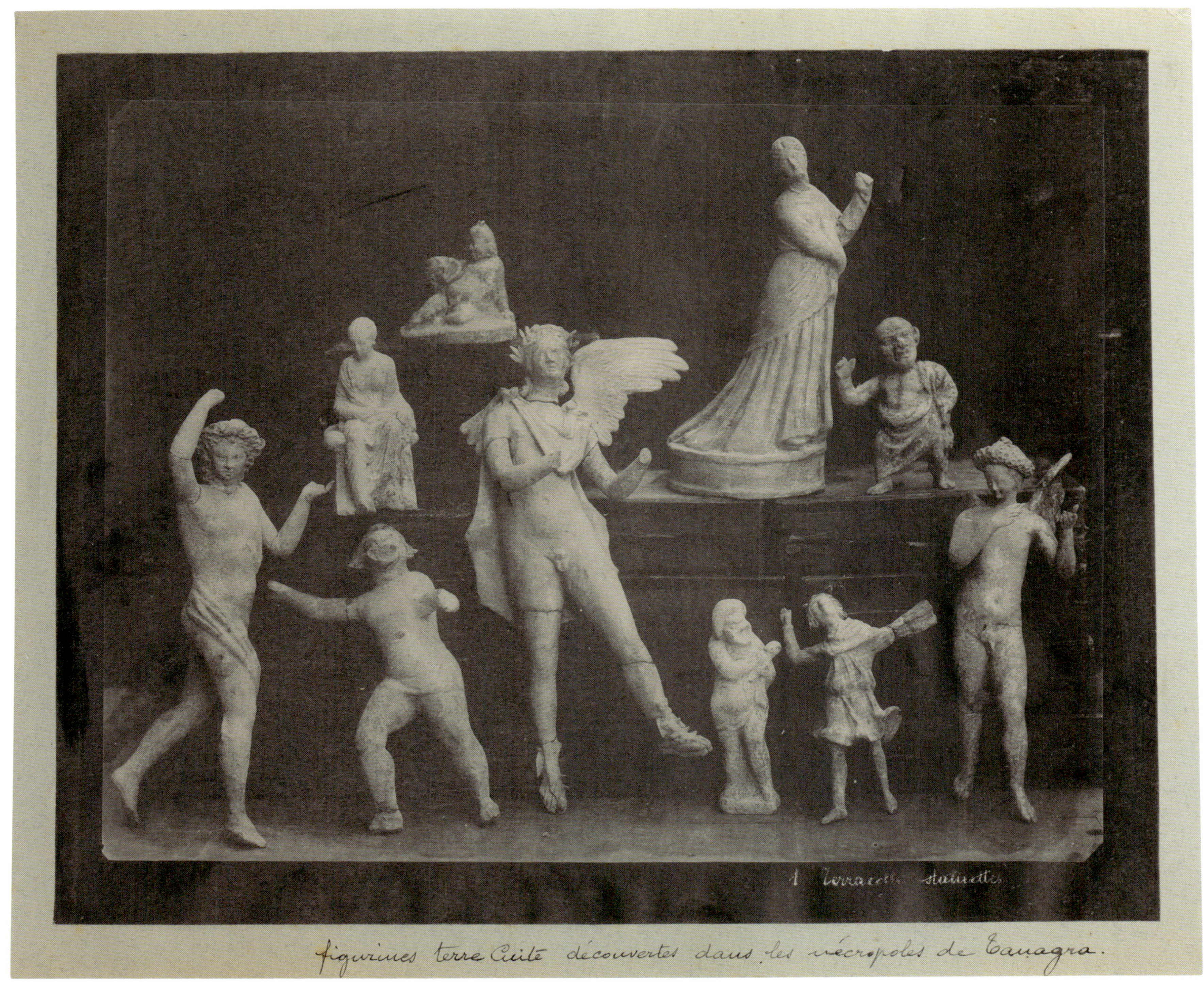

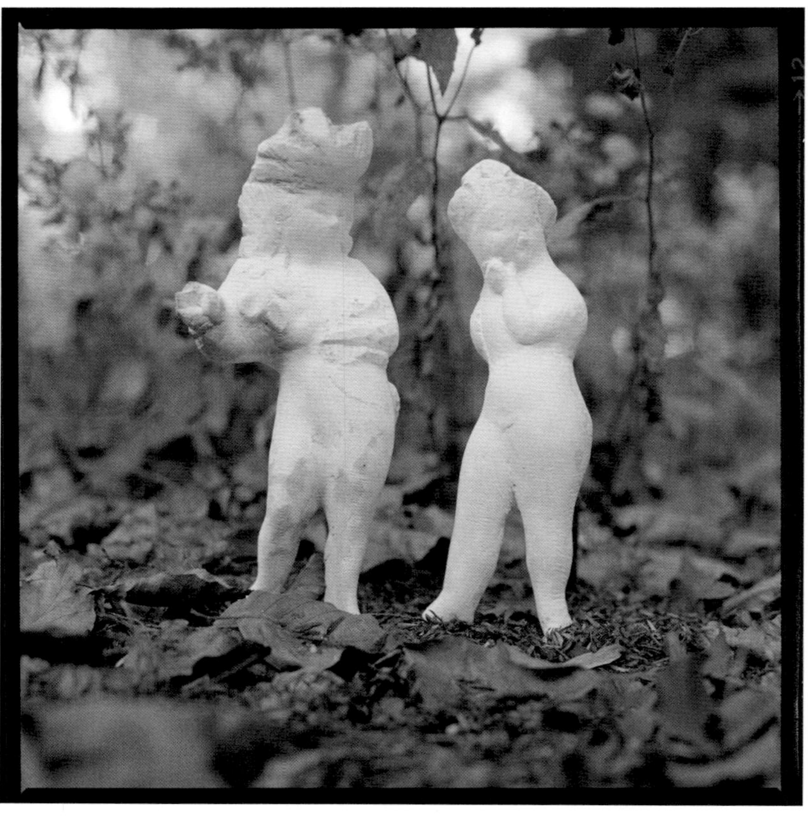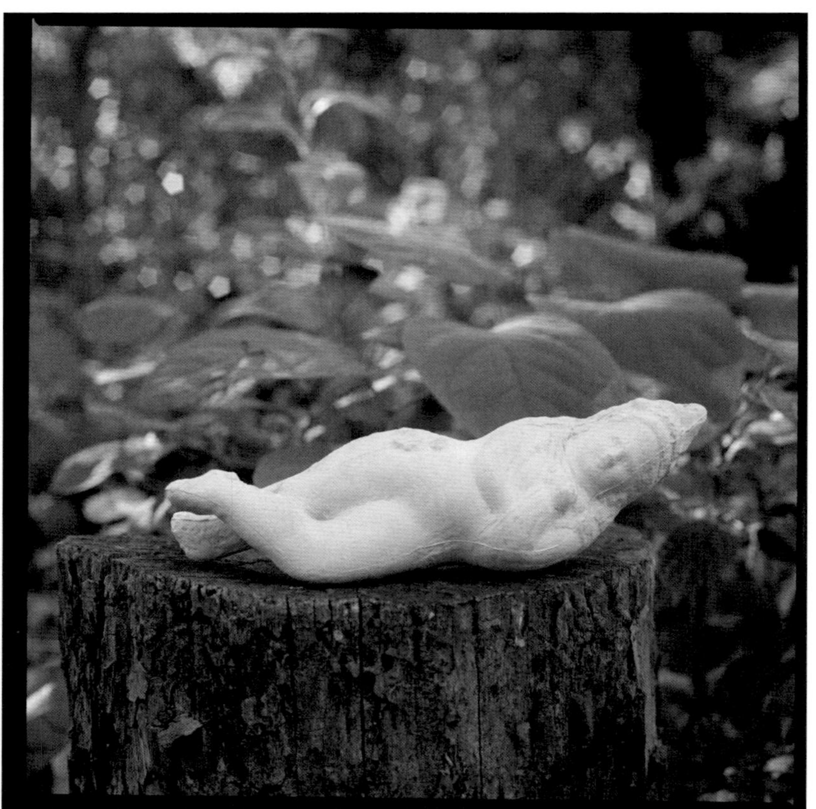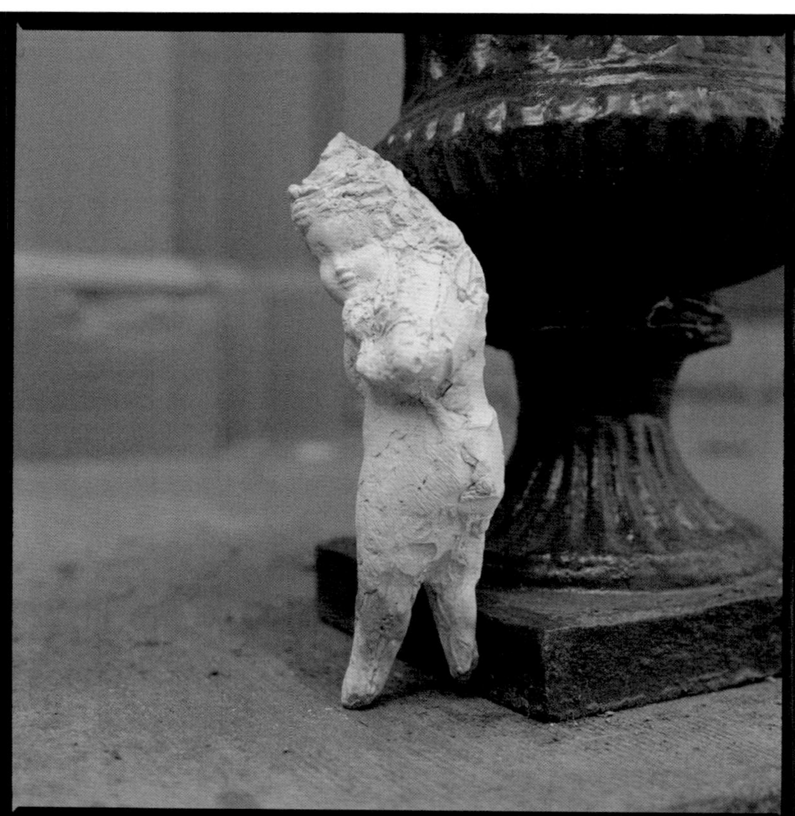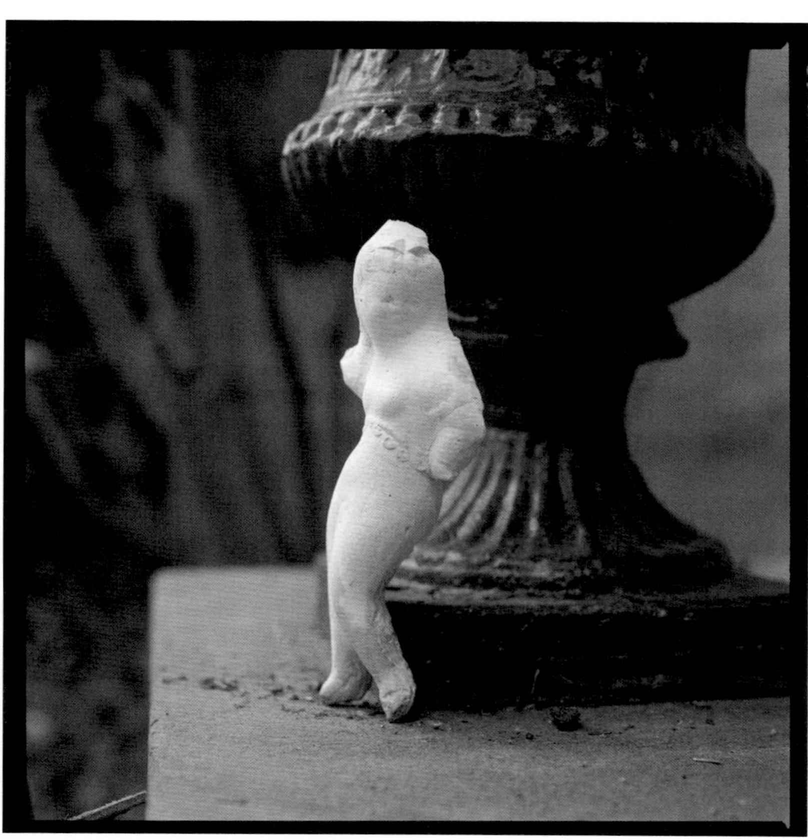

Peter Hujar photographs of Elie Nadelman plaster figurines, 1984. Scan from original negative. Courtesy Pace/MacGill Gallery, New York and Fraenkel Gallery, San Francisco

Opposite: Installation view of *Transmissions*, with plaster figurines by Elie Nadelman (c. 1938–46). Photo: Ron Amstutz

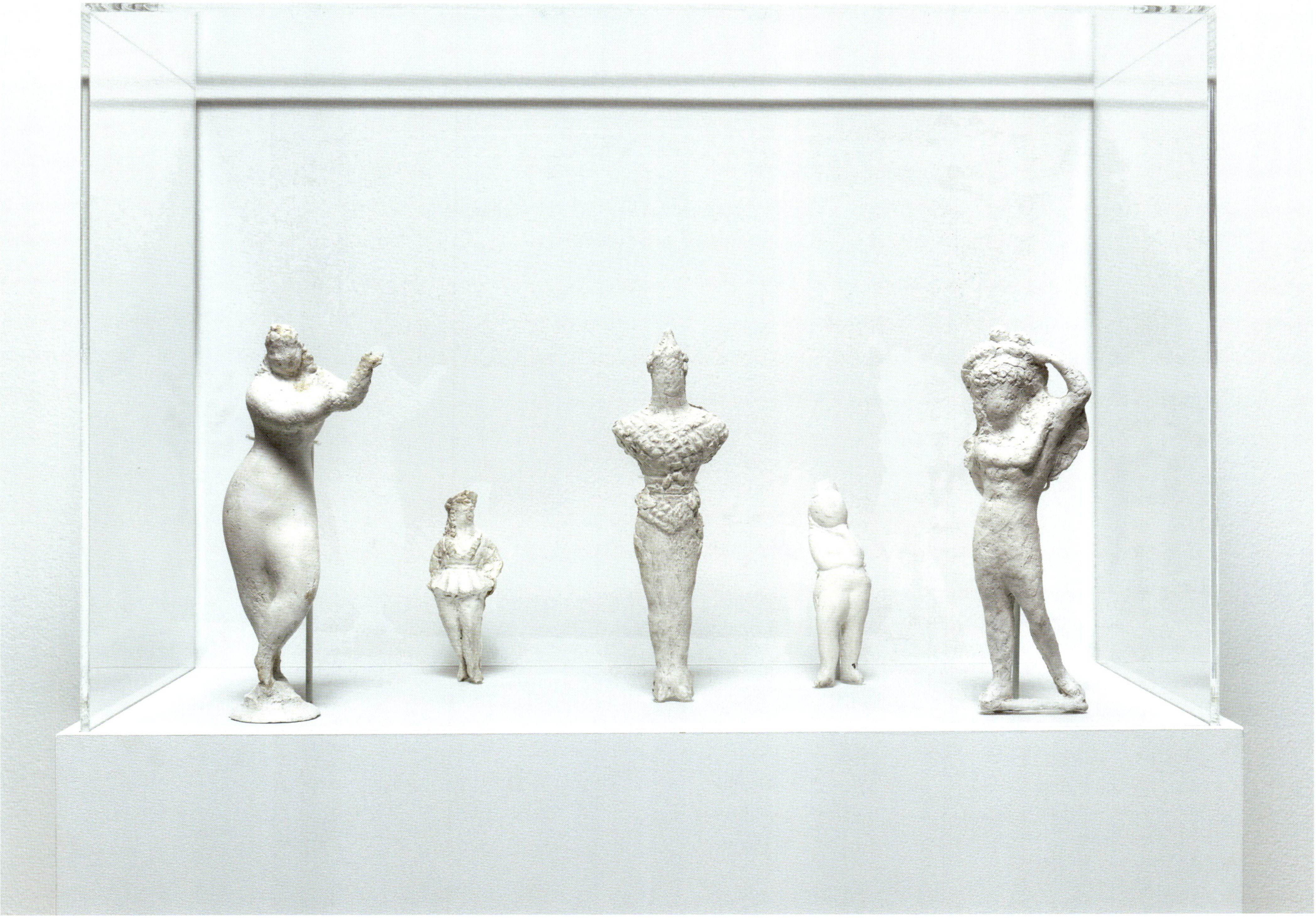

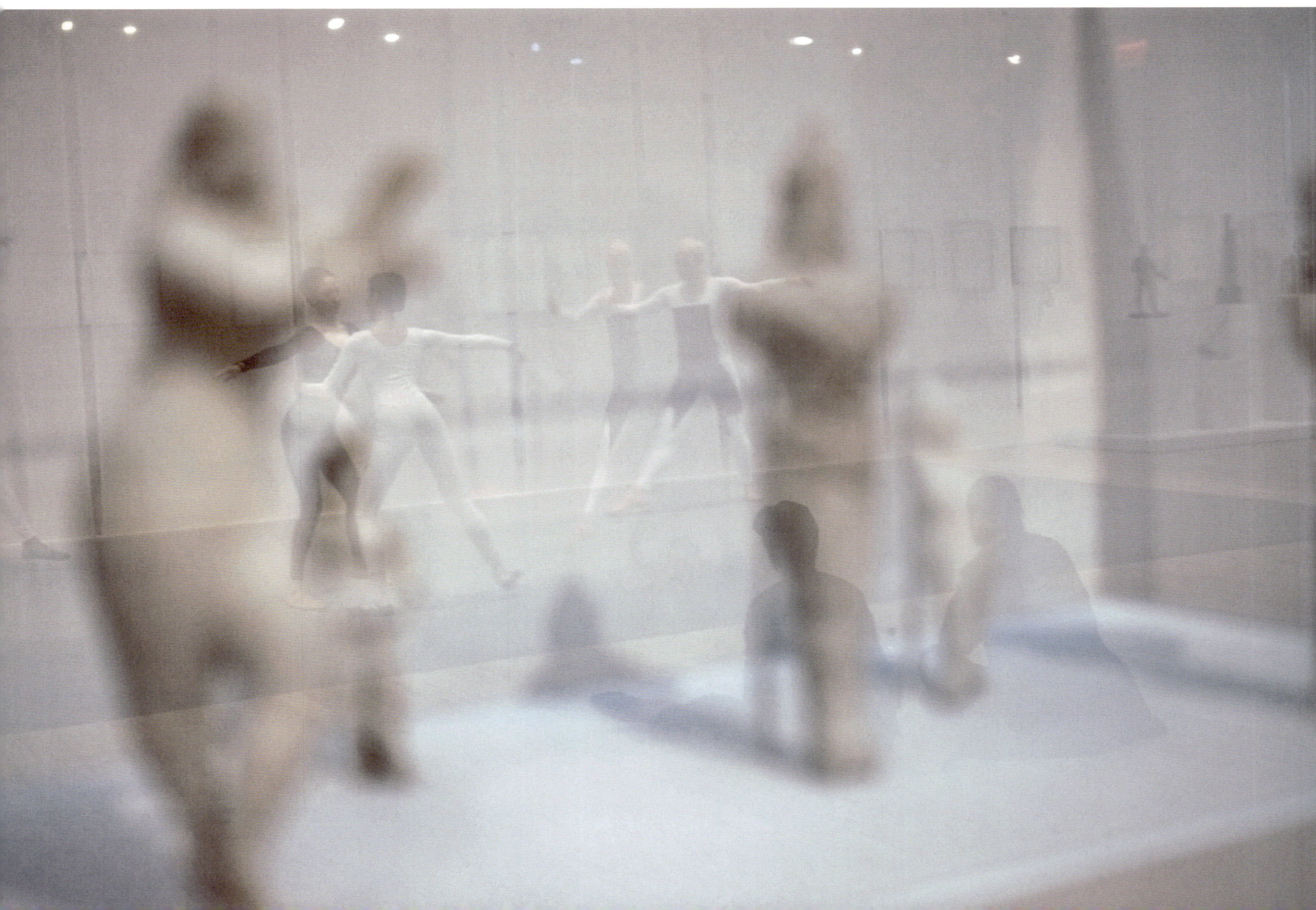

Pages 150–63: *Nick Mauss: Transmissions*, 2018. Photographs by Ken Okiishi

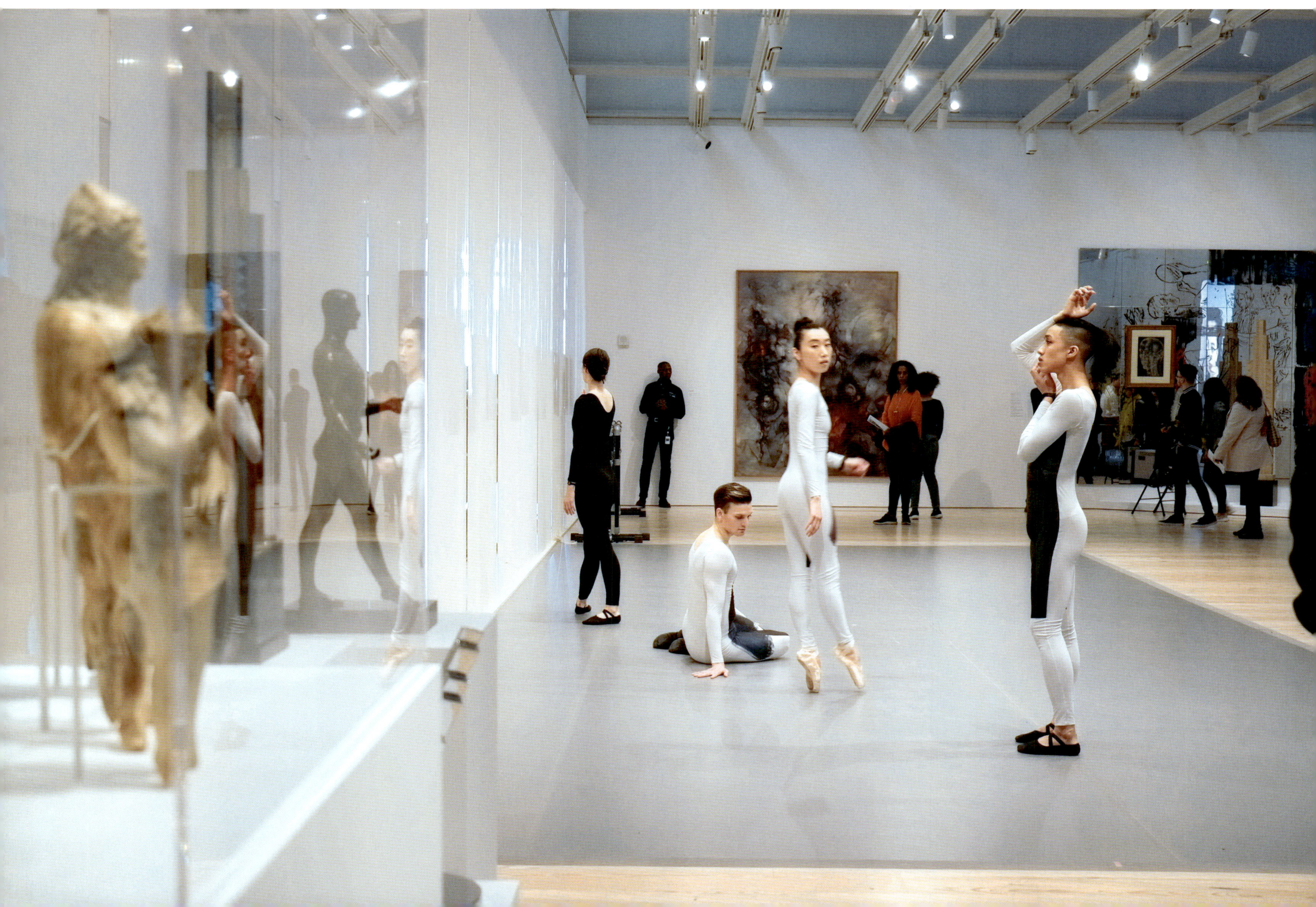

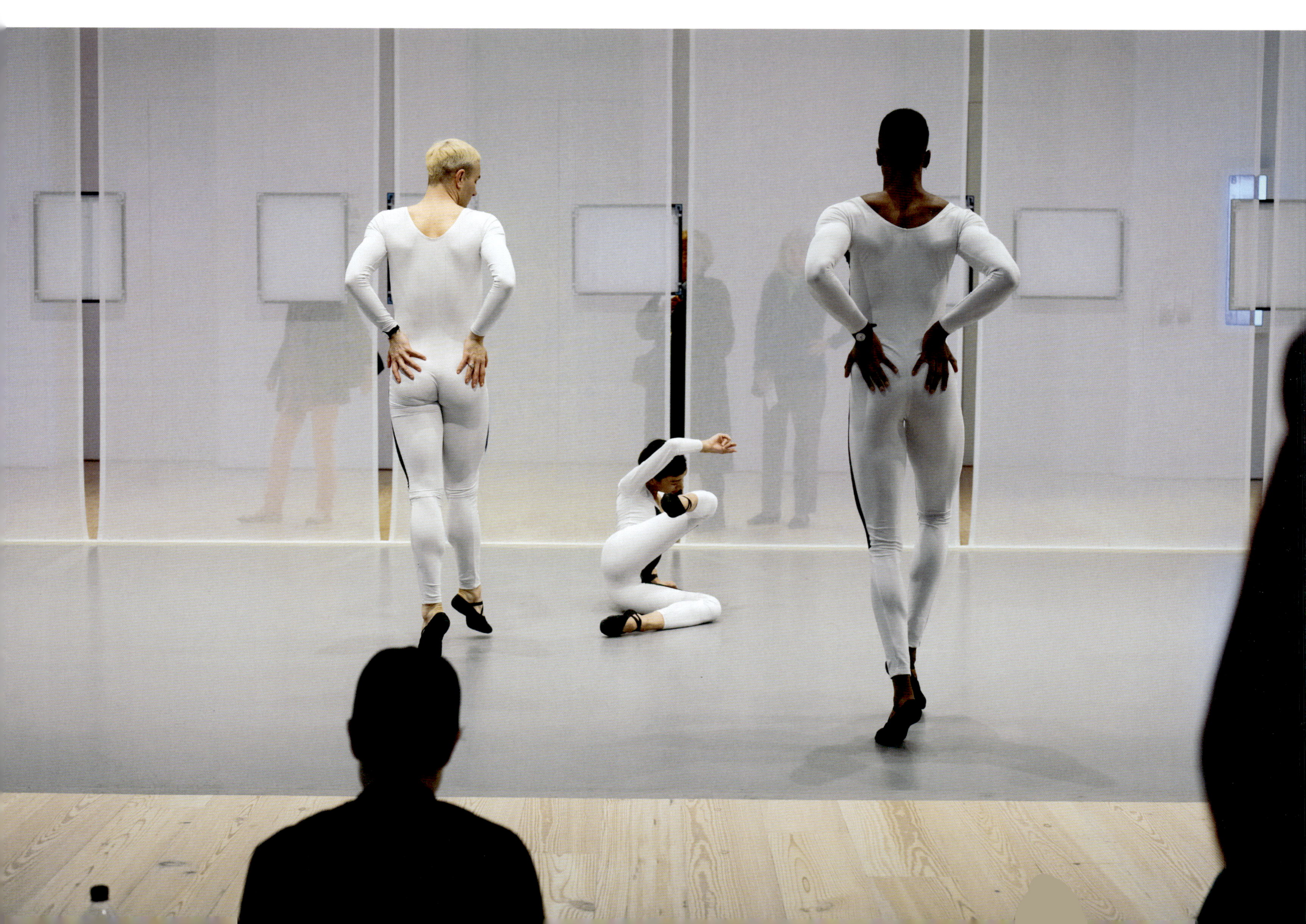

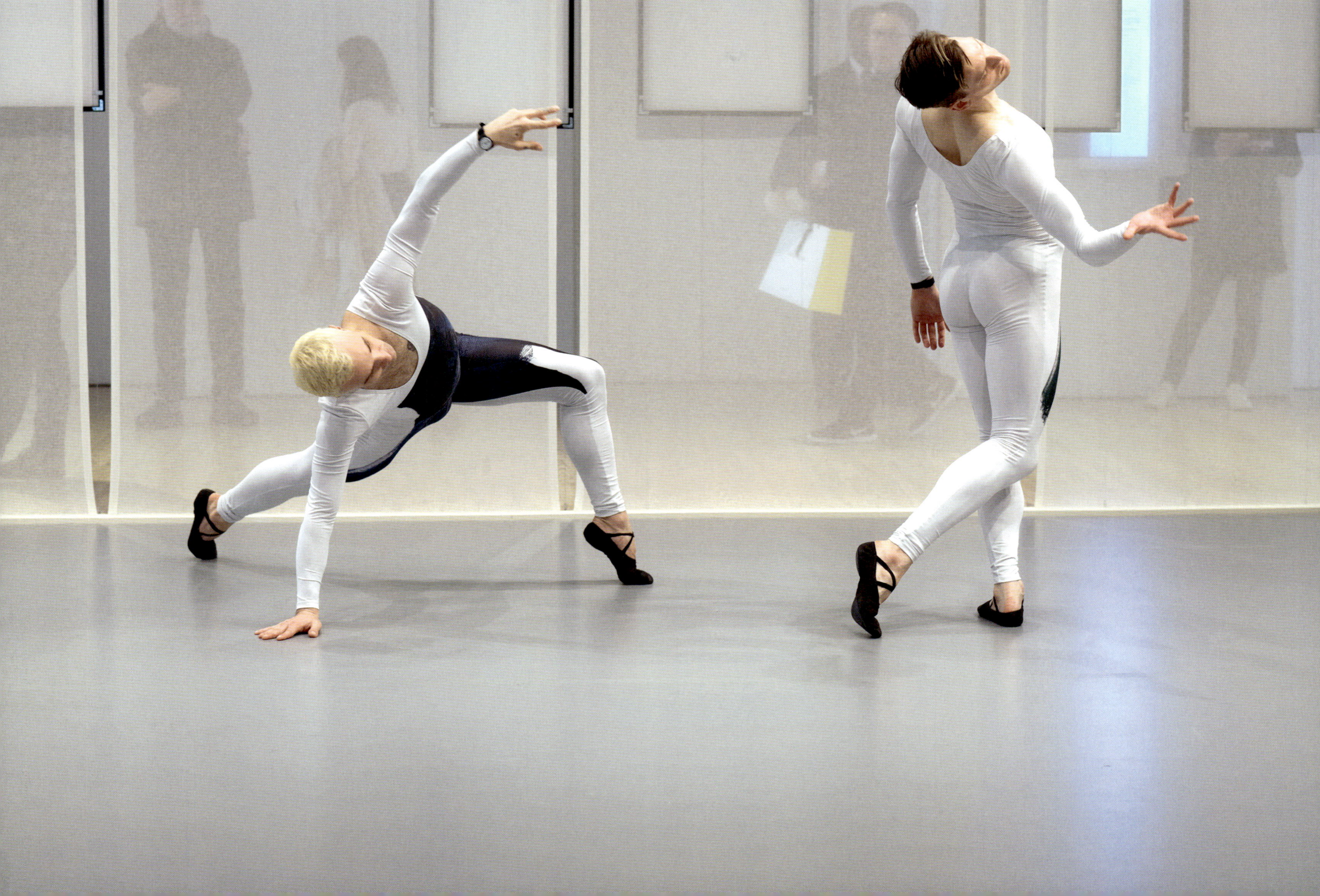

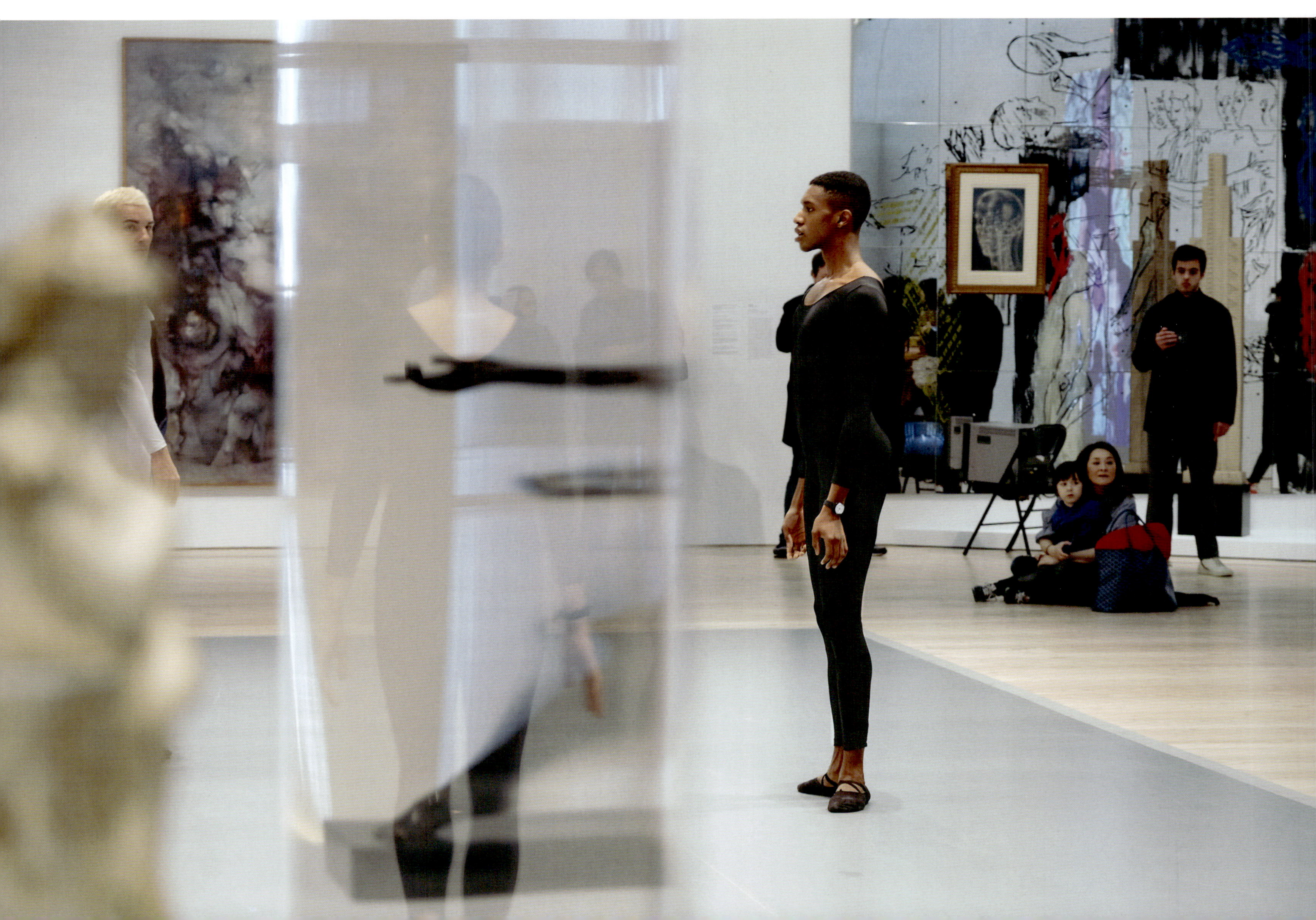

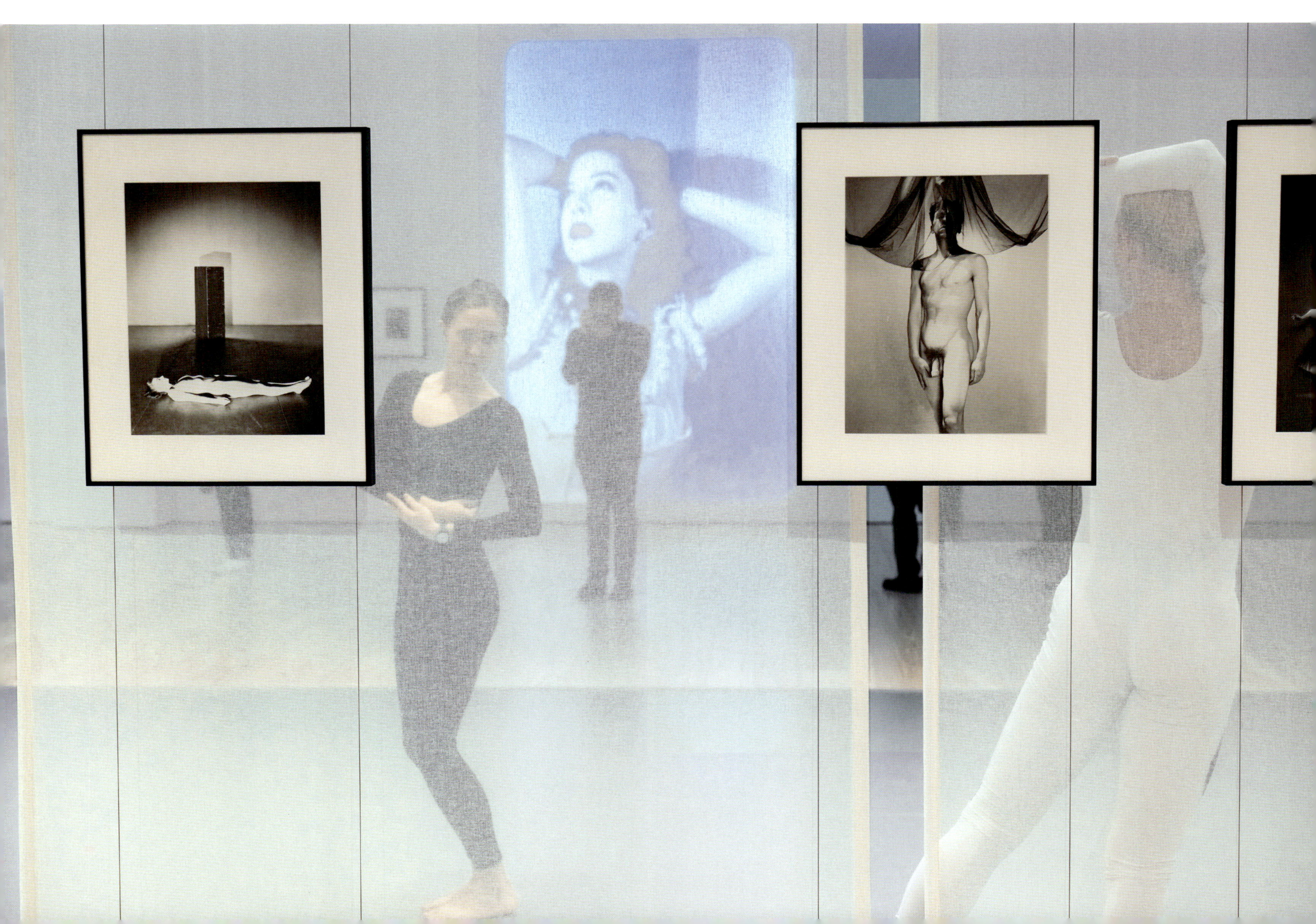

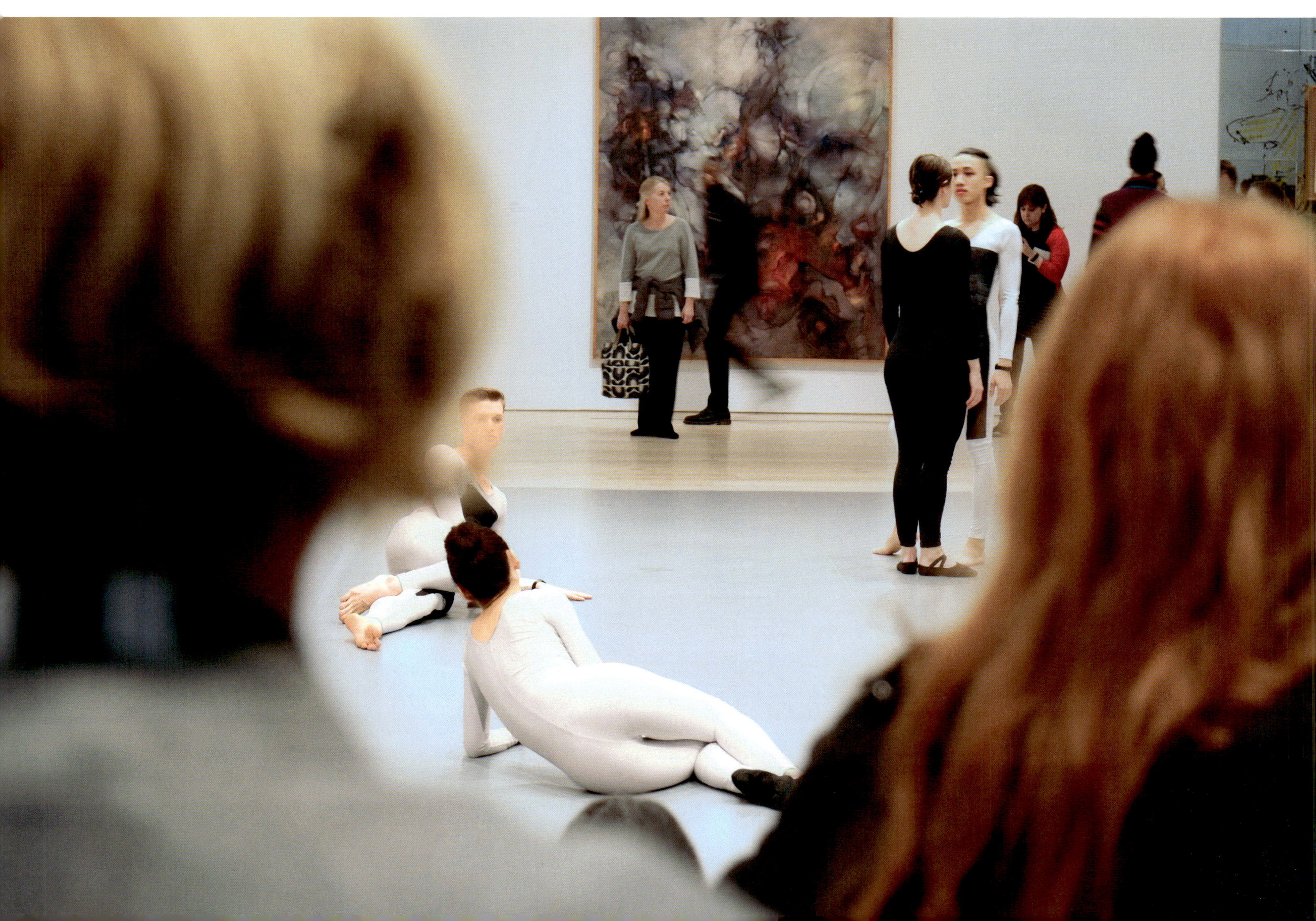

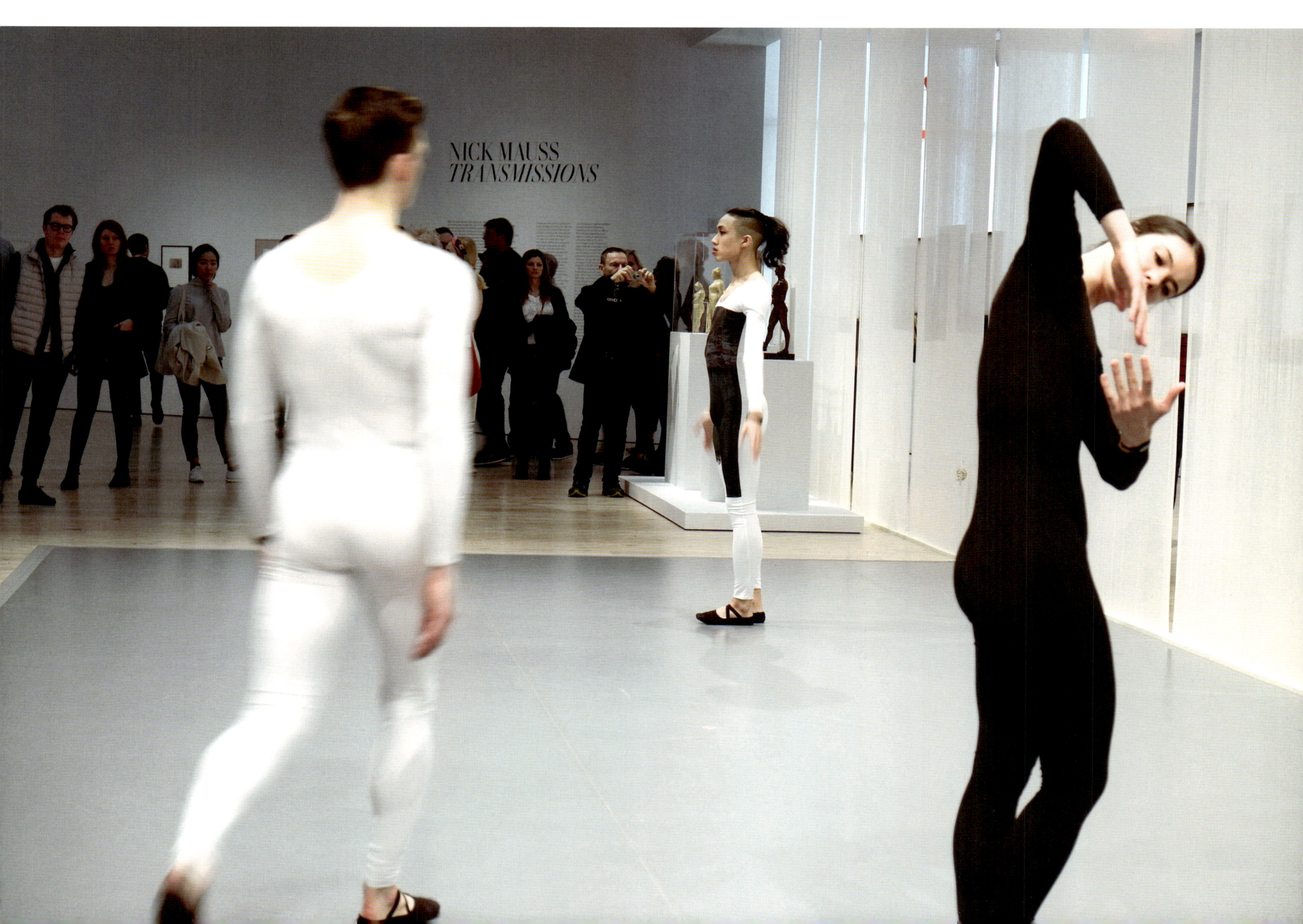
NICK MAUSS
TRANSMISSIONS

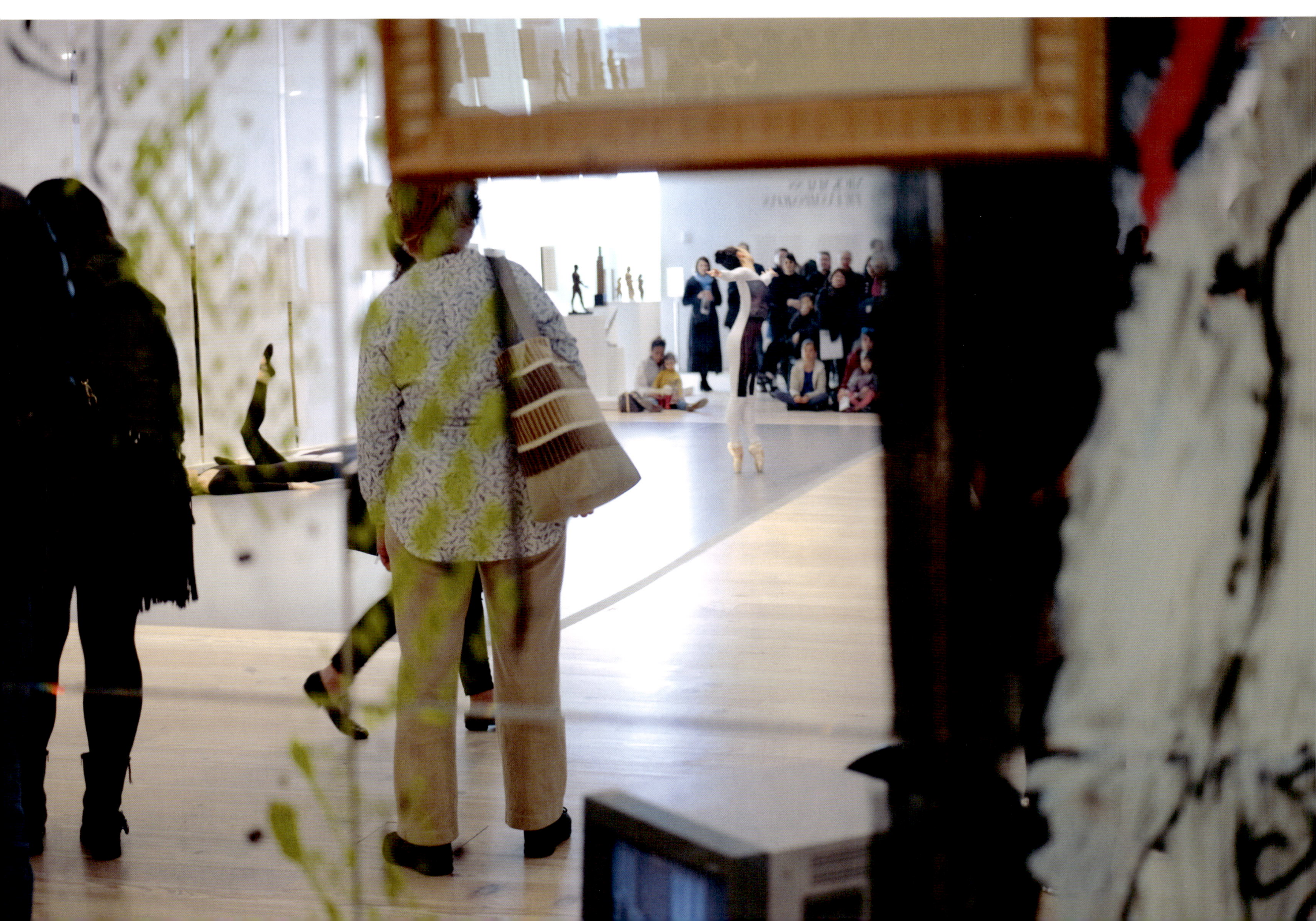

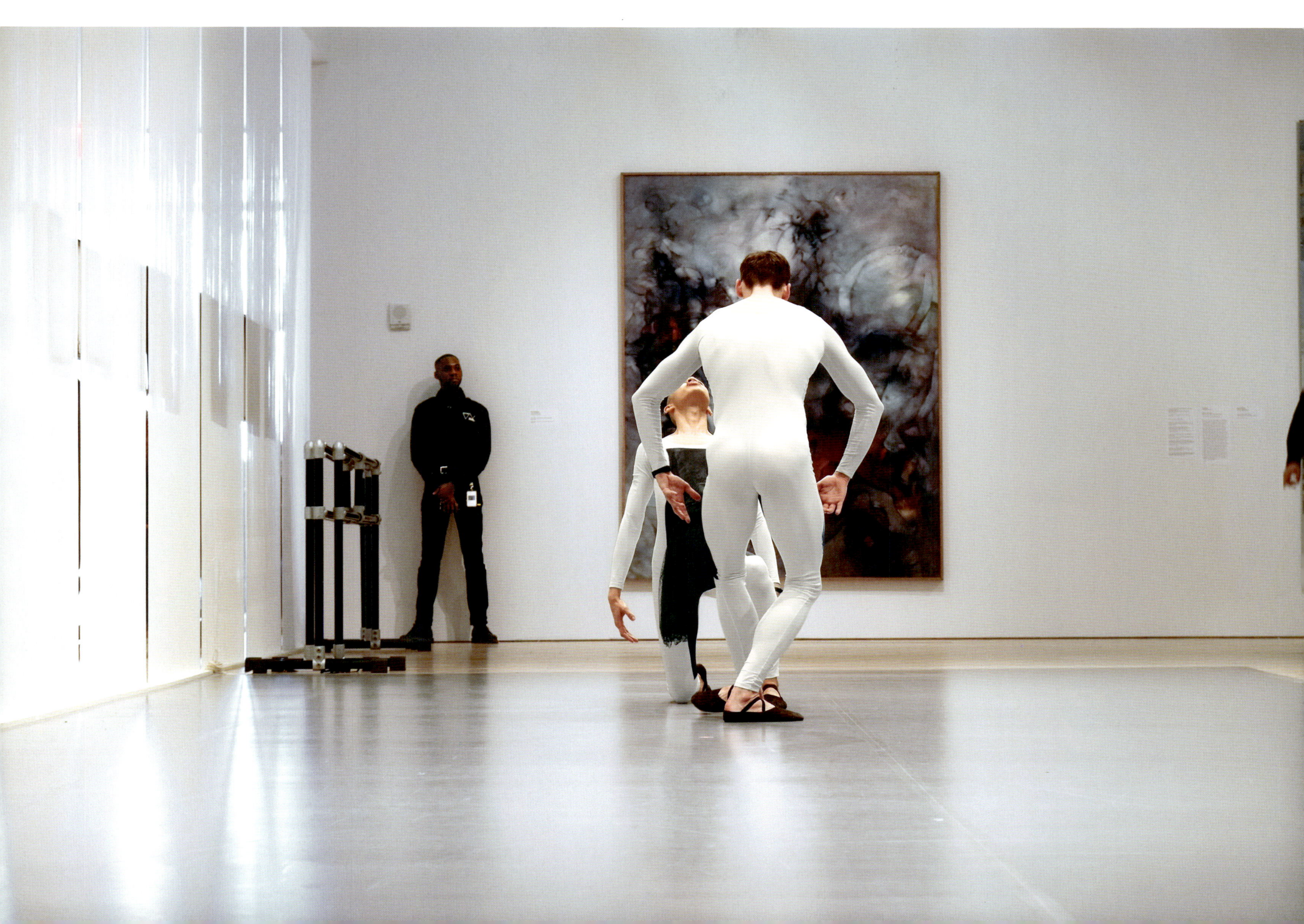

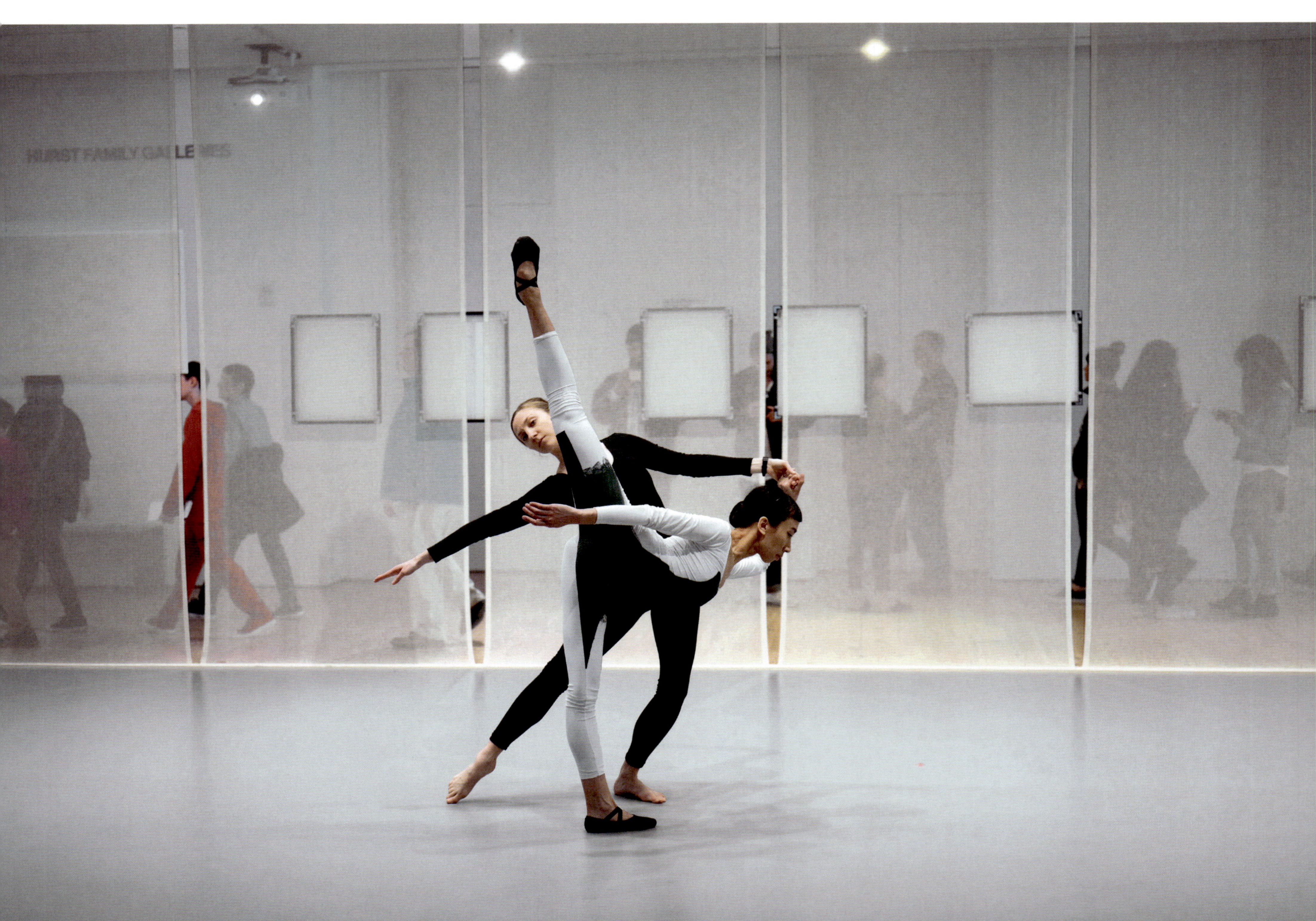
HURST FAMILY GALLERIES

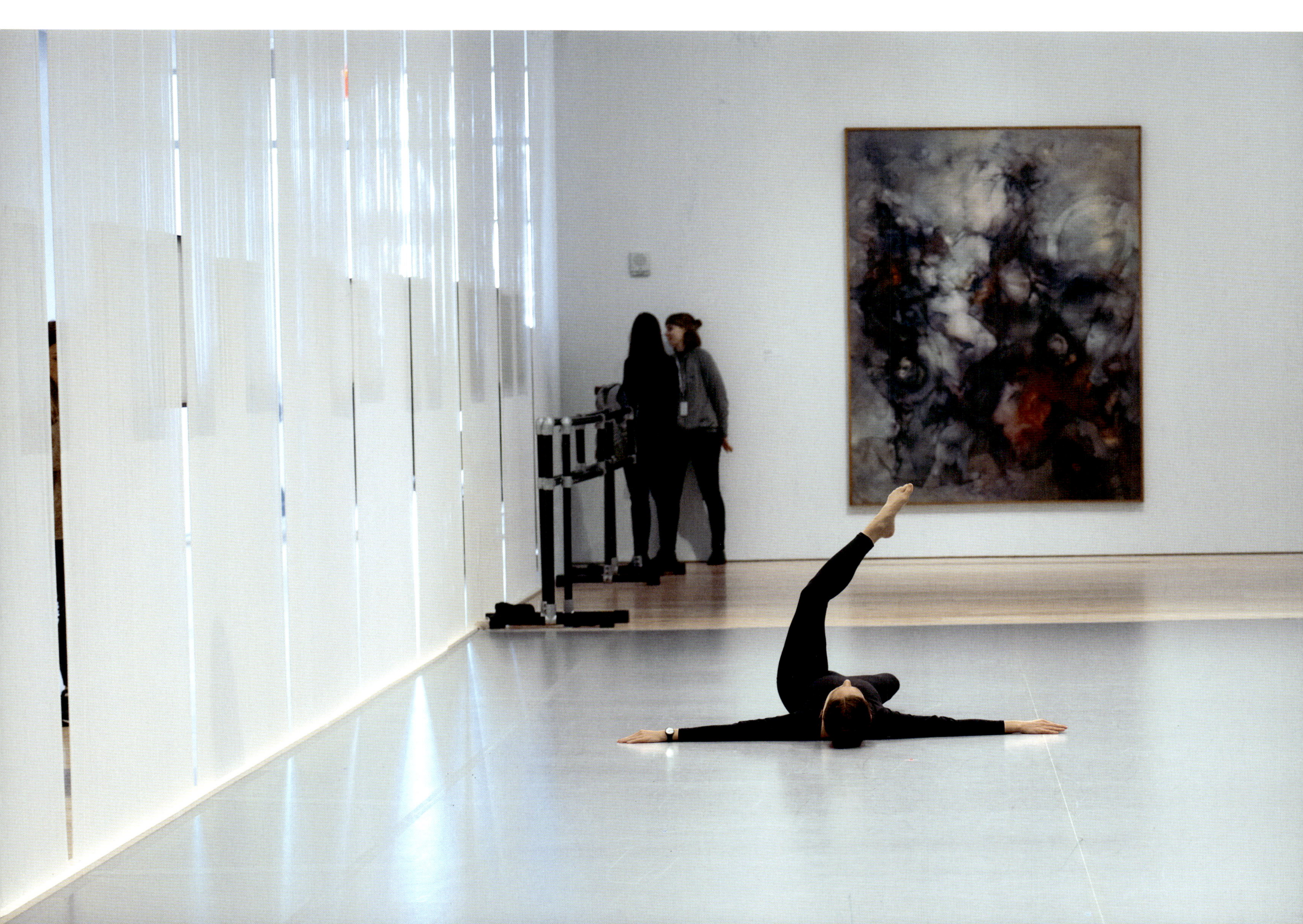

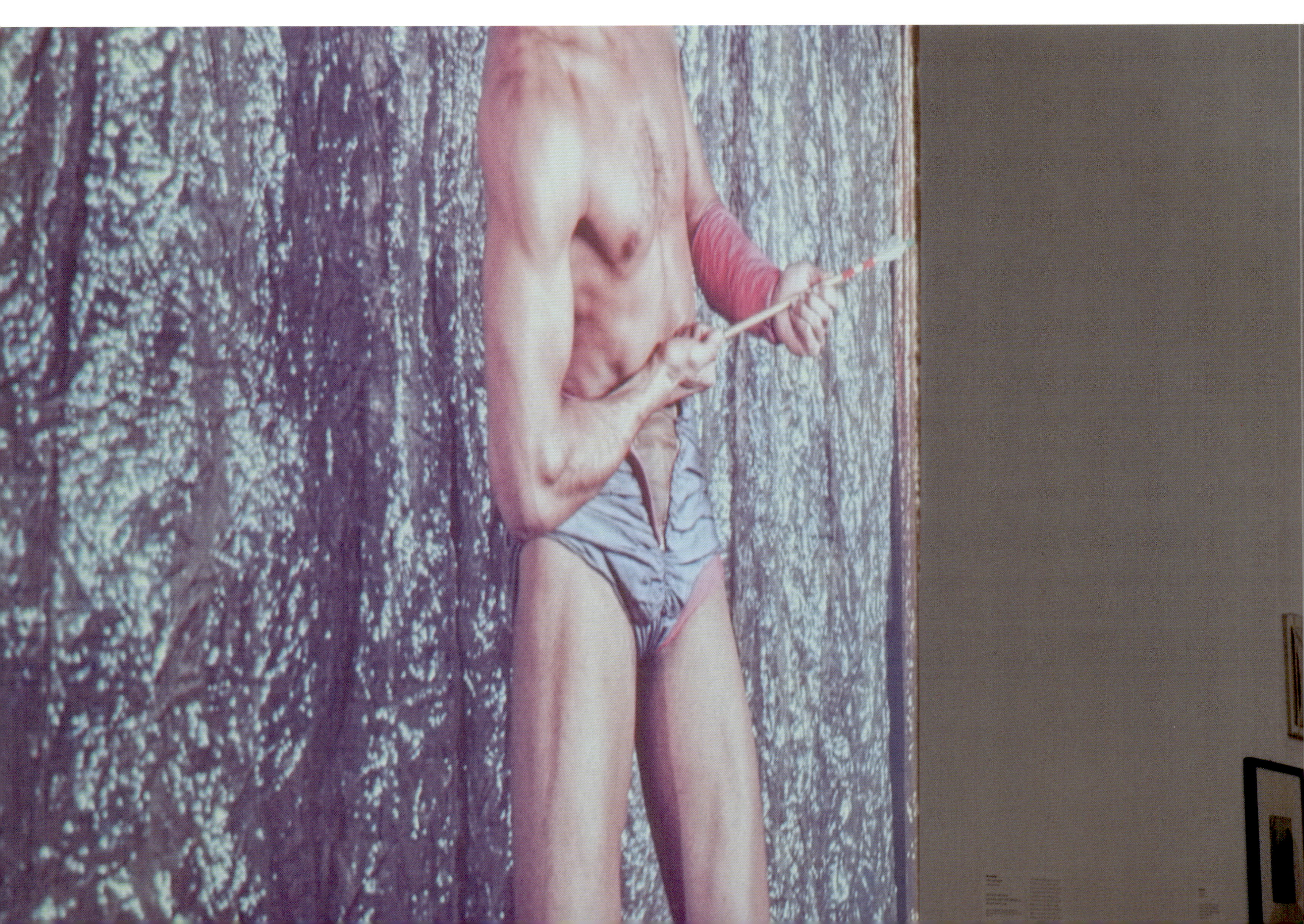

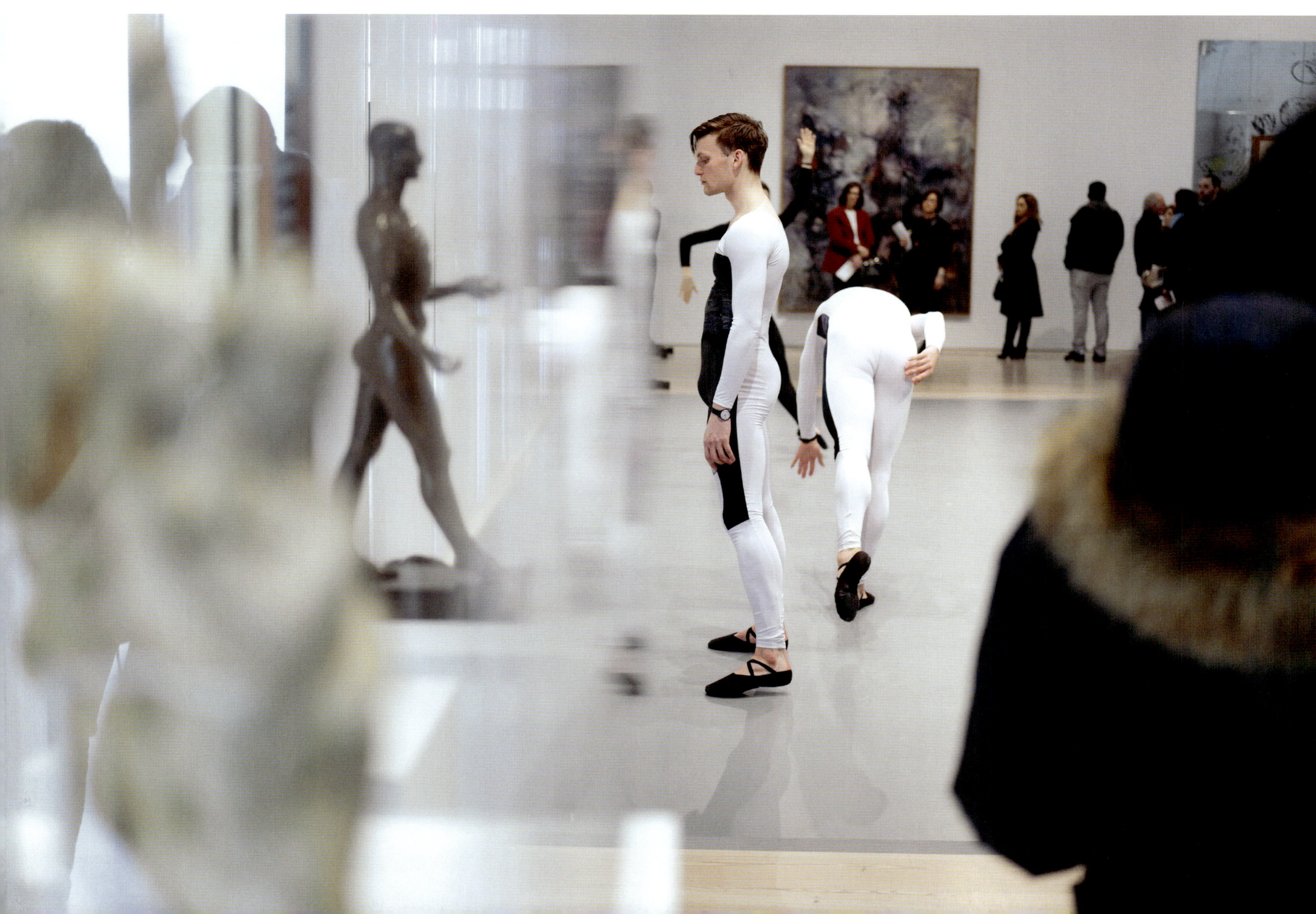

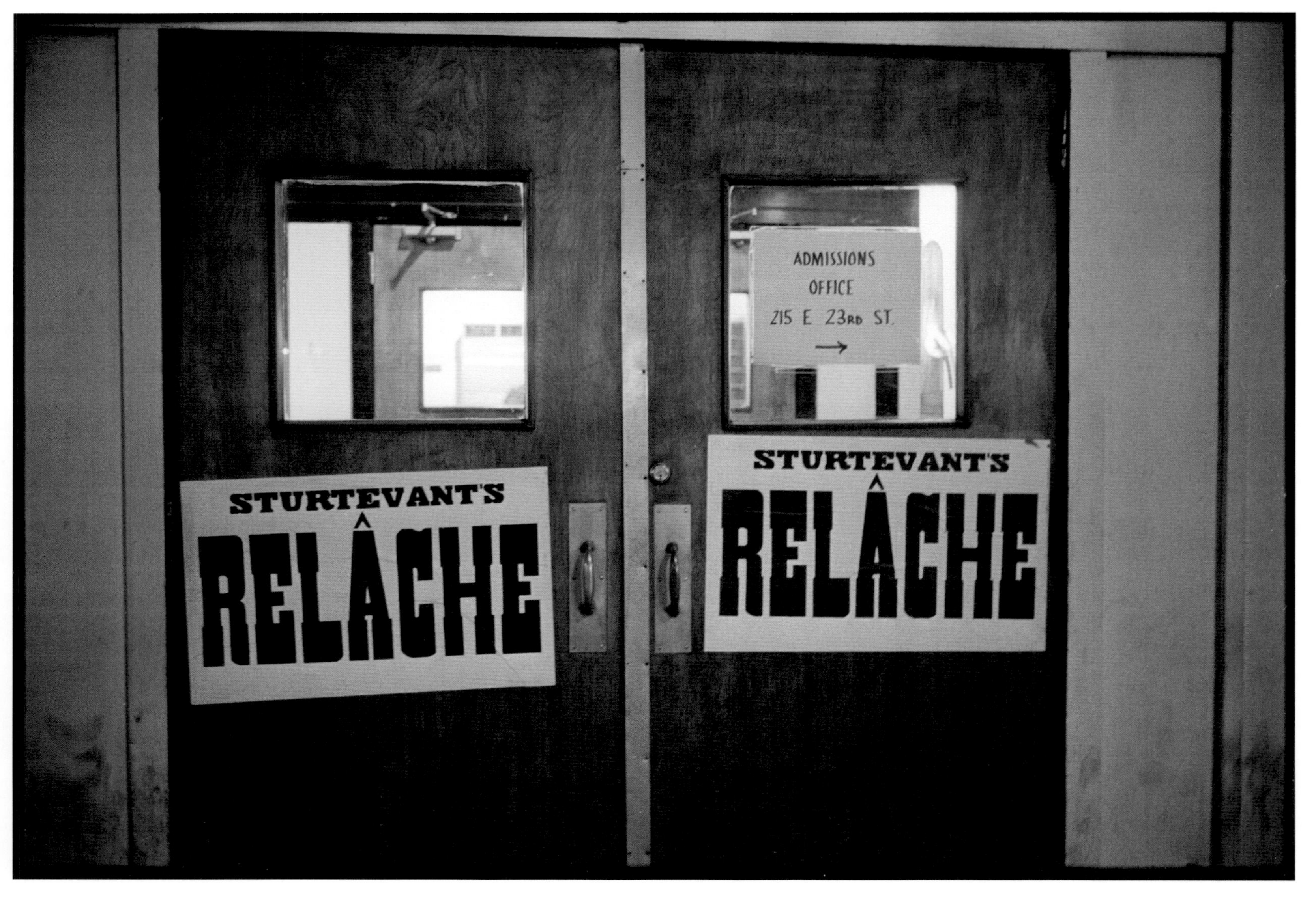
ADMISSIONS
OFFICE
215 E. 23RD ST.
STURTEVANT'S
RELÂCHE
STURTEVANT'S
RELÂCHE

In 1967, audiences arrived at the School of Visual Arts in New York for what was advertised as an event by the artist Elaine Sturtevant only to find a sign reading "Sturtevant's Relâche" on the locked auditorium doors. *Relâche*, a French colloquialism for a canceled performance, turned the viewers away at the precipice of the theater, denying them the spectacle of dancing bodies. Flagging Sturtevant's position within a Dadaist legacy of aesthetic negation, dancer and critic Jill Johnston described the work as "cancellation art."[1] Indeed, Sturtevant's *Relâche* borrows its title from a work originally staged by Francis Picabia in 1924 with the Ballets Suédois.[2] *Cancellation art* is a catchy epithet, calling to mind not only Sturtevant's unique activation of the avant-garde legacy but also broader demands to upend or alter the tradition of ballet itself, censuring its scopophilic relation to the body and the way it reinforces certain racial, gender, and sexual norms.[3] There have been many attempts across dance history to construct new forms of dancing bodies to replace those of the old ballet regime (including the postmodern performances in which Johnston herself participated).[4] Even the literal meaning of *relâche*, "release," gestures to the release techniques of modernist dance, which could be said to stage its own disruption of the tension held in the body of the ballet dancer. Nevertheless, ballet goes on.

Sturtevant's poster takes the stage again in *Transmissions*, where Nick Mauss explores ballet's persistence despite—or by way of—attempts to release the grip of its disciplinary regimen. Looking specifically at work from the mid-twentieth century, Mauss focuses on an era known for stripping balletic form of its accoutrements and emphasizing the raw musculature and virtuosic speed of the dancer. Recent scholarship has observed the queerness of this age of dance (when male dancers were often cast in starring roles), particularly concerning the open secret of homoerotic display. *Transmissions* highlights a different sense of queerness, one that emerges through complex layers of history and is made visible in a slideshow Mauss assembled from photographs taken by Carl Van Vechten.

Over the course of fourteen years, from 1940 to 1964, the writer, photographer, and connoisseur produced more than 2,800 mounted slides, many of ballet dancers. Captured in Van Vechten's home studio, most of these are portraits staged in relation either to the dancers' stage roles or to roles they never performed but that derive from iconic ballets (for instance, *Giselle* [1841] or *The Afternoon of a Faun* [1912]). A personal archive that was rarely printed, these works circulated only among Van Vechten's friends, either by mail or by invitation, through slideshows staged at his home. Mauss digitized 826 of these images to restage one such slideshow for their first public exhibition in *Transmissions*. As fleeting glimpses of dancers haunted the gallery space, the rhythmic rotation of the slides recalled the syncopated counts of a dance studio. Their flickering beat performed a battement,[5] often the foundation of ballet training, though rather than a limb it was images from ballet's past that were extended to be just as quickly withdrawn. They articulated a push against the static space of the gallery, tripping up the viewer's attempt to gain hold of either the dancer or the dance, and this, I argue, is the queerness *Transmissions* articulates in layering past and present, as well as dancer and role.

To be sure, many of Van Vechten's photographs stage openly homoerotic scenes, featuring such dancers as Anton Dolin, John Kriza, and Donald Saddler in formfitting costumes or nothing at all. The images highlight an archive of iconic male figures and are perhaps even traces of the way dancers and lovers of dance built nascent queer communities around the spectacle of these homoerotic forms. But in making bodies available for trade (trafficked, that is, through imagery), they appear to utilize the same signifiers long associated with American masculinity's rugged individualism. Sailors, soldiers, and cowboys present, as Hiram Pérez argues, "collectively, the rough trade of US imperialism."[6]

At the helm of building the queer male body of American mythology was Lincoln Kirstein, cofounder of New York City Ballet. Kirstein supported, both financially and through his writing, stripping ballet of its formal attributes and supplanting classical and avant-garde performances with new dances that revolved around popular narratives meant to appeal to wider audiences. In this vein, Kirstein also published a dictionary, *Ballet Alphabet* (1939), meant to lay bare ballet's particular language and even explain the symbolic meaning of various positions and movements. This drive toward accessibility aligned with the period's broader anxieties about hidden meanings and subconscious messages in the many transmissions flying through and across wires and airwaves, as well as in enigmatic forms of cultural production.

One can, however, read between the lines of *Ballet Alphabet* to its queer undertones, particularly visible in the accompanying illustrations by Paul Cadmus, which feature mostly male dancers alone or in sets of three (two men and a woman), wearing nothing more than briefs.[7] *Ballet Alphabet* mocks the feigned naivete that theorist Eve Kosofsky Sedgwick, a foundational thinker for queer theory, has called the "the powerful mechanism of the open secret," which is "made perfectly congruent with the smooth, dismissive knowingness of the urbane and pseudo-urbane."[8] The mockery is made even more evident in Kirstein's dedication of the book: "For my Father and Mother, who sometimes pretend they don't know what I'm talking about."[9]

The midcentury Americanization of ballet had its own ancillary repercussions on Sedgwick's understanding of queer politics. One of the scholar's abiding arguments, for instance, is that queer (unlike gay) politics "embraces, instead of repudiating, what have for many of us been formative childhood experiences of difference and stigmatization."[10] In her essay "A Poem Is Being Written" (otherwise about her predilection, as a child in the 1950s, for writing poems that broke with the cadence of the complete sentence or phrase), she offers a footnote on her voracious consumption of "the girl culture (of that class and time) of ballet."[11]

1. Jill Johnston, "Dance Journal," *Village Voice*, November 30, 1967, quoted in full in Bruce Hainley, *Under the Sign of [sic]: Sturtevant's Volte-Face* (Los Angeles, CA: Semiotext[e], 2013), 43.

2. Francis Picabia's *Relâche* bears little resemblance to Sturtevant's, though both have been described as an assault on the visual. Rosalind E. Krauss argues, for example, that "*Relâche* strikes out at the audience directly—absorbing it, focusing on it—by lighting it. So the audience is blinded even while it is illuminated, and that double function demonstrates that once the watcher is physically incorporated into the spectacle, his dazzled vision is no longer capable of supervising its events." Rosalind E. Krauss, "Mechanical Ballets: Light, Motion, Theater," in *Passages in Modern Sculpture* (Cambridge, MA: MIT Press, 1977), 212–13. This antivisuality has been read as an attempt to dismantle both bourgeois subjects—dancer and spectator—that ballet has historically sustained. On this, see Noël Carroll's description of Réné Claire's film *Entr'Acte* as "born in the spirit of negation." Noël Carroll, "*Entr'Acte*: Dada and Paris," in *Interpreting the Moving Image* (Cambridge, UK: Cambridge University Press, 1998), 26–33.

3. On scopophilia and the "male gaze," see Laura Mulvey, "Visual Pleasure and Narrative Cinema," *Screen* 16, no. 3 (October 1975): 6–18.

4. On ballet's role in shaping both the individual and social bodies, see Jennifer Homans, *Apollo's Angels: A History of Ballet* (New York: Random House, 2011).

Peter Moore, *Sturtevant's Relâche*, School of Visual Arts, New York, November 20, 1967

5. "BATTEMENT: Beating is the action of the extended or bent leg. There are *grands battements*, the straight lift of the leg to front, side and back which is a preparation for leaps. The *petits battements* are *battements degages*, *frappes*, *relevés*, or *tendus*—separate or disengaged, full out from the knee, struck, raised on half-toe, or extended from a *plié*." Lincoln Kirstein, *Ballet Alphabet: A Primer for Laymen* (New York: Kamin, 1939), 18.

6. Hiram Pérez, *A Taste for Brown Bodies: Gay Modernity and Cosmopolitan Desire* (New York: New York University Press, 2015), 13.

7. This trifecta bears a notable resonance with PaJaMa, a collaborative formed by Paul Cadmus and Jared and Margaret French, whose work is also represented in *Transmissions*. While Jared and Margaret were married, Jared and Paul were lovers—together the three undertook an extensive and experimental photography that remains a tribute to the crossing of queer and abstract art early in the twentieth century. On Cadmus, see Richard Meyer, "A Different American Scene: Paul Cadmus and the Satire of Sexuality," in *Outlaw Representation: Censorship and Homosexuality in Twentieth-Century American Art* (Boston: Beacon Press, 2002), 33–94.

8. Eve Kosofsky Sedgwick, *The Epistemology of the Closet* (Berkeley: University of California Press, 1990), 53.

9. Dedication page, in Kirstein, *Ballet Alphabet*.

10. Eve Kosofsky Sedgwick, "How to Bring Your Kids Up Gay: The War on Effeminate Boys," in *Tendencies* (Durham, NC: Duke University Press, 1993), 157n8.

11. Eve Kosofsky Sedgwick, "A Poem Is Being Written," in *Tendencies*, 186n6.

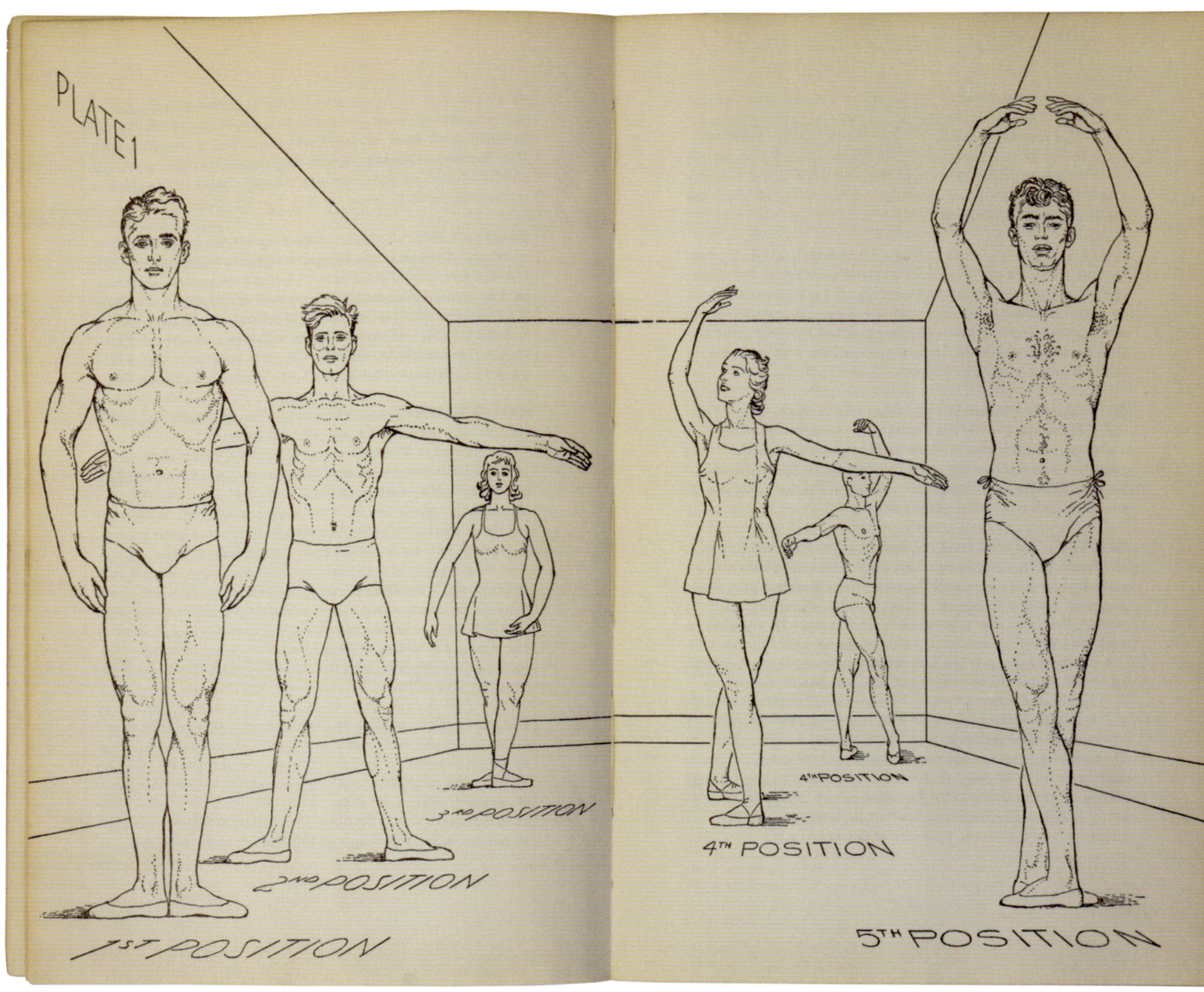

Interior spread from *Ballet Alphabet* by Lincoln Kirstein, illustrated by Paul Cadmus (New York: Kamin, 1939)

In the same moment Kirstein was popularizing the ballet as a mechanical and teachable system, Sedgwick was practicing its discipline. It is only years later, however, that the ballet she absorbed (through classes, performance, and literature) would appear alongside her articulation of queerness as more than an identity—as a strategy of surviving and dismantling the norms enforced on the body. As she goes on to write, ballet was (and perhaps still is) an "arch-mediator of one's relation to half-ritualized violence . . . a rhythmic, prestigious, exhibitionistic, and highly theatricalized way of choosing the compelled and displayed body . . . , an intensively though impossibly gendered one." She concludes, "The potential for sustained and productive, if costly, play between power and impotence, through the medium of sanctioned spectacle, was not lost on me or on many other girls."[12]

Without denying ballet's oppressive hierarchy, Sedgwick argues that the rhythm that its "sanctioned spectacle" instilled in her was at cross-purposes with other conditioning rhythms—namely obedience and learning to fit in. This is different than the masterful illusion of hiding queer sexuality in plain sight. It is, instead, a kind of wedging apart of one disciplinary regime with another, a disruption that can be as pleasurable as it is painful for those who perform and encounter its

12. Ibid.

13. The gas station, as a liminal social space, is also a notable ground of queer cruising. For a thorough discussion of *Filling Station* and queer sexuality, see Jennifer L. Campbell, "Dancing Marines and Pumping Gasoline: Coded Queerness in Depression-Era American Ballet," in *Queer Dance*, ed. Claire Croft (New York: Oxford University Press, 2017), 125–45.

14. Lincoln Kirstein, quoted in Mark Franko, "The Ballet-versus-Modern Wars as Ideology," in *The Work of Dance: Labor, Movement, and Identity in the 1930s* (Middletown, CT: Wesleyan University Press, 2002), 121. As Franko and others have argued, Kirstein engaged in an ideological struggle against expressive modernism, which was evinced in his drive to turn the ballet into popular spectacle by importing—in his own words, "grafting"— the formal rigor and athleticism onto symbolic narratives of American life. The problem with Kirstein's project should be obvious: it perpetuated not only American nationalism but also imperialism in its colonizing and redeployment of existing art forms in service to the US nation-state.

15. "ECHAPPE: From the French, to slip or escape. A slipping movement, in which the body in *fifth* position bends both knees equally and jumps, regaining the floor in *second* position. Feet retouch the ground toes first, heels last." Kirstein, *Ballet Alphabet*, 24.

forms. Alongside questions of representational violence are the issues of what is transmitted around the compelled and displayed body and what sort of *relâche*, suspension or temporary release, may come from choosing such a spectacularly queer mode.

Mauss's work in *Transmissions* similarly sets at cross-purposes modern American ballet's ostensible straightforwardness—or transparency. Literalizing this idea is Mauss's re-creation of a costume Cadmus designed for the one-act ballet *Filling Station* (1937), a coverall made of entirely see-through fabric. Choreographed and originally performed by Lew Christensen, *Filling Station* tells the story of Mac, a gas station attendant who dances his way through a series of vaudevillian acts that threaten to disrupt the routine function of the gas pump.[13] A private photograph George Platt Lynes captured of Jacques d'Amboise (who reprised the role of Mac for television in 1953) in the coverall, sans dance belt, gregariously tipping his hat, captures the eroticism of the costume. According to Kirstein, however, the ballet is about "work today," and Mac embodies a "self-reliant, agreeable, and frank American working-man."[14]

Hung in the window of the Whitney Museum of American Art's eighth-floor gallery, the transparent costume contains not only the cityscape and the West Side piers (and its history as a site for queer sex and artistic experimentation) but also the window itself, the most basic and ubiquitous feature of the modern office tower. Large glass windows like these signal the surveillance culture of an allegedly benevolent transparency. Mac's nearly naked echappés[15] may position him as an object of desire, but the potential joy of his exhibitionism is tempered by an understanding of the panoptic control under which Mac (whether a gas station attendant or a dancer onstage) does his work today. Indeed, what may be most pornographic about Mac is not his fleshy presence but the way his body is controlled by the services he performs: the flow of gas he pumps and the demands of keeping things moving at the station. Mauss's display reveals

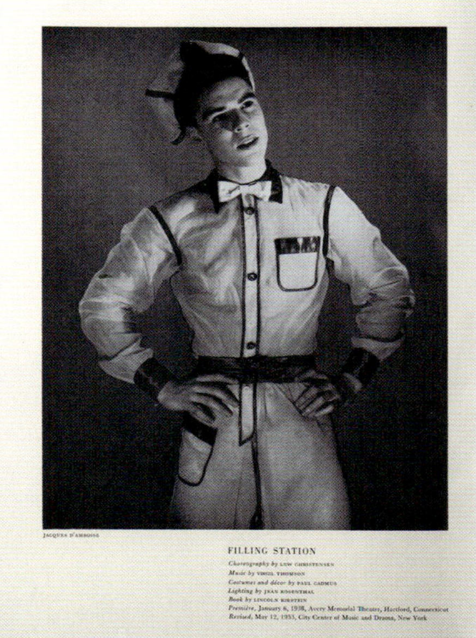

Jacques d'Amboise as Mac in *Filling Station* (1937), photographed by George Platt Lynes, reproduced in the souvenir program *The New York City Ballet: A Portfolio of Photographs by George Platt Lynes*, 1954

16. I'm gesturing here at Kirstein's interest in a very different kind of photography than Van Vechten's studio portraits. Kirstein championed, for example, the documentary work of Walker Evans, who himself proposed that the photograph was a transparent means of communication.

17. "ARABESQUE: A pose of the classic theatrical dance, taking its name from a style of renaissance leaflike ornament, in which the dancer's body is supported on one foot either straight (*tendu*) or half-bent (*demiplié*) with the other in the air, extended at right angles to it, and the arms composed to further a harmonious horizontality, creating the longest possible line from toes to finger tips. . . . A feeling of effortless suspension can be gained by a dancer's final Arabesque, posed at the end of a variation, just before quitting the scene, a finality rendered breathlessly infinite." Quoting Carlo Blasis (1829), Kirstein continues, "*Arabica ornamenta*, as a term in painting means those ornaments, composed of plants, shrubs, light branches and flowers, with which the artist adorns pictures, compartments, frises, panels. The taste for this sort of an ornament was brought to us by the Moors and Arabs.' . . . But Carlo Blasis, as usual, is probably right." Kirstein, *Ballet Alphabet*, 9–10.

Mac—"self-reliant, agreeable, and frank"—to be the ideal subject of late capitalism, a self-managed individualist operating as the affective and somatic arm of the corporation.

The word *transparency* can also be applied to the photographic slide, a medium meant not to be seen through but to be looked at through projection—one that, in its ephemerality, suggests not the clarity but rather the instability of vision.[16] Van Vechten's slides acknowledge the mediation that has occurred as dance has historically been documented. Two photos show dancer Hugh Laing in front of a life-size poster featuring two bullfighters standing together in the middle of an arena. In the first, Laing looks in the same direction as the matadors, aligning himself with their ceremonial pose. In the second, he twists himself around to look back at the scene, becoming not only the matadors' audience but potentially their bull.

Not all of Van Vechten's works can be so easily parsed. Another slide shows Laing in arabesque,[17] again mirroring a poster that hangs behind him. The poster features a drawing by Jean Cocteau of Vaslav Nijinsky in the titular role for *Le Spectre de la rose* (1911). The drawing highlights the deconstruction of the gender binary Nijinsky's performances are best known for: his muscular legs are

firmly planted on the ground while his upper torso holds a loosened port de bras (a pose more traditionally associated with female dancers). The dancer's face, however, looks nothing like Nijinsky's: Cocteau used a single, slanted line to depict his eye. If this exemplifies Cocteau's barely-there style, it is also a racialized marking that suggests, as Peter Wollen first argued, that Nijinsky's play with gender is situated at a "complex imbrication of the sexual and the political," filtered through orientalism and a Western fantasy that displaces queerness onto a phantasmatic "East."[18] Laing mirrors only the arabesque, leaving behind the costuming and makeup, which Van Vechten's photograph ensures is nevertheless visible in the background. It's a disorienting exchange that seems to mark a tension between what Laing desires to capture from the poster with his body and what Van Vechten wishes to see with his camera. From Cocteau to Laing to Van Vechten's analog slide and finally to Mauss's digital slide, dance moves from body to image and back again in an exchange that has endless potential. Yet in the projection on the gallery walls, the scene of transmission is momentarily suspended, frozen between the body and its embodiment of the archive.

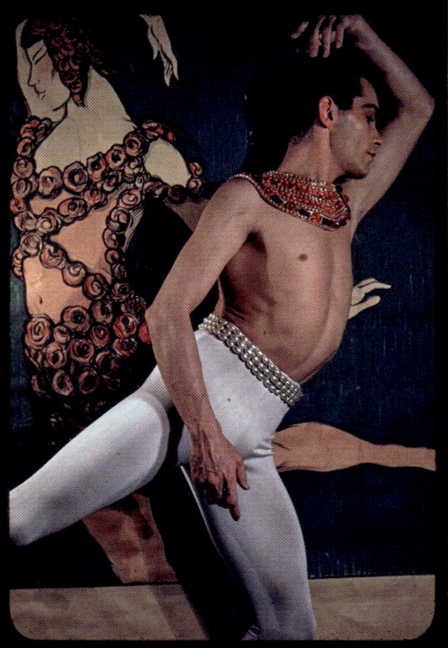

18. See Peter Wollen, "Fashion/Orientalism/The Body," *New Formations*, no. 1 (Spring 1987): 18.

Hugh Laing with Jean Cocteau's poster of Vaslav Nijinski, photographed by Carl Van Vechten, 1940. Kodachrome slide with hand-labeled frame. Jerome Robbins Dance Division, The New York Public Library for the Performing Arts, Astor, Lenox and Tilden Foundations

19. "PAS: Theoretically, the *pas* is not a single but a combination of steps or movements of the feet. . . . Choreographers and individual dancers for five hundred years have contributed to build on one another's work until we have been given the dancing practice of our contemporary stage. The two prime categories of *pas* govern the twin provinces of earth and air. Steps predominantly the gift of the seventeenth century demonstrated the resources of the plane stage-surface with adaptations of ballroom walk or march. By the middle of the eighteenth, new steps began to predicate the conquest of air. As time went on, greater subtlety, variety and plasticity evolved themselves into a fluid idiom. The nineteenth century provided a language accentuated by heel and toe beats borrowed from the characteristic national dance sources (polka, mazurka, cachucha, etc.), which gave color to the corpus of steps which had tended to become theatrically sterile. If the twentieth century has provided new steps, these have been appropriated from popular entertainments, public ball-rooms and music-halls. The steps of traditional social or ballroom dancing have always been amplified by theatrical gesture, but as for their execution from the minuet down to our two-step, it is more a question of tempi than of complex physical activity. By a 'step' in theatrical dancing, we usually refer to a combination of movements which has become popular enough to enjoy written definition or inclusion in dance manuals. The step thus defined becomes canonical, part of the material of dancing, which can be taught. But there are innumerable steps created by choreographers for their own private and transient uses, which may never bear a name." Kirstein, *Ballet Alphabet*, 57–58.

20. The term *alfresco* is taken from Van Vechten's hand-labeled description on the slide frame.

With the slideshow in *Transmissions*, Mauss publicly and abundantly reimagines what had previously been seen only in private, presenting nearly one-third of Van Vechten's archive. Irreducible to a single genre, let alone meaning, Mauss's collection of photographs adds complexity to, for instance, images that Van Vechten took of Laing and Alan Meadows engaged in a pas de deux.[19] In a troubling depiction of racial fantasy, the duo is staged alfresco[20] in beaded loincloths and flowered headdresses, in what appears to be Central Park, right outside Van Vechten's home on Central Park West. The pairing appears again in similar costume in Van Vechten's studio, where the mostly naked dancers hold various positions across and alongside each other. As their images flit by, one sees them playing and performing with each other in a series of mutable positions. Then, in an unusually candid and banal photograph for Van Vechten, the two dancers are back outdoors, resting on a tree in a wooded area, wearing fashionable shorts and looking off into the distance. They appear at rest, or at least performing rest, for they have leis draped around their necks as though they are tourists in Hawaii. Almost always twinned in costume, Laing and Meadows seem reflections of each other, their posed bodies entangled.

What Mauss's reanimation of this archive reveals is that Van Vechten might have done his best work despite himself, if not as a photographer then as an archivist. Within the aggregate of these slides, one finds a movement between dancers being compelled and choosing to display their bodies. Shortly after her New York premiere in 1949, in which she presented two lauded solos, Janet Collins modeled the costumes from the event in photos for Van Vechten: one a high-waisted and long-sleeved leotard made to look like a matador's *traje de luces*, and the other a red ruffled skirt and cropped top decorated with a white floral pattern and lace. The two solos showcased Collins's versatility as a dancer of both ballet and modern dance, the former set to Mozart's *Rondo* and the latter to the spirituals "Nobody Knows the Trouble

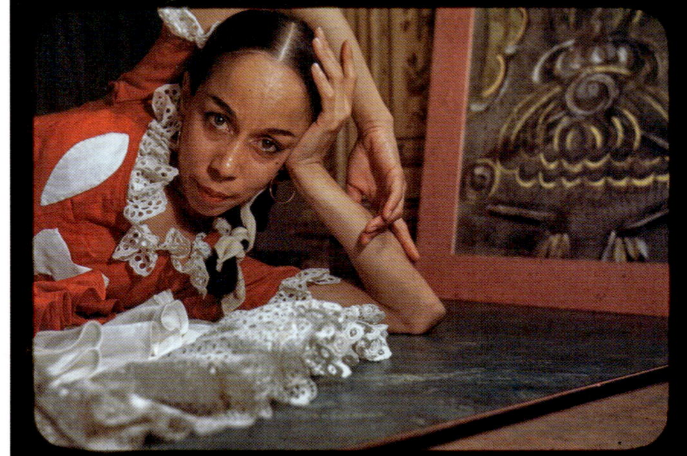

Janet Collins in *New Orleans Carnival*, photographed by Carl Van Vechten, 1949. Kodachrome slide with hand-labeled frame. Jerome Robbins Dance Division, The New York Public Library for the Performing Arts, Astor, Lenox and Tilden Foundations

I've Seen" and "Didn't My Lord Deliver Daniel."[21] Critic John Martin saw her performance as more than a display of versatility and interpreted it as a single dance, describing her as dancing "whole-souledly" in a "markedly personal approach which will undoubtedly come sooner or later into complete control of all the divergent influences and emerge as a style of its own."[22] Van Vechten's slides of Collins make possible a different reading of the relation between her two performances. The disparity between her stiff poses in the *traje de luces* and her more languid poses in the ruffled skirt call to mind protagonists of the opera *Carmen*, in which the bull and the female character Carmen become foils for misogynist fantasies of taming female desire. In Van Vechten's photos, Collins occupies both roles, that of the bull (femme fatale) and that of the matador, staging a kind of struggle with the camera on two fronts. Denied the power to style herself, Collins—staring into and away from Van Vechten's lens—shifts between these preassigned, anachronistic roles of seduction and refusal.

Years after the photo shoot in Van Vechten's studio, in 1952, Collins took on the lead role in *Carmen* as the Metropolitan Opera's first prima ballerina, the only black dancer ever to hold that role. Intended as an evening-length work, the piece was shortened just before its premiere, scaled down to a duet between Collins and Loren Hightower late in the fourth act, in a balcony set that occluded the dancers' lower halves with a balustrade. Collins later commented:

There's a lot of material that choreographers have to throw out, and dancers have to throw out, too, if something doesn't fit. But the wonderful thing is, if it doesn't fit in that part, you might use it again, so you don't have to throw anything away. It's like food you put on the shelf or in the ice box—you use it tomorrow. Dancers, of all people, actually, you might think of them as romantic, but they're very practical. They better be, because they work so hard. And they have to sometimes—you might have to give up a movement you just think is so beautiful, but it doesn't fit. And I assure you, you can use it some-where else. You lose nothing.[23]

Are Van Vechten's slides that somewhere else? The extreme economy of the remix that Collins describes, the practical and not-at-all-romantic capacity to use the vestiges of a dance, transforms into an almost menacing statement in which she assures that "you" will lose nothing. Amid these compelled and displayed forms, in this archive of images galvanized by the real and imaginary attachments and entanglements brought to the dancing body, Collins describes what I would argue is at the root of queer practice whether onstage or off, brought to the forefront or buried in the back.

Kirstein defined the balletomane as "a ballet-maniac or enthusiast for theatrical dancing," further arguing that this "rabid public balletomania is not so much the fault of the art as of the class of society whose idleness or frustrations affords them hysterical compensation," which "prejudice[s] many laymen against dancing."[24] This was, in short, the problem he sought to solve: ballet's association with wealth and its exclusion of those he called "ignorant." He worried that the fervent enthusiasm, commitment, even desire for dance appears as "flagrant approbation." But his definition of the flagrant class and his call to masculinize and popularize the medium were restrictive: What would ballet's syntax be if Kirstein had imagined the social field more broadly and without such a sense of mastery? Or if Collins had written its visual dictionary? Indeed, how have power and impotence played out through dance, and what does a dancer stage within a dance?

Transmissions folds its viewer into layers of such questions by locating within the archive an illusory space where history is not so easily disclosed. Mauss's version of Van Vechten's slide-show releases specters into the gallery space who stage a rhythmic and highly theatrical display that layers their bodies with ours. More than a work about ballet, *Transmissions* opens up the possibilities its ephemera allows. In ballet's panoply of fantasies, it speaks to what, for better or worse, cannot be so easily canceled or foreclosed.

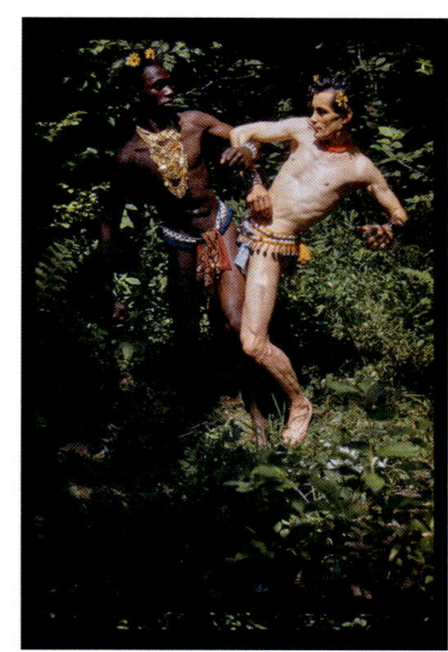

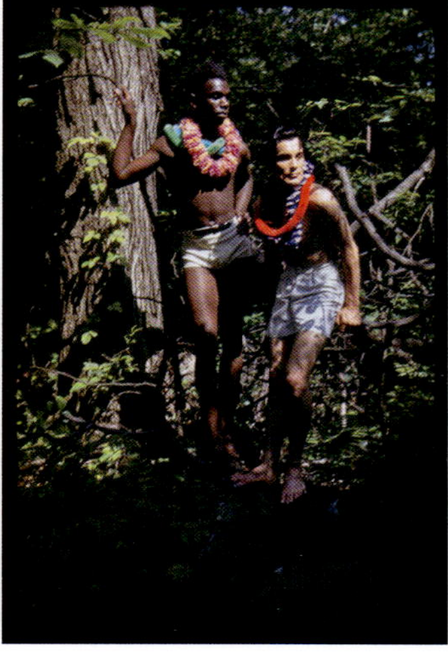

24. Kirstein, *Ballet Alphabet*, 15.

Hugh Laing and Alan Meadows, photographed alfresco by Carl Van Vechten, 1940. Kodachrome slides with hand-labeled frames. Jerome Robbins Dance Division, The New York Public Library for the Performing Arts, Astor, Lenox and Tilden Foundations

21. Collins first performed these works in Los Angeles in 1947, in an evening-length concert that the dancer described as presciently mapping a history of black life from colonialism through slavery and imprisonment, ending on the hopes and longing for a kind of freedom. See Yaël Tamar Lewin, *Night's Dancer: The Life of Janet Collins, with Her Unfinished Autobiography* (Middletown, CT: Wesleyan University Press, 2011).

22. Ibid., 122.

23. Ibid., 193.

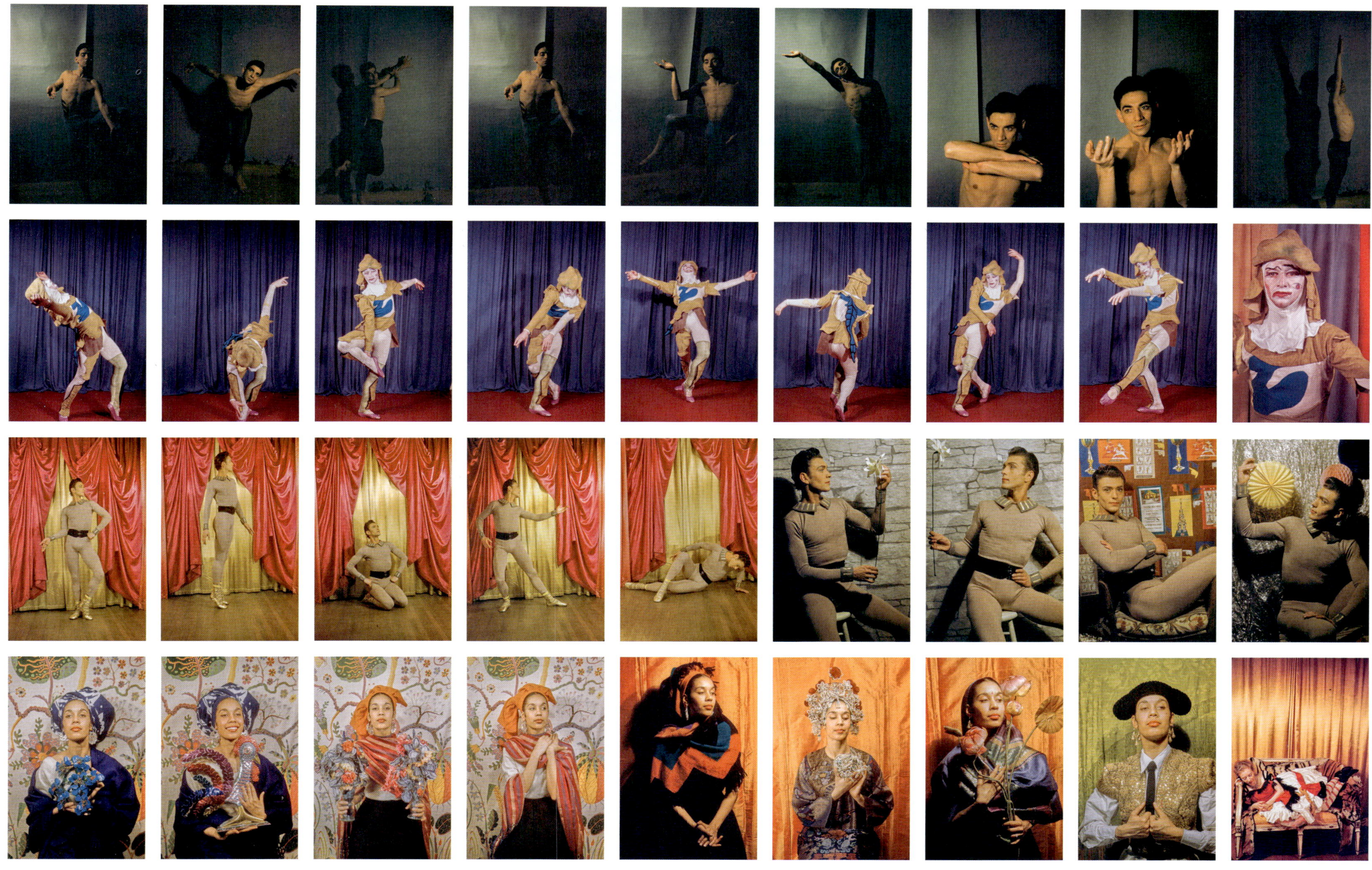

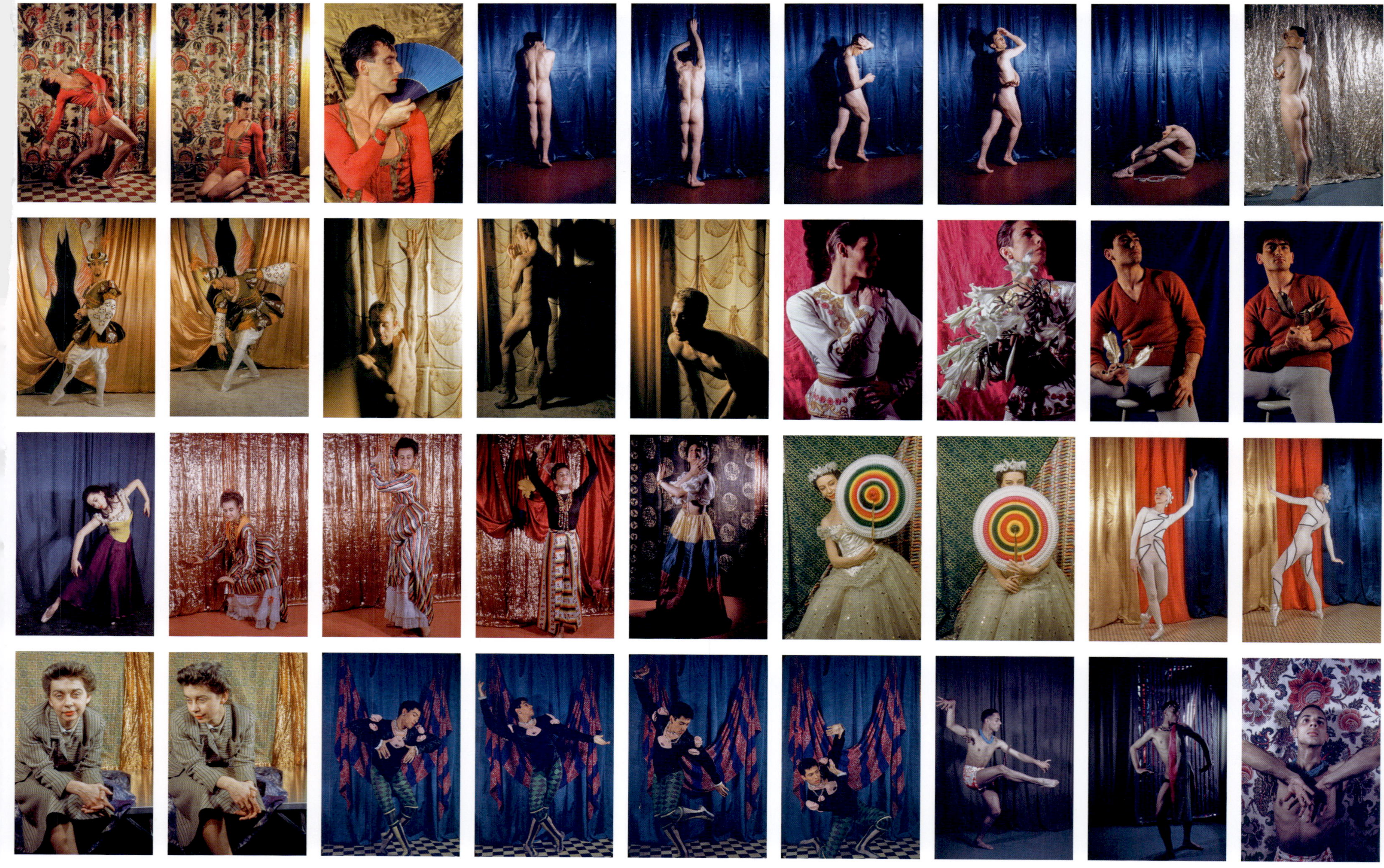

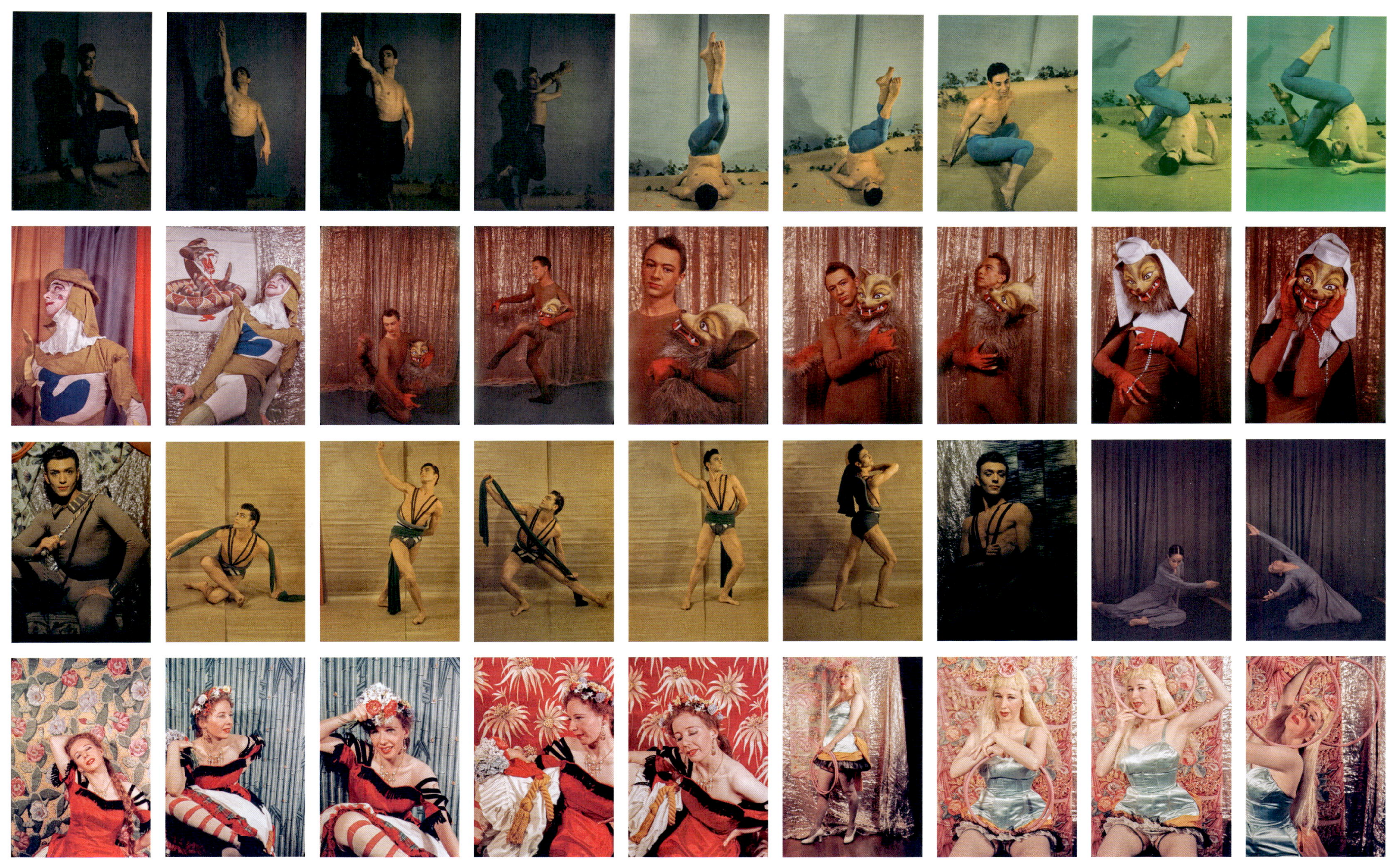

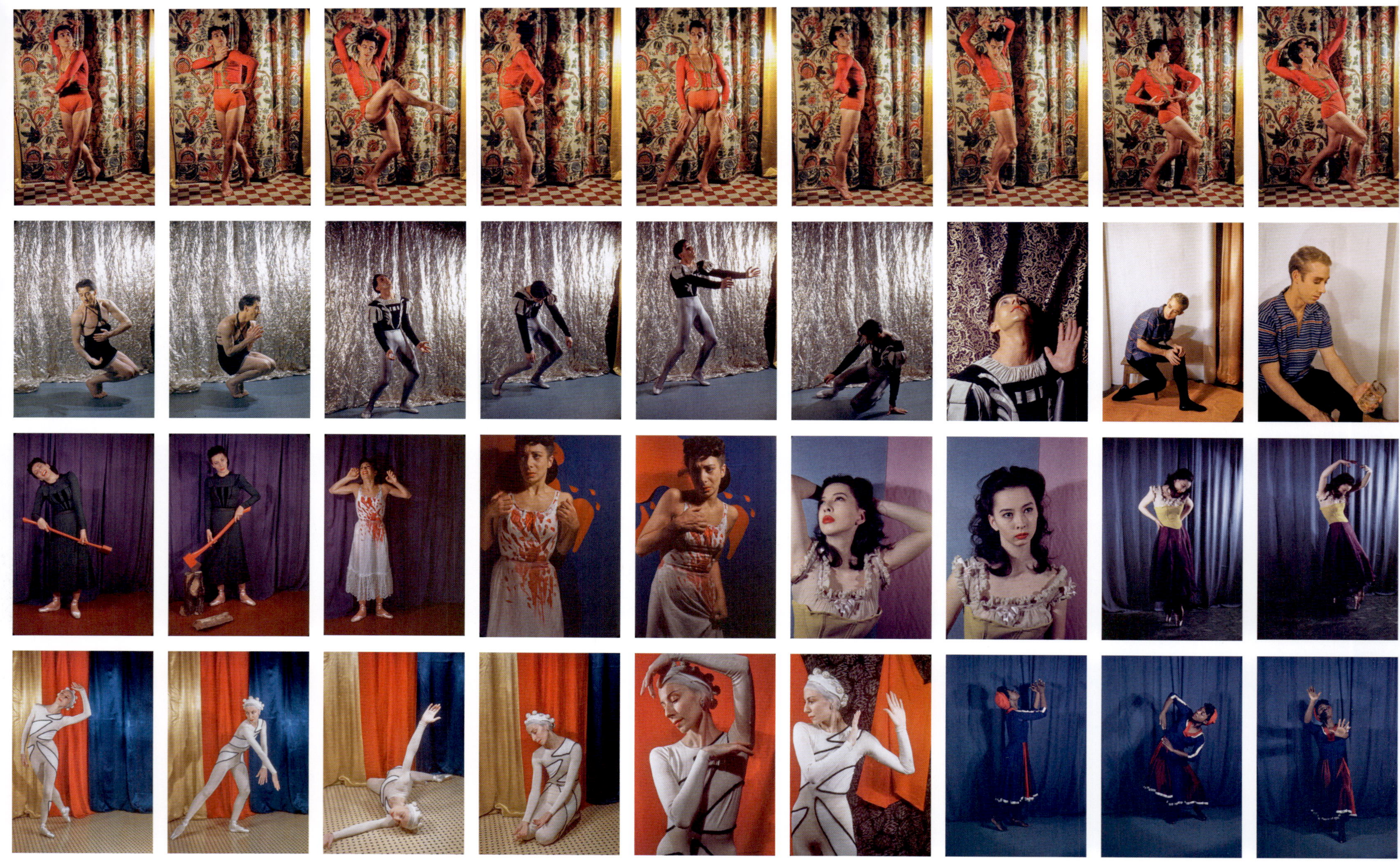

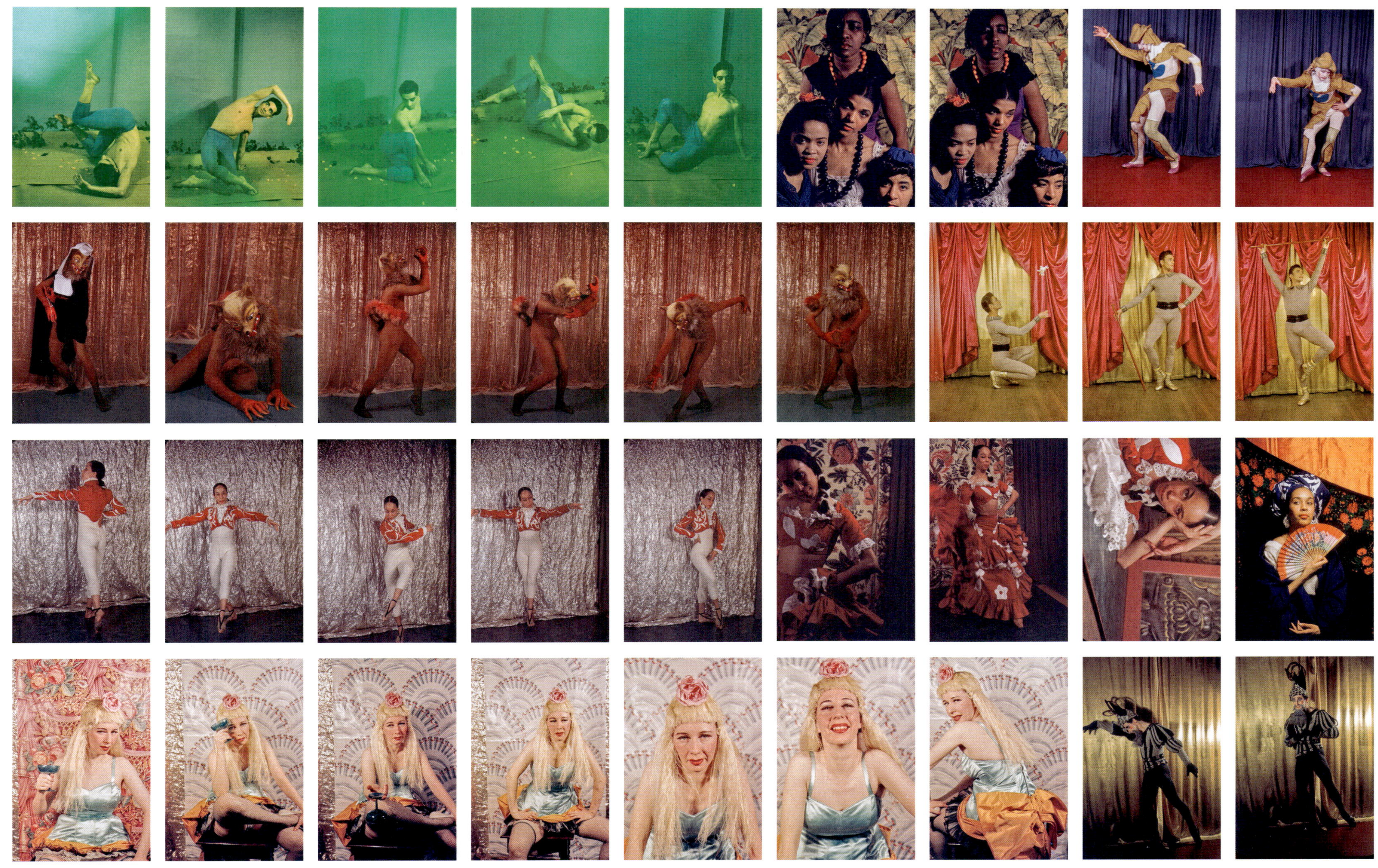

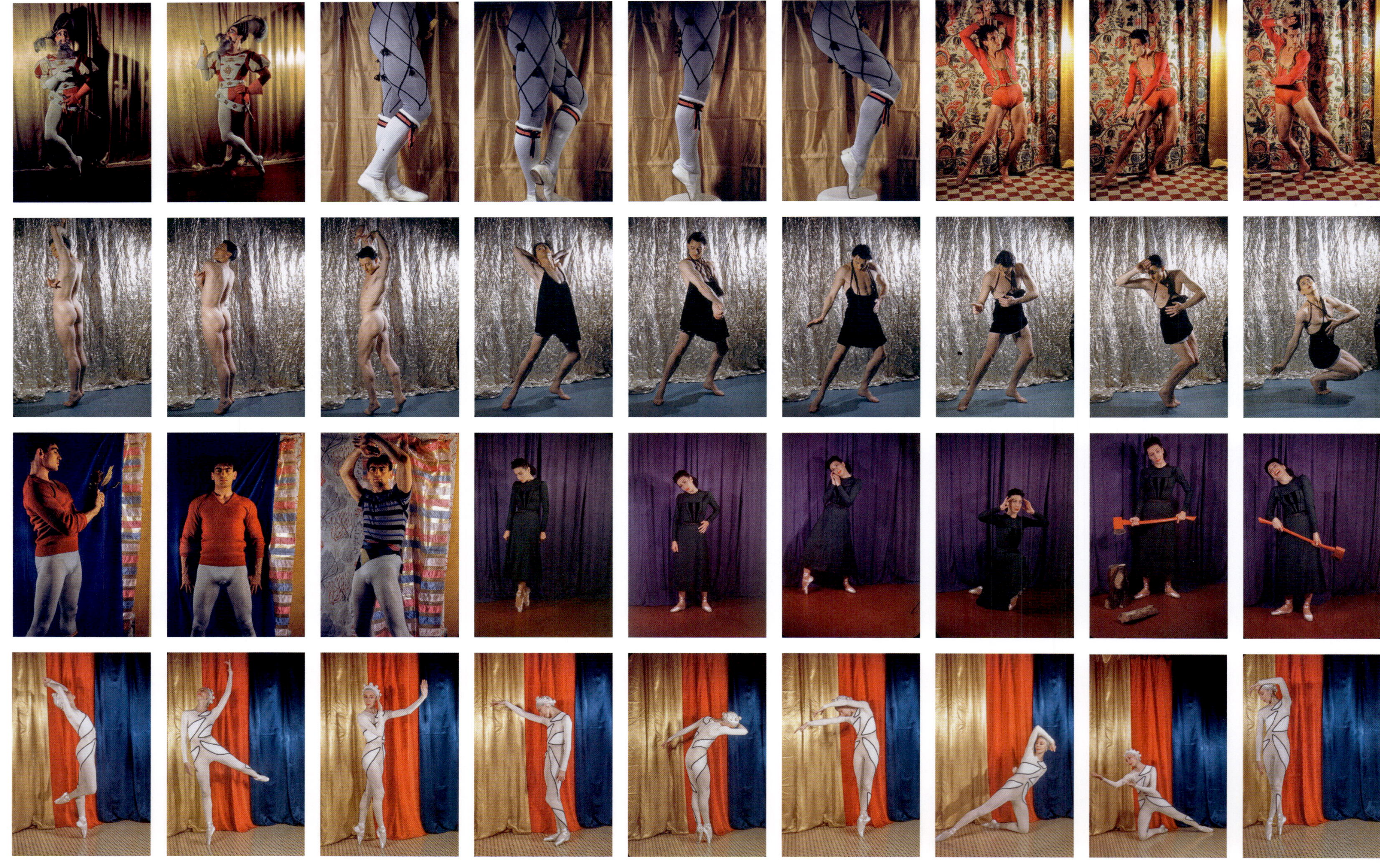

Recto

1	2	3	4	5	6	7	8	9	10	11	12	13	14	15	16	17	18	19	20	21	22	23	24	25	26	27
28	29	30	31	32	33	34	35	36	37	38	39	40	41	42	43	44	45	46	47	48	49	50	51	52	53	54
55	56	57	58	59	60	61	62	63	64	65	66	67	68	69	70	71	72	73	74	75	76	77	78	79	80	81
82	83	84	85	86	87	88	89	90	91	92	93	94	95	96	97	98	99	100	101	102	103	104	105	106	107	108

Verso

109	110	111	112	113	114	115	116	117	118	119	120	121	122	123	124	125	126	127	128	129	130	131	132	133	134	135
136	137	138	139	140	141	142	143	144	145	146	147	148	149	150	151	152	153	154	155	156	157	158	159	160	161	162
163	164	165	166	167	168	169	170	171	172	173	174	175	176	177	178	179	180	181	182	183	184	185	186	187	188	189
190	191	192	193	194	195	196	197	198	199	200	201	202	203	204	205	206	207	208	209	210	211	212	213	214	215	216

1–13: Hernan Baldrich in *Progression*, 1962

14–23: Hernan Baldrich in *On the Beach*, 1962

24, 25: Muriel Cook, Dorothy Williams, Maudell Bass, and Lewanne Kennard in *Black Ritual*, 1940

26–38: Todd Bolender as the Phlegmatic Temperament in *The Four Temperaments*, with original costume by Kurt Seligman, 1947

39–51: Todd Bolender in *Renard the Fox*, 1947

52–59: Robert Cohan in *Every Soul Is a Circus*, 1955

60–64: Robert Cohan

65–70: Robert Cohan as the Wind in *Canticle for Innocent Comedians*, 1955

71, 72: Janet Collins in *The Spirituals*, 1949

73–77: Janet Collins in Mozart's *Rondo*, 1949

78–80: Janet Collins in *New Orleans Carnival*, 1949

81–89: Carmen de Lavallade, 1955

90–95: Agnes de Mille in *Hell on Wheels*, 1940

96–106: Agnes de Mille as Venus in *Judgment of Paris*, 1940

107–10: Anton Dolin in *Bluebeard*, 1944

111–14: Legs of Anton Dolin in costume for *Capriccioso*, 1940

115–29: Anton Dolin in *Danse Espagnole*, 1940

130–51: Anton Dolin, 1940

152, 153: William Earl, 1961

154, 155: William Earl in *The Figure in the Carpet*, 1961

156–58: William Earl, 1961

159, 160: Ian Gibson in *Princess Aurora*, 1941

161–65: Harald Horn, 1956

166–76: Nora Kaye as Lizzie Borden in *Fall River Legend*, 1948

177–81: Sono Osato in *Pillar of Fire*, 1942

182, 183: Beryl McBurnie (La Belle Rosette) in Martinique costume, 1941

184, 185: Beryl McBurnie (La Belle Rosette) in African costume, 1941

186, 187: Alicia Markova in *Die Fledermaus* costume, 1955

188–204: Alicia Markova in *Rouge et Noir*, with costume designed by Henri Matisse, 1948

205–7: Pearl Primus dancing *Hard Time Blues*, 1943

208, 209: Jean Rosenthal, 1951

210–13: Francisco Moncion as Sebastian in *Sebastian*, 1944

214–16: Lenwood Morris, 1940

All images: Kodachrome slides with hand-labeled frames. Jerome Robbins Dance Division, The New York Public Library for the Performing Arts, Astor, Lenox and Tilden Foundations

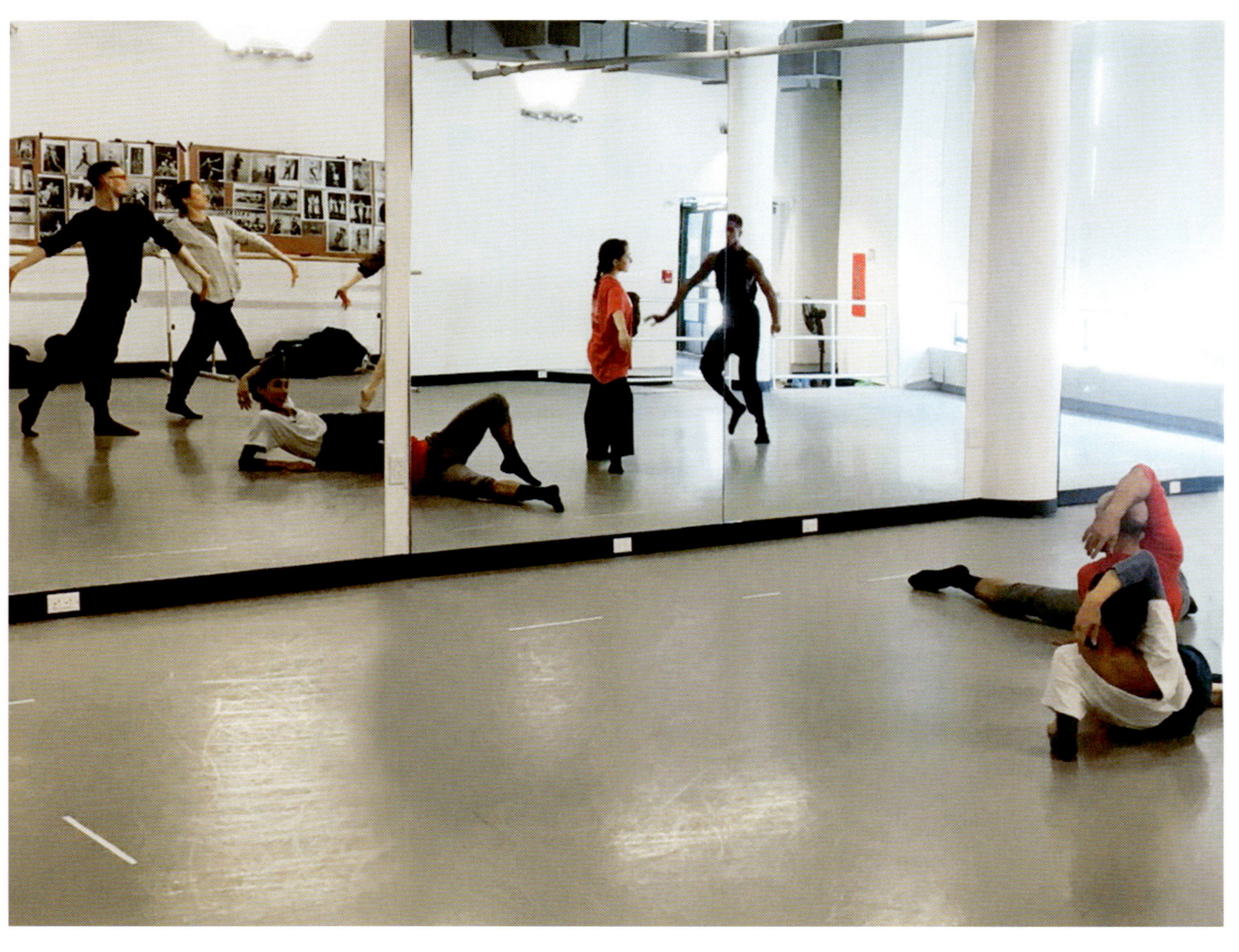

In orienting his exhibition *Transmissions* toward presence and exchange, Nick Mauss abandoned chronology in favor of moments of poetic, energetic, and spontaneous relation. A monitor propped on a folding chair plays a selection of Balanchine rehearsal tapes into a mirror: the subtle gesture, borrowed from the rehearsal studio, implicates, through reflection, our own bodies in the learning of a dance. Averse to the notion of historical reenactment, Mauss approached *Transmissions*'s daily performances—so integral to his project—as an investigative process, using the historical emergence of American modernist ballet as an open framework for developing experimental and improvisatory approaches to generating new movement. In a conversation about making *Transmissions*, the artist emphasized that the exhibition is "by no means comprehensive, and quite fragmentary, but . . . that does speak in some ways also to the way that ballet is carried forward and transmitted. It relies very much on memory and on a personal point of view."[1] Transmission, in this sense, implies not exactly replication, or even continuity, but a carrying forth that is subjective and transformative, kinetically embodied by particular individuals, and at times indicative of loss. As anthropologist Paul Connerton notes in his book *How Societies Remember*, "Transmission occurs only in the time that the bodies are present to sustain that particular activity."[2]

Through an open-call and auditioning process, Mauss cast sixteen dancers with distinct practices and training, who were interested in participating in a dialogic process of creating new movement against the background of their own (often distant) ballet training. The plurality of perspectives within the group, combined with the fact that most had not worked together before, required a building of trust over time. It also required an openness to incorporating disparate ways of knowing and learning into a dance, without conforming to a single style or approach. Starting from the premise that a dance is more often made by its dancers than by a single choreographer, the movement in *Transmissions* was collectively generated by all sixteen performers in conversation with Mauss through a period of intensive workshopping at the Center for Ballet and the Arts—forging an aesthetic that decentered attention, away from a single performer as much as from a single author.

Mauss guided the process by proposing a frame of reference anchored by artworks and documents that would be exhibited in *Transmissions*. Early on, the group visited the Jerome Robbins Dance Division of the New York Public Library for the Performing Arts, where they watched films by the dance historian and filmmaker Ann Barzel that captured a frenetic, emergent form of theatricalized modern ballet, shot from the wings—a view of ballet before it was codified into the repertoires we see today. This inventive spirit was carried into rehearsals, where questions of style, historical specificity, and affect were negotiated. On the studio wall hung a long scroll-like image board indexing gestures and poses into a lexicon. Dancer Anna Thérèse Witenberg contributed a copy of Arnold Haskell's 1950 *Baron at the Ballet* as a further source of ideas and melodramatic images. Jasmine Hearn shared a deeply meaningful encounter with Carmen de Lavallade upon seeing a portrait of the young artist by Carl Van Vechten. In weekly rehearsals held over the course of two months, the dancers worked in pairs or trios in relation to a set of images or videos, presenting their movement to the larger group for informal critiques. The process generated an excess of material that was ultimately incorporated into a choreographic sequence: a pliable rubric that highlighted each performer's artistic contribution and would form the basis of four-hour performances presented daily within the exhibition, four dancers at a time.

Deliberately, the dance presented in *Transmissions* defied expectations of ballet as a genre. The very presence of ballet in a museum has been relatively unexplored, and the dances in *Transmissions* were uniquely brought into direct relation with a complex of imbricated histories. As the late queer theorist José Esteban Muñoz reminds us, all gesture is recursive. Gesture signals "a refusal of a certain kind of finitude"—it persists long after its performance.[3] Throughout *Transmissions*, the live dance became an extension of the preceding rehearsal period, and of rehearsals some eighty years ago, as physical language was constantly reexamined, tried on, shared, and invented in real time, posing more questions than answers. How might a museum, for instance, reshape its own vision of modernity to accommodate art forms that are immaterial and polyvocal? Art forms whose traces are knotted in archives, or in the fleeting testimony of those who were there to experience them? And how might such histories exist prominently in the museum's galleries for the duration of an exhibition, rather than be relegated to its ancillary spaces and programming? How can we collectively—as observers, arts workers, or performers—work to retain and transmit a dance's teachings? Foregrounding process over narrative, movement in the gallery always began with class, with one dancer sharing a legacy of instruction to the group, as a way to warm up. Burr's lesson invoked Merce Cunningham, and Matilda's class was always the most strenuous. The choreographic sequence that followed changed expression across *Transmission*'s duration but was always performed in repetition, twice daily: a repertoire of prolonged poses performed by the dancers as a group, which bookended a selection of solos, trios, and duets. Stitched together freely through improvisation, the forms and gestures in the posing sequence at times rhythmically recurred across dancers, documents, and artworks in the room—reverberating momentarily as a new present.

1. Nick Mauss, in "Transmissions: Nick Mauss in Conversation with Elena Filipovic, Jennifer Homans, and Elisabeth Sussman," Whitney Museum of American Art, May 4, 2018.

2. Connerton's description refers specifically to knowledge transference through bodies, which he refers to as "incorporating practice," as opposed to transmission through documentary techniques. Paul Connerton, *How Societies Remember* (Cambridge, UK: Cambridge University Press, 1989), 72.

3. José Esteban Muñoz, "Gesture, Ephemera, and Queer Feeling," in *Cruising Utopia: The Then and There of Queer Futurity* (New York: New York University Press, 2009), 65.

Forrest Hersey, Elizabeth Hepp, Alexandra Jacob, Matilda Sakamoto, Quenton Stuckey, and Burr Johnson in rehearsal for *Transmissions*. Photo: Nick Mauss

Nick Mauss in Conversation with Dancers Alexandra Albrecht, Kristina Bermudez, Maggie Cloud, Brandon Collwes, Jasmine Hearn, Elizabeth Hepp, Forrest Hersey, Alexandra Jacob, Burr Johnson, Maki Kitahara, Evelyn Kocak, Benedict Nguyen, Matilda Sakamoto, Quenton Stuckey, and Anna Thérèse Witenberg

Edited from a series of conversations with different casts that took place in May 2018 at the Whitney Museum of American Art, New York

Nick Mauss: I'm interested in your experience of the transition from the rehearsal space into the space of the museum, and what it was like to confront and perform for an audience like this, or even for multiple audiences with different degrees of attention. I'm curious to hear how that felt, or how it affected your performance, or if it brought up any interesting questions to work with.

Matilda Sakamoto: I was saying last night after finishing the day's performance in the museum that in the beginning the thing that surprised me the most was not the performance—that's something I'm very used to—but rather doing ballet "class" while being watched. Usually if people are watching class, then they are watching *knowing* it's class, but a lot of people who come to see this exhibition are just like, "When is the show?," which makes the dynamic very interesting and unexpected. I felt kind of uncomfortable at first doing class when people were expecting to *get* something from watching it, that it wasn't just for yourself. Then, as time went on it changed and didn't feel as trying. But it was surprising at first—I didn't realize how personal and intimate class is.

Nick: Many of you have said that you are used to thinking of a performance as having a beginning, a middle, and an end, and that in this four-hour performance arc those time markers fall away.

Matilda: The pressure from yourself in the beginning to be like, "Oh, this is the middle climax part," when it's like, "Oh no, it's not, it's a four-hour duration." There is definitely more of that pressure just from my own—you know, what I'm used to.

Alexandra Albrecht: I think that I feel calmer in this performance context than I do in concert dance, because there isn't the setup that many of us are used to, where you have a three-show run for a piece that's been worked on for a year. It's so rare to have equal parts process and performance and not to have the pressure of performing only three shows.

This creates a general sense of calm for me. I haven't had the same level of performance anxiety. Even though I've been dancing since I was twelve years old, I still get super nervous. That's not to say that I never get nervous here, but it's really different from what I have experienced in basically every other work I've performed in throughout my life. It could also be something about the audience and their attention that I don't *feel* in the same way. It's not the same pressure as when people are only watching me, the dance, and the other dancers. I know that some people want to watch the choreography as they can see it—or as they imagine it to be—but the coming and going of the audience and the emphasis on all the objects in the room create a kind of release.

Evelyn Kocak: The audience is not shrouded in darkness. The typical boundaries between audience and performer aren't there, which I think is a great thing, though it took some getting used to, for sure. Figuring out how to create your own boundaries if that's what you wanted, or to be comfortable with them not being there, or some balance between the two—I played around with that a lot, like why *do* I need a boundary between myself and the audience? Do I even need to create one? I definitely haven't wanted to tell people to come to see our warm-up, because that's just something I normally do on my own. I mean, my mom loves being able to see the ins and outs of the behind-the-scenes, and other people love it too, but I haven't *encouraged* people to come see that part of it.

Jasmine Hearn: The warm-up section became a way for me to acclimate myself to being witnessed. So as much as I'm like, "I'm doing a ballet class in front of everybody" (which is a deep fear), in the end I really feel like it has been a preparation for eyes to be on me—for this idea of being consumed, or however we want to think about that. As I continue to invite folks, I make sure they are aware of what it is. I've actually appreciated having that time to be able to be seen and also to look at others. It's interesting to track the trajectory of how I've felt in this, and it's been *so, soo, soooo* telling regarding what it is that I'm comfortable with, and what it is that I'm not. It definitely backs up the one thing that I find consistent in what I do, which is doing the things that make me most fearful and letting others see that. I'm assuming that folks aren't expecting someone that dances like I do and looks like I do to be in this thing. That's my own insecurity, I understand that. So to confront folks' reactions to some of the things that I'm doing has been exciting. And I have a lot more confidence now, which is pretty dope.

Maggie Cloud: I was aware of somebody I knew walking through today during class, but I felt that they were engaged. It was someone who works in the dance world, who has probably seen a lot of us perform but hasn't seen us warming up. I found it interesting and think it must have been a really different experience for her. In a lot of performances the warm-up is in a separate space, and it's intimidating to walk into a room that feels like it belongs to whoever's already there. Here we've cultivated our own space, and I think that was empowering for us to start from zero and then build and build and build.

Alexandra A.: When I see dance people in the audience, I actually do want them to see the full performance. I want them to see the duet transition into the quartet and so forth. I want that experience for them—and I don't know why, exactly.

Matilda: But then with "regular" people it's like, "Yeah, great, don't watch. Whatever."

Alexandra A.: No, it's not just for dance people who are here, but also for my friends who come to see me. When I see someone I know, I think, "I hope they watch it start to finish."

Nick: So in that sense, the decision to include within the four-hour duration so much else that really is more related to process or to getting ready to do the work felt a bit like . . . not what you want to show to your peers?

Alexandra A.: Well, I want them to see the greatest hits, to see what we really worked on. I guess I want to understand how they see it as choreography—if they see it as a work of choreography or if they're thinking that it is a bunch of different phrases or that it's improv. I'm interested to know how they see it and to hear from them. I want them to get the full picture of what we imagine as the "set" choreography.

Forrest Hersey: Initially I separated the sections in my mind; this is choreography and this is improvised. But from what I've heard from nondancers who've seen the shows is that they can't make any distinction between what they've seen, that it's all just a performance to them except for the class. Most people say, "How did you know all that choreography?" thinking that I've learned four hours of choreography. It appears that way to them, even though they probably only watched thirty or forty minutes of it. They assume it was *that* intense the whole time.

Benedict Nguyen: It's been enlightening to have bodies moving in space to respond to energetically. The energies and feelings that come from direct address or confrontational energy or a gaze that I am aware of receiving—I feel that feedback from the audience. It's such a contrast to my experience during the project's video documentation yesterday when no one was there. There was no feedback during the filming. It was kind of like being in the space and yet not.

Alexandra A.: Did you just do the set choreography?

Benedict: We did the whole four hours with two videographers.

Nick: I don't love that solution for documentation, and it struck me once we moved into the space yesterday for filming how much the audience is a part of this. There is a strong dynamic in the space, and the different energies between performers and audience, intentionally or not, create a tension. Clean, airless documentation is hard for me to take. I imagine

it was difficult to perform in that situation and attempt to conjure the energy you need to give without receiving any.

Matilda: The audience really does affect this show. When you are on a stage and the audience is dark, you can't sense the different ways people are viewing you dancing. Here, you can see everyone and see what they're taking in. At one point, you might feel that no one is watching you during the posing section, and it feels free; then, all of a sudden, somebody will be close to you, but they might have a neutral energy, so it doesn't feel like they're too close. And then there are people who are intense, and you can feel them no matter where they are in the room. Posing feels different, being watched and not watched.

Quenton Stuckey: I think today I was more playful with the audience. Normally I don't make eye contact with people, but today I was looking into people's eyes and trying to shake them up in some way.

Anna Thérèse Witenberg: There will be some days where I feel super porous and kind of vulnerable and distracted, and I feel the need to look at everyone who walks through the doors: "Who is this person? What are they here for?" Then other days, I'm totally in my own world, rarely make eye contact, and am kind of disinterested. Also I have never explicitly realized before how much you can tell when someone is focused on you, and how you can read so much from even just a momentary glance. Sometimes you can really tell that someone is engaging—you keep your eyes scanning and then you look and there's that one person keeping their focus. Those are often the moments when I feel most safe. Of course, some gendered aspects come up, like, "Do I feel safe looking back at men who are looking at me?" You can tell when it's a more sexualizing gaze, which honestly hasn't come up that much. Or there's the time someone spoke to Jasmine and me in a vulgar way—like a drunk Friday-night thing. It's interesting to realize how sensitive I am to the way people look at me and how my response to that can vary depending on how I'm feeling that day. It's funny when there are dancers in the audience who come and stand up straighter and are, say, watching your face. You can make some assumptions based on the way people are watching, just in their acts of seeing.

Matilda: There are times when I feel a little ego and think, "They should be watching me, I'm performing right now." But most of the time it actually gives me solace and feels freeing not to be the only thing getting attention. A lot of people here don't even know what they are seeing; they just happened upon this while visiting the museum. So most of the time I feel like the situation has helped me explore my own sense of freedom, because the audience is just exploring too.

Forrest: The idea of the audience being surprised to stumble upon a dance performance is so unfamiliar to me. When I go to a show as an audience member, I come to the performance with plenty of background information. My viewing experience is so loaded already. I don't like when I'm being watched by someone like a deer in headlights. I'm not thinking that they have to adjust and catch up to what's going on or that a lot of it might be new and interesting to them.

Alexandra A.: This makes me think about how performance is defined by the audience's presence: Is it a performance if the audience isn't there? When I'm feeling those moments when the attention isn't on me, it's not as if I'm thinking, "Okay, I'm now in my own internal space and the performance is not happening." I don't trail off that far. This is a weird dichotomy for me that I've always struggled with. I'm a performer, I'm an exhibitionist, that's been my identity my whole life, but I'm also weirdly shy and have anxiety about performance and still have mild panic attacks onstage. This in-between space that can feel sometimes neutral and sometimes charged—those vacillations—is unique to this performance.

Nick: You can kind of modulate it, but you're also being modulated by it?

Alexandra A.: Totally! That's what always keeps me coming back to the performance as it's happening. It's so singular in its effect. It's beyond my control sometimes, how an audience impacts what your body does and how viewership can affect this thing that you rehearse for months or years. You do it in front of people who make it the performance, and you're suddenly altered.

Anna: We've talked about the phones, and how intense it is to feel people coming up, taking an Instagram story, and then walking away—that feeling that you are social capital and that people are consuming you as a decorative object. There's been a lot of that here, but it seems like it's coming mostly from tourists. I wonder how different it would be if phones weren't allowed in the space.

Quenton: I found that audience members who were behind the scrim—there's that barrier—took way more liberties in saying things.

Nick: They would *speak* to you through the scrim?

Elizabeth Hepp: Yeah, they speak as though we can't hear them. Like we can't hear or see them. It's like the scrim is their safety shield.

Nick: Like, what *kinds* of things?

Quenton: Well one woman said, "What if I just kissed you right now?" That was a joke, I suppose. She was trying to make me break my facial expression or something. Other people would just make obnoxious noises.

Nick: It's almost as if behind the scrim is the subconscious, in front of the scrim is the social.

Elizabeth: Behind the scrim is online, anonymous, and you can say whatever you want.

Anna: There's the initial confusion—"Is this ballet?"—which came up in so many conversations I overheard. "They're

barefoot, it's not ballet." There is also one volunteer guard on Mondays, an older gentleman, who says, as soon as the elevator doors open: "Welcome to the ballet. The ballet starts at 2:00 p.m. Sharp."

Kristina Bermudez: I've heard people say similar things, like "These are the dancers!"—those words in a really intense voice. I wish the audience members were a bit more courageous. When we're improvising, I like to look at the audience a lot to make eye contact, behind the scrim or not, and I wish they would respond to us. Maybe on days when we are feeling shitty and quiet, they would just be calm, but on days when we are more playful and open, they would sit closer. Today there was a guy who randomly started clapping in the middle, and then everyone started clapping. It was right before the quartet even started. That was hilarious! Like, finally, let's get some clapping instead of that in-between energy of whispers.

Nick: Nancy Dalva from the Merce Cunningham Trust was saying today that people will make anything into a proscenium. They'll make an open field into a proscenium. I was talking to her about my initial anxiety over what might happen with the audience, and she said, "Look at them, they're great. They're like lambs."

Elizabeth: I actually really liked having children in the audience, which is funny because I generally hate kids. It was cool— their reactions were so real. I could get more from them by watching their expressions and what they were seeing than from the adults who seemed to feel that they had to maintain this stoic way of looking.

Maki Kitahara: Some people move their bodies with us, and some just watch. I love to see that. Since this exhibition's title is *Transmissions*, I feel that as dancers we can send something to them. Also, since we are in the museum and I am not onstage, I feel that the audience is also part of the exhibition. As if we just exchanged transmissions.

Nick: You told me about how one night you and Ahmaud [Culver] bowed because it felt like the right thing to do, and the audience responded and seemed to feel that they had had some closure or connection or that they were being acknowledged, just as you were working and being acknowledged. I was so happy you brought this to my attention, because I initially had another idea—which was maybe too strict—to create antigestures that would force visitors to deal with their own expectations rather than let them get lost in whatever fantasy of dance that they came in with. Your gesture—your feeling that bowing was the right thing to do that day—reminded me that this is a shared experience, that you're making the work *with* people in the space, and that it can also be appropriate to make contact in that way and signal the end of what you are doing, to draw a line.

Forrest: Yeah, we did bow one time, and then the next day I thought that if we had moved the bars as we normally do to signal the end, it would have felt abrupt—like a hand in the face. It feels nice to bow, if they applaud.

Nick: I asked you to do a lot of things at the same time as we were initially developing this work in the studio. On the one hand, to revisit your individual relationships to ballet, and on the other, to generate new movement in relation to the historical material in the exhibition. Did you find this process productive? Is that something you were already doing in your own work?

Brandon Collwes: Initially I was trying to put on some sort of ballet front, and it felt inauthentic to me. While I do have so much classical ballet technique training in a different way from the modern, Merce Cunningham–y vibe, I didn't want to be too much of anything. I found responding to the room always gave me the impetus for something that I wanted to show. The Carl Van Vechten slides hold so much energy in the room. Also the reflections of some of the things in the space, even the faraway photographs behind glass—glimmers of light would always catch my eye and in those images

there was something very resounding and classical.

Quenton: When I'm in the space with, for example, the photos of the American Negro Ballet, I think about my relationship to ballet and black people's relationships to ballet in general, how it's a very white form that lots of black people don't have access to. Even growing up, when I told my friends I was doing ballet, they'd be like, "What?" I'm always thinking about that. Obviously technique can save you in certain situations, and you can always fall back on it, but for me growing up ballet was a distant fascination. I didn't have access to it, but I intuitively wanted to do it. I always go with, as a body, intuitively, how would I move? I go back to, "Oh, this is me doing ballet when I'm thirteen, by myself," and to, like, "You need to be here *in* here." I'm playing with, "Look, I'm the black body here and I can do this," but also, "I'm going to show you a little bit of how I interpret what the space is for *me*."

Kristina: That just made me think of the kids in the audience, because while I'm improvising and playing around, it's almost like a memory I'm activating and when you see the kids you're thinking about yourself in that situation, what you felt when you were that age or how you danced or improvised then. That playfulness is definitely interpreted into movement. Ninety-five to ninety-eight percent of the choreography I was taught in college had nothing to do with ballet. So then when we try to apply improvisation with ballet technique and choreographing with a ballet technique, it becomes playful. It's all so different. It's hard.

Brandon: Using that playfulness, thinking that I'm making fun of ballet really does work for me rather than going with it full on. Embodying it felt so incredibly insincere. In the beginning, I started having weird flashbacks to my old ballet-boy days, and I was, like, "Oh no!" I quickly figured out that I had to be more genuine, even if it was me being happy doing a bourrée. I couldn't go halfway because then I would lose my character—because

it felt as if every day I had a kind of character role. That feels natural. I actually preferred when we started off more stoic and not talking, to be honest. I felt that as we've broken down the initial set choreography I've had more interactions with people that have kind of pissed me off. It's created the opportunity for people to come up and say things like, "What time does it start?" or, "Is it happening?" And my response has been surprising to me, but it's always a little bit curt, like, "It's happening."

Nick: I told you, once you open the door, everyone just wants to talk.

Brandon: I am *that* guy, too, who gets stopped on the street every five seconds because I look people in the eye. So then I was being nice and open and at the same time being kind of bitchy, and I didn't like that. So I've gone back to stoic. As long as I can figure out a way of making it authentic in the moment, it has worked out.

Quenton: There was a group of black students that came in and were all taking photos of me, and I thought, "You too can be here." That was a really nice feeling, because I remember going to school and seeing dance and ballet and there was never a black body. And then you're thinking, "Is that something that we're supposed to, you know, do?"

Kristina: When my little brother came down from upstate New York, I could tell that he was moved by seeing men dancing. Coming to the city and seeing two females and two guys dancing together and working together without any actual gender roles—I could really see that he appreciated that, and I imagine other people appreciate it as well.

Nick: I am surprised by how powerful that has been for people—how people hold on to gender roles in dance as necessary conveyors of meaning. The roles *can* be displaced.

Kristina: I feel that a lot in the "AB" duet as well, because of that muscular moment. The way that it's choreographed, the type A has the "female" role. That part feels vulnerable to me, especially when we split off and do our own things. I definitely feel an awareness in the audience, and I feel myself as a tall, strong dancer doing the lifting.

Quenton: I'm always cast as the lifter, and so when I'm being caught in our duet, it's like, "Oh, I'm never this girl, and it's really nice! I can have a romantic duet." That's fun—you know, that never really happens.

Brandon: I feel that play with gender and dance is almost commercialized now that so many artists are doing it. I thought the way you approached it in this environment was pretty unique. It didn't feel forced. It felt really natural.

Nick: This morning someone asked me why the dancers aren't in the space during all the exhibition hours. I said that you are in the space for a long time every day, and it's work. Also I want people to experience the absence of the dance and realize that if they want to witness the performance, they should return—that it's not always available. Another thing that I discovered and found interesting was that the rehearsal and generating process was partially a kind of social experiment, trying to get to know one another and how to work together.

Burr Johnson: This has been a process in which there hasn't been someone at the top, like a master, saying, "You're doing it wrong, you need to strive to be better." This has been more like, "Just strive to be yourself in the space, so then you can actually be better."

Evelyn: Which can be terrifying, because I found I didn't necessarily know what to do with that freedom at first. I haven't usually been given that freedom so I was just—"What?"

Alexandra Jacob: I came into this after being in a ballet company for ten years. In that world, even when a new piece is set on you, you are still generally expected to match a certain uniform body. I was at first terrified here—there's no ballet master

or rehearsal director, and everyone's just doing this together. But then I thought, "This is kind of cool. This is what I feel I was built for." Those ten years of doing this one thing made me see what I wanted to do. Even though I was stuck in that vocabulary, my heart wasn't fully invested, and I think I've always craved this independence. I've only experienced this kind of freedom maybe one other time in the company with a choreographer, but even then there was always a ballet master saying, "You created this, but you have to keep within this frame."

Evelyn: It's been really fascinating to see, after the point of leaving the rehearsal studio, how each of us relates to one another and the score and how the pieces have evolved. I saw that the most when I was placed into a different group of dancers from the ones I was usually performing with, and realized that they were doing the same parts very differently, and that was really cool. Even if I didn't initially know where to put myself into the piece or feel like I had a personality within it, I've been able to find more of that through the course of doing it. The freedom to find yourself and change yourself, to not be married to one thing—you don't get that in a ballet company most of the time. You find your own covert ways to inject personality into what you're doing. It's been interesting to see how I can push myself out of my comfort zone, because my safety blanket is ballet. To say, "It's okay, I don't need to know exactly what I'm doing and I can be wrong."

Kristina: I've had a more structured background as a performer. I have always been the rebellious type, but a lot of us here are rebellious. So it's been a matter of listening, because we all have these things that we want to do. If all of us are doing them at the same time, it can be too much.

Elizabeth: It feels pretty natural in the way that it has developed. For example, Maki and I in the "AB" duet: we started adding a lot of things at the end, and it was funny how easy it felt because I know so well now how she dances. I know her

instincts and impulses, and it was easier than I thought it would be to let it roll and see what happens.

Burr: There's a big spectrum among all the groups that I have been with here. Some of us really want to do it right and be consistent and do the same thing every time, so then it becomes very clear; other people want to unhinge things. Maggie, for instance, you are so clear and are such a conduit. You are able to show yourself through clarity. Maggie and I are so familiar with each other, and it's interesting to see her taking risks that I don't see her taking in other contexts, because there is an open space in which to do that.

Nick: During the course of working together in the studio I felt as if another language was being invented, maybe as a bridge to my lack of access to a standard dance language but also tailored to the new movements being generated among you.

Brandon: I feel like that happens in almost every circumstance where you're creating movement. Nearly every choreographer has a name for a move, a name for a section. It's just a way for dancers to remember it, track it, and refer to it to each other, which is really important when it comes to creating those movements. Even if it's something we call the "spinach kale"—we all have some idea of what that means. Often in our different groupings, there was one person who homed in on a scene to keep it neutral and not let it get too far off path, which I think is interesting. I can tell when someone is thinking of those words, like "spinach kale."

Elizabeth: If I don't understand what a choreographer wants, I generally feel like that's on me as the dancer to figure out what they're thinking. I worked with a choreographer for a bit on a solo that she made for me with a harpist. If I didn't understand what she was saying, she'd say, "Let me say this a different way." So we kept trying to put language to a certain feeling or movement until we reached a place where a word worked for both of us and we achieved an image. I hadn't really thought about how much language can impact movement. Also the harpist—who is not a dance person—had a whole different language, which referred to music. We had to find communal vocabulary.

Nick: How would you relate the role played by language to the role played by technique?

Burr: I think of technique as a systematized way of doing things, and I don't think of ballet technique as being the penultimate technique. I think it's one way of moving, but that there are many other ways of empowering your body. What do you mean by technique?

Nick: It's a question that I get asked a lot, so I thought I'd put it to all of you. It's a term that I associate with "skill" and other things like that that I don't actually find interesting when isolated. But I also associate the practice of *technique* with a way of being articulate, which I think is crucial. I see each of you as being articulate in singular ways. And I'm trying to renegotiate my own relationship to technique and what that could mean.

Burr: It's interesting for me to think about the idea of articulation, and how it relies on either an informed judge or someone just trying to understand. Someone looking at ballet technique or someone who performs and knows ballet technique in a certain way might feel that they don't understand what they're looking at in what we've made here, or they might find it totally abstract because I don't "speak" that language the way they understand it.

Maggie: When using it in an improvisational way, I feel that *articulation* provides a bigger vocabulary for expression. It provides more options, in a foundational way.

Evelyn: Yes, it's like having more nuanced words to express what you're saying. If you're thinking of ballet or dance as a form of expression and as a language, you could view technique as enlarging the vocabulary or ways of articulating yourself.

Burr: I guess I should have just gone the other way and said what I really wanted to say: when someone looks at a dancer, say, on the street busking for money, you wouldn't necessarily say that that person has hip-hop technique. We tend to reserve that word for ballet or pointed feet and turns.

Maggie: But that's still training.

Burr: That's what I'm trying to say; it is still technique. Someone may not look at that dance on the street and think they have technique, but in my mind they do.

Evelyn: It's just specific to what they're doing.

Nick: Also, to be clear, I'm not even asking about "good" technique or "bad" technique. I'm just trying to access how you resource yourselves.

Burr: I think about technique as being able to do anything that's thrown at me— being the clearest conduit for whatever the author has in mind.

Forrest: Technique is injury prevention. If you use your body improperly then you are more likely to get injured, and then you have to stop altogether. Your body is an instrument that you can make more articulate—you can just, like, upgrade it. If you keep upgrading your body, you don't have to use ballet rotation all the time. I suppose it can be helpful to have more options in creating any kind of movement. I might be wrong, but sometimes if you're too rotated then you can't do other things. So then it's not really an upgrade. It's just—I don't know—a strengthening in whatever language you want to strengthen.

Matilda: That's been a big struggle in terms of how I feel about dance lately. I often feel that I'm too technical or something. When a choreographer wants really grounded contemporary dance, all of a sudden I think I'm too technical—and I'm like, "No, I can't do that." But I'm not technical enough for something else. It's a weird place. In one way, I think technique is one of the most important things and it

does prevent injury and create the ability to know how to do things and do them easier on your body, but it also creates crazy habits that are empty defaults. And if you didn't have those to fall into, you might be doing something completely new. The whole deskilling thing is really happening in dance right now, where people are liking the raw body.

Nick: What does that mean, raw body?

Matilda: It's like, "Just do what's natural," you know? And then you're like, "Oh, I trained to be unnatural, so what is natural?" Some dancers are trained in less technique than I have, and it just works, but then they can't do a tendu. But is a tendu even important? Is the *extra* look of the tendu important? Or is it more important that they know how to work their bodies into something that is their own form of a tendu? I've been thinking about that a lot lately, and it's a struggle but I need to do it.

Nick: It takes so long to unlearn the really bad things.

Benedict: Technique is good placement, which I didn't understand for a long time, and I think I'm coming back to this with a much clearer idea of it. Technique is labor. It's work. Having a first position is like stacking things in the right place. It's uncomfortable. I know where it's supposed to go. There's a rigor to *doing* that even if I know I understand it. It's not easy.

Nick: And what is the value in that rigor?

Benedict: Making ballet look the way it is supposed to look. But it's not as though all rigors are challenging in the same way. I think the aesthetic values of ballet rigor—having long legs and you turn out, you extend your leg in a tendu because it looks longer than it does when your legs are parallel, or the logic behind, "We *point* our feet"—sometimes I don't . . .

Matilda: Even people who are, say, not doing ballet technique. Let's say they're not technical dancers. They're still practicing whatever their nontechnical thing is, which also has its rigor, its form of training, right? So maybe technique is just that all artists are kind of crazy, and we're just constantly trying to do things to prove we can do them.

Jasmine: I'm also thinking about how long you have been practicing this way of moving, or this way of being. Was it based on a specific ideal and within your own expectation of yourself? I'm hearing words like *technique* and *training*, and I'm thinking about what it means to have time to practice something specific. I remember as a kid, folks saying, "Oh, you've got technique. You can kick your legs high and have clear lines," or, "You can be trusted in the completion of the form." And then being able to practice so many different kinds of techniques since then, while continuing to be immersed in ballet and Westernized dance techniques and forms. It's been interesting to understand, for example, the technique of listening to my womb—that's a technique. And I'm like, "Okay, how do all of these things blend together?" On top of that, there are questions of confidence, questions about where you live and how you can be seen, and how you can be fully in your body while you do whatever forms or techniques or styles that you've been training in. How much time have you had to practice so that you can gain the kind of comfort to then be able to offer or share or perform?

Evelyn: Technique gets the reputation of being about how many jumps you can do, how many turns, etc., which I hate. I think I always unconsciously have thought of technique as about specializing in a certain way of moving or combining types of movement, like the way I devoted myself to becoming a specialist in how Balanchine wanted his ballets danced. I'm not married to the concept of technique. I'm more married to honoring the specificity of his movement style, which is why that is important to me as a dancer, because I've dedicated everything I do to that. I've enjoyed the chance to have a departure from that but know it's not going anywhere—I always have that

training. Training with such specificity can make you fearful of abandoning it, because you've given yourself over to form and sacrificed yourself to it, and of course it's deeply, deeply important to you. I've felt in this process that I've sometimes been defensive of my training, and then I thought, "No, calm down, nobody's challenging it." It can seem like a narrow way to realize one's career—and it is specific—but it was also important to me to follow that training for as long as I did, even though I don't follow it as much anymore.

Jasmine: Yes, and then also understanding that certain things are unearthed. Throughout this process, I was like, "Oh right, I did go to school for three years, where I did an 8:00 a.m. ballet class five times a week. . . . Oh right, I did do pointe privates when I was child. . . ." It's just so funny. I thought, "Oh, oh, oh!" I love the remembering. That was enjoyable and at the same time startling.

Evelyn: I have insecurity about abandoning what I do know. To just move in space and make shit up, to totally abandon shapes and ideas of movement that feel natural to me. I was terrified of that, but it's gotten easier.

Burr: Something that has jumped out to me in this process is, simply, sexuality. One of the reasons why I got into dance in the first place was because I was a closeted kid and found these dance videos of people who I suspected were gay. I was so interested in that, and I knew that dance could be a gateway—that this life could be a gateway into that kind of expression. There's also a closeted thing within ballet itself, like you're supposed to perform your sexuality for the stage and also perform it for the patrons who are in control of ballet.

Alexandra J.: I was happy that you exhibited the picture of the ball sack. Aesthetically, everything I live for has been derived from sexuality, and I didn't really realize it until now. Everything—my fashion, my music—has been based on the leather daddies in the Castro District in San Francisco who I watched growing

up. There was something that I wanted to unearth for myself in ballet. It felt very superficial—like, "Oh, I can have this kissy-kissy relationship onstage"—it just felt very PG. It felt cool seeing these pictures to have a visual taste of the people who created earlier platforms for what I know now. It is a nice unearthing. I was already tapping into this sexuality and felt it there before—it was like a magnet on the other side of the wall, but I never really saw it. You removed that wall for me, Nick. Visually, it was really cool seeing everything, homosexuality and bodies, like what dance is to me instead of this fake pretentious thing. It felt more raw.

Evelyn: But Balanchine ballets *don't* follow that narrative. I just want to offer that because I also hate the narratives you're referring to. I think they're so antiquated and predictable and heteronormative, like every damsel in distress is like falling in love with her prince. But there is kind of an inherent eroticism in Balanchine's work.

Burr: In the way that we see ballet on the stage, the portrayal of sexuality is two-dimensional, while the dancing is erotic, it's multidimensional.

Jasmine: Entering into this experience, I read the audition notice and was, like, "Whatever, I'm going to audition." I remember telling you that I had a chance to be around Carmen de Lavallade. The one thing that Carmen told me was, "Say yes to everything as an artist, go project to project, just to see what happens"— not *everything*, not if you're going to get harmed. She broke that down. So that's what I did—I said yes to everything. So it's been interesting here: during moments when I felt tension, especially in the beginning, Carmen's face would sometimes come up in the Van Vechten slide projection during those exact moments. I don't think it's a coincidence, and I would think, "Oh, right, just say yes, Jasmine." That was a direct link between my personal history and what was actually in the space. I thought that was pretty unbelievable. It has also been interesting talking about the erotic within the space while being in the unitards, and then also performing on the Friday nights when folks are tipsy as ever. And having people tell you about yourself and hit on you as you're performing.

Burr: It has been very cruise-y in there for the boys. We've talked about this.

Jasmine: It's been really, like, "Oh, let me tell you about you."—Huh? But that's been fun—kind of—for me, because then I just get real. But at the same time, it does affect the performance in a way that takes a lot of labor to navigate.

Evelyn: My favorite thing is to sit on the last stair facing the stage, where people around the corner don't expect to see you. People have jumped back before.

Burr: I like to be up at the top of the "tree house" and just look down at people.

Nick: It's as if you're in a castle tower, and you're about to pour boiling oil down it.

Evelyn: You have to find ways to reclaim your agency or control the situation. It's been fun to play with.

Nick: What significance does the historical dimension of this work have?

Burr: I think about this a lot, because one of my dance-history professors in college said the reason why ballet is so successful is that it doesn't throw out its traditions the way modern dance and postmodern dance do. We always feel pressure to make something completely new—I need to distinguish myself from whomever. He said that in ballet, making something new isn't the primary goal; instead it is entertainment or storytelling, so then it's a little more like building on top of itself. In the work that I do and the processes that I'm a part of, there is a sense of referencing history and trying not to make addressing the past clinical but finding ways to look at it with fresh eyes.

Alexandra A.: I expected to be dealing with history even more directly than we did. I thought we would spend more time

with the film footage, extracting more specific material and reimagining it for this group—figuring out how we could alter something specific. I guess I'm curious how people see the dance and the choreography in relation to the works in the exhibition, and if they can find relationships for themselves. I don't know.

Nick: I didn't anticipate how hard it would be to access the historical material in advance of the exhibition. I had a fantasy that we would work almost archaeologically with these documents before realizing that we wouldn't be permitted to do that. It ended up that we were doing things by substitution, but it was so exciting to see how eloquently you made choices and incorporated the slivers that could be gleaned from what was available to us. It seemed like maybe *that*—inventing in the absence of fully visible "original"—was ultimately the work.

Alexandra A.: I still remember you saying one day in rehearsal that for you our narrative is the process. I think it was a more classical duet that was being worked out, and we were talking about how narratives seem to arise in more classical content and asking what the narrative for this piece would be, how we would home in on the overarching concept when there are sixteen or seventeen choreographers. When you said that our narrative is the process itself, it was reassuring.

Matilda: That was a nice turning point in the rehearsals, because narrative is so much a part of ballet. In the beginning, I was trying to create ballet and it felt cheesy, because my mind automatically went to something Romantic. As the process went on, I remember in my mind going from, "Okay, I'm trying to do ballet," to, "Oh, I'm trying to create a process, an investigation."

Jasmine: Recognizing my own cravings and priorities, I understand that what I'm doing isn't new—like someone did this step already. The way that it's arranged might be different, but I trust that it has happened already. I believe I've been on this earth before, but in *this* body and

this time with all of its different kinds of contingencies, how do those contingencies intersect with one another and what happens? What kind of magic gets conjured there?

Anna: I think a lot about how the body holds so much subconsciously. We're constantly mining from these wells within ourselves that we may not be conscious of and that might be coming from a collective or personal history. I think language is so essential for dance. Part of the reason why it's considered an ephemeral form is often grounded in language, so writing about dance is important. There are so many theories and ways of processing that provide reference points and context for dances. Reviews try to capture dance in words. How does that shape the way we see the work and engage with it?

Benedict: Even audiences who stumble into the exhibition are able to place buzzwords on what we're doing—*ballet* being one of the first after *dance*. I'm thinking about our response to this archive and about how loaded many of the gestures are, the histories of where they came from in the world and physiologically why we do things, you know, within a class but also how elements of that are reflected in the choreography . . .

Nick: Are you talking about examining authority on the body?

Benedict: Examining the significance of the narratives that are loaded into those gestures, even if we're dissociating them from narrative.

Nick: Can you give an example?

Benedict: A gesture of the hands twisted around the head might hold an element of supplication. While it has its roots in eras of ballet, and it also does something particular.

Nick: Where does the gesture of the hands twisted around the head come from?

Matilda: Always an "Arabian" something. Something "exotic."

Benedict: Yes, not nonmeaning, but *this* in between *this* in between Romantic. What does it mean to string those together in *that* order in *that* moment?

Nick: I remember showing Jasmine a gesture that I particularly like in a Bronislava Nijinska ballet—I think it was *Les Noces*. She said she didn't like it at all and found it offensive. I had assumed it was taken from Russian folk art, a representation of a chicken or something. But of course, it can be read differently, and in that moment I realized these gestures and shapes signify across time or maybe cross wires with other forms of signification. I'm happy that you're asking everyone to think about how this gesture reads to people now and how that reading comes up against knowledge of where it originates.

Forrest: I think it still does have an "other" feeling for people because of Britney Spears and Shakira. I think people still like belly dancing.

Matilda: This process was intuition-based in its approach to creating movement, even though it came from a place of analyzing pictures in history. I'm sure we all have had different thought processes, but because we made things that weren't trying to represent anything it would be interesting now to take what we created and pull out the things that should be delved into further. Now that we have a baseline understanding of what was instinctual, we could pull out the things that have one meaning and then see the things that we just went to as a default, and then see the things that actually maybe mean something more. We went into this without an exact idea of what it was going to be. We could probably create another piece based on what we've created, the information we've learned and the information received, and then pull out and delve into what everything is and why we chose it. In hindsight, it's easy to say that we should have thought about this or that. But sometimes you can't, you just don't realize some things until after.

Nick: Benedict, do you think you would want to go into and research the

legacy—or the muffled echo—of these persistent gestures? To follow, for example, one strain of exoticized gesture in classical repertoire. Or have you already?

Benedict: I don't know. I could watch one of the classics and find so much information there. In almost any classical work, specific gestures get appropriated on top of the formalisms of ballet. Like: fifth position, fifth position, pointe shoe, pointe shoe, pointe shoe, and this arm, which together somehow communicates that I'm a slave dancer in India. And then, arabesque, arabesque, waltz, waltz, waltz, and another gesture . . .

Matilda: I wonder if you just did those moves plainly or in a different way— usually, when you do this, you also do a little hip and you know . . . When does it start to become something that you can't separate from just being movement?

Quenton: Are you talking about dance history? Or history in general?

Nick: It doesn't have to be dance history.

Quenton: I find that if I'm creating, I'm always referencing history. I'm always trying to shake off the trauma of history. I'm referencing actions that people have done in the past in the choreography, so we can continue to remember. Creating something new is great, but I also think that memory is important.

Matilda: To this day, I would secretly love to be a principal dancer. There's this desire that's been a part of me for so long. It's more physical—the feeling—as it's really not worked for me. Ballet has been such a part of my life, but it was detrimental in some ways to the way I view myself. It was so forced, and since I wasn't what you're "supposed" to be, I started to go in the opposite direction. I still have form in what I explore, but I also like trying to rebel against the idea of ballet. The process of working on this has helped me figure out how I feel about ballet—that it doesn't have to be what it was or something that I need to go against, but it can just be and I can find a way to make it work.

In creating work, practicing, or in self-exploration, it can be more of a marriage, and less like the feeling that I'm doing my own nonballet versus doing ballet. I can explore that relationship more organically. Maybe I was trying to be a little too extreme in my rejection. Ballet does carry a lot of emotional energy in me.

Anna: It can feel like such a trap to strive for originality when our bodies are trained. I often find myself frustrated when I'm in the studio trying to make something. Things can feel derivative, and it drives me crazy. I am influenced by whatever I'm currently doing. I look back at what I was making in college, trying to make something like Trisha Brown's *Set and Reset*, for example, because that's what I was studying. And now I've been trying to shake Sarah Michelson's work out of my mind. Those are things that have shaped me and many of us. How do I incorporate those ideas into my work, find what's still relevant to me about it? I can feel trapped—how could I possibly be original when it feels like everything's been done? Really—everything.

Kristina: I personally don't mind that at all because if something feels good on your body, why not keep on doing it? Just because you showed a work one time doesn't mean it's the final work. You can keep on developing it, and it ends up being something that's inside of you that you keep on wanting to talk about. This experience has shaped a piece that I recently showed. It's okay to take material that you've worked on if you feel connected to it and if it's connected into your body, and then also ask questions like, "What did I like about that piece? Was it the structure, the feeling? Was it the way the movement developed?" I try to take those tiny things and apply them to new things and reapply them again and again and again.

Biographies of *Transmissions* Performers

ALEXANDRA ALBRECHT is a performer and curator based in New York. She has collaborated on original works by Hilary Easton, Stacy Grossfield, Ryan McNamara, Jillian Peña, Sam Pinkleton, and Ani Taj/The Dance Cartel. She holds a BFA in dance and a BA in journalism from New York University.

KRISTINA BERMUDEZ is from Queens, New York, and received her BFA from the Boston Conservatory at Berklee School of Music as a Jan Veen Scholar, after attending Walnut Hill School for the Arts in Natick, Massachusetts. She has performed in New York City Center's production of *Evita*, worked with Anne Teresa de Keersmaeker during the Broadway developmental lab of *West Side Story*, and performed for Opera Philadelphia under the direction of Bill T. Jones for the musical workshop of *We Shall Not Be Moved*. Other influential teachers include choreographers Diane Arvanites and Danielle Polanco. Bermudez's work has been presented at various venues and festivals such as Judson Memorial Church and the Martha Graham Dance Company's NEXT@Graham. She is currently producing a short documentary about her experiences touring Europe as a solo artist.

MAGGIE CLOUD is a performer and acupuncturist living in Brooklyn, New York. She grew up in Sarasota, Florida, and graduated from Florida State University with a BFA in dance. Cloud has performed in the work of many choreographers, including Moriah Evans, Beth Gill, John Jasperse, Sarah Michelson, Pam Tanowitz, and Gillian Walsh.

BRANDON COLLWES trained at the Pittsburgh CLO in musical theater and jazz dance. He studied the George Balanchine technique at the Pittsburgh Ballet Theatre and the Creative and Performing Arts High School of Pittsburgh, where he started making his own choreography. He continued his studies at the Juilliard School, New York; and Purchase College, State University of New York. In 2003, he became a member of the CDF Repertory Understudy Group, where he trained under Merce Cunningham and Robert Swinston. He danced with the Merce Cunningham Dance Company from 2006 until the company's closing in 2011. He currently dances with the Liz Gerring Dance Company, teaches internationally, and continues to develop and perform his own work. Collwes is also a self-taught painter.

AHMAUD CULVER was raised in Lancaster, California, and began his formal training at California Institute of the Arts, Valencia. After working as a freelance dancer in Los Angeles for several years, Culver moved in 2009 to New York, where he has worked with national and international dance companies and choreographers such as Karole Armitage, Augusto Soledade Brazzdance, José Limón Dance Foundation's Collin Connor, Danza Concerto of Colombia, Eglevsky Ballet, and Opera Saratoga.

JASMINE HEARN is a native Houstonian who received a BA in dance from Point Park University, Pittsburgh. A Brooklyn, New York–based performer, curator, director, choreographer, organizer, and teaching artist, she is a company member with Urban Bush Women and a 2019 Jerome Foundation Jerome Hill Fellow. She frequently collaborates with BANDportier, Vanessa German, MBDance, Samita Sinha, and Alisha B. Wormsley. Hearn teaches, performs, and collaborates around the world. She received a 2017 Bessie Award for her performance with Skeleton Architecture, and has shared her work at Camargo Foundation, Cassis, France; Danspace Project, New York; LaMaMa, New York; and New York Live Arts.

ELIZABETH HEPP is a freelance dance artist based in Brooklyn, New York. After receiving her BFA from New York University's Tisch School of the Arts, she studied Cunningham technique with the Merce Cunningham Trust and participated in multiple repertory workshops. She has worked with many choreographers, including Molly Gorin, Erick Montes, Lynn Neuman, and Dusan Tynek.

FORREST HERSEY was raised in Ghent, Kentucky, and trained at University of Louisville Dance Academy and the Youth Performing Arts School, both in Louisville, Kentucky. While earning a BFA from the Conservatory of Dance at Purchase College, State University of New York, he performed repertory by Aszure Barton, Shannon Gillen, and Ohad Naharin. Hersey was a freelance dancer for Rashaun Mitchell and Nelly van Bommel before representing the Merce Cunningham Trust as part of the celebration of thirty-five years of the MacArthur Fellows Program. He currently dances for Liz Gerring Dance Company, Pigeonwing Dance, and ZviDance.

ALEXANDRA JACOB began ballet training at the age of eight in Berkeley, California. In 2004, she joined the Dance Theatre of Harlem, then under the direction of Arthur Mitchell and later that of Virginia Johnson. During her ten years at the company, she performed featured roles by George Balanchine, Donald Byrd, Michel Fokine, Christopher Huggins, Royston Maldoom, Arthur Mitchell, Peter Pucci, and Lowell Smith. She has recently collaborated with Zana Bayne,

Beacon's Closet, Lou Dallas, Dirty Churches, DSTM, Jaguar USA, Ladyfag, Charlie Le Mindu, Susanne Bartsch's Love Ball III, Sarai Mari, Tag Heuer, Mika Tajima, Art Production Fund's Psycho Graphics digital billboard video campaign, Things Power Themselves, Vie Active Activewear, Kanye West's Yeezy "We Got Love" campaign, and Wide Rainbow. She also stars in Annelise Ogaard's forthcoming independent film *Our Colleagues*.

BURR JOHNSON has danced for Christopher Williams, Helen Simoneau Danse, John Jasperse Projects, Kimberly Bartosik/daela, and Shen Wei Dance Arts. He has worked with Marina Abramović/Givenchy, Walter Dundervill, Mark Fell, Jack Ferver, Isabel Lewis, Ryan McNamara, Min Oh, Peter Sellars, and Yozmit. His choreographic work has been presented at Abrons Art Center, New York; Danspace Project, New York; Dixon Place, New York; Elizabeth Dee Gallery, New York; Josée Bienvenu Gallery, New York; Movement Research at Judson Memorial Church, New York; and New York Live Arts. In 2019 Johnson performed in the Merce Cunningham centennial event *Night of 100 Solos* in Los Angeles.

MAKI KITAHARA is from Fukushima, Japan, and is an award-winning dancer, choreographer, and teacher. She has performed lead roles in ballets and contemporary dance works and has collaborated with professionals from other artistic fields in Japan and internationally. She has been nominated for a New Face Award by the Agency for Cultural Affairs, Government of Japan. Her own solo work *Michi* (2017) has been performed three times in New York. She recently performed a new collaborative work at the Ace Hotel, New York. Kitahara is currently a faculty member at Gibney Dance, New York.

EVELYN KOCAK studied for three years at the School of American Ballet before joining New York City Ballet as an apprentice in 2004. She joined the Staatsballett Berlin as a member of the corps de ballet in 2006 and danced there for four seasons. Kocak returned to the United States to join Pennsylvania Ballet for the 2010–11 season and was promoted to soloist for the 2012–13 season. She has danced with the Suzanne Farrell Ballet, Tom Gold Dance, Claudia Schreier and Company, and Seattle Symphony, and in *Something to Dance About*, directed by Warren Carlyle. She has also collaborated on projects with visual artist Alex Prager and performance artists Michèle Graf, Selina Grüter, and Madeline Hollander.

BENEDICT NGUYEN is a dancer, writer, and curator based in the South Bronx, New York. Their writing has appeared in the *Brooklyn Rail*, Asian American Writers' Workshop's *The Margins*, and *Shondaland*, among other publications. As the 2019 Suzanne Fiol Curatorial Fellow at Issue Project Room, New York, Nguyen devised Soft Bodies in Hard Places, a platform for transdisciplinary collaborations in dialogue with astrological movements.

MATILDA SAKAMOTO is a New York– and Los Angeles–based choreographer, dancer, and artist. She received her BFA from the Juilliard School, New York, and has danced for artists including Esmé Boyce, Hivewild, Ashley Robicheaux, and Nicole von Arx. In 2019 she performed as an actor in Richard Nelson's newest play, *The Michaels*, at the Public Theater, New York. Sakamoto choreographed a dance opera in Ostrava, Czech Republic, for composer Petr Kotik at the NODO Festival, which was also presented in New York at Paula Cooper Gallery. Her choreography has been presented at venues such as Dixon Place, New York; Judson Memorial Church, New York; and Triskelion Arts, Brooklyn, New York. Sakamoto is a choreographer for the Juilliard School's summer dance program.

QUENTON STUCKEY is a dancer and musician. Originally from New Orleans, he is largely a self-taught dancer. He has performed at the Museum of Modern Art, New York; Museu Nacional de Arte Contemporânea, Lisbon; Philip Johnson's Glass House, New Canaan, Connecticut; and the Solomon R. Guggenheim Museum, New York, among other venues. He also choreographed a piece for the Guggenheim's Young Collectors Council in 2017. Stuckey is currently a music resident at Pioneer Works, a Brooklyn, New York–based arts and science space. He is in the process of recording a debut album under the guise of an only child.

ANNA THÉRÈSE WITENBERG trained with Sarah Michelson at Bard College, Annandale-on-Hudson, New York, performing in her works, such as *tournamento* at the Walker Art Center, Minneapolis; *September 2017* ∧ at Bard; and *October 2017* ∧ at the Kitchen, New York. At the American Dance Festival, Witenberg was selected to perform in works by Beth Gill and Anna Sperber. She has performed with the Stephen Petronio Company in a restaging of Trisha Brown's *Glacial Decoy* at the Durham Performing Arts Center, North Carolina, performing Brown's role. She also danced Brown's solos in *Cutbacks* and *Set and Reset*, restaged by the Trisha Brown Company. Since moving to New York, she has performed in Douglas Dunn's *Portal* at Queensbridge Park, Long Island City, New York; Anna Sperber's *Again the Wolves* at the 92nd Street Y in New York and the Yard in Chilmark, Massachusetts; Doug Le Cours's *Fraying Tether* at Weis Acres, New York; and

Maya Lee-Parritz's *Tribute to Angels* at the Shed, New York. She currently freelances for Anna Sperber and Katie Workum, and collaborates on dance and video work with Tal Eshel and Doug LeCours. Her own choreography has been presented in New York at the Brooklyn Ballet and the Performance Mix Festival 33.

Selected Biographies of Performers and Choreographers Pictured in *Transmissions*

DIANA ADAMS (1926–1993) was a principal dancer for New York City Ballet and American Ballet Theatre. Adams performed in many of George Balanchine's major works and was considered to be an archetypical Balanchine dancer (the choreographer made the precarious pas de deux in *Agon* [1957] on Adams and Arthur Mitchell). In the 1960s, while still performing, Adams began teaching at the School of American Ballet, ultimately becoming dean of students until retiring in 1971. She was married to dancer Hugh Laing from 1947 to 1953.

MAXWELL BAIRD was a dancer in the 1934 cast of Virgil Thompson's *Four Saints in Three Acts* (choreographed by Frederick Ashton), which opened on Broadway at the 44th Street Theatre. He was photographed by George Platt Lynes.

HERNÁN BALDRICH is an internationally acclaimed Chilean dancer and choreographer. Baldrich was the codirector and choreographer of the Chamber Ballet of the Institute of Musical Extension of the University of Chile (1966). He also founded in 1977 the legendary Mobile company, one of the first independent dance groups in Chile, establishing it under a political dictatorship. Mobile, which existed until 1991, brought together artists from many disciplines—dance, sculpture, photography, theater, and poetry, among them—toward the common goal of making dance. Baldrich traveled to the United States in the early 1960s, presenting original works at Jacob's Pillow and the Harkness Ballet. He was photographed during this period several times by artist Carl Van Vechten.

BRADBURY BALL was a model for George Platt Lynes. He was photographed alongside Charles "Tex" Smutney and Charles "Buddy" Stanley circa 1942.

MAUDELL BASS (1908–1989) was a concert dancer, model, and distinct cultural figure in the Los Angeles art community of the mid-twentieth century. As a teenager touring Mexico and Latin America with the Folklórico group, Bass was painted by Diego Rivera. After moving to Los Angeles around 1933, she became the first black dancer to study with Lester Horton, the prominent contemporary choreographer; was photographed by Johan Hagemeyer and Edward Weston; and modeled for sculptor Beulah Woodard. Bass danced in Agnes de Mille's *Black Ritual* (*Obeah*) for the American Ballet Theatre in 1940, performed with Pearl Primus in the 1950s, and continued performing well into her seventies.

AL BLEDGER was a lead dancer, together with Lavinia Williams, of the short-lived Eugene Von Grona's American Negro Ballet Company. He performed in the 1941 off-Broadway musical *La Belle Hélène* and in Beryl McBurnie's *Antiliana*, a program of Caribbean dancing, in 1943.

BILL BLIZZARD was a model and the subject of several erotic photographs by George Platt Lynes. For a period, he was Lynes's lover. He was introduced to the photographer by John Leaphart.

TODD BOLENDER (1914–2006) was an acclaimed Ohio-born ballet dancer, teacher, choreographer, and director. After relocating to New York in 1936, he was recruited by George Balanchine and Lincoln Kirstein to join the American Ballet Theatre. Bolender is known for his breakthrough performance in the 1946 experimental ballet *The Four Temperaments*, and for roles in *Agon*, *Billy the Kid*, *Renard*, and Lew Christensen's *Filling Station*. He became a key figure in New York City Ballet and its forerunner companies before leading the Kansas City Ballet from 1981 to 1996. A prolific choreographer, Bolender created thirty-six works for the Kansas City Ballet and elsewhere. He is considered a crucial influence in the development of ballet as an American art form.

RUTHANA BORIS (1918–2007) was born in Brooklyn, New York, and was the first American ballerina to star in the famed Ballet Russe de Monte Carlo, where she danced from 1943 to 1950 in ballets such as *Frankie and Johnny* and *Swan Lake*. She was among the first students of George Balanchine and Lincoln Kirstein's School of the American Ballet when it opened in 1934. In 1935, she made her solo debut with the Metropolitan Opera, performing in *Carmen*, and continuing on as prima ballerina from 1937 to 1942. Boris is known particularly for her comedic performances and versatility in dancing both classical and contemporary ballet roles. As a choreographer, she created seventeen works, including the widely recognized pieces *Cirque de deux* (1947) and *Cakewalk* (1951).

ROBERT COHAN (b. 1925) is a Brooklyn-born choreographer and dancer who began his professional career with the Martha Graham Dance Company, which he joined in 1946 and performed with for many years as a soloist. After leaving the company in 1957, he started his own dance group, working as a choreographer. He returned to Graham's company in 1962 for its European tour and became a codirector in 1966. Since then, Cohan has lived and worked abroad and has become a leading figure in the development of modern British dance. He was the first artistic director of the Contemporary Dance Trust in London, and founding artistic director of the Place—Britain's first contemporary dance school—and the London

Contemporary Dance Theatre (LCDT), which he directed for twenty years.

JANET COLLINS (1917–2003) was a New Orleans–born, Los Angeles–raised American ballet dancer, choreographer, and teacher. One of the few classically trained black dancers of her era, she revolutionized traditions of American dance. Collins performed in the companies of Adolph Bolm, Katherine Dunham, Lester Horton, and Carmelita Maracci, among others, and refused to join Ballets Russes de Monte Carlo at age fifteen, when asked to disguise that she was black. She debuted her own choreography in 1949 at the 92nd Street Y and performed the following year in the Cole Porter Broadway musical *Out of This World*. In the early 1950s, she became the prima ballerina of the Metropolitan Opera, becoming known for lead roles in *Aïda*, *Carmen*, the Dance of the Hours in *La Gioconda*, and the Bacchanale in *Samson and Delilah*.

MURIEL COOK performed title roles in Broadway shows, including *Flying Colors* (1932), *Big White Fog* (1940), Lew Leslie's *Blackbirds of 1939* (1939), and *Swingin' the Dream* (1939). As part of American Ballet Theatre's short-lived "Negro Unit," she performed in Agnes de Mille's *Black Ritual (Obeah)* in 1940, alongside fifteen other African American dancers.

MERCE CUNNINGHAM (1919–2009) was a visionary choreographer and dancer, widely considered one of the most influential artists of the twentieth century. Deeply influenced by his experimental education at Black Mountain College, Cunningham went on to dance for Martha Graham, who sent the young modern dancer to study technique at the School of American Ballet. Over his seven-decade career, Cunningham choreographed 180 works and more than 700 choreographic "events," revolutionizing dance both technically and conceptually. Cunningham was known for his audacious collaborations with visual artists and composers, including Jasper Johns, Robert Rauschenberg, and, most notably, his partner John Cage. With Cage, Cunningham composed works in which dance and music were brought together as independent, autonomous forces. Both absorbing and rejecting the influences of George Balanchine and Martha Graham, Cunningham's radical approach to choreography revealed how dance can be classical, yet unlike ballet.

JACQUES D'AMBOISE (b. 1934) was a principal dancer with New York City Ballet and also choreographed works for the company. After his acrobatic performance in 1953 as Mac, the gas station attendant and all-American hero of Lew Christensen's *Filling Station* (1937), d'Amboise was promoted to soloist. In 1976, while dancing as a principal, he created the National Dance Institute to engage children with dance, no matter their background or ability. He also danced in films, including *Seven Brides for Seven Brothers* (1954), *The Best Things in Life Are Free* (1956), *Carousel* (1956), and *Off Beat* (1986).

ALFREDO CARLO ("FRED") DANIELI (1917–1997) was an Italian American dancer who performed with the American Ballet Caravan and worked extensively with George Balanchine, performing with New York City Ballet and in Broadway musicals. In 1949, he cofounded with his wife, Evelyn Danieli, the Garden State Ballet School, New Jersey's first professional ballet school; in 1961, he founded the Garden State Ballet. The company presented its dances in community spaces across the state. As Danieli said to the *New York Times* in 1973: "We have no Lincoln Center in New Jersey. We go out to the people with all our productions."

LEON DANIELIAN (1920–1997) was an Armenian American ballet dancer best known as a soloist in Ballet Russe de Monte Carlo in the 1940s and 1950s. During his early years, he performed with American Ballet Theatre, in Colonel W. de Basil's Original Ballet Russe, and in Broadway musicals. Danielian was admired for his spirited dancing, classical technique, and gift for comedy. He excelled in roles such as Harlequin in *Le Carnaval* and the Peruvian in *Gaîté parisienne*. Danielian later became a respected teacher, working at the Ballet Russe School in New York and as director of American Ballet Theatre School in the 1970s.

JAMES LESLIE ("JIMMIE") DANIELS (1908–1984) was a cabaret and nightclub performer who began his career singing in Harlem and became a sensation in Paris. After singing throughout Europe during the 1930s, he returned to the United States and opened Jimmie Daniels' Nightclub in Harlem, which operated from 1939 to 1942. Daniels was briefly partnered with the architect Philip Johnson and became a muse to sculptor Richmond Barthé. Carl Van Vechten and George Platt Lynes also captured his likeness. A major fixture of New York nightlife, Daniels became the lead performer at the Bon Soir in Greenwich Village, known for attracting a black, white, and gay clientele during the 1950s. In the 1960s, he performed at the Tiffany Room, now the Ice Palace in Cherry Grove on Fire Island and the Blue Whale Bar in the Fire Island Pines, until a cross was burned in front of his home, which compelled him to drop the engagement. Daniels continued to record and perform in the West Village throughout the 1970s.

CARMEN DE LAVALLADE (b. 1931) is a celebrated dancer and choreographer whose career began in her hometown of Los Angeles, where she performed with the Lester Horton Dance Theater. She is the cousin of the famed Metropolitan Opera prima ballerina Janet Collins and succeeded Collins in the same role in 1955. At a young age, she appeared in films including *Carmen Jones* (1954) and *Odds against Tomorrow* (1959). She left Los Angeles with Alvin Ailey in 1954 to make her Broadway debut with him the same year in Truman Capote's musical *House of Flowers*. In 1955, she married dancer and actor Geoffrey Holder, with whom she shared an intimate, galvanizing creative life. Notably, she has danced in ballets created for her by Alvin Ailey, John Butler, Agnes de Mille, Geoffrey Holder, Lester Horton, and Glen Tetley. She has choreographed many works, for venues including the Alvin Ailey American Dance Theater, the Dance Theatre of Harlem, the Metropolitan Opera, Philadanco, and Yale Repertory Theater.

AGNES DE MILLE (1905–1993) was an American dancer and choreographer who was born in New York's Harlem neighborhood. As a member of American Ballet Theatre, she created her first ballet, *Black Ritual (Obeah)*, which was performed by sixteen black female dancers, in 1940. Notably, she also created the ballet *Rodeo* (1942) with a score by Aaron Copland for Ballet Russe de Monte Carlo and the choreography for the Rodgers & Hammerstein musical *Oklahoma!* (1943), after which she choreographed works for more than a dozen other musicals. In 1973, she founded the Agnes de Mille Dance Theatre, which she later revived as Heritage Dance Theatre. She was the author of several books, including a personal memoir, *Dance to the Piper* (1952), and a biography of her lifelong friend Martha Graham, *Martha: The Life and Work of Martha Graham* (1991).

ANTON DOLIN (1904–1983) was an English choreographer and dancer. Dolin began his ballet career in 1921 when he joined Serge Diaghilev's Ballets Russes. There he was a principal starting in 1924 and later became a principal with the Vic-Wells Ballet (now the Royal Ballet) in the early 1930s. At Vic-Wells, he danced with Alicia Markova, who was his partner in founding the Markova-Dolin Ballet and the London Festival Ballet. During American Ballet Theatre's formation in 1940, he joined as a dancer and choreographer, remaining until 1946.

WILLIAM ("BILL") EARL was a dancer in New York City Ballet. He performed in *The Figure in the Carpet* (1961) and *La Sonnambula* (1960).

JOHN FERENZ was photographed by George Platt Lynes in 1936.

LOIE FULLER (1862–1928) was a Chicago-born dancer and actress, known for a pioneering synthesis of modern dance and theatrical lighting techniques. She invented the "serpentine dance," an evolution of the skirt dance (a form of burlesque dance that incorporated elements of folk and popular dances like the can-can). Performing in billowing silk drapery, illuminated by multicolored lighting of her unique design, Fuller transcended ballet and forged an innovative technique of her own. After emigrating to Paris, she performed at the Folies Bergère. Her influence on the visual arts in early twentieth-century Europe cannot be overstated—the craze for Loie Fuller registered in the poetry of Stéphane Mallarmé; in the artwork of Henri de Toulouse-Lautrec, Jules Cheret, and August Rodin; and even in the architecture of of Art Nouveau.

IAN GIBSON was a dancer in American Ballet Theatre. Born in Scotland and raised primarily in Canada, Gibson began ballet training under Dorothy Wilson in Victoria, British Columbia, and continued his studying under June Roper in Vancouver. He began his career at the Hollywood Bowl in 1938 and soon joined Ballet Russe de Monte Carlo. Gibson later signed with American Ballet Theatre in 1942, where he performed the Bluebird pas de deux in *The Sleeping Beauty* (1943). He also performed in the 1941 world premiere of *Slavonika*, as well as the 1942 US premiere of *Petrushka.*

MARTHA GRAHAM (1894–1991) was a dancer and choreographer whose name has become synonymous with modern dance. The "Graham technique" is the first enduring opposition to the idiom of classical ballet. Based on the dynamics of contraction and release and the spiraling of the torso around the spine, Graham's technique aims to expose human emotion through movement, or, in Graham's own words, to "give visible substance to things felt." Collaborating with artists, designers, and composers to create more than 180 works, Graham also created roles for classical ballet stars such as Margot Fonteyn and Rudolf Nureyev, though Graham cast herself at the center of her dances until 1969. Her most well-known works, such as *Appalachian Spring* (1944), are inspired by "American" themes and landscapes. Among many others, Merce Cunningham, Erick Hawkins, Paul Taylor, and Twyla Tharp were members of Graham's company.

LAURIE DOUGLAS HARBACH (1914–2015) was an Oklahoma-born model and member of the Chickasaw Nation. She was featured in publications such as *Vogue, Modern Photography*, and *Modern Romance*, and was notably photographed by her former lover George Platt Lynes. She was briefly married to the television producer and director William Harbach and lived her later life in Tangier, Morocco, from 1971 to 2013.

ERICK HAWKINS (1909–1994) was a dancer and choreographer who studied at the School of American Ballet. He performed in Balanchine's American Ballet, choreographed for Ballet Caravan, and later joined Martha Graham's modern dance troupe as its first male member. He was married to Graham for a short period. Hawkins's own choreography, which he developed after working with Graham, was inspired by forms of ritual and mysticism and kinesthetic responses to human, animal, and natural phenomena. Throughout his career, he collaborated with many visual artists, including Helen Frankenthaler, Robert Motherwell, and Isamu Noguchi; and with many composers, including Henry Cowell, Lou Harrison, and Toru Takemitsu.

(KATHERINE) GERTRUDE HOFFMANN (1883–1966) was born in San Francisco and became a celebrated vaudeville dancer and choreographer. She is widely known for her seductive performance as Salome in *A Vision of Salome*, which repeatedly led to her arrest for allegedly violating the Comstock Laws. She began her career working as a rehearsal director of vaudeville routines at Oscar Hammerstein's Victoria Theater, later performing onstage herself. In 1911, Hoffmann brought a pirated version of the Ballets Russes to North America. She later formed an acrobatic dance troupe of chorus-line dancers known as the Gertrude Hoffmann Girls.

HARALD HORN was a dancer who performed with the Berlin Dance Theatre and Ballet Russe de Monte Carlo. He also performed at the Broadway Theatre as part of the original cast of *Tovarich* (1963). He appeared in the film *Die Große Starparade* (The Great Star Parade), made in Germany, with Katherine Dunham's company in 1954.

NORA KAYE (1920–1987) was an American prima ballerina, often referred to as the "Duse of Dance," after acclaimed actress Eleonora Duse. She worked in films as a choreographer and producer and performed on Broadway. At age fifteen, she joined the Metropolitan Opera's corps de ballet and, after training under Michel Fokine and George Balanchine, became a part of American Ballet Theatre. There she danced in the major roles of Antony

Tudor's works. She joined New York City Ballet in 1951, performing in Jerome Robbins's *The Cage* and Tudor's *La Gloire*. In 1959, Kaye married choreographer Herbert Ross, with whom she founded the Ballet of Two Worlds. She was later named the assistant to the director of the American Ballet Theatre and served as associate artistic director of the company from 1977 to 1983.

LEWANNE (LAWUANE) KENNARD, also known as Lawuane Ingram after her marriage to actor Rex Ingram, was a dancer in the American Ballet Theatre who had studied under Martha Graham. She was part of the short-lived "Negro Unit" of Ballet Theatre, which performed Agnes de Mille's *Black Ritual (Obeah)* in 1940. Soon after, she moved to Katherine Dunham's company, where she performed in *Cabin in the Sky* (1940), a choreographic collaboration between Dunham and George Balanchine.

HUGH LAING (1911–1988) studied dance in London with Margaret Craske, Olga Preobrajenska, and Marie Rambert, joining Antony Tudor's London Ballet in 1938. In 1939, Laing accompanied Tudor to New York, where Laing was celebrated as a star dancer of Ballet Theatre. He went on to dance with New York City Ballet in the 1950s, later embarking on a career as a commercial photographer. Laing was married to dancer Diana Adams from 1947 to 1953.

JOHN LEAPHART was a model and lover of photographer George Platt Lynes, to whom he was introduced by writer and tattoo artist (and fastidious chronicler of his own complex sex life) Samuel Steward, with whom Lynes maintained an epistolary exchange of photographs in return for Steward's narrative memorializations of his "experiences."

NICHOLAS MAGALLANES (1922–1977) was born in Santa Rosalía de Camargoa, Mexico, and immigrated to the United States at the age of five. When he was sixteen years old, he was spotted at the New York Boys' Club on East Tenth Street by artist Pavel Tchelitchew, who recommended him to Lincoln Kirstein as a scholarship student at the fledgling School of American Ballet. Magallanes would later go on to become the principal dancer of New York City Ballet. Along with Tanaquil Le Clercq, Francisco Moncion, and Maria Tallchief, Magallanes was among the core group of dancers with whom George Balanchine and Lincoln Kirstein formed Ballet Society, the immediate predecessor of New York City Ballet.

ALICIA MARKOVA (1910–2004) was a British ballerina, director, choreographer, and teacher of classical ballet. Markova was widely recognized as one of the twentieth century's greatest ballet dancers, performing with Serge Diaghilev's Ballets Russes and touring globally. The first British dancer to become a principal in a ballet company, she was known for her purity of line, precision, and grace. She became one of the only two British dancers to be considered a prima ballerina assoluta. In 1935, she founded the Vic-Wells company with Anton Dolin and Ninette de Valois. She was also a founding dancer of the American Ballet Theatre, the Rambert dance company, and the Royal Ballet, as well as a cofounder and director of the English National Ballet. After retiring from dancing, Markova directed the Metropolitan Opera Ballet for six years.

JOSÉ ("PETE") MARTINEZ (1913–1997) was born in Mexico and was an early student at the School of American Ballet, founded in New York in 1934 by George Balanchine, Lincoln Kirstein, and Edward M. M. Warburg. In the 1940s, he danced with the American Ballet Caravan and Ballet Society, precursors of the New York City Ballet. A lover of Lincoln Kirstein, he was the subject of Kirstein's 1943 novel, *For My Brother*. He was also a frequent model for the painter Paul Cadmus, artist Fidelma Cadmus Kirstein, and photographer George Platt Lynes.

BERYL MCBURNIE (1913–2000) was a Trinidadian dancer who lived and worked in New York in the late 1930s and 1940s. While in New York, she enrolled at Columbia University's school of drama, studied dance with Martha Graham, and worked with choreographers Charles Weidman and Katherine Dunham—to whom she privately taught dances from the West Indies. In 1941, McBurnie began performing under the stage name La Belle Rosette at venues including the 92nd Street Y, New York; the Museum of Modern Art, New York; and the Brooklyn Academy of Music, Brooklyn, New York. A pioneer of Trinidad and Tobago's folk dance scene, she established in 1947 the Little Carib Theatre, the first permanent folk-dance theater and company in Trinidad and Tobago.

RALPH MCWILLIAMS (1926–1981) was a dancer whose versatile career encompassed ballet, modern dance, musical comedy, and television. He danced with American Ballet Theatre from 1949 to 1952 and again in 1957, and was stage manager for the company from 1966 to 1970. He studied music at the Juilliard School and took private ballet lessons with George Chaffee and Igor Schwezoff. In modern dance, he was the frequent partner of Myra Kinch, on tour and at the Jacob's Pillow dance festival. He danced on Broadway in *High Button Shoes* and *Allegro* and appeared

in off-Broadway and national productions. He was a frequent subject for artists such as Paul Cadmus and George Platt Lynes.

ALAN (JUANTE JERGERHADUTHA) MEADOWS was introduced to Carl Van Vechten by Harlem Renaissance sculptor Richmond Barthé. Virtually nothing is known about Meadows's background. In *The Homoerotic Photography of Carl Van Vechten*, James Smalls characterizes Meadows as "probably a young dancer [who] circulated among Harlem's black and white gay cultural elite, if not physically, then certainly through Van Vechten's photographs."

(MATTHEW) FLOYD MILLER was a dancer in the 1934 cast of Virgil Thompson's *Four Saints in Three Acts* (choreographed by Frederick Ashton), which opened on Broadway at the 44th Street Theatre.

ARTHUR MITCHELL (1934–2018) was a legendary ballet dancer who performed in New York City Ballet. Born in Harlem in 1934, he joined New York City Ballet in 1955, becoming the first African American dancer to be named a permanent member of the company. He danced in major roles in ballets, including *Agon*, *Arcade*, *Bugaku*, *A Midsummer Night's Dream*, and *The Nutcracker*, and inspired these lines in poet Marianne Moore's tribute to his performances: "contagious gem of virtuosity—make visible, mentality." Following the assassination of Martin Luther King Jr., Mitchell cofounded the Dance Theatre of Harlem with his mentor Karel Shook, and later founded additional companies in Spoleto, Italy; Washington, DC; and Brazil.

FRANCISCO MONCION (1918–1995) was a dancer with New York City Ballet. Born in the Dominican Republic, he began training in 1938 at the School of American Ballet, where he learned to dance in the style of the Russian School of ballet under the likes of George Balanchine, Anatole Oboukhoff, and Pierre Vladimiroff. He began performing in the Ballet Society in 1946 and stayed with the company as it became New York City Ballet in 1948. In his nearly forty-year career, he performed in major works by George Balanchine and Jerome Robbins. He was noted for his performances as the Dark Angel in *Orpheus* and in the title role of Balanchine's *Prodigal Son*, as well as for his role alongside Mary Ellen Moylan in the Broadway production of *The Chocolate Soldier* (1947).

LENWOOD MORRIS (d. 1981) was for many years the ballet master and a character actor in the Katherine Dunham Company. Deemed the "Matriarch of Black Dance," Dunham was trained as an anthropologist, forging an

innovative technique—which Morris would master and teach—that fused Caribbean, African, and African American dances with traditional European ballet. Morris was known for his precision and photographic memory of dances; in lieu of a camera, Dunham took Morris into the jungles of Brazil to learn dances of headhunter tribes. Fearless and openly gay, Morris would often joke with "Miss D" about his status as a "queen." He was master instructor and ballet master at the Performing Arts Training Center of Southern Illinois University, which Dunham founded.

MARY ELLEN MOYLAN (b. 1926) is an American dancer born in Cincinnati, Ohio. As a teenager, she moved to New York, where she studied ballet at the School of American Ballet. In 1942 she debuted as première danseuse in the musical *Rosalinda*, choreographed by George Balanchine, and danced in Balanchine works with the New Opera Company. Moylan was a soloist in Ballet Russe de Monte Carlo, from 1943 to 1944, performing in *Ballet Imperial*, *Le Bourgeois gentilhomme*, *Études*, *Serenade*, *Snow Maiden*, and *Les Sylphides*, among others. In 1997, Maria Tallchief described her work as "brisk and fleet and classically pure," claiming, "I wanted to be just like her and use my legs the way she used hers."

BRONISLAVA NIJINSKA (1891–1972) was a Polish dancer and choreographer born into a family of traveling performers. Her brother and earliest collaborator, Vaslav Nijinsky, was the star performer of the Ballets Russes. Nijinska's dancing career began when she was a student at the Imperial Ballet School in Saint Petersburg, after which she joined the Ballets Russes in Paris. Nijinska was forced from her brother's production of *The Rites of Spring* in 1913 for getting married, which Nijinsky understood as a betrayal of their confidence. In the 1910s, Nijinska moved to Kiev, where she began a fruitful collaboration with the Constructivist artist Alexandra Exter, made her first plotless modernist dances, and established the School for Movement, which aimed to educate dancers in becoming creative artists rather than dancers for hire. Rejoining the Ballets Russes in 1921 as sole choreographer of the company, Nijinska created nine ballets, including the neoclassical masterpieces *Les Noces* and *Les Biches*. Characterized by an adamantly modernist approach to ballet, Nijinska's work was technically and conceptually radical, making her one of the most important ballet choreographers of all time and one of few exceptions in a profession dominated by men. World War II forced Nijinska to relocate from Paris to Los Angeles, where she choreographed dances for Max Reinhardt's film *A*

Midsummer Night's Dream (1935), founded her second school of ballet and trained a new generation of dancers, including Maria Tallchief and Allegra Kent.

SONO OSATO (1919–2018) was an American ballet dancer and actress. At fourteen years old, she became the youngest member of Ballets Russes de Monte Carlo and refused to "Russianize" her Japanese name. Osato toured the world with the company for six years, after which she studied at the School of American Ballet and then joined American Ballet Theatre. Isamu Noguchi sculpted her portrait, as one among several subjects from the worlds of dance. At the outbreak of World War II, Osato's father was imprisoned as an "enemy alien"; though she took on her mother's maiden name, the federal government barred Osato from touring with Ballet Theatre owing to her Japanese heritage. By 1944 Osato had found success as an "all-American girl" in Leonard Bernstein and Jerome Robbins's *On the Town*, which is credited as the first Broadway production featuring a nonsegregated cast. In 2006, she founded the Sono Osato Scholarship Program in Graduate Studies at Career Transition for Dancers to help former dancers finance graduate work in both the professions and the liberal arts.

RUTH PAGE (1899–1991) was an American dancer and choreographer considered the grand dame of dance in Chicago from the 1920s to the 1980s. Known for her contributions to modern dance, she forged a highly experimental style that often combined elements of poetry, opera, avant-garde, classical, and modernist expressions. Page trained with Adolph Bolm in New York, appeared briefly with Anna Pavlova's company in 1914, and performed in the Ballet Intime and Allied Arts Ballet during the 1920s. She performed with and often choreographed works for Ballet Russe de Monte Carlo, Les Ballets Americains, the Chicago Opera, the Metropolitan Opera, and the Ravinia Opera.

PEARL PRIMUS (1919–1994) was a dancer, choreographer, and anthropologist known for her contributions in bringing African dance to American audiences. Born in Port of Spain, Trinidad, and raised primarily in New York City, Primus began dancing as an understudy in a National Youth Administration group while she was a graduate student in biology at Hunter College. In 1943, she performed her first composition, *African Ceremonial*, along with *Strange Fruit*, *Rock Daniel*, and *Hard Time Blues*. She traveled to West Africa in 1948, bringing back with her a deeper familiarity with traditional African dance. Primus's choreography was rooted in black American traditions, often bringing together elements from spirituals, jazz, and blues and frequently incorporating language drawn from black literature.

JEAN ROSENTHAL (1912–1969) was a pioneer in theatrical lighting design, known primarily for her lifelong collaborations with Martha Graham, whom she met at the Neighborhood Playhouse School of the Theater in 1929. In her long and illustrious career, she also worked with George Balanchine, as well as with John Houseman and Orson Welles at the Federal Theatre Project. She was known for helping to turn the role of lighting designer into a formalized position in theater, and for her use of floodlights to eliminate shadows.

BILLIE SMITH was a dancer in the 1934 cast of Virgil Thompson's *Four Saints in Three Acts* (choreographed by Frederick Ashton), which opened on Broadway at the 44th Street Theatre. He had previously performed in the chorus of Cole Porter's *Fifty Million Frenchmen* (1929).

CHARLES ("TEX") SMUTNEY was a gymnast who later became a choreographer and dance instructor at Smith College in Northampton, Massachusetts.

MARIA TALLCHIEF (1925–2013) was born on an Osage reservation in Oklahoma and grew up in Los Angeles, where she began dancing at an early age. When she was seventeen, she moved to New York and joined Ballet Russe de Monte Carlo, where she met George Balanchine, who was then the company's resident choreographer. Tallchief quickly became Balanchine's muse, and the two were married briefly, starting in 1946, the same year he cofounded New York City Ballet. Tallchief joined the company and rose to prima ballerina, through her inimitable roles in *The Firebird* and as the Sugar Plum Fairy in *The Nutcracker*. She performed internationally and was the first American to dance at Moscow's Bolshoi Theatre. Later, in the 1970s, she served as director of ballet for the Lyric Opera of Chicago and founded the Chicago City Ballet in 1974.

BEATRICE TOMPKINS (1918–2003) was a member of Ballet Russe de Monte Carlo and Ballet Caravan, where she was part of the original cast of Balanchine's *Four Temperaments*, among many other works. She was the ballet mistress in Robert Joffrey's first ballet troupe, the Joffrey Ballet, where she was charged with artistic presentation, adapting ballets to diverse touring venues, from gymnasiums to living room–size stages. According to dance critic Sasha Anawalt, Tompkins was "capable, efficient, droll, and wise, she wore natty wool knit skirt-suits and short black gloves to receptions and smoked cigarettes with an aristocratic air." She later relocated with her husband to San Francisco, where she performed with the San Francisco Ballet in William Christensen's *Hansel and Gretel*.

TAMARA TOUMANOVA (1919–1996) was a prima ballerina and actress known best for her performances with Ballet Russe de Monte Carlo and the American Ballet Theatre. She began her career at age six, when she was invited by Anna Pavlova to perform in a gala concert. In 1931, when Toumanova was only twelve years old, she was invited by George Balanchine to perform in Ballet Russe de Monte Carlo. There, she performed along with teen dancers Irina Baronova and Tatiana Riabouchinksa. The trio became known as the "baby ballerinas." She performed regularly in Balanchine's work throughout the 1940s, until 1947, when she began performing with the Paris Opera Ballet.

JOHN VAN SIKKEN was photographed by George Platt Lynes circa 1940.

SHIRLEY WEAVER (1920–2014) was a dancer born in Kansas City, Missouri, who performed with the Metropolitan Opera, Ballet Russe de Monte Carlo, the Slavenska-Franklin Ballet, and as a ballerina at Radio City Music Hall. She later became a dancer and choreographer with the Kansas City Ballet and taught for many years at the University of Missouri–Kansas City Conservatory of Music.

DOROTHY WILLIAMS was a dancer in the American Ballet Theatre. She was part of the short-lived "Negro Unit" of American Ballet Theatre, which performed Agnes de Mille's *Black Ritual* (*Obeah*) in 1940. She also performed in the 1943 production of *Carmen Jones* at the Broadway Theatre.

This book is the sum of countless conversations and collaborations with artists, dancers, art historians, curators, dance historians, designers, editors, archivists, conservators, educators, art workers, estates, institutions, and friends. *Transmissions* was conceived from the beginning as an open-ended exploration, one that has been guided and shaped by these many contributors in what is ultimately an ensemble effort. But neither the exhibition nor the book would have materialized without Elisabeth Sussman. Over the course of many years, her determination, curiosity, and absolute trust gave shape to the urgency of my questions and allowed me to reimagine the museum. This book is dedicated to her.

Scott Rothkopf brought visionary focus and scale to my proposition and embraced the challenges posed by its many moving parts, even if it meant testing some of the limits of the museum's capacities and structures. I am indebted to Elisabeth and Scott's curatorial partnership for so carefully drawing out and supporting my ideas without compromise. Sustaining and catalyzing my work in parallel to the development of *Transmissions*, Karin Althaus, Marie-Claude Beaud, Célia Bernasconi, Suzanne Cotter, Milovan Farronato, Nicola Lees, Matthias Mühling, and João Ribas are also implicated in its realization.

Morgan Arenson, Lola Harney, Greta Hartenstein, Jamie Krasner, and Allie Tepper—the core *Transmissions* exhibition team—showed enormous dedication to this unpredictable endeavor. The intelligence, flexibility, and personal investment they brought to every step of its development carried the work from the archives to the rehearsal studio to the museum itself. Allie has my additional thanks for her total commitment to bridging the very different demands of making an exhibition, a performance, and a book.

I am more grateful than I can say for the opportunity to have worked with and learned from dancers Alexandra Albrecht, Kristina Bermudez, Maggie Cloud, Brandon Collwes, Ahmaud Culver, Jasmine Hearn, Elizabeth Hepp, Forrest Hersey, Alexandra Jacob, Burr Johnson, Maki Kitahara, Evelyn Kocak, Benedict

Nguyen, Matilda Sakamoto, Quenton Stuckey, and Anna Thérèse Witenberg. Their rigor, frankness, and eloquence changed the way I think about artists and touched not just me but so many visitors to the exhibition. Thank you to Paula Court for so sensitively capturing their daily performances in the exhibition and to Patricia Beaman for her incisive input during rehearsals.

In the early stages of my work, I benefited enormously from advice and feedback from Frances Chiaverini, Stuart Comer, Adrian Danchig-Waring, Silas Farley, Alex Fialho, Kaitlyn Gilliland, Kim Gordon, Trajal Harrell, Pati Hertling, Ana Janevski, Martha Joseph, Will Rawls, Scott Roben, Sam Roeck, and Farris Wahbeh. A fellowship at the Center for Ballet and the Arts at New York University helped anchor my project in the city that formed me and in the prehistory of the cultural legacies I inherited. I am grateful to Jennifer Homans, Lauren Kiel, Allan MacLeod, Laura Quinton, Andrea Salvatore, and Sabrina Yudelson for their support and enthusiasm during and beyond my fellowship, which extended to the use of the center's rehearsal studios for several months. Fellow colleagues at the center, including Juliet Bellow, Julia Foulkes, and Gia Kourlas, gave important critical feedback regarding methodology and my position as an artist reappraising historical material through gesture and display. Heather Watts's wildly intertextual disquisition on learning *Agon*—a dance she described as a formal French garden superimposed with Mondrian's *Broadway Boogie Woogie*—still throws sparks in my memory.

Linda Murray and Arlene Yu at the Jerome Robbins Dance Division of the New York Public Library for the Performing Arts shared their unparalleled knowledge of the library's astonishing collections with me, suggested crucial divagations from my original lines of inquiry, and ultimately shepherded the loans of so many works and documents from the library for exhibition at the Whitney. Jennifer Eberhardt, Cassie Mey, and Daisy Pommer were unreasonably patient with my countless requests and queries. Shawn Wilson at the Kinsey Institute in Bloomington, Indiana, gave me full access to the institute's holdings of George Platt Lynes material during my visit and facilitated the reproduction of Lynes's works for the exhibition and this book; thank you also to Steven Haas and Joshua Lynes. Beth Rudin DeWoody welcomed me into her own vast collection and generously loaned crucial works—thank you to Dong Austria, Wendy Grogan, and Maynard Monroe for enabling my many visits and fielding countless e-mails. Edward M. Burns of the Van Vechten Trust and Peter Kayafas made possible the first public projection of Carl Van Vechten's dance photographs and showed me what it means to safeguard and maintain fragile art forms and social histories. Thank you to Nicole Cornell and Ellen Sorrin of the George Balanchine Trust, and to Katherine E. Brown and Katharina Plumb of New York City Ballet. Thank you to all the lenders, including Jack Shear; the Philadelphia Museum of Art; the Yale University Art Gallery, New Haven, Connecticut; and those who wish to remain anonymous.

The logistics of the exhibition were brilliantly overseen and executed by Brenna Cothran, Amanda Davis, and Zoe Tippl. Caitlin Bermingham, Anna Martin, and Mark Steigelman brought their remarkable sensibilities and attention to detail to the design and installation of the exhibition. Bryan Savitz transformed problems into opportunities and contributed crucial elements to the exhibition design. Rosana Chang and Reid Farrington made sure all the moving images looked their best. Andrea Solstad's refabrication of Paul Cadmus's transparent *Filling Station* costume became emblematic of the exhibition as a whole. Thank you to Louise Lawler for letting me transpose her photographs onto the dancers' leotards and to Blake Palmer for overseeing the costume fabrication and fitting. Thank you to Hilary Greenbaum and Beth Turk for so beautifully rethinking (and editing) the wall labels in multiple voices, and to Anne Byrd and Emma Quaytman for asking such important questions.

I am grateful to Max Chester, Isabelle Dow, Megan Heuer, and Christine Howard Sandoval for facilitating vibrant public programing, and to Fran Lebowitz for not only entertaining my cold call but also sharing with a new audience her unsparing reflections on the changing and eradicated cultures of New York. Thank you to Kathryn Potts, as well as to Justin Allen, Eduardo Restrepo Castaño, Elena Ketelsen Gonzalez, Heather Maxson, Dyeemah Simmons, Billie Rae Vinson, Sasha Wortzel, and Madison Zalopany of the Whitney's education department for developing and hosting opportunities for people to engage with the exhibition.

So many others at the Whitney—the entire museum, it often seemed—were part of this work. Thank you to Sofie Andersen, Danielle Bias, David Breslin, Donna De Salvo, Adrian Hardwicke, Barbara Haskell, Nick Holmes, Zoe Jackson, Kelley Loftus, Aliza Sena, Elisabeth Sherman, Stephen Soba, and Adam Weinberg.

This book reflects the care and passion of Barbara Schroeder and Karen Kelly of Dancing Foxes Press, Joseph Logan and Katy Nelson of Joseph Logan Studio, and Whitney editor Beth Huseman, who brought us all together in the first place. It has been an utter joy and privilege to work on constructing this book with them. Thank you to Anita Duquette and Micah Musheno for their patience and expertise with regard to image rights.

My heartfelt thanks to 303 Gallery in New York and Campoli Presti in London and Paris for their unfailing support and representation of my work, as well as to Erin and Peter Friedland for their spontaneous generosity in supporting the full realization of this book. Thank you to Matthew Higgs for the gift of Marianne Wex's *Let's Take Back Our Space: "Female" and "Male" Body Language as a Result of Patriarchal Structures*, which left its stamp both formally and conceptually on the structure of this book.

Many friends and new acquaintances encouraged and challenged my thinking during and after the exhibition's run: Shelley Fox Aarons and Philip E. Aarons, Matthew Jeffrey Abrams, Negar Azimi, Anne Bass, Hamish Bowles, A.K. Burns, Dan Byers, Catherine Chevalier, Lynne Cooke, Douglas Crimp, James Crump, Brigid Doherty, Anne Dressen, Andrew Durbin, Catherine Facerias, Elena Filipovic, Stephen Robert Frankel, Jeanne Graff, Kathy Halbreich, Jodi Hauptman, Lucy Ives, Russell Janzen, Alex Kitnick, Alex Kwartler, Marci Kwon, Élisabeth Lebovici, Zoe Leonard, Julian Lethbridge, Benjamin Liu, Alastair Macauley, Emma McCormick-Goodhart, Richard Meyer, Angela Miller, Samantha Miller, Simone Montemurno, Kathy Noble, Laura Regensdorf, Elaine Reichek, Olivia Shao, Kianja Strobert, Megan Francis Sullivan, Emily Sundblad, Gloria Sutton, Lanka Tattersall, Lynne Tillman, Julia Trotta, Chloe Wyma, Erika Vogt, Thea Westreich, and Ethan Wagner, and Joshua Lubin-Levy, whom I also thank for the trenchant insights in the essay he wrote for this book. Special thanks to Emmelyn Butterfield-Rosen, whose friendship and scholarship animate my life, and, finally, Ken Okiishi, with whom I see and reflect back an experience of this world. His photographs of the exhibition and its audience strike at the core of my search, as only he could know, since *Transmissions* was born out of half a lifetime of collaboration, threaded with our conversations between classes, clubs, exhibitions, dances, movies, memorials, lectures, readings, protests, and concerts.

Nick Mauss

In reproducing the images contained in this publication, the publisher obtained the permission of rights holders whenever necessary and possible. Reasonable efforts have been made to credit the copyright holders, photographers, and sources; if there are any errors or omissions, please contact the publishers so that corrections can be made in any subsequent edition.

Cover, pp. 30–45, 69 (left), 141, and 142: © 2019 Estate of Paul Cadmus / Artists Rights Society (ARS), NY. Photo from the Collections of the Kinsey Institute, Indiana University. All rights reserved. Used with permission of The George Platt Lynes Estate; pp. 2, 4, and 91–98: © Paula Court; p. 15 (all images): © 2018 Louise Lawler, courtesy the artist and Metro Pictures, New York; p. 16: © Estate of Elie Nadelman and © 2019 Man Ray Trust / Artists Rights Society (ARS), NY / ADAGP, Paris; pp. 18 (middle and right), and 117–21: © Condé Nast; pp. 19 (both images), 167 (right), 168 (all images), and insert (all images): © Van Vechten Trust; pp. 22 (left), 108–11, and 123 (top and bottom), 167 (left): courtesy of New York City Ballet; pp. 46 (left), 55 (top left), 85, and 149: © Estate of Elie Nadelman; p. 46 (right): used with permission of The George Platt Lynes Estate; pp. 48, 55 (bottom left), 112 (right), and 166: © 2019 Estate of Paul Cadmus / Artists Rights Society (ARS), NY; pp. 49 and 54: © Walker Evans Archive, The Metropolitan Museum of Art, New York. Image source: Art Resource, NY; p. 50: courtesy of Swann Auction Galleries; p. 52 (bottom): courtesy of DC Moore Gallery, New York; p. 53: courtesy Gitterman Gallery and DC Moore Gallery, New York; pp. 58 and 59: courtesy of Doyle Auctioneers & Appraisers; p. 60 (top right): Collection Steve Turner; p. 60 (bottom left), 82 (left and right), 83 (all top images), and 146: © 2019 Artists Rights Society (ARS), New York / ADAGP, Paris; p. 61 (left and right): © Association

Marcel Duchamp / ADAGP, Paris / Artists Rights Society (ARS), New York 2019; pp. 62 and 63 (all images): courtesy Anthology Film Archives, New York; p. 65: photograph by Maurice Seymour courtesy of Ronald Seymour; p. 66 (left, both): courtesy Chicago Film Archive; p. 67 (right): courtesy the Noguchi Museum, © 2019 The Isamu Noguchi Foundation and Garden Museum, New York / Artists Rights Society (ARS), New York; p. 68 (left) and 69 (right): photo by Kevin Noble. Courtesy of the Isamu Noguchi Foundation and Garden Museum, © 2019 The Isamu Noguchi Foundation and Garden Museum, New York / Artists Rights Society (ARS), New York; p. 68 (right): © 2019 The Isamu Noguchi Foundation and Garden Museum, New York / Artists Rights Society (ARS), New York, image © Philippe Halsman / Magnum Photos; p. 70: courtesy and © TAJAN; p. 72: photo by George Platt Lynes used with permission of The George Platt Lynes Estate; pp. 74 and 75: courtesy Galerie Bassenge, Berlin, © Estate of Ilse Bing; p. 76 (both): courtesy National Gallery of Art, © Estate of Ilse Bing; p. 84: photo by Martha Swope, © Jerome Robbins Dance Division, The New York Public Library for the Performing Art; p. 86: © Estate of Elie Nadelman, photo © The Estate of Leslie Gill; p. 87: © Man Ray 2015 Trust / Artists Rights Society (ARS), NY / ADAGP, Paris 2019; p. 88: © Estate of John Storrs, courtesy Richard Gray Gallery, Chicago/New York; p. 90 (left and right): © The Lachaise Foundation; pp. 99 (all images), 100, and 101 (top left): courtesy Ballet Society/Eakins Press Foundation; p. 101 (top middle and right): courtesy Ballet Society/Eakins Press Foundation © Estate of Elie Nadelman; p. 101 (bottom left and right): courtesy Ballet Society/Eakins Press Foundation, © 2019 The Joseph and Robert Cornell Memorial Foundation / Licensed by VAGA at Artists Rights Society (ARS), NY; p. 103 (left): © 2019 Succession H. Matisse / Artists Rights

Society (ARS), New York; p. 103 (right): © 2019 Salvador Dalí, Fundació Gala-Salvador Dalí / Artists Rights Society, New York; p. 115: courtesy the Noguchi Museum, © 2019 The Isamu Noguchi Foundation and Garden Museum, New York / Artists Rights Society (ARS), New York; and © 2019 Succession H. Matisse / Artists Rights Society (ARS), New York; p. 116: © Condé Nast and © Man Ray 2015 Trust / Artists Rights Society (ARS), NY / ADAGP, Paris 2019; pp. 130 and 131: courtesy and © Van Vechten Trust; pp. 132–35: © Estate of Ilse Bing; p. 140: courtesy School of American Ballet / Jerry L. Thompson; pp. 143 (left and right), 144: courtesy School of American Ballet; p. 148 (all images): © Estate of Elie Nadelman, photo © 1987 The Peter Hujar Archive LLC; courtesy Pace/MacGill Gallery, New York and Fraenkel Gallery, San Francisco; p. 164: © 2019 Barbara Moore / Licensed by VAGA at Artists Rights Society (ARS), NY, Courtesy Paula Cooper Gallery, New York.

Transmissions performance photographs:

p. 2: Quenton Stuckey, April 8, 2018. Photo by Paula Court
p. 4: Brandon Collwes, Quenton Stuckey, and Kristina Bermudez, March 31, 2018. Photo by Paula Court

pp. 24–29, performance photos by Ken Okiishi

pp. 24, 26: Elizabeth Hepp, April 8, 2018; p. 27: Quenton Stuckey and Brandon Collwes, April 20, 2018; p. 28: Forrest Hersey, March 31, 2018; p. 29: Benedict Nguyen, March 31, 2018

pp. 91–98, performance photos by Paula Court

p. 91: Kristina Bermudez and Burr Johnson, May 9, 2018; p. 92: Matilda Sakamoto and Kristina Bermudez, March 31, 2018; p. 93: Anna Thérèse Witenberg, Ahmaud Culver, Jasmine Hearn, and Evelyn Kocak, March 13, 2018; p. 94: Kristina Bermudez, Brandon Collwes, Quenton Stuckey, and Matilda Sakamoto, March 31, 2018; p. 95: Burr Johnson and Alexandra Albrecht, May 9, 2018; p. 96: Burr Johnson, Alexandra Albrecht, Matilda Sakamoto, and Kristina Bermudez, May 9, 2018; p. 97: Kristina Bermudez and Burr Johnson, May 9, 2018; p. 98: Anna Thérèse Witenberg, April 21, 2018

pp. 150–63, performance photos by Ken Okiishi

p. 150: Maggie Cloud, Alexandra Jacob, and Brandon Collwes, April 20, 2018; p. 151: Elizabeth Hepp, Forrest Hersey, Maki Kitahara, and Benedict Nguyen, March 31, 2018; p. 152: Brandon Collwes, Alexandra Jacob, and Quenton Stuckey, April 20, 2018; p. 153: Brandon Collwes and Forrest Hersey, April 8, 2018; p. 154: Brandon Collwes, Kristina Bermudez, and Quenton Stuckey, April 6, 2018; p. 155: Maggie Cloud and Brandon Collwes, April 20, 2018; p. 156: Forrest Hersey, Maki Kitahara, Elizabeth Hepp, and Benedict

Nguyen, April 8, 2018; p. 157: Forrest Hersey, Benedict Nguyen, and Elizabeth Hepp, April 8, 2018; p. 158: Elizabeth Hepp and Maki Kitahara, April 8, 2018; p. 159: Benedict Nguyen and Forrest Hersey, April 8, 2018; p. 160: Maggie Cloud and Alexandra Jacob, April 20, 2018; p. 161: Maggie Cloud, April 20, 2018; p. 162: Installation view of *Transmissions* with detail of projection of Carl Van Vechten's portrait of Francisco Moncion as Saint Sebastian; p. 163: Forrest Hersey, Brandon Collwes, and Elizabeth Hepp, April 8, 2018

p. 170, photo by Nick Mauss: Forrest Hersey, Elizabeth Hepp, Alexandra Jacob, Matilda Sakamoto, Quenton Stuckey, and Burr Johnson in rehearsal for *Transmissions*

The publication of this volume follows the exhibition *Nick Mauss: Transmissions*, which was on view at the Whitney Museum of American Art, New York, March 16–May 14, 2018, and organized by Scott Rothkopf, Senior Deputy Director for Programs and Nancy and Steve Crown Family Chief Curator; and Elisabeth Sussman, Curator and Sondra Gilman Curator of Photography, with Greta Hartenstein, former senior curatorial assistant, and Allie Tepper, former curatorial project assistant.

Generous support for the exhibition was provided by Deutsche Bank and the Performance Committee of the Whitney Museum of American Art.

In-kind support was provided by The Center for Ballet and the Arts at New York University.

Support for the publication was provided by Peter and Erin Friedland.

Cover: Paul Cadmus holding his painting *Arabesque* (1941), photograph by George Platt Lynes, n.d. Scan from original negative. Collections of the Kinsey Institute, Indiana University

Page 192: Unknown photographer, *Dance of the Eyes (Portrait of Loie Fuller)*, c. 1907. Gelatin silver print, 4⅜ × 6⅝ inches (11.1 × 16.8 cm). Jerome Robbins Dance Division, The New York Public Library for the Performing Arts, Astor, Lenox and Tilden Foundations

For additional credits and copyright notices, see page 190.

Whitney Museum of American Art
99 Gansevoort Street
New York, NY 10014
whitney.org

Dancing Foxes Press
16 Lefferts Place
Brooklyn, NY 11238
dfpress.us

Distributed by
Yale University Press
302 Temple Street
P.O. Box 209040
New Haven, CT
06520-9040
yalebooks.com/art

Cataloging-in-publication data is on file with the Library of Congress.

ISBN:
978-0-300-24684-1

Edited by Karen Kelly and Barbara Schroeder

Design by Katy Nelson for Joseph Logan Design, assisted by Erica Getto

Photo research and rights clearance: Allie Tepper

Editorial assistant: Victoria Nebolsin

Research assistant: Sam Benezra

Copyediting and proofreading: Dierdre O'Dwyer and Polly Watson

This book is typeset in Sabon and Untitled Sans and printed on 150 gsm Condat matt Périgord

Printed and bound in Belgium by die Keure, Bruges

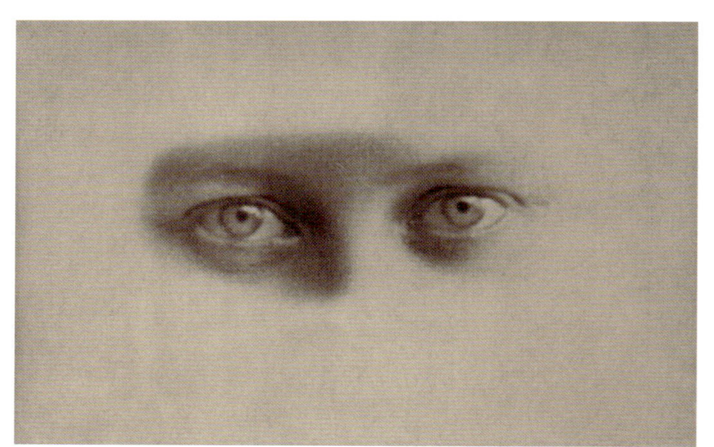